D1597921

ROWAN UNIVERSITY
CAMPBELL LIBRARY
201 MULLICA HILL RD.
GLASSBORO, NJ 08028-1701

Enemies and Familiars

A VOLUME IN THE SERIES

Conjunctions of Religion and Power in the Medieval Past

Edited by Barbara H. Rosenwein

A list of titles in the series is available at www.cornellpress.cornell.edu.

ENEMIES and FAMILIARS

SLAVERY AND MASTERY IN FIFTEENTH-CENTURY VALENCIA

Debra Blumenthal

CORNELL UNIVERSITY PRESS   Ithaca and London

This book was published with the aid of a grant from the Program
for Cultural Cooperation between Spain's Ministry of Culture
and United States Universities.

Copyright © 2009 by Cornell University

All rights reserved. Except for brief quotations in a review, this book, or parts
thereof, must not be reproduced in any form without permission in writing from
the publisher. For information, address Cornell University Press, Sage House,
512 East State Street, Ithaca, New York 14850.

First published 2009 by Cornell University Press

Printed in the United States of America

Library of Congress Cataloging-in-Publication Data

Blumenthal, Debra, 1969–
    Enemies and familiars : slavery and mastery in fifteenth-
century Valencia / Debra Blumenthal.
        p. cm. — (Conjunctions of religion and power in the
medieval past)
    Includes bibliographical references and index.
    ISBN 978-0-8014-4502-6 (cloth : alk. paper)
    1. Slavery—Spain—Valencia (Region)—History—To 1500.   2.
Slaves—Spain—Valencia (Region)—History—To 1500.   3.
Slaveholders—Spain—Valencia (Region)—History—To 1500.   4.
Master and servant—Spain—Valencia (Region)—History—To
1500.   I. Title.   II. Series: Conjunctions of religion & power in the
medieval past.

    HT1219.V3B58 2009
    306.3'6209467609024—dc22   2008045804

Cornell University Press strives to use environmentally responsible suppliers
and materials to the fullest extent possible in the publishing of its books. Such
materials include vegetable-based, low-VOC inks and acid-free papers that are
recycled, totally chlorine-free, or partly composed of nonwood fibers. For further
information, visit our website at www.cornellpress.cornell.edu.

Cloth printing   10 9 8 7 6 5 4 3 2 1

3 3001 00955 5359

This book is dedicated
to my grandmothers,
Hannah Bank Blumenthal
and Reba Robbins Frankel

Contents

Maps

Acknowledgments

This book is the product of more than ten years of research in the archives of Valencia. It simply would not have been possible without the patient and knowledgeable assistance of archivists and staff members at the Arxiu del Regne de València, the Archivo de Protocolos del Patriarca, and the Arxiu Municipal de València. This project also received critical financial support from the University of Toronto, the Regents of the University of Kansas, and the National Endowment for the Humanities. A yearlong residency at the Center for the Study of Cultures at Rice University enabled me to complete an earlier version of this project. Its transformation into a book was greatly facilitated by a year at the Radcliffe Institute for Advanced Study.

For introducing me to Valencia—along with the joys and frustrations of doing archival research—I am forever indebted to Mark Meyerson. This book also owes much to the unflagging support, encouragement, and keen insight of David Nirenberg. Martin Klein steered me through the vast historiography of comparative slavery and epitomizes the sort of scholar and colleague I hope to be.

The genesis of this book can be traced back to a seminar paper I wrote for Andrew Watson as a first-year PhD student at the University of Toronto. Stumbling upon an article by Iris Origo discussing the tensions generated by the presence of Tartar and Circassian slave women in the households of fourteenth-century Tuscany, I wondered what the dynamics of master-slave relations might have been like in Reconquest Spain. J. N. Hillgarth challenged me to find sources equally as rich as Origo's *ricordanze* and his sensible advice helped shape the initial research proposal. Once in Valencia, I benefited from the expertise and hospitality of local scholars including Isabel Amparo Baixauli Juan, Andrés Díaz i Borrás, Vicent Giménez Chornet, Vicente Graullera Sanz, Manuel Ruzafa, and Luis Pablo Sanmartín.

I am also indebted to the following scholars who—at pivotal steps along the way—took the time to read and offer comments on grant proposals, conference papers, the dissertation, or preliminary drafts of chapters of the book manuscript: Linda Northrup, Kay Reyerson, Sean Hawkins, David Brion Davis, Eva Haverkamp, Paula Sanders, Benjamin

Ehlers, Marcia Colish, Luis Corteguera, Marta Vicente, Elizabeth MacGonagle, Gwyn Campbell, Alejandro de la Fuente, and Valerie Ramseyer. For pointing out the important differences between grabbing someone's *cull* and grabbing someone's *coll*, I owe a special thanks to James Brundage. Barbara Rosenwein and the anonymous readers for Cornell University Press carefully read the entire manuscript. Their generous suggestions helped sharpen my arguments and substantially improved the organization of this book; any errors and oversights that remain are, however, entirely my own. Finally, I am extremely grateful to Barbara Rosenwein, John Ackerman, and Ange Romeo-Hall at Cornell University Press, who shepherded me through the publication process with extraordinary fortitude and grace.

Friends and colleagues have likewise made important contributions to this book. For knowing how to drive a stick shift and being an enthusiastic companion on excursions in Valencia's *huerta* (and points beyond), I owe a thousand *besos* to Oliver Todt. For providing important sources of inspiration (be it in the form of food, drink, and/or conversation), I am beholden to Tammy Dwosh, Leonard Rotman, Adam Wahlberg, Judith Williams, Laura Hines, Tony Rosenthal, Mary Catherine Davidson, Adebisi Agboola, Adrienne Edgar, Gabriela Soto Laveaga, Stefan Kraemer, Roman Baratiak, Hilary Bernstein, and Xiao-Bin Ji. For giving me the time, space, and encouragement to finish this book, I thank my medievalist colleagues at the University of California at Santa Barbara: Sharon Farmer, Carol Lansing, Edward English, Stephen Humphreys, and Carol Pasternak.

Ultimately, though, I owe the greatest debt to my family. It is no exaggeration to say that this book is the product of the indulgence of my parents, Malcolm and Marsha Blumenthal, the examples set by my sister, brother, and sister-in-law, Susanna Blumenthal, Jacob Blumenthal, and Susanne Goldstein, the diversions offered by my nephew and niece, Samuel and Hannah Blumenthal, and the good humor of Stephen White.

Abbreviations

AMV	Arxiu Municipal de València
APPV	Archivo de Protocolos del Patriarca de Valencia
ARV	Arxiu del Regne de València
B	Bailia
CSIC	Consell Superior d'Investigacions Científiques
Furs	Furs de València
G	Gobernación
JCiv	Justicia Civil
JCrim	Justicia Criminal
M.	Manus (=quire)
MR	Maestre Racional
P	Protocolos

Editorial Method

I have numbered the kings according to the Aragonese numeration, rather than the Valencian or Catalan numeration—thus, Pedro IV (rather than Pere III) and Alfonso V (rather than Alfonso IV).

The currency of the fifteenth-century kingdom of Valencia consisted of *diners*, *sous*, and *lliures*. One *sou* was worth twelve *diners*, and twenty *sous* made up one *lliura*. A *real* was worth one *sous*, 6 *diners*. A *florín* was worth 15 *sous*.

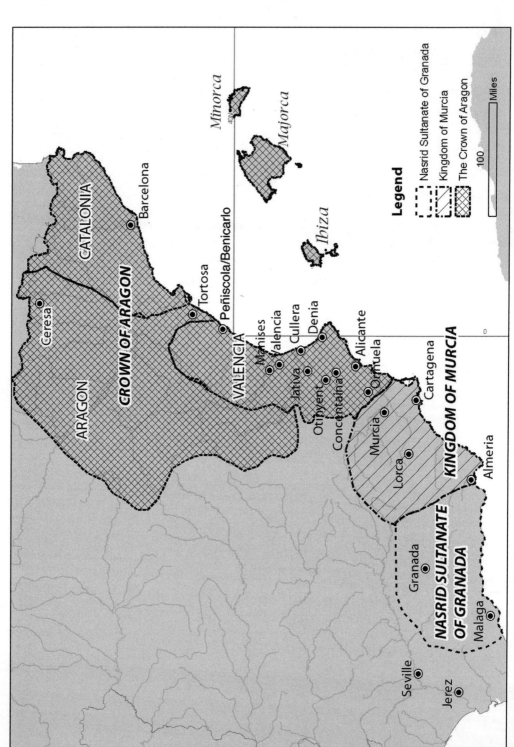

The Kingdom of Valencia and its vicinity. (Map prepared by C. Scott Walker, Harvard Map Collection.)

Legend

- Nasrid Sultanate of Granada
- Kingdom of Murcia
- The Crown of Aragon

Miles
0   100

CROWN OF ARAGON

ARAGON

CATALONIA

Barcelona

Ceresa

Tortosa

Peñiscola/Benicarlo

VALENCIA

Manises

Valencia

Cullera

Denia

Jativa

Otinyent

Concentaina

Alicante

Ormuela

KINGDOM OF MURCIA

Murcia

Lorca

Cartagena

Almeria

NASRID SULTANATE OF GRANADA

Granada

Malaga

Seville

Jerez

Minorca

Majorca

Ibiza

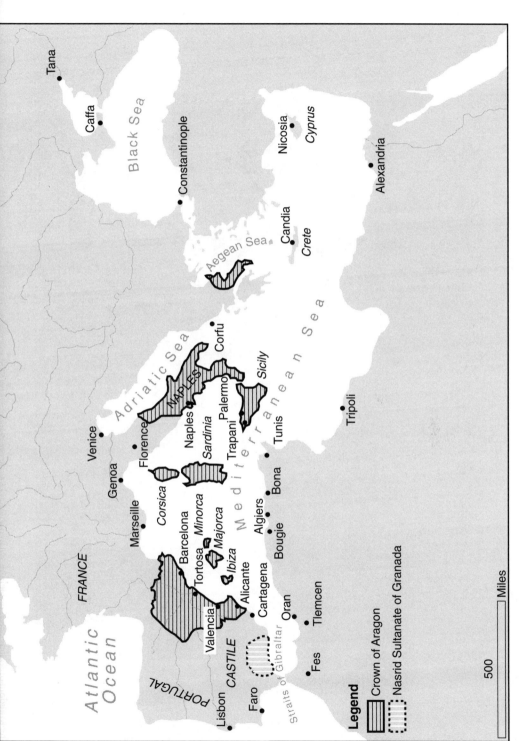

The Mediterranean in the late fifteenth century. (Map prepared by C. Scott Walker, Harvard Map Collection.)

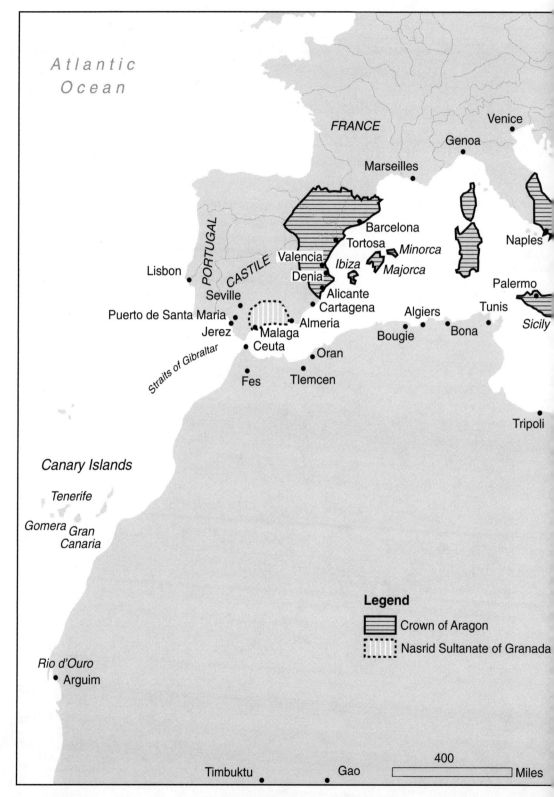

Atlantic Ocean

FRANCE

Venice
Genoa
Marseilles
Barcelona
Tortosa
Minorca
Valencia
Ibiza
Majorca
Naples
Lisbon
PORTUGAL
CASTILE
Denia
Alicante
Palermo
Seville
Cartagena
Tunis
Puerto de Santa Maria
Algiers
Sicily
Jerez
Almeria
Bougie
Bona
Malaga
Straits of Gibraltar
Ceuta
Oran
Fes
Tlemcen
Tripoli

Canary Islands

Tenerife

Gomera Gran
Canaria

Legend

Crown of Aragon

Nasrid Sultanate of Granada

Rio d'Ouro
Arguim

400

Timbuktu   Gao   Miles

Berbería, West Africa, and the Canary Islands. (Map prepared by C. Scott Walker, Harvard Map Collection.)

Enemies and Familiars

INTRODUCTION

In the fifteenth century, Valencia was an important Mediterranean port that rivaled, and for a time surpassed, Barcelona in its prominence as a commercial center. Merchants and corsairs, correspondingly, came to Valencia from all points of the compass, bearing captives to be put up for sale. Although the "*moro*" arguably was the most popularized slave figure in contemporary literature, those enslaved included Tartar, Circassian, Russian and Greek Orthodox Christian women and children, as well as black Africans and Canary Islanders. Valencians procured slaves not only by physically capturing them—waging warfare against so-called enemies of the faith and Crown, but also purchased them, already enslaved, from foreign traders operating out of eastern Mediterranean and then, subsequently, Atlantic ports. In addition, an important source of slaves throughout this period were judicial processes whereby free Muslim subjects (Mudejars) convicted of certain crimes were sentenced to perpetual servitude.

This book is about how these enslaved men, women, and children were bought, sold, and treated. It challenges the prevailing view that slavery in premodern Mediterranean societies was predominantly, if not exclusively, domestic and artisanal in character and, for this reason, ought to be characterized as a "kinder, gentler" form of slavery than that which appeared later. It argues that slaves were active agents in seeking freedom, precisely because their lives were not easy. Though they might have continued to identify themselves as "Muslims," "Greeks," "Tartars," or "black Africans," as slaves they shared the experiences of being separated forcibly from their homes and families, collectively endured the indignities of being exposed publicly and put up for sale, and struggled similarly against a system that empowered slaveholders to exploit their labor and abuse them sexually—particularly if they were female.

Enslaved men and women, however, did not all experience equal success in surmounting the social, economic, and cultural barriers that had been constructed to constrain them. Muslim captives and penally enslaved Mudejars perhaps had the easiest time resisting, if not reversing the "deracination" or natal alienation that Orlando Patterson has designated as one of the "constituent elements of slavery."[1] They, unlike most other slaves, had a realistic chance of returning "home," or, at the very least, could join the kingdom's sizable free Muslim community. In contrast, Tartar, Greek, Circassian, Russian, and black African freed persons had little alternative but to try to build new lives for themselves on Valencian soil. Given the reality that contemporaries increasingly were associating dark skin with slave status, one would expect that black Africans would have the most difficult time erasing the stain of their former status. Although we ought not to ascribe these differences in experiences to simple differences in skin color (religion, gender, and economic status, for example, arguably played equally significant roles), the discussion and representation of Muslim, "eastern," and black African slaves and freed persons in late medieval Valencian sources illuminate the medieval roots of modern racism.

The History of the Question

Up until the mid-1980s, the bulk of scholarly investigations of medieval slavery had focused on the question of its supposed extinction. Although Marc Bloch had posited the disappearance of slavery from most of western Europe by the eleventh century, subsequent historians argued that the transition from slavery to feudalism occurred over several centuries and that, in certain areas, namely southern and central Europe, slavery never completely disappeared.[2]

The persistence of the Mediterranean slave trade had been extensively documented by Charles Verlinden as early as the 1950s.[3] In contrast to the rural slavery of the ancient world and the plantation slavery of the modern period, however, slavery as practiced in the ports of the late medieval Mediterranean was predominantly urban and domestic. In consequence, scholars have tended to portray it as "a rather benign institution" that brought disparate peoples into close contact.[4] Indeed, Jacques Heers suggested that Greek, Tartar, and Circassian slave women acquired in marketplaces bordering the Black

---

1. Orlando Patterson, *Slavery and Social Death: A Comparative Study* (Cambridge: Harvard University Press, 1982).

2. Marc Bloch, "How and Why Ancient Slavery Came to an End," in *Slavery and Serfdom in the Middle Ages: Selected Essays*, trans. William R. Beer (Berkeley: University of California Press, 1975), 1–31. See Pierre Bonnassie, *From Slavery to Feudalism in South-Western Europe*, trans. Jean Birrell (Cambridge: Cambridge University Press, 1991), and Susan Moshe Stuard, "Ancillary Evidence on the Decline of Medieval Slavery," *Past & Present* 149 (November 1995): 3–32.

3. Charles Verlinden, *L'esclavage dans l'Europe médiévale*, 2 vols. (Bruges: De Tempel, 1955–77).

4. In an article published in 1994, Stephen Bensch observed that "the slave blocks of Venice and Genoa and even Valencia and Mallorca have begun to take on the character of miniature Ellis Islands." Stephen Bensch, "From Prizes of War to Domestic Merchandise: The Changing Face of Slavery in Catalonia and Aragon, 1000–1300," *Viator* 25 (1994): 85.

Sea were, like free female servants recruited from the immediate countryside, almost seamlessly integrated into their new urban surroundings. These predominantly white enslaved women would convert to Roman Catholicism, earn their freedom, and intermarry with members of the local population. According to Heers's model, in the Christian-dominated territories of the medieval Mediterranean, slavery worked more toward the socialization and integration of religiously and ethnically distinct peoples than toward their subjugation.[5]

Heers's picture of slavery in the medieval Mediterranean, however, does not accurately reflect the situation in late medieval Iberia. The fifteenth century was a particularly tense time for intercultural relations in this "land of three religions."[6] Not only were troops being marshaled to conquer the last remaining Muslim stronghold on the peninsula (the Nasrid Sultanate of Granada), but the cultural and religious assimilation of both conquered Muslims and Jewish converts (many of whom had been forcibly baptized) provoked considerable anxieties. Fears of widespread crypto-Judaism led to the establishment of the Spanish Inquisition and, ultimately, the expulsion of the Jews from Castile and Aragon in 1492. Nevertheless, suspicions regarding the sincerity of Muslim and Jewish converts to Christianity persisted, prompting the promulgation of "purity of blood" (limpieza de sangre) laws barring individuals of Jewish, and subsequently Muslim, descent from holding public office and from membership in certain institutions. In such an atmosphere, one can hardly assume that enslaved Muslim, Greek, Tartar, Circassian, and black African men and women enthusiastically embraced conversion or that, once converted, they were welcomed into these communities with open arms.

Caution seemed especially merited for the kingdom of Valencia. In addition to being located in close proximity to Islamic territories, the kingdom of Valencia also harbored within its borders a sizable free Muslim population that Valencian Christians never completely trusted. Making up 30 to 40 percent of the kingdom's population in the fifteenth century, Mudejars not infrequently were seen as a potential "fifth column" in the event of an attack by a Muslim enemy.[7] Confronted by an infidel enemy without as well as within,

5. Jacques Heers, *Esclaves et domestiques au Moyen Ages dans le monde méditerranéen* (Paris: Librairie Arthème Fayard, 1981), 287. In a more recent book, Heers tackled the trade in black African slaves from the seventh to the sixteenth centuries. However, he limits his discussion of the experiences of black African slaves to their exchange, employment, and status in Islamic territories. Jacques Heers, *Les négriers en terres d'islam: La première traite des Noirs VIIe–XVIe siècle* (Paris: Editions Perrin, 2003).

6. For a recent critique of the polarized images of medieval Iberia as, alternatively, an interfaith utopia or a persecuting society, see Jonathan Ray, "Beyond Tolerance and Persecution: Reassessing Our Approach to Medieval Convivencia," *Jewish Social Studies* 11, no. 2 (Winter 2005): 1–18.

7. Mudejars were approximately a third of the kingdom's total population in the fifteenth century. See Mark Meyerson, *The Muslims of Valencia in the Age of Fernando and Isabel: Between Coexistence and Crusade*

Valencian Christians viewed their slaves—some of whom had been Muslim corsairs—with intense ambivalence.

A second historiographical question, that of the relationship between slavery and "race," is also illuminated by the Valencian experience. In recent years, an expanding body of scholars has been concerned with investigating medieval notions of difference and the so-called medieval roots of modern racism.[8] I selected the city of Valencia in the fifteenth century as the focus for my research because it boasted a slave (and free) population of considerable diversity. While "eastern" white female slaves seem to have been the norm in the ports of Genoa and Venice, in Valencia war and corsair activity continued to provide a steady stream of Muslim captives, more than half of whom were male.[9] Portuguese exploration of the western coast of Africa, moreover, had resulted in the introduction of a significant population of black Africans into the Iberian Peninsula. By the end of the fifteenth century, black Africans made up as much as 40 percent of the slave population of Valencia.[10] Given the religious, linguistic, and ethnic diversity of its slave community, Valencia offers an ideal case study for exploring the role of "racism" in medieval slavery. Although some medievalists have argued that value discriminations *were* based

---

(Berkeley: University of California Press, 1991), 7, and Jacqueline Guiral-Hadziiossif, *Valencia, puerto mediterráneo en el siglo xv (1410–1525)* (Valencia: Edicions Alfons el Magnànim, 1989), 435.

8. Most notable are George Frederickson, *Race: A Short History* (Princeton: Princeton University Press, 2002); James H. Sweet, "The Iberian Roots of American Racist Thought," in "Constructing Race: Differentiating Peoples in the Early Modern World," a special issue of *William and Mary Quarterly* 54 (January 1997): 143–66; and David Nirenberg, "Was There Race before Modernity? The Example of 'Jewish' Blood in Late Medieval Spain," in *Origins of Racism in the West*, ed. Ben Isaac, Yossi Ziegler, and Miriam Eliav-Feldon (Cambridge: Cambridge University Press, forthcoming). My thanks to David Nirenberg for generously providing me with an advance copy.

9. Based on my own research in the notarial registers of the city of Valencia (records found both in the ARV and the APPV), of 511 references to slaves or former slaves between 1460 and 1480, 276 were male, 235 were female. Francisco Javier Marzal Palacios makes a similar observation in an article comparing the demographic makeup of the slave populations in, respectively, late medieval Genoa, Palermo, Palma de Mallorca, Barcelona, Marseilles, and Valencia. Noting the high number and nearly constant presence of Muslim captives in Valencia, Marzal contends this was a distinguishing feature, setting Valencia apart from other major slave-holding cities in the western (Christian) Mediterranean. Francisco Javier Marzal Palacios, "Una presencia constante: Los esclavos sarracenos en el Occidente Mediterráneo bajomedieval," *Sharq al-Andalus* 16–17 (1999–2002): 73–93.

10. Of the aforementioned 511 slaves and former slaves, 204 were blacks or mulattos. D. Bénesse, in an unpublished dissertation, notes how the number of black slaves being imported into the city of Valencia increased steadily throughout the fifteenth century, constituting a significantly higher percentage of the slave population in the last decade of the fifteenth century. Seventy percent of the slaves being imported into the city of Valencia between 1489 and 1500 were black. D. Bénesse, "Les esclaves dans la société ibérique aux XIVe et XVe siècles," University of Paris X, 1970. Cited in Jacques Heers, *Family Clans in the Middle Ages: A Study of Political and Social Structures in Urban Areas* (Amsterdam: North-Holland Publishing, 1977), 64.

on color, no slavery was race neutral.[11] Others, however, claim that relative to religious, linguistic, and cultural differences, color was insignificant "as a crucial marker" in the Middle Ages.[12] What the Valencian evidence demonstrates is that over the course of the fifteenth century, skin color increasingly came to be associated with slave status.

Finally, this book contributes to the ongoing debate among historians of slavery concerning "slave agency."[13] Throughout this work I emphasize the myriad ways in which slave owners as well as royal and municipal officials presented the enslaved as historical actors. Although I acknowledge that accepting contemporary descriptions of a slave's actions as "voluntary" or "by choice" is highly problematic, I place myself firmly in the camp of cultural-legal historians who, in contrast with past generations of scholars who tended to portray slaves "as people acted upon by legal institutions—mostly unjustly," stress the "interaction between 'subjects' of law (judges and legislators) and 'objects' of law (slaves)." As Ariela Gross has observed, such research complicates "earlier models of law as a hegemonic force" and challenges the assumptions of social historians who emphasized slave agency and slave resistance but thought that it took place only extra-legally and "on a private or unconscious level with no public or political dimensions."[14] My research in the archives of Valencia has uncovered a wealth of previously unexploited archival sources. In addition to examining the voluminous Crown records documenting the movement of captives into and out of the kingdom as well as more thoroughly investigating contemporary notarial registers for details regarding the material conditions of slavery and the position of slaves in the household, I have encountered hundreds of civil and criminal court cases. Slaves and freed persons figure prominently in these records as witnesses, defendants, and even plaintiffs. Criminal court records not only document instances in which slaves were the victims of violent assaults but also feature

11. See Thomas Hahn, "The Difference the Middle Ages Makes: Color and Race before the Modern World," *Journal of Medieval and Early Modern Studies* 31, no. 1 (Winter 2001): 1–37, and Jeffery Jerome Cohen, "On Saracen Enjoyment: Some Fantasies of Race in Late Medieval France and England," *Journal of Medieval and Early Modern Studies* 31, no. 1 (Winter 2001): 113–46.

12. Robert Bartlett, "Medieval and Modern Concepts of Race and Ethnicity," *Journal of Medieval and Early Modern Studies* 31, no. 1 (Winter 2001): 39–56. See also Bartlett, *The Making of Europe: Conquest, Colonization, and Cultural Change, 950–1350* (Princeton: Princeton University Press, 1993), esp. chapters 8 and 9, 197–242.

13. My treatment of the issue of "slave agency" has been influenced by the work of Ariela Gross, *Double Character: Slavery and Mastery in the Antebellum Southern Courtroom* (Princeton: Princeton University Press, 2000); Rebecca J. Scott and Michael Zeuske, "Le droit d'avoir des droits: Les revendications des ex-esclaves à Cuba (1872–1909)," *Annales: Histoire, Sciences sociales* 59, no. 3 (2004): 521–45; and Walter Johnson, "On Agency," *Journal of Social History* (Fall 2003): 113–24, and Johnson, *Soul by Soul: Life Inside an Antebellum Slave Market* (Cambridge: Harvard University Press, 1999).

14. Ariela Gross, "Beyond Black and White: Cultural Approaches to Race and Slavery," *Columbia Law Review* 101, no. 3 (April 2001): 655–59.

sensational accounts of attempted flights, thefts, and murders committed by slave perpetrators. Civil court cases, in turn, treat a wide range of slaveholders' concerns: squabbles
between heirs concerning property rights over slaves; altercations between disgruntled
buyers and sellers of allegedly "defective" slaves; and protests filed by slaveholders soliciting the court's assistance in invalidating contracts of manumission due to a conditionally freed slave's purported acts of ingratitude. In most cases, we see the Valencian legal
system reinforcing the rights of slaveholders over their slaves, which, of course, is not
altogether surprising. The naked brutality of slavery was often cloaked in a language of
legal niceties. Nevertheless, the respect given to due process and the consequent access
to the kingdom's courts it afforded enslaved men and women is striking given the formal
definition of slaves as the legally disenfranchised. Some of the most informative records
I encountered were lawsuits in which enslaved men and women themselves were the
plaintiffs. In these cases, termed *demandes de libertat*, enslaved men and women literally
sued for their freedom.

The Contours of This Book

In seven chapters, this book traces the varied experiences of Muslim, eastern, and
black African slaves from capture to freedom. In addition to examining how these men,
women, and children were acquired and brought to the Valencian marketplace, in this
book I explore the substance of slaves' daily lives: how they were sold and who bought
them; what sorts of labor they performed and the degree to which they participated in the
social, religious, and cultural life of this community. Thus, while previous scholars have
outlined the mechanics of the institution of slavery in the city and kingdom of Valencia,[15]
documented the vagaries of the medieval and early modern Mediterranean slave trade
(counting the number of slaves bought and sold in various markets),[16] or examined slavery within the broader context of Muslim-Christian relations,[17] this book, in contrast,

15. See Vicenta Cortés Alonso, *La esclavitud en Valencia durante el reinado de los reyes Católicos (1479–1516)*
(Valencia: Ayuntamiento de Valencia, 1964), and Vicente Graullera Sanz, *La esclavitud en Valencia en los siglos
XVI y XVII* (Valencia: Consejo Superior de Investigaciones Científicas, 1978).

16. See, for example, Verlinden, *L'esclavage dans l'Europe médiévale*; Domenico Gioffré, *Il mercato degli
schiavi a Genova nel secolo XV* (Genoa: Fratelli Bozzi, 1971); and Michel Balard, "Remarques sur les esclaves
à Gênes dans la seconde moitié du XIIIe siècle," *Mélanges d'archéologie et d'histoire publiés par l'École française
de Rome* (1986): 627–80.

17. See José Maria Ramos y Loscertales, *El cautiverio en la Corona de Aragón durante los siglos XIII, XIV, y XV*
(Zaragoza: Publicaciones del Estudio de Filología de Aragón, 1915); Mark D. Meyerson, "Slavery and the
Social Order: Mudejars and Christians in the Kingdom of Valencia," *Medieval Encounters* 1, no. 1 (1995):
144–73; Olivia Remie Constable, "Muslim Slavery and Mediterranean Slavery: The Medieval Slave Trade
as an Aspect of Muslim-Christian Relations," in *Christendom and Its Discontents*, ed. S. L. Waugh and P. Diehl
(Cambridge: Cambridge University Press, 1996), 264–84; and Bensch, "From Prizes of War to Domestic

explores the social and human dimensions of slavery in a religiously and ethnically plu-
ralistic society.[18]

The first chapter, "Defining *de bona guerra*," discusses the ways in which the domination of a master over his or her slave was established, legitimated, and understood in
fifteenth-century Valencian society. Despite significant changes in both the slave population's demographic composition and the methods employed for acquiring slaves, the
language used to justify the institution of slavery remained remarkably static throughout
the fifteenth century, firmly rooted in the rhetoric of holy war. Black or white, Mudejar or
Moor, Greek or Guanche (aboriginal inhabitants of the Canary Islands), male or female,
all were "captives of good war," infidels, enemies of the Catholic Church and Crown.

Chapter 2, "Talking Tools: Slaves in the Marketplace," contrasts a captive's initial public and official sale into slavery with the more private resales and exchanges of slaves
between households. I show how slaves were often active participants in their resales, a
crucial part of the negotiation process being an "interview" between the slave and his or
her potential buyer.

The third chapter, "Slave Labors," examines the role of slaves in the Valencian economy. Countering the popular image of the late medieval Mediterranean slave as a pam-
pered white female domestic, it reveals the participation of slaves in a broad range of
economic activities: from building construction to silk spinning, bread baking to agricultural production.

In the fourth and fifth chapters, my focus shifts to the dynamics of the master-slave relationship. Calling into question the common view that there was fairly rapid integration
of slaves into their newly adopted communities, these chapters highlight the underlying
tensions in the master-slave relationship. Although baptism, naming, and testamentary

---

Merchandise." See also James William Brodman, *Ransoming Captives in Crusader Spain: The Order of Mer-
ced on the Christian-Islamic Frontier* (Philadelphia: University of Pennsylvania Press, 1986); Mark Meyerson,
"Slavery and Solidarity: Mudejars and Foreign Muslim Captives in the Kingdom of Valencia," *Medieval
Encounters* 2, no. 3 (1996): 286–343; Andrés Díaz Borrás, *El miedo al Mediterraneo: La caridad popular Valenciana y la redención de cautivos bajo poder Musulmán, 1323–1539* (Barcelona: Consell Superior de Investigacions
Científicas, 2001); and Jarbel Rodriguez, *Captives and Their Saviors in the Medieval Crown of Aragon* (Washing-
ton D.C.: Catholic University Press, 2007).

18. For a few noteworthy exceptions, see A. C. de C. M. Saunders, *A Social History of Black Slaves and
Freedmen in Portugal, 1444–1555* (Cambridge: Cambridge University Press, 1982); Iris Origo, "The Domestic Enemy: The Eastern Slaves in Tuscany in the Fourteenth and Fifteenth Centuries," *Speculum* 30 (1955):
321–66; Stephen A. Epstein, *Speaking of Slavery: Color, Ethnicity, and Human Bondage in Italy* (Ithaca: Cornell University Press, 2001); and Heers, *Esclaves et domestiques.* In addition, Alessandro Stella endeavors
to present the experience of slavery from the enslaved men's and women's perspectives; his evidence
(wills, parish registers, and marriage dossiers), however, dates primarily from the seventeenth and eigh-
teenth centuries. Alessandro Stella, *Histoires d'esclaves dans la Péninsule Ibérique* (Paris: Éditions de l'École des
Hautes Études en Sciences Sociales, 2000).

practices all reveal how slaves were incorporated and considered members of their master's households, these customary practices were eagerly embraced by masters at least partly because they served to naturalize and legitimate their authority; they ought not be accepted on face value as evidence of integration. Analysis of contemporary court records exposes the surprisingly prominent role played by enslaved men and women in disputes over "honor" in fifteenth-century Valencia. Precisely because they were considered members of the household, slaves, through their actions and behavior, could threaten as well as enhance their master's (and mistress's) reputation. Although on the one hand masters called upon their slaves to defend their honor by attacking their enemies, on the other, just as frequently, they distinguished themselves from their slaves by depicting them as unruly or sexually promiscuous others.

The sixth chapter, "Paths to Freedom," examines a slave's prospects for liberation relative to his or her religious and ethnic background and gender. Although black African slaves were largely dependent on the beneficence of their masters or on the Valencian legal system to win their freedom, the local free Muslim community had more resources and, consequently, was much more active in ransoming coreligionists. Moreover, although notarial formulae suggest that all slaves could reasonably expect to win their freedom, consultation of contemporary court records reveals that heirs often ignored deathbed bequests of liberty, slave owners not infrequently dangled disingenuous promises of future liberation as incentives for better service, and slave owners retained the right to cancel and nullify a contract of manumission due to a conditionally freed slave's perceived "ingratitude." Indeed, as we see in the seventh and final chapter, even when slaves did manage to recover their freedom, their status remained insecure and their prospects as freed persons were not necessarily very bright. The boundaries that had been drawn to distinguish slaves from their masters were not so easily erased.

CHAPTER 1 DEFINING *DE BONA GUERRA*

Although Caçim Benhamet had been a linen weaver in his native Tunis, on 16 July 1434, thirty-year-old Caçim entered the city of Valencia as a slave. Purchased four days later by Orfresina, the wife of Marti de Sayes, Caçim was one of several thousand slaves living in this city.[1] Caçim's fellows in captivity included not only Muslims but Eastern Orthodox Christians and sub-Saharan Africans, women like Maria, a twenty-six-year-old Greek female born on the island of Cyprus, and boys like Johanico, a ten year old described as "Jalof" (Wolof) by Crown officials. How did they get here? Why did they end up here? In this chapter I examine how men, women, and children of varied ethnic and social backgrounds became slaves in the late medieval Mediterranean world. While Maria vividly recalled the Genoese pirates who had captured her more than eighteen years earlier while she was playing with some other children in her neighborhood, Johanico's memories of his homeland and the circumstances surrounding his capture, significantly, were left unrecorded.[2]

In the fifteenth century, Valencia's slave population was drawn from three principal sources: war and corsair activity, penal servitude, and trade. Valencian, Catalan, Majorcan, Castilian, and Portuguese corsairs brought in a steady stream of Muslim captives, seized

---

1. As Vicente Graullera has observed, "It is very difficult, if not impossible, to give a figure, even an approximate one, for the number of slaves living in Valencia." The research of both Vicenta Cortes and Vicente Graullera suggests that they likely numbered in the thousands (out of an estimated total population of around forty thousand). Graullera, for instance, encountered some 2,999 slaves in Crown records and speculates that the total number of slaves living in Valencia was probably much higher, for not all slaves were presented before the bailiff general. See Graullera, *La esclavitud*, 176. For a discussion of the available evidence concerning the population of Valencia in the fifteenth century, see Augustín Rubio Vela, "Sobre la población de Valencia en el cuatrocientos (Nota demográfica)," *Boletín de la Sociedad Castellonense de Cultura* 56 (1980): 158–70.

2. For Caçim's "confession" before Crown officials upon his arrival in Valencia, see ARV B 193: 186v–197r. For Maria's complaint, filed before the governor after spending more than eighteen years living in servitude, see ARV G 2331: M. 16: 3r–8v. For Johanico's presentation before Crown officials, see ARV B 194: 252r. Maria's case is discussed more extensively below, as well as in chapter 6.

in land and sea raids directed against residents, alternatively, of the Nasrid Sultanate of Granada or the "Moorish kingdoms" of Bougie, Fes, Tlemcen, and Tunis (see map 1). Royal and seigneurial officials, in addition, routinely issued sentences of perpetual enslavement to members of the kingdom's local Muslim population. Though Mudejars, in contrast with "foreign" Muslims, were subjects of the Crown, hence to be protected from capture and enslavement by Christian corsairs, they nonetheless could be penally enslaved by local administrators as a punishment for certain crimes. Local and foreign merchants, moreover, added to this mix by bringing slaves from more distant lands to the Valencian marketplace. Basing their operations first in the eastern Mediterranean and Black Sea region and then, subsequently, in Atlantic ports, merchants resold these "eastern," Canary Islander, and black African slaves to Valencian buyers for a profit.

Over the course of the fifteenth century, Valencians witnessed significant changes in both the composition and primary mode of acquisition of the local slave population. Most notable was this shift from a Mediterranean to an Atlantic-centered slave trade. Did changing patterns in slave procurement affect contemporary understandings of slavery's legitimacy as an institution? Under what circumstances did fifteenth-century Valencians believe an individual could rightfully be enslaved? Through an analysis of the language utilized by Crown officials and slave owners in court rulings and notarial contracts as well as testimony taken from the captives themselves, this chapter considers how subjugation was both justified by captors and purportedly understood by their victims.

Sources of Supply

Generated by corsair activity and war, augmented by penal servitude, and enriched by trade, the slave population of Valencia was drawn from a variety of different sources.

War and Corsair Activity

Although the mass reduction of conquered Muslim communities into slavery had always been the exception rather than the rule in the Crown of Aragon, a not insignificant segment of the local slave population had been acquired directly through capture. As the pace of the Reconquest slackened in the late thirteenth century and the boundaries between Christian and Muslim territories stabilized, however, the kingdom of Valencia was no longer, strictly speaking, a frontier state. The Castilian kingdom of Murcia now stood between it and the Nasrid Sultanate of Granada (see map 1).[3] Indeed, the bulk of captives entering the kingdom of Valencia in the fifteenth century were the victims of a rather amorphous and loosely defined war taking place on the high seas and along the coasts of

---

3. See Maria Teresa Ferrer i Mallol, *La frontera amb l'Islam en el siglo XIV: Cristians i sarraïns al País Valencià* (Barcelona: CSIC, 1988).

the Mediterranean Sea. Waged by pirates and corsairs alike (between which it was often difficult to distinguish), these were not campaigns directed toward territorial conquest, but surprise land raids and naval assaults whose principal motivation was the seizure of booty and captives. Rafael Cariñena i Balaguer and Andrés Díaz i Borrás have noted how the war against the infidel, particularly in the form of naval expeditions directed against Granadan and Maghriban corsair vessels, took on new urgency in Valencia starting in the last quarter of the fourteenth century. Local observers noted a "perilous increase" in Moorish corsair activity along the kingdom's littoral, reflective of a new dynamic in relations between the Crown of Aragon and the Maghrib.[4] The kingdom of Valencia, due to its physical location, seems to have been particularly vulnerable to such attacks. Thus, in 1388, the *jurats* (Valencia's six annually elected city counselors or executive officers) of the city of Valencia exhorted the city council to take action against Moorish corsairs, declaring:

> Tolerating such things would not only bring confusion and shame upon Christians—especially those of this nation who, in past times, were veritable lords of the seas, even making certain coastal towns of *Berbería* [North Africa] its tributaries—but also bring notable damage to this city and kingdom, as every day infidels would capture and seize the persons, vessels, and merchandise of this city and kingdom, hampering the trade of grain as well as other commodities of this land.[5]

To combat this menace, municipal and Crown officials had experimented with a variety of measures, the easiest and most cost effective of which was to encourage the arming of private vessels to patrol its shores. As José Maria Ramos y Loscertales observed, royal licenses authorizing the arming of private vessels to defend the kingdom's coasts, waters, and trade routes (and, in the process, take captives) were "*numerosísimos*" during the fourteenth and fifteenth centuries.[6] Cut off from Muslim territory by land, Valencians took to the seas to pursue war against the infidel.

4. Rafael Cariñera i Balaguer and Andrés Díaz i Borrás, "Corsaris valencians i esclaus barbarescs a les darreries dels segle XIV: Una subhasta d'esclaus a València en 1385," *Estudis Castellonencs* 2 (1984–85): 439–56. See also Andrés Díaz i Borrás, *Los orígenes de la piratería islámica en Valencia: La ofensiva musulmana trecentista y la reacción cristiana* (Barcelona: CSIC, Institución Milà y Fontanals, 1993); Charles-Emmanuel Dufourcq, *L'Espagne Catalane et le Maghrib au XIIe et XIV siècles* (Paris: Presses Universitaires de France, 1944); and John H. Pryor, *Geography, Technology, and War: Studies in the Maritime History of the Mediterranean, 649–1571* (Cambridge: Cambridge University Press, 1988).

5. AMV, Manual de Consells, A–17: 257v–258r. Cited in Cariñera i Balaguer and Díaz i Borrás, "Corsaris valencians," 447.

6. José Maria Ramos Loscertales, *El cautiverio en la corona de Aragón durante los siglos XIII, XIV, y XV* (Zaragoza: Publicaciones del Estudio de Filología de Aragón, 1915), 10–11. Jacqueline Guiral-Hadziiossif has pointed out that corsair activity could be directed not only against Muslims but also against Christian

Thus, on 25 August 1422, Berthomeu Silvestre, a resident of Cullera, arrived in the port of Valencia bearing eleven captives (ten "Moors" and one Jew), his share of twenty-seven captives taken in a joint corsair expedition in the waters off the Strait of Gibraltar.[7] Such activities persisted throughout the fifteenth century. Decades later, in October 1494, Jaume Dixer, a nobleman and the owner of a *galeota* (a small oared vessel, used frequently in corsair activity), returned to Valencia bearing sixteen male captives (one Jew and fifteen "Moors") seized from a merchant vessel captured (along with its cargo of wheat, barley, and raw and spun cotton) "in the waters of Berbería."[8] More representative of the activities of the "petty" or part-time corsairs discussed by Jacqueline Guiral-Hadziiossif were a pair of artisans from Denia who, in October 1495, brought back two captives to Valencia, the fruits of an expedition along the coast of North Africa. According to the testimony of one of the so-called "catius de bona guerra" (captives of good war), a seventy-year-old laborer named Abbes, the two Denian artisans had surprised and captured him and his fourteen-year-old daughter, Mansora (who, incidentally, was blind), while they were threshing wheat.[9] Living within striking distance of proclaimed enemies of the faith, Valencian corsairs, both part-time and professional, took advantage of their easy access to Granada and North Africa to launch raids directed at capturing the infidel.

Cariñera i Balaguer and Díaz i Borrás have speculated, in fact, that corsair activity spurred the growth of the local slave market. In their eagerness to recruit private individuals to patrol Valencia's waters, municipal officials indirectly promoted the expansion of the slave trade. By lending financial and material support to Christian corsairs and paying top dollar for any captives seized, municipal officials increased its profitability.[10] Thus, as Guiral-Hadziiossif has observed, by the fifteenth century, "corsairs from all

---

enemies of the Crown, that is, Castile and Genoa. Guiral-Hadziiossif, *Valence*, 138–40. For the licensing of corsairs elsewhere in the Crown of Aragon, see María Dolores López Pérez, *La Corona d'Aragón y el Magreb en el siglo XIV (1331–1410)* (Barcelona: Consell Superior de Investigacions Científicas, Institución Milà y Fontanals, 1995).

7. Berthomeu recounted how (in conjunction with ships armed in Alicante and Cartagena) they had cornered and then captured this armed Moorish vessel that was in transit from Malaga to Tangiers. Bearing a cargo of silk, pepper, tartar, and alum, this vessel had also carried (in addition to its Muslim crew) five black female slaves and their two young sons. Berthomeu acknowledged that, in order to amass the funds necessary to compensate one of his partners who lost his vessel during the attack, he had already sold part of his portion (two black female slaves) in Alicante. ARV B 193: 49r–59v.

8. ARV B 194: 156r–162r.

9. ARV B 194: 304r–v. For Guiral-Hadziiossif's discussion of "petty" corsairs, see Guiral-Hadziiossif, *Valence*, 160.

10. Cariñera i Balaguer and Díaz i Borrás note how it became the policy of the municipality to purchase any Moorish corsairs captured for the purpose of publicly executing them. Between 1381 and 1389, the municipality purchased and publicly executed at least thirteen Moorish corsairs, for the express purposes of "terrifying and serving as an example to others." Cariñera i Balaguer and Díaz i Borrás, "Corsaris valencians," 499.

parts came to the marketplace of Valencia." In addition to those recruited and licensed by local officials, corsairs from Majorca, Cartagena, Portuguese-controlled Ceuta, and even Trapani, Sicily, came to Valencia to auction their spoils to the highest bidder.[11] With some bringing in as many as forty-five "Moorish" captives at one time, twenty-three corsairs introduced a total of 234 *moros* into the Valencian marketplace between 1419 and 1434. The vast majority of these captives were "foreign" Muslims—subjects, alternatively, of the Nasrid Sultanate of Granada or the kingdoms of Bougie (modern-day Béjaïa, Alge-ria), Fes (modern-day Fez, Morocco), Tlemcen, and Tunis (see map 3).[12] Thus, in July 1434 a group of Christian corsairs based in Peñiscola captured Caçim Benhamet (along with a dozen other *moros*) off the coast of Tortosa. All twelve had been passengers aboard a Moorish *galiota* armed in Bougie to engage in corsair activity against Christians.[13]

Penal Servitude

Constituting as much as 80 percent of the population at the time of its reconquest by Christians under King Jaime I (ca. 1238) and about 30 percent of the population by the end of the fifteenth century, the kingdom of Valencia's free Muslim community re-mained vulnerable to enslavement despite their status as protected subjects.[14] Mudejars were routinely deprived of their liberty by royal and seigneurial officials as a punishment for crimes ranging from begging without a license to adultery to abandoning their lords. Enslavement either was the official penalty stipulated in the kingdom of Valencia's legal code or a substitute penalty imposed in lieu of the corporal punishments prescribed by Islamic law.

11. Guiral-Hadziiossif, *Valence*, 232. For some examples of "foreign" corsairs bringing captives to the port of Valencia, see, for Majorca, ARV B 193: 97v–104v; for Castilian Cartagena, ARV B 193: 33r–37r; for Portuguese-controlled Ceuta, ARV B 193: 88v–93v; and for Trapani, Sicily, ARV B 194: 278r–279r.

12. These figures are based on my analysis of Crown documents recording the presentation and con-fessions of the 234 captives presented before the bailiff general between 1419 and 1434; see ARV B 193. This is one of only two volumes of *presentaciones e confessiones de cautivos* extant from the fifteenth century. For the presentation of the lot of forty-five captives, see ARV B 193: 144r–168r.

13. ARV B 193: 186r–197v.

14. In a series of surrender treaties negotiated between the Aragonese kings and the conquered Mus-lims of Aragon, Catalonia, and Valencia in the twelfth and thirteenth centuries, Muslims had been guar-anteed their religious, judicial, and communal autonomy. As Mark Meyerson has explained, Mudejars "could practice Islam, maintain their mosques with their adjoining properties (*waqf* endowments), rule on litigations between Muslims in Islamic courts according to Islamic law, and select their own officials for the governance and administration of their communities, or *aljamas*. The Muslims' sustenance was ensured by the terms allowing them to retain their homes, lands, and movable goods." For the most part, Meyerson emphasizes, the Crown respected the protections granted in these treaties, "each king shrewdly balancing religious scruples with fiscal necessity. Mudejarism survived, not out of deference to an ideal of tolerance, but because the Muslims were valuable to the Crown as a source of taxation and as the agricultural and industrial substrata of local economies." Meyerson, *Muslims of Valencia*, 13–14.

It is important to note that only Muslims—not Christians, or even Jews—could be penally enslaved. Mark Meyerson has pointed out that this suggests that Mudejars were targeted more for their "potential for political sedition" than for their "essential religious dissidence." Despite the relatively stable religious, sociopolitical order in the kingdom of Valencia, Meyerson argues that "the Christians' continual anxiety about Mudejar insurgency produced and perpetuated behaviors and institutions that had the submission and control of Mudejars as their goal." Thus the enslavement of Mudejars was institutionalized, "becoming a common feature of Valencian life and not just the result of war and rebellion."[15]

According to the dictates of the *Furs de València*, the Kingdom of Valencia's law code, Mudejars apprehended while attempting to depart from the kingdom without royal license were to be considered "captives of good war" (*catius de bona guerra* or lawfully seized captives). Whether their destination was Granada, "Berbería," or anywhere outside the kingdom, fugitive Mudejars were to be enslaved and their property confiscated.[16] Thus, in 1484, a Mudejar couple was enslaved for "secretly and without license" boarding a vessel headed for Berbería (North Africa). Upon discovering the stowaways, the Genoese captain alerted port security (the Justicia del Grau), who subsequently turned the couple over to the bailiff general. Pronounced "slaves of the Crown," the penally enslaved Mudejars were put up for sale alongside "foreign" Muslim captives in an auction supervised by the bailiff general.[17] Similarly, on 11 April 1482, the nobleman Altobello Centelles purchased a twenty-four-year-old Mudejar named Abrahim, originally from Albaida, a town about eighty-five kilometers south of Valencia, near Ontinyent. According to the sales receipt, Abrahim had been penally enslaved "since he had traveled and gone into Muslim territories without the license of the bailiff general."[18]

The *Furs de València* also stipulated enslavement for any Muslim caught *acaptar sin licencia*: begging or soliciting alms without a royal permit.[19] Maymo Cabez, a thirty-five-year-old Mudejar from Ceresa in Aragon, for example, was penally enslaved "since he was discovered in the Vall d'Alfandech [a region with a predominantly Mudejar population] . . . begging [without a license]."[20] Similarly, on 4 July 1485, twenty-four-year-old Mahomat Alcohari was pronounced a slave of the Crown "because he was soliciting alms throughout the present kingdom without a license." It took the bailiff general, however,

---

15. Meyerson, "Slavery and the Social Order," 147–48.
16. *Furs de València*, ed. Germà Colon and Arcadi Garcia, (Barcelona, 1990), V: 123.
17. ARV B 217: 680r–681r, 699r–700r.
18. The sales receipt read "per ço com sens licencia del magnifich batle general s'en seria anat e passat en terra de moros." ARV B 217: 500v–501r.
19. *Furs de València*, Colon and Garcia, eds. (Barcelona, 1970), I: 218–20.
20. ARV B 217: nonpaginated insert: 8 March 1480.

more than four months to find a willing buyer. Mahomat allegedly was "crazy, a bad captive, and a fool."[21]

Foreign Muslims as well as Mudejars could be enslaved for unauthorized begging. Statutes in the *Furs de València* specified that redemption and emigration fees for "Moorish" captives had to be raised *outside* the territories of the kingdom of Valencia. Crown authorities did not want the funds raised to purchase their freedom and buy passage back to Islamic territories to come from local Mudejar communities (*aljamas y morerías*). Rather, they intended to have the loss in manpower that Muslim redemptionist activities implied at least partially compensated by an influx of money coming from the "lands of Moorish kings" (*terra de reys moros*). Foreign Muslims thus were prohibited from attempting to redeem themselves from captivity using local resources. North African and Granadan Muslims caught begging within the boundaries of the kingdom were to be apprehended and declared "slaves of the Crown."[22] On 19 November 1479, Ali, a thirty-five-year-old man from Tunis (described as llor, or of darker skin color), was declared a slave of the Crown "since he was discovered begging for alms in the vicinity of the town of Cocentaina." Back in captivity, Ali was purchased seven days later by a Valencian carpenter for twenty-four lliures.[23] On 10 February 1485, Muça Almedini and Ali Olbedini, both formerly of the kingdom of Fes, were pronounced slaves of the Crown "because they were begging for alms in the present kingdom." Seized near the castle of Beselga (near Estivella, about forty kilometers north of Valencia), Muça and Ali were not transferred into the bailiff general's custody in Valencia until more than two months later. The lord of Beselga initially tried to claim the two captives for himself. Muça and Ali eventually were sold to the carpenter Jacme Lombart for a combined price of sixty-three lliures and ten sous.[24]

The bailiff general, nevertheless, was not the only official authorized to pronounce sentences of penal servitude. Seigneurial lords possessed similar, if slightly more restricted, powers to punish their Muslim vassals with enslavement. Although seigneurial lords could not prohibit individual Mudejars from changing lords, in 1446 Juan II promulgated a statute empowering them to issue sentences of perpetual servitude against fugitive Mudejars in the event they fled en masse from his holdings. The statute specified that if four or more Mudejar households left simultaneously without their lord's permission,

---

21. ARV B 218: 116r–v. The buyer, a Valencian merchant, purchased Mahomat for a mere fifteen lliures.

22. *Furs de València*, I: 218–20. In 1403, the statute was amended to prohibit individual Christians, Jews, or Muslims (or Christian, Jewish, and Muslim collectives) from using local monies to help finance a foreign Muslim captive's redemption. Even so, it was not uncommon for Valencians to purchase foreign Muslim captives as a form of investment, acting as middlemen for these foreign *moros* while they raised money locally to secure their redemption.

23. ARV B 217: 175r–177r.

24. ARV B 218: 56v–57v.

they, along with their wives and children, could be captured and sold into slavery.[25] Mark Meyerson has argued that while the Crown targeted illegal emigration, seigneurial lords were preoccupied with restricting the movement of Mudejar vassals *within* the kingdom. The seigneurial lord's concern, after all, was much more local in character: ensuring that he had enough Mudejar vassals to work his lands.

Meyerson insists that restrictions on the free movement of Muslims, considered collectively, were predicated more on protecting Valencia's economic interests than on ensuring the kingdom's security. The kingdom's continued prosperity, after all, was believed to be heavily dependent on the contributions of Mudejar farmers, artisans, and laborers.[26] What prompted the issuance of this legislation, then, was not fear of a mass uprising (and/or Mudejar collaboration in a "Moorish" invasion) but rather fear of a mass exodus. These measures were largely directed toward preventing the depopulation of royal and seigneurial holdings. Thus, it seems hardly coincidental that enslavement was the preferred penalty for unauthorized Muslim movement. Royal and seigneurial officials thereby acquired for the kingdom an even more secure source of Muslim labor: Mudejar slaves.

Why didn't royal and seigneurial officials exercise their power to penally enslave to an even greater degree? Meyerson reminds us that heightened competition between lords for Muslim laborers militated against "the grossly arbitrary enslavement of their Mudejar vassals." Royal and seigneurial officials were highly cognizant of the fact that in response to "blatant oppression," Mudejar vassals (despite the aforementioned legislation) could pick up and leave. Because demand for Muslim laborers was particularly high, Meyerson contends that seigneurial lords in the fifteenth century were less likely than their predecessors to sentence their Mudejar vassals to penal servitude.[27]

A supplementary, though still important, source of Mudejar slaves was the practice of royal and seigneurial officials of commuting sentences of corporal punishment to sentences of perpetual servitude. Thus, a Mudejar convicted of a capital offense, such as theft or adultery, rather than being punished with the penalty prescribed by Islamic law (sharī 'a or xara in contemporary sources)—that is, stoning, lashing, or loss of limb—could instead have the penalty changed to perpetual enslavement.[28] On 28 February 1484, Fatima,

---

25. The proceeds of this sale were to be divided equally between the Crown and the aggrieved lord. *Furs de València*, V: 115. Thus on 14 January 1478, a group of Mudejar vassals from Dos Aguas appointed a representative to appear before the bailiff general and ask for help negotiating the release of "certain Muslim men and women who fled from said place [Dos Aguas]" and had been detained. APPV 15939 (nonpaginated): 14 January 1478.

26. See Meyerson, *Muslims of Valencia*.

27. Meyerson, "Slavery and the Social Order," 164.

28. The treaties negotiated in the thirteenth century between Jaime I and the conquered Muslims of Valencia granted Muslims legal autonomy and the ability to administer justice according to çuna and

a Mudejar woman whom the bailiff general had sentenced, in accordance with Islamic law, to death by stoning, instead agreed to "give herself to the royal majesty as a captive." Fatima's penalty was changed to enslavement (*mudada la pena a captivari*) and she was subsequently sold to a Genoese merchant.[29] Similarly, when a Mudejar vassal from Gilet was sentenced to receive seventy-five lashes in punishment for an unspecified crime he allegedly committed near the town of Petrés, rather than endure the prescribed penalty, the Mudejar instead "gave himself as a slave" to the lord of Petrés.[30]

Unfortunately since there was no formal hearing recording the entry of penally enslaved Mudejars into the local slave population parallel to the presentation of foreign Muslim captives before the bailiff general, it is difficult to give any estimates concerning the overall number living in the city of Valencia in the fifteenth century. Be that as it may, whether "voluntary" or imposed, penal servitude constituted a potentially more convenient, less costly, and relatively constant source of slaves for Valencians. Not only were Mudejars closer at hand than their "Moorish," "eastern," or west African counterparts, they also offered the presumed benefits of already being conversant in the local language, customs, and agricultural production techniques.

---

xara—that is, according to the *Sunna*, or the Muslims' local customary law and Shariah. The right of Muslims to have their civil and criminal cases judged according to the Shariah would be reiterated by Pedro IV in 1337 and the Aragonese Crown also took steps to ensure that there were a sufficient number of Muslims judges or *qadis* to man the Islamic courts both in royal towns and rural seigneuries. Noting how "at the pinnacle of Valencia's Islamic judiciary was the *qadi* general, or royal *qadi*...who exercised appellate jurisdiction over the kingdom's Islamic courts," Meyerson stresses how "beyond this court, the Mudejar satisfied with the decision of the local *qadi* could have recourse only to the bailiff general or the king." By the mid-fourteenth century, however, the intervention of Christian magistrates in Muslim disputes had become frequent and, in fact, John Boswell found that Christians were constantly "meddling" in Muslim disputes. Although some contemporary observers clearly bemoaned this development as a violation of their privileges, Meyerson sees "a progressive accomodation between the Islamic and Christian legal systems" as "Valencia's Muslims became more accustomed to the participation of Christian magistrates in their judicial affairs and more willing to plead their suits before Christian courts," a natural consequence, perhaps, of the dwindling population of Valencia's *morería*, particularly after its sack in 1455. See Meyerson, *Muslims of Valencia*, 185–93, and John Boswell, *The Royal Treasure: Muslim Communities under the Crown of Aragon in the Fourteenth Century* (New Haven: Yale University Press), 364–69.

29. The record specified how Fatima "fonch condempnada a mort a pedregat [had been condemned to death by stoning]." However, "a la suplicacio de moltes persones aquella donant se per cativa a la magestat reyal li fonch mudada la pena a captivari [at the request of many people, the penalty was commuted to enslavement, with that one (Fatima) giving herself to the royal majesty as a captive]." ARV B 217: 667v–668r.

30. Reflective of how penal enslavement was often a tool exploited by individual lords to secure Muslim labor, this Mudejar vassal's original lord, Manuel Lancol of Gilet, subsequently filed a complaint before the governor, claiming that his vassal had been falsely convicted and that the *qāḍī* who sentenced his vassal to seventy-five lashes was prejudiced in favor of Manuel's rival, the lord of Petrés. ARV G 2355: M. 15: 24r–29r.

Trade

Charles Verlinden documented in exhaustive detail how Catalan-Aragonese expansion in the eastern Mediterranean (i.e., the "conquests" of Sardinia, Corsica, the duchy of Athens, and the kingdom of Naples) had significant repercussions on its slave population. Verlinden's analysis of contracts of sale culled from the notarial archives of Barcelona revealed that while the slaves exchanged in the thirteenth century were nearly exclusively "Saracens" captured in the Reconquest, by the fourteenth century Russians, Circassians, Tartars, Turks, Bosnians, Bulgarians, and Greeks had taken their place—also considered infidels, "enemies of the Catholic faith and Crown."[31] As Catalan merchants challenged Italian hegemony in the eastern Mediterranean, slaves acquired in the Black Sea ports of Tana and Caffa flooded into Iberian ports (see map 2).

Although Valencia would never import "eastern" slaves in large enough numbers to supplant Muslim captives procured through corsair activity and penal servitude, they nonetheless constituted a notable segment of its slave population. Indeed, having eclipsed Barcelona as the most important port in the Crown of Aragon, the city of Valencia had, by the latter half of the fifteenth century, established itself as a major hub in the revitalized slave trade of the later Middle Ages. Although the Ottoman conquest of Constantinople in 1453 put a significant damper on Catalan traffic in the eastern Mediterranean, examination of notarial records dating from 1460 to 1480 reveals that about a quarter of the slaves bought and sold in Valencia continued to be identified as coming from these regions.

In sharp contrast with the gender breakdown for "Moorish" captives acquired through corsair activity, these Greek and Russian Orthodox Christians and pagan Tartars and Circassians were overwhelmingly female. Eighty-four percent (thirty-seven) of the forty-four transactions I found involved women.[32] Only seven featured males, three of which recorded the sale and resale of the same Turkish male, a thirty-five-year-old baptized Christian

---

31. Verlinden, L'esclavage, 319.

32. These figures are based on my consultation of 182 volumes of notarial registers dating from 1460 to 1480, preserved in the collections of both the ARV and APPV. Considering the fact that the overall male/female ratio for the slave sales documented in these notarial registers for this period was almost 50/50, with, if anything, a slightly higher number of male slaves, this notable gender imbalance with respect to the sales of "eastern" slaves takes on even greater significance. By way of comparison, 52 percent (131) of the 252 sales encountered in this sample concerned male slaves. Forty-eight percent (121) involved female slaves. It remains debatable whether this indicates a special or heightened demand for "eastern" female domestic slaves in the wake of massive demographic losses in postplague western Europe, as some have argued. Others have argued that this was simply a quirk of supply. Since male slaves coming from the Black Sea regions were in high demand in Islamic territories to serve in Mamluk and Ottoman armies, the Turkish, Russian, Circassian, and Tartar slave women turning up in European ports ought to be regarded as "spillover" from this trade. See William D. Phillips, Slavery from Roman Times to the Early Transatlantic Trade (Minneapolis: University of Minnesota Press, 1985).

named Pau.[33] Three of the remaining four transactions concerned boys between the ages of two and eleven; the two year old, moreover, was sold along with his pregnant mother.[34]

Toward the latter half of the fifteenth century, with the conquest of the Canary Islands and the beginning of Portuguese exploration of the coast of west Africa, however, the city's slave population underwent further diversification as ships arriving in Valencia's port (*grau*) unloaded Canary Islander and ever increasing numbers of black African slaves. Vicenta Cortés Alonso found that the average cargo of vessels carrying these predominantly Wolof men, women, and children oscillated between eighty to 130 slaves. The merchant most heavily engaged in this traffic was the Florentine Césaro de Barchi. Working on behalf of Bartolomeo Marchionni, a Florentine merchant based in Lisbon, de Barchi conveyed no fewer than two thousand black African slaves to Valencia between 1489 and 1497.[35]

Valencians, moreover, traveled to the Atlantic ports as well as to other Castilian and Portuguese cities that served effectively as clearinghouses for Canary Islander and black African slaves. In June 1495, a former cobbler turned merchant traveled to the Castilian city of Jerez to buy Caterina, a seven-year-old girl from the Canary Islands.[36] Nadal Ferrer, in contrast, sent an agent to Lisbon to purchase a ten-year-old Wolof boy named Johanico on his behalf.[37]

As the center of the slave trade shifted from the Mediterranean to the Atlantic, the city of Valencia found itself further removed from the sources of supply. Inasmuch as the Canary Islands now fell under Castilian jurisdiction, Canary Islander slaves came to Valencia via Puerto de Santa María, Cádiz, Jerez, or Seville (see map 3).[38] Given the Portuguese monopoly over trade with west Africa, most black African slaves coming to Valencia passed through Lisbon first.[39]

Toward the end of the fifteenth century, then, corsair activity against Muslims in Granada and North Africa declined in importance with respect to supplying the city's

33. See ARV P 1099: nonpaginated, 13 December 1459 and 13 May 1460 and ARV P 9986: nonpaginated, 21 May 1461.

34. ARV P 11436: nonpaginated, 5 March 1470.

35. Cortés, *La esclavitud*, 112. Césaro de Barchi also appears frequently in notarial records dating from this period, selling, almost invariably, black African slaves "de genere de Gelof." His dealings, however, were not only with other merchants. He frequently sold slaves to individuals, including, for example, a baker, a widow, and a barber. See, respectively, ARV P 2005: 184v–185r, ARV P 2006: 304v–305r, and ARV P 2007: 289r–v.

36. ARV B 194: 252r.

37. ARV B 194: 248r–v.

38. For Canary Islander slaves arriving in Valencia by way of Puerto de Santa María, see ARV B 194: 48r–50v and 68r–69v; for Caliç, see ARV B 194: 120r–v and 128r–129v; for Jerez, see ARV B 194: 164r–165r; and, for Seville, see ARV B 194: 461r–462r.

39. See, for example, ARV B 194: 10r–12r, 24r–25v, 150r–151r, and 153r–154v.

slaves. Although, between 1419 and 1434, twenty-three of thirty-five presenters of captives before the bailiff general had been corsairs, corsairs numbered only eight out of 114 presenters between 1494 and 1497. During this same period, the bailiff general declared just over 100 North African or Granadan Muslims *"catius de bona guerra"* as compared to 253 Canary Islanders and 622 black Africans.[40] Increasingly, the "captives" entering the kingdom of Valencia had been acquired from traders in the kingdoms of Castile or Portugal. Indeed, in the wake of the conquest of Granada, Valencians traveled to Malága, Córdoba, and Almería to purchase Muslim captives.[41]

Sources of Legitimacy

Given this diversity in slave origins, status distinctions were not obvious in the late medieval Mediterranean world. At a time when pirates and bandits ran rampant across the Mediterranean (and parts of the Atlantic), in a context where Valencian Christians could just as easily find themselves captives of North African Moors,[42] Valencian Christians perhaps felt especially compelled to articulate rules of enslavement (and continually reaffirm them). Selling a "free" person as a slave, for example, was a serious crime in fifteenth-century Valencia. According to the kingdom's legal code, knowingly being party to the unlawful seizure and sale of a free person into slavery constituted the crime of *collera*, punishable by a sentence of death without possibility for pardon.[43]

Confessions in the Court of the Bailiff General

Indeed, before a captive could legitimately be sold as a slave within the kingdom of Valencia, he or she first had to be presented before the bailiff general (*batle general*), the Crown official entrusted with investigating the legitimacy of all captures and collecting the Crown's cut of the booty. (Initially, this had been a fifth of any captured item's sales price; hence this tax was called the *quinto*). To determine whether a captive was *de bona guerra* (that is, lawfully captured and enslaveable), the bailiff general received testimony

40. These figures were derived from my analysis of the two volumes of *presentaciones y confessiones de cautivos* extant from the fifteenth century, ARV B 193 and 194.

41. ARV Baliía 194: 54r–v, 230v–231v, 282r–283r, 327r–328v, 465r–466r. See also M. A. Ladero Quesada, "La esclavitud por guerra a fines del siglo XV: El caso de Málaga," *Hispania* 27 (1967): 63–88.

42. For works discussing Muslim corsair activity against Christians and Christian captivity in Islamic territories, see Díaz Borrás, *Los orígenes de la piratería islámica;* Rodriguez, *Captives and Their Saviors;* and Brodman, *Ransoming Captives in Crusader Spain.* The threat of captivity persisted, of course, into the early modern period: see also Robert C. Davis, *Christian Slaves, Muslim Masters: White Slavery in the Mediterranean, the Barbary Coast and Italy, 1500–1800* (London: Palgrave Macmillan, 2003), and Ellen Friedman, *Spanish Captives in North Africa in the Early Modern Age* (Madison: University of Wisconsin Press, 1983).

43. *Furs de València*, V: 107–109. For a discussion of the crime of *collera*, see also Ferrer i Mallol, *La frontera amb l'Islam*, 50–64.

not only from the individual seeking confirmation of their slave status—most commonly the very corsairs who captured them—but also from the captives themselves. In their "confessions" before the bailiff general—frequently taken with the assistance of an interpreter (*torcimany*) and in the presence of prominent members of the local Muslim community, including the Crown-appointed qāḍī or chief judge of Valencia's Muslim community or *aljama*—captives related their personal histories. Besides stating their name, age, faith, parentage, and place of birth, these captives recounted, often with great poignancy, how they had been captured, enslaved, and brought to Valencia. Although a captive's "confession" was limited and, to a large extent, determined by the questions posed, this hearing nevertheless constituted an opportunity for a captive to offer his or her side of the story and, in extremely rare cases, issue a plea for release. The very existence of these records is emblematic of how slavery was presented as an institution regulated by a well-defined set of legal procedures.

Charged with investigating the circumstances of every captive put up for sale within the kingdom's borders, the bailiff general was the Crown official invested with the authority to distinguish licit corsair activity from illicit piracy.[44] Thus, on 23 June 1433, a notary acting on behalf of the nobleman Galceran de Requesens appeared before the bailiff general with forty-five captives in tow. He asked the bailiff general to declare these *moros* seized from two Moorish corsair vessels "captives of good war...just as was customary with similar Saracens, especially those engaged in corsair activities against Christians."[45]

Although the bailiff general's principal concern in policing corsair activity may have been to protect the Crown's diplomatic and commercial interests, this ought not to obscure a very real concern with maintaining slavery's moral legitimacy. Although it would seem that the presenters of captives expected from the bailiff general nothing less than a rubber-stamp on their ability to trade, sell, and possess these captives as slaves, the time, resources, and energy that were invested in these proceedings suggests that they were more than calculated maneuvers whereby the bailiff general could assert his authority and garner more revenues.

44. Although in practice the methods and tactics employed by pirates and corsairs may have seemed virtually indistinguishable, the pirate (in the words of the bailiff general) *"ne teme a Dios ni a Rey"* (fears neither God nor king). He attacked and captured vessels indiscriminately without authorization or justification. The actions of a corsair, in contrast, were (at least in theory) strictly regulated. For example, he would not have legal possession of any booty captured unless he first physically presented it before the appropriate authorities and gave a full account of his actions. Indeed, for Michel Mollat, the distinction between the pirate and the corsair hinged on this very act. It symbolized the corsair's recognition of a higher authority. Michel Mollat, "Essai d'orientation pour l'etude de la guerre de course et la piraterie (XIII–XV siècles)," *Course et Piraterie: Études présentées à la Commission International d'Histoire Maritime* 15 (Paris: CNRS, 1975). Cited in Guiral-Hadziiossif, *Valence*, 101.

45. ARV B 193: 144r–168r.

The *presentaciones de cautivos*, after all, were formal hearings explicitly designed to make public arguments justifying an individual's capture and sale into slavery. The testimony of corsairs, the confessions of captives, and the bailiff general's sentences provide us with valuable insight concerning contemporary understandings of the circumstances under which individuals could lawfully be enslaved. The court of the bailiff general constituted perhaps the most important venue in which slavery's legitimacy was officially, publicly, and repeatedly proclaimed. These records, therefore, not only describe fifteenth-century experiences of enslavement, ultimately they defined the process by which the "naturally free" could be transformed into slaves.

Conquest in warfare had long been the standard accepted mode of acquiring slaves along the Muslim-Christian frontier. It is no coincidence that the term used to describe a legitimately enslaved individual was "captive of good war" (*catiu de bona guerra*). In the early part of the fifteenth century, the bulk of captives entering the port of Valencia had been the victims of corsair activity. Masterminded by seamen of a multitude of different origins, these attacks were often, although not always, part and parcel of the interminable struggle between Islam and Christianity. One gets a general sense of the atmosphere in which these seizures took place by reading the testimony of captives and corsairs. The more or less formulaic series of questions and answers meticulously documented in the volumes of *presentaciones y confessiones de cautivos* is, at times, interrupted by compelling bits of narrative, vivid tales of attacks made by Christian corsairs on both land and sea.

On 16 July 1434, a group of Christian corsairs from Peñiscola and Benicarlo (coastal towns located in the northern part of the kingdom) appeared before the bailiff general to present the twelve surviving captives of the sixteen seized from aboard a Moorish corsair vessel. They related how, a few weeks before then, the city councilmen of Vinaroz, "as was customary," had issued a general warning, alerting neighboring municipalities that they had spotted a *galeota de moros* lurking in its waters and headed in their direction. Heeding this advice to take the appropriate precautions "on land as well as at sea," the men of Benicarlo and Peñiscola quickly mobilized a defense, dispatching four armed vessels in pursuit of the Muslim galley.

Among those aboard this Muslim galley was the aforementioned thirty-year-old linen weaver named Caçim Benhamet, who provides our most detailed account of what turned out to be the ship's last voyage. Caçim testified that about a month earlier, he, along with nineteen other Moors, had boarded a ship (*bergant*) armed in Bougie "for the purposes of going to win [i.e., capture] Christians." The expedition had started off promisingly. They cornered three Christian vessels at the mouth of a river near Tortosa. Two of these ships gave chase, however, pursuing the Moorish vessel out into the open sea, where its situation quickly degenerated. In the course of a prolonged sea battle, Caçim reports that three of his fellow crewmembers were killed and seven more injured before they surrendered to the Christians.

In such a clear-cut case of Christians combating Moorish corsairs, the bailiff general had no problem affirming Caçim's *de bona guerra* status—particularly since, immediately upon their return to Peñiscola, their Christian captors had secured from them confessions affirming that "they had gone to sea in order to capture the persons and goods of Christians." Indeed, under questioning from the local bailiff, "each and every Moor" had admitted, "with not one disputing this," that "just before they were captured, they had forcibly boarded a [Christian] vessel." Moreover, they acknowledged, "had not the men aboard said vessel taken flight, they would have taken them captive."[46]

Muslim corsairs, however, were not the only victims of Christian corsairs. The activities of corsairs licensed by the bailiff general or other authorized officials were hardly limited to "defensive" maneuvers—that is, the pursuit of Muslim corsair vessels prowling the kingdom's coastline. Judging from the *presentaciones y confessiones de cautivos*, fishermen, lone travelers, and Muslim jurists (*faqīhs*) were equally fair game. For example, Abrahim Ben Muça, a thirty-year-old fisherman, described how he and his brother were captured off the coast of Monecha (Granada). Shortly after sunrise, as he and his brother set out in their skiff to secure the day's catch, they were surprised by a Christian corsair vessel that had been hiding behind a pile of rocks.[47] Similarly, Faraig Benali, a thirty-five-year-old laborer from Motril (Granada), related how he had been assaulted and taken captive while traveling alone along a footpath bordering the sea. The group of six or seven Christians had jumped out suddenly, surrounded him, and then gave him a blow to the head with a knife.[48] Finally, sixty-year-old Ali, a native of Bone (modern-day Annaba, Algeria) who described his occupation as "reading the Qur'ān in mosques," was captured along with three other *faqīhs* traveling aboard a Muslim merchant vessel carrying a cargo of wheat, barley, and raw and spun cotton.[49] None of these captives posed an obvious military threat to the Crown. Nonetheless, the bailiff general expressed no hesitancy in judging these civilian noncombatants "captives of good war." In this war on the seas, where surprise land raids and naval assaults were the norm, legitimate captives included both violent aggressors and innocent bystanders caught in the crossfire. "Enemies of the faith and Crown" seemingly included anyone residing in hostile territories.

In the more than twelve hundred confessions extant from the fifteenth century, only five captives ever contested the legitimacy of their seizure. They did so by protesting that

---

46. "Tots concordes e degu no discrepant dixeren ells esser venguts per guanyar e pendre les persones e robes de xristians e de fet ans que fossen presos muntaren en un leny al cap de Tortosa e sino com la gent era fuyta ells los hagueren cativats." ARV B 193: 186r.

47. ARV B 193: 30v–32v.

48. ARV B 193: 97v–104v.

49. ARV Baliía 194: 156r–162r.

their presence in hostile territories was involuntary or only temporary. In 1423, a captive named Abdalla claimed that he was a long-lost Christian. Born in Greece, Abdalla, alias Nicholau, testified that he was taken captive by a group of Moors from Algiers while serving as a crewman aboard a Valencian galley. Forced by his Muslim masters to deny his Christian faith publicly, Abdalla/Nicholau protested that "at heart, he is [still] a Christian." Among the forty-four others seized from aboard this Moorish vessel was another captive claiming that he was a long-lost Christian. Though Azmet Alazla admitted he was born a Muslim in the kingdom of Valencia, he testified that he had converted to Christianity just before being kidnapped by Moorish pirates. Azmet, alias Jacme Bertran, insisted that he had been forced to board the Muslim corsair vessel in which he had been captured. Indeed, Azmet/Jacme maintained that he had been plotting his escape. As soon as the vessel neared Christian territory, he had intended to jump ship, fleeing his Muslim oppressors so that he could reembrace the Christian faith.[50]

In an atmosphere of mutual suspicion, the bailiff general perhaps had good reason to question the veracity of Abdalla and Azmet's claims. After all, one of their companions had been caught in a lie[51] and three others confessed they were fugitive Mudejars who had illegally emigrated into Muslim territories for the purpose of joining forces with Moorish corsairs to wreak havoc on Christians.[52] Ultimately, therefore, the bailiff general paid little heed to their protests and lumped the forty-five captives together, declaring them all *catius de bona guerra*. Whether fugitive Mudejars or victims of kidnapping, all of them, at the time of capture, were residents of the city of Bougie and subjects of the "king" of Tunis. Forcibly conscripted or volunteers, all were aboard a Muslim vessel engaged in corsair activity against Christians. Hence, they were lawfully enslaveable as "public enemies of the Catholic faith and Crown."

The claims made about a decade later by three Muslim captives that their permanent residence was in territories currently under treaty with the Catalan-Aragonese Crown were less easy for the bailiff general to ignore. With eight captives in tow, the Valencian

50. ARV B 193: 144r–163r.

51. In his first hearing before the bailiff general, Ali Abencayt, a forty-year-old native of Sale, testified that he was a mere porter. Upon further questioning, however, Ali admitted that he was the ship's captain. ARV B 193: 144r–163r.

52. Mahomat Abacayzar (who, at the time of his capture, was reportedly twenty-five years in age) had been born in Gandia; Abraffim Benjahem (also twenty-five) was originally from Gondara, near Denia; and Çaat Xexoni (twenty-three) testified that he was born in Panies, also near Denia. Çaat's testimony is particularly illuminating. Çaat explains that while he and several other Mudejars were attending a wedding in the Vall d'Eslida, they were approached by a Christian who offered to smuggle them into the Nasrid Sultanate of Granada for a fee of five florins apiece. ARV B 193: 144r–163r. See also the testimony of the fifty-year-old Farig Abellim, who, up until about a year earlier, had been living in Barcelona as the slave of a tanner. This dark-skinned (llor) Muslim had fled his master's custody and, in the company of five other Muslim fugitives, traveled back to Islamic territories in a stolen fishing boat.

corsair Bernat Font appeared before the bailiff general on 14 July 1434, seeking the *de bona guerra* ruling that would facilitate their sale in the Valencian marketplace. Captain of a midsized galley licensed "to engage in corsair activity against Moors," Font habitually prowled the waters off the Strait of Gibraltar. While he was in Ceuta, "awaiting further fortune and a chance to capture more booty," Font learned of a Muslim merchant vessel bearing wheat, clothing, and other merchandise due to depart the port of Bediz de la Gomera in the kingdom of Fes. Setting off in hot pursuit, by the following morning Font was about fifteen miles from Bediz when he spotted not just one but two vessels, the second trailing close behind the first. Font soon discovered that this second vessel was piloted by a Portuguese corsair who also had his sights on the richly laden Moorish vessel. Rather than brush his rival off, the Portuguese captain sought Font's assistance, making him and his crew the following proposition: if they should prove "a good partner in this endeavor," they would be richly rewarded. Thus, about forty miles from Bediz, they had jointly assaulted and captured this Muslim vessel, seizing its cargo as well as taking its twenty-four passengers as captives. Font subsequently brought his share of the spoils to Valencia, where he hoped to make a tidy profit.[53]

Soon enough, however, a wrinkle developed in Font's plan. In direct contradiction with the testimony they had initially given before the local bailiff of Alicante, three of the seven captives now claimed to be residents of the sultanate of Granada, hence protected from enslavement by virtue of a treaty between the Crown of Aragon and the Nasrid Sultanate.

Font initially attempted to deflect these protests by shifting responsibility for the vessel's capture entirely onto the shoulders of the Portuguese captain, which, if successful, would have meant that these three passengers would not be protected by any treaty between the Nasrid Sultanate and the Crown of Aragon. Font and his crew, after all, had not been the ones who had captured them. Rather, they had been *given* to them, already captured. The Portuguese captain had given the captives to them "out of courtesy" for the aid they had lent him in fighting the infidel. However ingenious this argument seems to us, the bailiff general was not satisfied with it. Font therefore tried a different (less creative) tactic: he insisted the three captives were lying. Font argued that they were feigning Granadan origins in an effort to secure their deliverance from captivity.

Font's entire case, however, hinged on the earlier testimony of these "liars": the statements they had made in the port of Alicante immediately after their capture: "Questioned by the nobleman [and bailiff of Alicante] don Pero Maça as to their place of origin, they said and were heard to say in the presence of others that they [respectively] were from Tunis, Fez, and Marrochs. Not one of them [said that they were] from the lands of Granada." It was Font's contention that these captives—having seen how other captives

---

53. ARV B 193: 210r–213r.

aboard the vessel escaped enslavement as a consequence of being subjects of the Nasrid Sultanate—had changed their stories.[54] Font continued:

> And if some of them say now that they are from Granada or Málaga, something which he does not believe, they would have said so only because they saw how the nobleman don Pero Maça had taken back four Moors from Málaga, reimbursing their buyers the prices paid for them and releasing said four Moors back into the custody of the king of Granada, delivering them from captivity.

Font's crewmembers, not surprisingly, backed up his claims, as did the bailiff of Alicante. Tapping into deep-seated suspicion and distrust of the infidel, Font urged the bailiff general to discount this new testimony:

> It would be an outrageous thing to have your wisdom rest on a sole assertion, especially that of an infidel.... It is unclear why more weight should be ascribed to the claims they make today than to those they had maintained up until now, especially when a record of what they said exists, a formal document drawn up in the town of Alicante by don Pero Maça in which he recorded those whom he found there who were from Granada, a document of which these persons are well aware and not ignorant. These matters, greatly attested to by said noble and others, ought to arouse your courage as well as that of all the land to issue a ruling affirming that these captives are not from Granada, but are, respectively, from Bougie, Tunis, etc.[55]

Although captives rarely contested the legitimacy of their seizures in the court of the bailiff general, protests made *after* the fact—including abjurations of prior testimony—

---

54. The bailiff of Alicante testified that these men had been present when he questioned some other captives concerning the circumstances of their seizure. Thus, they had overheard how these other captives protested that they could not be enslaved since they were "protected" subjects of the Nasrid Sultanate of Granada. The bailiff recounted how "as they were there before him, he asked the captain, as well as the four other Moors, one by one, where they were from. The captain responded that he was from Tenez. The others, however, responded that they were from Málaga. Thus, he [the bailiff] told the slave sellers, 'Well, then, you can take the captain, but you must leave me these ones,' referring to the four Moors who said they were from Málaga." The bailiff then related how the captain, hearing this, suddenly decided to amend his testimony. "He said that he had a wife in Málaga in addition to the one he had in Tenez." His suspicions raised given the circumstances under which this new piece of information had been revealed, the bailiff of Alicante ordered the slave seller to bring the captain back and said to him, "Smart one, tell me the truth. Who is your [true] lord, the king of Granada or the lord of Tenez?" The bailiff related how the captain ultimately admitted he was a subject of the lord of Tenez, "acknowledging how he had sworn his oath of vassalage there." ARV B 193: 235r–v.

55. ARV B 193: 215r–223v.

were hardly unheard of. Indeed, this was a significant enough problem in the kingdom that legislation was written to prohibit it. In the Cortes celebrated in Valencia in 1301, Jaime II promulgated the following statute concerning "those Saracens who are taken at sea by corsairs or others": "Once, in the presence of the bailiff general of the lord king they have testified and are judged *de bona guerra*, from that moment on, any subsequent confession they should make alleging the contrary ought not to be received. If they later state the contrary, they ought not to be believed. Rather, the first confession ought to stand."[56] Inasmuch as, in this case, the "first confession" contradicted testimony given in the court of the bailiff general, this statute did not offer much in the way of an easy resolution.

Compounding the bailiff general's difficulty was an awareness that Christian corsairs displayed an equally strong propensity for giving false testimony. Jacqueline Guiral-Hadziiossif has noted how Christian corsairs appearing before the bailiff general frequently lied about how they had acquired a captive in order to secure a *de bona guerra* ruling.[57] Thus unlawfully seized Mudejars were routinely pressured to say that they were from Fes or North Africa. Given the obvious bias of the witnesses produced by Bernat Font, the bailiff general sought corroborating testimony from individuals who seemingly had nothing to gain: the five Moors who were captured aboard the same cargo ship. Although four of the five slaves demurred, claiming that they knew nothing about these captives' personal backgrounds, having only recently made their acquaintance, a twenty-four-year-old dark-skinned (llor) porter named Caet Benmahomat proved more cooperative. Caet affirmed that he had "certain knowledge" that two of the three captives had not been born in the sultanate of Granada. Rather, they were natives, respectively of Bougie and Algiers. He knew this, he continued, because he had been friends with them. For the past several years they had all lived, eaten, and worked together in Bougie.

Although Caet was the only witness whose testimony directly contradicted the captives' claims, the bailiff general felt satisfied enough with his assertions to overlook the contradictory and inconclusive statements of the others. In fact, the bailiff general harmonized the witnesses' testimony in his ruling, glossing over the places where witnesses had disagreed. According to the bailiff general's final summation, all five witnesses had confirmed Font's contention. The three captives were lying and, in truth, they were subjects of the king of Fes.

The only investigation of its kind encountered in over one thousand presentations, the effort expended by the bailiff general here to verify Bernat Font's claims is noteworthy. Particularly revealing is the trial's final scene. With the principal notables of the Muslim

---

56. Cited in Graullera Sanz, *La esclavitud*, 67. This provision would later be repeated in the *Llibre Negre*, the *Aureum Opus*, and in the *Furs de València*.

57. Guiral-Hadziiossif, *Valence*, 138.

community once more in attendance, the three captives were hauled back into the bailiff general's court and obliged to sit and listen as interpreters read aloud the testimony of witnesses discrediting their claims to protected status as subjects of the Nasrid Sultanate of Granada. At the conclusion of this extensive and meticulously constructed presentation of the "evidence," the captives were asked if what had been read aloud to them was, in fact, true. All three captives reportedly replied in the affirmative, admitting "it was true, just as has been recounted." Immediately following this carefully orchestrated ceremony, the bailiff general pronounced them *catius de bona guerra* and a few days later they were sold to a Valencian merchant for a tidy sum. Font, we can assume, took the cash and set off on yet another adventure.[58] What this episode ultimately highlights is an almost pathological concern with securing the slave's admission of the legitimacy of his condition. Despite all the "evidence" that had been marshaled against them, it was only when the three captives themselves acknowledged the legality of their seizure that the bailiff general (as he had done hundreds of times before) issued a ruling sanctioning their enslavement. Captives were brought before the bailiff general to publicly "confess" their condition. At the climax of this command performance, they were asked, point blank, "Are you a captive or are you free?" The "voluntary" character of their confessions, moreover, was repeatedly stressed in the bailiff general's ruling. Thus, with respect to the eight captives presented by Bernat Font, the bailiff general concluded:

> After having seen the presentation of the said eight Moors made before him, with each and every one of said eight Moors testifying before him voluntarily and without any force being put on them . . . it has been clearly proven and established, having been confirmed by the captives' own testimony, that all eight men are from the land of the Moors, public enemies of the holy Catholic faith and the lord king.[59]

Contracts of Captivity (Cartas de Cativeri) and Commutations of Corporal Penalties

On 11 February 1476, a Mudejar couple from Gata, Çahat Mahomatdell and his wife Fatima, were sold to the nobleman Joan Dixer for forty lliures. In the contract of sale, their former lord, Pedro Ladro, affirmed his ownership of the couple by citing the terms of a contract. He explained to the seller that "they were put into captivity and pertain to me in accordance with the terms of a certain contract." Although Pere does not give any more details concerning this contract, he likely was referring to a contract of debt in

58. ARV B 193: 243r. On 4 August 1434, Font sold the captives to a local merchant of Valencia for 10,010 solidos. This merchant also purchased the Moorish vessel with all of its furnishings for an additional eleven hundred solidos.

59. ARV B 193: 238r–239r.

which Çahat and Fatima pledged their persons as security for its repayment. Indeed, the document immediately subsequent to this sale in the notarial register is a contract of debt in which Çahat and his wife promised to pay their new "owner" the forty lliures he "lent" them "out of pious love for us" in order to "redeem" them from Pere Ladro's custody. They acknowledged that if they failed to pay Joan Dixer back within the time stipulated, "they will be and shall remain in captivity and servitude."[60]

Although Crown protections assured Mudejars a certain amount of freedom of movement within the kingdom, seigneurial lords, nonetheless, were empowered to seize a Mudejar vassal who failed to pay off debts and/or seigneurial dues before changing residence or swearing an oath of vassalage to another lord.[61] In a document drawn up on 19 October 1474, a Mudejar couple from Picaçent—a cobbler named Abdulcaçim al Marques and his wife Axux—confessed that they had left their lord's lands without satisfying a one hundred florin debt. When these fugitive Mudejars were apprehended, however, their lord did not simply pronounce Abdulcaçim and Axux *catius de bona guerra*. Rather, a "contract of captivity" was drawn up. Abdulcaçim and Axux promised to return to Picassent "within the next eight days" where they would live "with all their goods and clothing... not departing from thence or leaving its boundaries without license of the said nobleman" until the debt had been paid in full.[62]

According to the Furs de València, enslavement for debt was illegal. What we might refer to as debt servitude was permissible in the kingdom of Valencia only if it was voluntary and, even then, it was supposed to be temporary:

A free person shall not serve creditors for any obligation or for any debt that he owes them *unless he wishes to put himself into service of his own free will for a set period of time*, [the duration of which should be] determined in accordance with the amount of debt. If at any time during this set period he should have the means to pay off the debt, [effective] immediately upon payment, he shall not be obliged to provide any further service. The creditor is also obliged to deduct [from the amount of debt] the amount of the debt already satisfied through service.[63]

---

60. ARV P 1844 (nonpaginated): 11 February 1476. Çahat and Fatima affirmed that if they failed to live up to any of the terms of this agreement "simus remaneamus in captivitate et servitute."

61. See the statute promulgated by Martín I in 1403, discussed in Meyerson, "Slavery and the Social Order," 158–59.

62. ARV P 2785: nonpaginated, 19 October 1474.

63. "Persona franch o liura no servescha als creedors per alcuna obligatió o per alcun deute que-ls deje, si donchs no s'l volrrà obligar de sa pròpia volentat que li servescha a cert temps per rahò d'aquel deute; e, si en aquell demig haurà de què pusque pagar, que-l pac e que no li sia tengut de servir més; e lo crehedor prenga'l-li en comte ço que li haura servit en paga del deute." Furs de València, ed. Colon and Garcia (Barcelona, 1983), IV: 27.

Çahat and Fatima or Abdulcaçim and Axux could be enslaved, then, not because of the debt itself, but because they had voluntarily entered a contract of service, pledging their own persons as surety. Mudejar vassals too impoverished to liquidate their debts "voluntarily" entered into contracts of captivity (*cartas de cativeri*). Sometimes their debts had been prompted by material necessities. At other times, the debt was a fine imposed in penalty for a certain crime. For many Mudejars, perpetual servitude seems to have been the effective end result of these contracts. For lack of anything else, they pledged their persons—or, sometimes, that of their children—in surety (*en penyora*). Any failure to comply with the terms of this agreement—violating the residence requirements, failing to make payments on time, or swearing homage to another lord—would, effectively, be punished with penal servitude. Thus, in 1466 a "very young" Mudejar girl had been transferred over into the custody of her father's lord as surety for his repayment of a debt. According to the terms of the debt agreement, if this father failed to "redeem" (*quitava*) his daughter from his lord's custody within a certain time period, she would become his perpetual slave. Two years later, since the girl's father had failed to satisfy the debt, she was declared a slave by the qāḍī of Beniargo and this nobleman (Ramon de Vilanova) sold the Mudejar girl to a silk weaver.[64]

According to contemporary notarial records, in fact, most Mudejars—even those convicted of crimes—were enslaved (at least officially) for breach of contract. In 1472, a Mudejar vassal of Manises named Ali was seized by his lord, Pere Boïl, for committing "certain crimes." "At the request of some friends and relatives of his," however, Ali was released from his lord's custody on the promise that he would pay a fine of forty lliures within the next four years. Under the terms of this agreement, a *carta de cativeri*, Ali, along with his brother Mahomat, "obliged themselves and swore homage to said nobleman, promising to be his vassals for the next five years." Vowing not to depart from his service "until he was content," the brothers assured Pere that if they ever "openly or secretly" left Manises to live somewhere else or swore homage to a different lord, "they would become the captives of the said lord." Henceforth Pere could treat them as his slaves, that is, "sell them, beat them, and imprison them in such a way that no one could defend them."[65]

Two years later, Pere would assemble a group of witnesses and a notary to record his enslavement of his fugitive vassals who, before fulfilling their obligations to him, had

---

64. The contract had specified that "si dins lo dit temps no la quitava, que fos cativa a totes passades" (if he did not redeem her within said time period, she would be a slave in perpetuity). ARV B Letra P #43 (1466).

65. The contract stipulated that the two brothers had agreed that "si fugiran publicament ni amagada en algun altre loch per abitar en aquell o avassallaran ab altre senyor que ells sien catius del dit noble senyor. E que puga fer de ells com de sclaus seus axi vendre'lls batre'lls o apresonar los en forma que negu no'ls puga deffendre de ell. Ans volen que si contravenen en res del que li an promes en lo dit acte all dit noble senyor ara per lavors se deuen per catius seus." ARV P 1914: nonpaginated, 22 August 1474.

sworn an oath of vassalage to another lord. Ali and Mahomat, as well as two other Mudejar brothers, Yaye Alquacho, alias "Picha," and Asmet, were being pronounced slaves. It was not enough, however, for Pere simply to affirm that these Mudejars contravened the contracts "they had made and to which they had consented." Once again, we see this obsession with securing the captives' "confessions":

> Said noble asked them if after having made and signed said contracts they became the vassals of the magnificent *micer* [66] Jacme Garcia de Aguilar, the lord of Alaquas. Each of the aforementioned four men and every one of them responded and told said most noble *en* Pere Boyill that it was true, that they had made and signed said contracts and then, afterward, broke and contravened them, becoming the vassals of the said magnificent *micer* Jachme Garcia de Aguilar.

Hence, Pere concluded, "Since they have violated said contracts, by virtue of having violated them, they are to be given as captives to the said lord. And, since they [themselves] have acknowledged this," he, "as the lord of the said castle and locality of Manises, informs them that he hereby judges them to be his captives and takes custody of them as his slaves, to do with all and every one of them as he wills and that he does so in accordance with the preinserted contracts."[67]

Described as "contracts of captivity," all of the documents I have mentioned here portray enslavement as the consequence of deliberate choices and conscious actions. We see a similar logic being enunciated in documents recording the commutation of corporal punishments to sentences of perpetual enslavement. The substitution of enslavement for the corporal penalties decreed by Muslim *qāḍīs* was invariably presented in the Christian documentation as a benevolent and generous act, if not a reprieve from certain death. Thus, on 7 July 1477, Çahat Alasmar, a Mudejar sentenced by Ali Bellvis, the *alcadi del senyor rey* (i.e., the chief *qāḍī* or judge of the Muslim community in Valencia) to lose his right fist, appeared before his lord, Francis de Menaguerra, to beg for his pardon. The notary called in to record this event described the scene taking place in the main hall of the lord's home:

> And Çahat Alasmar (alias Aladobuc), dreading an injury so great as losing his right hand or fist, fearing very much a punishment so severe, and wishing to redeem

---

66. An honorific title, often ascribed to men of letters.

67. "Lo dit noble interroga a aquells si apres fets e fermats los dits contractes si seren fets vassalls del magnifich micer Jachme Garcia de Aguilar senyor de Alaquas. Los quals tots los sobredits quatre e cascu per si respongheren e dixeren al dit molt noble en Pere Boyill que veritat es que ells an fet e fermat los dit contractes e apres trenquant e venint contra aquells se eren fets vassals del dit magnifich micer Jachme Garcia de Aguilar." ARV P 1914: nonpaginated, 22 August 1474.

himself from suffering this as well as other, monetary, penalties … gave himself up as a captive to his lord, begging him to be willing to accept him and waive said penalty and penalties both corporal and monetary. Thenceforth his lord would be able to sell, donate, or bequeath him as his captive, acquired lawfully in good war. [Furthermore, he urged his lord to commute this penalty to enslavement] especially because it could not be doubted that, as a result of such a punishment, he would lose his life.[68]

Thus, Cahat's lord, in response to this plea, benevolently pardoned his sentence to suffer both pecuniary and corporal penalties and "accepted" him as his slave.

The notary called in to record and formally certify the penal enslavement of Fatima, a Mudejar woman from Navarres sentenced to receive fifty-five lashes by Yusuf Benaye, the qāḍī of Xativa, painted a similar scene:

Seeing before her the executioner (moro de vaques), ready, with all of his equipment, to administer the said sentence on her person, considering the said sentence of lashing to be a very cruel and grievous punishment, one that she could not endure or withstand, thus, in order to redeem and protect her person from said punishment of lashing, Fatima decided to offer herself up as a captive. Therefore, for this reason, she now willingly and knowingly gives herself as captive to the nobleman and lord of Navarres, Miquel Joan Tolza, as well as to his dependents. He can sell, donate, alienate, as well as transport her in any manner, doing with her person as he wills, just as can be done with a female captive acquired and won in good war (de bona guerra).[69]

It is most certainly true, as Mark Meyerson has suggested, that "it was not so much mercy that moved royal officials in these cases as a desire to obtain the proceeds from the

68. "E com lo dit Cahat al Asmar alter Adobuc temes lo tant dan com es li seria perdre la dita ma dreta e o puny dret e per quant tem molt la dita tant gran pena e per rembre aquella e altres pecuniaries en les quals aquell era condempnat ab la dita sentencia se dona per catiu al dit senyor e pregan lo vulla acceptar e perdonar li la dita pena e penes axi corporal com peccuniaries en axi que lo dit senyor lo puxa vendre donar e alienar com a catiu seu comprat de bona guerra e majorment com stiga en dubte per la dita pena no perdes la vida." The nobleman Francis de Menaguerra, in turn, "acceptant lo dit Cahat la Asmar en catiu seu perdona a aquell a prechs de diverses persones axi les penes corporal com peccuniaries muntant e transportant aquells en cativeri puix al dit Cahat era permes rembre les ab cativeri." APPV 25003: nonpaginated, 7 July 1477.

69. "Ves damunt si lo moro de vaques aparellat ab tots sos arreus per executar la dita sentencia en la sua persona e aquella dita Fatima ves la dita sentencia e pena de açots molt greu e crua e tal que aquella no poria passar ni sostenir per ço per rembre e reservar la sua persona de la dita pena de açots delibera ans donar se a captiva. Per tal de grat e de certa sciencia se dona per captiva al dit magnifich mossen Miquell Johan Tolza cavaller senyor del dits loch de Navares e als seus en axi que la puixa vendre donar alienar e en altra qualsevol manera tresportar e fer de aquella a les sues propries voluntats si e segons poria fet de una captiva adquesida e guanyada de bona guerra." APPV 20515: nonpaginated, 18 July 1478.

sale of the Mudejars themselves."[70] Nevertheless, what stands out most strikingly here is the emphasis being placed on the condemned Mudejar's role in his or her enslavement. Delivering their persons "willingly and knowingly" to their new masters, it was at the request, if not urgent pleas, of Mudejars, that Christian lords "accepted" them as their slaves.

Self-Sale

Since they were already slaves when they entered the kingdom, "eastern" slaves acquired in eastern Mediterranean ports were not presented before the bailiff general. Having been sold and resold as slaves, usually by Genoese, Venetian, Catalan, or Majorcan merchants in port cities scattered across the Mediterranean (or perhaps elsewhere in the Iberian Peninsula), their "slave" status was well established by the time of their arrival in Valencia. Nevertheless, each time a slave changed hands, buyers, sellers, and notaries took care to certify his or her legally enslaved status. Part of the notarial formulary for any slave sale was a clause in which the seller assured the buyer that the slave in question was "*de bona guerra*." Thus, in a contract of sale drawn up in 1470, a widow selling a fifty-year-old Russian slave, a Christian named Maria, assured her buyer that Maria was a *catiu de bona guerra*, explicitly affirming that she had been "acquired and captured in good war and not in violation of any truce or peace treaty of the lord king."[71] Although Orthodox Christians, as "schismatics," could be classified as "infidels, enemies of the Catholic faith," the enslavement of fellow Christians provoked a certain amount of discomfort. In labeling her a *catiu de bona guerra*, Maria's seller put this Christian female in the same category as Moorish infidels.

In his Europeanwide study of medieval slavery, Charles Verlinden detected signs of uncertainty with regard to the legitimacy of the enslavement of Orthodox Christians and observed that these doubts seem to have been particularly acute in the territories of the Crown of Aragon during the fourteenth century.[72] Discomfort with respect to Catalan trafficking in Greek slaves was evident almost immediately after the Catalan Company began its exploits in the eastern Mediterranean.[73] Perhaps because some of the Orthodox

70. Meyerson, "Slavery and the Social Order," 150.

71. "De bona guerra habitam et captivam et non de pace nech treuga domini regis." ARV P 1911: nonpaginated, 26 October 1470.

72. Charles Verlinden, "Orthodoxie et esclavage au bas Moyen Age," *Mélanges Eugène Tisserand* 5 (1964): 428–42. Verlinden, though, also found special dispositions favoring the enfranchisement of Orthodox Christian slaves being issued in Genoa.

73. Although the so-called Catalan Company (in reality a more motley crew of Catalan, Aragonese, Sicilian, and other mercenaries under the command of the German Roger the Flor) had originally been contracted by the Byzantine Emperor, Michael IX, to drive the Turks out of its border lands in Asia Minor. Subsequently, Michael IX became so threatened by their successes that he had Roger de Flor (along with several of his key commanders) assassinated. In retribution, the surviving members of the Catalan Company went on a rampage, terrorizing the western and southern regions of the Greek peninsula. Eventually,

Christian captives seized by Catalan *almogàvers*[74] were being purchased by Muslim buyers, Jaime II issued a royal edict dictating that, henceforth, Greek slaves were no longer to be traded by Catalan merchants. In 1314, however, "at the request and entreaty of the honored citizens of Barcelona," Jaime II amended this ordinance so that Greek slaves could still be exchanged *within* the territories of the Crown of Aragon. So long as they were not exported, Greek slaves could continue to be bought and sold in Aragonese territories.[75]

Citing royal ordinances and decrees issued between 1314 and 1388 and directed toward both restricting the trade in Greek Orthodox Christian slaves and facilitating (if not securing outright) the manumission of enslaved Greeks and other Orthodox Christians, Verlinden argued that these Crown initiatives (dictated, respectively, by Jaime II, Pedro IV, and Juan I) were inspired, principally, by ideas circulating in ecclesiastical circles. Suggesting that the renewed prospect of mending the schism between the eastern and western churches provoked Latin (i.e., Roman Catholic) ecclesiastical officials to reconsider the ethics of enslaving their fellow Christians, Verlinden stressed, for instance, how in a decree awarding provisional freedom to a group of Greeks detained as slaves in Tortosa (dated 1382), Pedro IV cited the "*constitutio et ordinatio*" of Pope Urban V calling for the universal liberation of Greek slaves after seven years of service.[76]

We ought not automatically assume, however, that Crown officials, in responding to the appeals made by slaves of Orthodox Christian origins, were motivated strictly (or even principally) by concerns regarding the morality of Christians enslaving Christians. Rather, these actions were not all that distinguishable from interventions made by Crown officials on behalf of Muslim subjects of Aragonese allies protesting that they had been unlawfully captured. In one of the letters Verlinden cites as proof for this new atmosphere of moral concern, the bailiff (*verguer general*) of the Catalan duchies of Athens and Neopatria demanded (in 1360) the release of five Greek men transported into the kingdom of

---

they carved out the Catalan Duchy based in Athens and Thebes, which they held onto into the 1380s. After a brief period under the successive rule of the Acciaioli family of Florence, the Venetians, and then Constantine Palaeologus of Morea, the remnants of the former Catalan duchy of Athens were conquered by the Ottoman sultan Mehmed II in 1456. On the exploits of the Catalan Company, see K. M. Setton, *Catalan Domination of Athens* (Cambridge: Medieval Academy of America, 1948), and Ramón Muntaner's *Crònica*, recently edited by Vicent Josep Escartí (Valencia: Valencia Institució Alfons el Magnànim, Diputació de València, 1999). See also Robert D. Hughes's recent translation into English of a portion of this work, *The Catalan Expedition to the East from the 'Chronicle' of Ramon Muntaner* (Woodbridge, U.K.: Tamesis Books, 2006).

74. Reputedly one of the most feared fighting forces in the Mediterranean, the *almogàvers* were mercenaries who typically fought on foot and were renowned for their skill with the javelin.

75. In this case, Verlinden acknowledged that, rather than being influenced by ideas circulating in ecclesiastical circles, Jaime II might have been inspired by the example of his younger brother, Frederick III of Sicily (Trinacria), who issued some very similar legislation in 1310.

76. Verlinden, "Orthodoxie et esclavage," 433.

Majorca for the purposes of being sold into slavery. In contesting their *de bona guerra* status, however, the bailiff makes no reference to their "Christian" identity. Rather, the bailiff argued that they could not lawfully be seized because they lived in territories that were at peace with the Crown of Aragon.[77] Similarly, in 1384, when Pedro IV demanded the immediate liberation of Michael Conde, a Greek boy taken captive along with his parents in Cephalonia, he did not argue that he was doing so because Michael was a "Christian," but because Cephalonia was under the jurisdiction of the Aragonese in Sicily. Pedro's decree states that "men of said country and kingdom, although they are Greeks, ought not to be taken captive since only Greeks under the dominion of the [Byzantine] emperor are to be considered those who, as Greeks, customarily can be taken captive."[78]

With the accession of Juan I, however, there is better evidence that some contemporaries were disturbed by the idea of Christians enslaving other Christians. Not only did Juan I issue an edict granting Orthodox Christian slaves special access to the courts to file suits demanding their liberty, but he also sent ambassadors to get the Avignonese pope Clement VII to issue a bull ordering the liberation of all Greek slaves, effective immediately (as opposed to following seven years of service). Indeed, what is most striking about Juan I's policies concerning these Orthodox Christian slaves is that he did not require conversion to Catholicism as a condition for their liberation. Though Juan I did acknowledge that their owners were entitled to some form of monetary restitution, he insisted that they should be compensated financially only if they could prove that their Greek slaves had been acquired indirectly through purchase. According to Juan I's reasoning, then, Greeks were no longer to be considered *de bona guerra* as schismatics. The only "legitimate" way a Christian could acquire a Greek Orthodox Christian slave was by purchasing one who had been captured by a Muslim Turk.[79]

Verlinden interpreted this shift in royal policy as a sign that "humanitarian" ideas emanating from ecclesiastical circles had won wider support. Whether or not this shift in policy was, in fact, attributable to pressure from members of the clergy, this "moral victory" was, Verlinden acknowledged, extremely short-lived. Juan's brother and successor Martin I reversed many of these provisions. In particular, "upon the strenuous urgings of the city council of Barcelona," he issued an order declaring that Eastern Orthodox slaves—whether Greek, Armenian, Albanian, Russian, Bulgarian, or natives of any region subject to the Byzantine emperor—would no longer be permitted special access

77. Verlinden, "Orthodoxie et esclavage," 431.

78. "Homines dicti comitatus et regni, quamvis sint greci non debent captivari cum solum in captivatio grecorum que fieri solebat intelligerent greci de dominio imperatoris." Cited and transcribed in Verlinden, "Orthodoxie et esclavage," 432.

79. Verlinden, "Orthodoxie et esclavage," 434. For the instructions given by Juan I to his ambassadors, see J. Miret y Sans, "La esclavitud en Cataluña en los últimos tiempos de la edad media," *Revue Hispanique* 41 (1917): 23.

to royal or municipal tribunals to file demands for liberty. Henceforth, they were to be treated like any other slave.[80]

Royal edicts, however, did not necessarily silence all the protests. Verlinden calls attention to the figure of Ramon de Escales, the bishop of Barcelona in the early part of the fifteenth century. Advocating the liberation of Greeks, Albanians, and, by extension, all Eastern Orthodox Christians, Ramon's preaching provoked strong opposition from the city's merchants and patricians. Complaints regarding his sermons reached Barcelona's city council. Portraying his activities as disruptive and threatening to public order, the city councilors ordered that he be strongly admonished and prevented from expressing such sentiments again publicly. Undaunted, Ramon de Escales continued preaching. In particular, it seems he was encouraging Eastern Orthodox slaves to file demands for liberty before the bishop's court. In 1401, the bailiff (verguer) issued an ordinance condemning to death any slave who sought recourse from a court other than the bailiff's to secure his or her freedom. Shortly thereafter, the bailiff sentenced a Greek male slave to death by hanging for seeking justice in the bishop's palace. Ramon de Escales, in response, promptly excommunicated the bailiff.

As the above example indicates, the ethics of Christians enslaving (or even owning) fellow Christians remained an open question and continued to be debated in the territories of the Crown of Aragon throughout the fourteenth and into the fifteenth centuries. I have encountered two suits dating from the latter half of the fifteenth centuries in which female slaves claiming "Greek" ethnicity demanded their liberation. In 1457, a 35—40-year-old woman named Caterina appealed to the governor of Valencia to affirm her free status since she was "of the nation (natio) of the Greeks, a native of the town of Corfú." Claiming that she had been kidnapped at a young age by Genoese raiders, Caterina demanded her freedom, citing not only the aforementioned papal bulls but also a directive issued by Pedro IV ordaining that "Greek persons or men or women of the Greek natio cannot be held, purchased, or sold as catius." Said privilege specified that "such persons are to be freed, with their buyers losing the price paid."[81] Similarly, in 1470, Maria, the aforementioned twenty-six-year-old woman from Nicosia, Cyprus, asked the governor to nullify her sale into slavery. Noting how she was a "Greek, born of parents who were free persons and members of a free people (gens)" such that she, too, had been born free, Maria asked the governor to affirm her free status.[82] Also claiming that she had been

---

80. Verlinden, "Orthodoxie et esclavage," 435–36.

81. "Per privilegis e bulles apostolicals e encara per privilegi del senyor rey en Pere es statuit e ordenat que persones gregues o de nacio de grechs homens o dones no puxen esser tenguts comprats ni venuts per catius ans los compradors perden lo preu e les tals persones son franques." ARV G 2289: M. 17: 46r.

82. "La dita venda deu esser declarada per vos dit spectable governador no esser de effecte algu ne la dita Maria podia esser stada venuda com sia grega ex libertis et in gentis parentibus procreada franca et libera." ARV G 2331: M. 16: 3r–8v.

kidnapped by the Genoese, Maria tugged at the governor's heartstrings by noting how she was only eight years old when she was taken from her parents. Indeed, she testified that she had been playing with some other little girls when she was taken captive.

Maria's sellers, of course, vehemently rejected Maria's claim that she was a Greek-born Christian. The truth of the matter was, they argued, that she was a Russian woman who had been taken captive by some Muslim Turks. Coming into Christian custody *after* she had already been enslaved legally by Muslims, these Genoese merchants insisted that they had acquired Maria legitimately via purchase. More interestingly, however, they also contested Maria's claim that she had been taken to Valencia by force and sold against her will. Denying Maria's charges that one of them had stripped her naked and given her many lashes to secure her "cooperation," they produced sales documents containing clauses in which Maria affirmed that she was being sold "with her express consent" as well as witnesses who testified that they saw Maria serve them "willingly" in their household in Valencia.

Maria retorted that though it was true that these documents ostensibly recorded her "assent" to her sale, her "assent" had been coerced. She recounted how on previous occasions when she proved less than cooperative with her sellers, they had responded by beating her and dragging her back into their households where she had been confined for several months. She claimed that they would not even let her stand near any doors or windows. Ultimately, however, Maria insisted that whether she "consented" to her sale or not was immaterial. Such actions could in no way compromise her birthright as a Greek-born Christian.

These two cases suggest that despite the existence of papal bulls and royal edicts granting them special protections, it was difficult and comparatively rare for Greek Orthodox Christian slaves to secure a hearing in the local courts. Indeed, while both Caterina and Maria contended that they were captured at a young age, they were "middle-aged" by the time they appeared in the court of the governor. They secured this court hearing only after spending the bulk of their lives—more than eighteen years—in servitude.

Securing official recognition of their Greek ethnicity, moreover, was hardly the ticket for an immediate emancipation. Less than a year earlier, Maria had filed a demand for liberty before the court of the *visrey* of Majorca. Though the *visrey* did affirm her Greek-born status, rather than order her immediate liberation he did no more than arbitrate a settlement whereby Maria was given the opportunity to buy her freedom, paying her owners the hardly insignificant sum of fifty-five lliures plus half of their legal expenses and the cost for her room and board in the municipal prison while the lawsuit was pending. Not surprisingly, Maria was unable to pay this sum. Thus, she was given the option of either being returned into her masters' custody and "working off" said sum in his service or having her services sold to a third party. She opted for the latter and was "purchased" by a nun in the Dominican convent of St. Mary Magdalen. This nun, Ysabel Bellvis, agreed to issue Maria a charter of freedom, but only upon completion of an eight-year term of service—a term of service thought to be roughly equivalent in value to her purchase price. When, several months later, Maria filed her second demand for liberty in Valencia, she was only marginally more successful. Though the governor, this time, granted an immediate enfranchisement (citing "justice" as well as the "decree of our holy father Pope Urban V"), her owner, the aforementioned nun, immediately filed an appeal, postponing indefinitely Maria's emancipation.[83]

Caterina's suit, in turn, was completely unsuccessful. The governor ultimately would dismiss Caterina's claim on the grounds that her owner had proven his contention that she was lying. Given the Circassian ethnicity attributed to her in a prior contract of sale, her inability to speak Greek, and her unfamiliarity with the churches and street names of her supposed place of birth, Caterina's owner managed to convince the governor that she was Circassian, not Greek.[84]

Thus, the impact of these so-called humanitarian ideas on actual practice in Valencia seems to have been negligible, at best. The testimony of witnesses in both of these trials, in fact, exposes an utter lack of consensus. Not everyone seems even to have been aware of the royal and papal decrees prohibiting the sale of Greeks and/or ordering their emancipation.[85] Upon finding himself at the center of this dispute over this enslaved woman's status, for example, the broker contracted to sell Caterina pleaded ignorance. He claimed he had been duped by Caterina into describing her as "Greek" in her most recent contract of sale. This broker explained that "since he did not know which *nacio* the slave was and since he did not have the [original] sales contract," he was forced to ask the slave herself to ascertain her ethnic identity (mandatory information in every slave sale). When he

---

83. "La qual per esser grega e de nacio de gregs exhigint ho justicia e senyaladament indult o concessio e decret de nostre sanct pare papa Urba Quint no ne ha pogut esser serve ne captiva ne venuda per cativa annullant e irritant qualsevol vendes que de facto sien e seran fetes dels dits gregs." ARV G 2331: M. 26: 1r–4v.

84. For the reference made to earlier contracts of sale in which Caterina was described as a "Circassian" (not Greek), see ARV G 2289: M. 17: 47r: "E per xarquesa es stada venuda per tots los qui han aquella venuda segons apar per carta de la venda." For the reference made to Caterina's evident lack of familiarity with the major landmarks of her hometown and her inability to speak Greek, see ARV G 2289: M. 19: 47r: "Que la dita sclava es estada interrogada de quin loch o ciutat era de greça e aquella non ha sabut dir e si pux ha dit que es de algun loch no sab dir res de aquell loch ço es de les sglesies e carrers de aquell loch. ... Item ... que la dita Catalina (sic) sclava no sab parlar grech." For the governor's sentence, see ARV G 2289: M. 20: 29r.

85. In the context of Aragonese Sicily, in contrast, Verlinden did stress a marked discrepancy between law and practice. Although Sicilian notaries frequently cited Frederick III's stipulations concerning the special privileges enjoyed by Greek and Orthodox Christian slaves, they often did so inaccurately. Thus, even when they claimed that they were observing these special dispensations, they were not doing so, presumably (in Verlinden's view) due to their deficient knowledge and/or lack of direct familiarity with this legislation. Verlinden, "Orthodoxie et esclavage," 446–47.

asked the slave "which *natio* are you?" Caterina "falsely and wickedly" had replied that she was Greek. This broker, "being inexperienced" and not knowing "that Greeks cannot be sold as slaves," told the slave's buyer that she was Greek. Although this broker protested that he did this "out of innocence," not realizing its potential repercussions, it is evident that neither the buyer nor the notary recording this transaction were terribly concerned about this either.[86] Indeed, consultation of contemporary notarial registers uncovers instances in which Greek and other Eastern Orthodox Christian slaves were sold just as Muslim and pagan slaves were—without the insertion of any clause restricting the buyer's rights of ownership.[87]

Be that as it may, some faint echo of these debates may be discerned in contemporary notarial registers. It could be argued that some sales contracts of Eastern Orthodox Christian slaves bear the imprint of Urban V's papal bull calling for the emancipation of Greek slaves after a seven-year term of service.[88] Many of these sales contracts were "temporary" in nature. On 11 March 1475, Joan Batista Gentil, a Genoese merchant residing in Valencia, sold a twenty-year-old Greek woman to Ançelmo de Prato, a Lombard merchant. According to the terms outlined in this contract of sale, this Greek woman, born in Candia on the island of Crete but now baptized according to the Latin rite and called Maria, was to be freed after an eight-year term of service.[89]

In stark contrast with the passive role ascribed to slaves in most sales contracts, here this Greek Christian female is presented as an active, willing participant. Thus, in the documents recording the agreements negotiated between two consecutive sets of buyers and sellers, the notary emphasized that Maria was also "present and consenting to said sale" (*presentem et dicte vendicioni consentientem*). Appended to both contracts, moreover,

---

86. "Com no tingues la carta de la compra... ignorant de quina nacio era la dita sclava lo dit n'Andreu interroga aquella de quina nacio era. E la dita sclava dix que era grega per falsia e maleca e com lo dit Andreu fos ignorant que gregues no poden venden vendre per sclava ab sa puritat dix que era grega segons li era stat dit per la dita sclava." ARV G 2289: M. 17: 47r.

87. See, for example, ARV P 1999: (nonpaginated) 22 November 1479 and 15 June 1479, in which (respectively) a tailor purchases a forty-year-old Greek woman named Margarita and a merchant purchases a ten-year-old Russian boy named Perot.

88. Urban V's bull was, in turn, based on the biblical injunction limiting the subjugation of Hebrew or Israelite (as opposed to Caananite) slaves to six years of service. If his master was a Gentile, the slave (or his kin) could buy out the contract even earlier. See the relevant passages in Exodus 21:2–6, Deuteronomy 15:12–18, and Leviticus 25:47–54.

89. ARV P 1995: 50r–51r. The contract, dated 11 March 1475, specified that "elapsis dictis octo annis dicta serva sit franca et libera." When, about a year later, Ançelmo's relative, Francisco, resold Maria to a new owner, Francisco reaffirmed the sale's temporary nature, specifying that as soon as the now seven-year term of service elapsed, Maria would be free (*elapsis dictis septem annis dicta serva sit franch et libera*). This contract, dated 19 February 1476, moreover stipulated that if, at any time during the next seven years, Maria managed to pay a redemption fee, set at 25 lliures, "in such a case she should immediately be freed" (*tali casu sit francha*). ARV P 1996: 56 r–v.

was a clause, written in the first person, in which the enslaved person herself approved the terms of the agreement. Stressing how she "was present during all the aforementioned things," Maria affirmed that "with my assent and of my own free will I praise, approve, ratify, and confirm each and every clause [of this contract]."[90] The efforts made by slave buyers, sellers, and notaries in securing from Eastern Orthodox Christians statements ratifying the terms of their sale could, arguably, be a reflection of the particular discomfort felt by Christians in enslaving and selling fellow Christians. Nevertheless, they were also reminiscent both of the efforts made by the bailiff general to secure testimony from Moorish captives affirming the legitimacy of their capture and the *cartas de cativeri* in which Valencian Mudejars similarly "confirmed, approved, and ratified" their enslavement.

Although certain Christians clearly had misgivings about enslaving other Christians, ultimately it is difficult to maintain the contention that the enslavement of Eastern Orthodox Christians was regarded dramatically differently from that of other slaves in fifteenth-century Valencia. Greek Orthodox Christian slaves by no means constituted the majority of slave plaintiffs suing for their freedom. Moreover, of the twenty-two slave sales I encountered in notarial registers dating from between 1460 and 1480 concerning Greek or Russian Orthodox Christians, only six were temporary in nature. The remaining eighteen slave sales contained no clauses limiting the term of service.[91] Contracts of sale for pagan or even Muslim converts to Christianity, indeed, were also, on occasion, temporary in nature. In a contract drawn up on 14 October 1479, a merchant from Naples inserted a clause limiting the buyer's authority to retain his slave, a Turkish woman named Mariella, eighteen years in age, in his power indefinitely. The contract specified that, after seven years of service, Mariella would be granted her freedom.[92]

"Judging from Their Appearance"

In the last decades of the fifteenth century, with the widespread introduction of Canary Islander and black African slaves into the Valencian marketplace, the bailiff general confronted a new dilemma in making his determinations concerning status. The bulk of "captives" being presented before him were no longer Granadan and North African

---

90. "Ad hec autem ego dicta Maria omnibus hiis presens predicta omnia et singula tanquam de meis assensu et voluntate facta laudo aprobo ratifico et confirmo." See ARV P 1995: 50r–51r and ARV P 1996: 56r–v.

91. These figures are based on my analysis of a random sample of notarial records dating from 1460 to 1480, based on the consultation of 182 volumes of notarial registers (*protocolos*) encountered in both the ARV and APPV.

92. ARV P 1999: 14 October 1479. Similarly, on 21 May 1476, a Genoese merchant sold Margarita, a baptized Christian woman from the Levant (likely a Muslim convert), under the condition that she be freed after seven years of service. ARV P 1996: 182v.

Muslims seized in corsair activity but black Africans and Canary Islanders acquired in Portuguese or Castilian markets.

Kenneth Baxter Wolf has drawn attention to how the fifteenth-century Portuguese chronicler, Gomes Eannes de Zurara (aka Azurara), consciously (mis)represented the west African victims of Portuguese slaving expeditions as "Moors." Infusing his account with "the images, motifs, and story lines of chivalric literature, popular histories and romances," Zurara presented slaving expeditions in west Africa "simply as a new chapter in the long history begun with the 'reconquista' of Spain." Likewise, Wolf observed how Zurara effectively "Mooricized" the west African victims. Although the Portuguese clearly recognized "the novelty of peoples of the Rio d'Ouro and Arguim," they nonetheless placed them "in a preexisting category that had meaning for them: 'Moors'." Despite the fact that they "dressed differently, showed no clear signs of being Muslims, spoke Azaneguya, and called their homeland 'Zaara'," Zurara constantly referred to them as "Moors." Wolf reasons that this was a conscious strategy:

> [This] crude categorization created a context for Portuguese aggression towards the west Africans. For the category "Moors"—in the mind of Zurara, and we assume, in the minds of [King] Afonso and the Portuguese sea captains as well—carried with it a very specific blueprint for action. Insofar as these people were regarded as Moors in some general sense, they found themselves being treated as Moors in a very specific sense: as an enemy to be fought, captured and sold into slavery.[93]

Indeed, perhaps the most striking reflection of the enduring strength of holy war rhetoric was the representation of Canary Islander and west African slaves as *moros* in the sentences issued by the bailiff general. By labeling them *moros*, the bailiff general made it easier for himself to declare them *catius de bona guerra*. Indeed, the procedure followed in these presentations, down to the payment of the quinto, was identical to that for Muslims seized in more traditional types of corsair activity. The purchasing of Canary Islander and west African slaves in Portuguese or Castilian clearinghouses, thereby, was rendered virtually indistinguishable from engaging in raids along the Granadan

---

93. Kenneth Baxter Wolf, "The 'Moors' of West Africa and the Beginnings of the Portuguese Slave Trade," *Journal of Medieval and Renaissance Studies* 24, no. 3 (Fall 1994): 468. A. C. de C. M. Saunders has also noted how the Portuguese depicted their actions in west Africa as the conquest of Muslim territory in an effort to legitimize, in the eyes of the papacy, their claims to exclusive trading rights in these regions. See A. C. de C. M. Saunders, "The Depiction of Trade as War as a Reflection of Portuguese Ideology and Diplomatic Strategy in West Africa, 1441–1556," *Canadian Journal of History* 17 (1982): 219–34. See also Gomes Eannes de Zurara, *The Chronicle of the Discovery and Conquest of Guinea*, trans. and ed. Charles Raymond Beazley and Edgar Prestige (New York, n.d. [1963]; orig. pub. 1896–99), 1: 54–55, and accompanying notes, 2: 319.

or North African coasts. As *moros*, therefore, Canary Islanders and black Africans were brought before the bailiff general to give testimony concerning the circumstances of their capture.

The first volume of *presentaciones y confessiones de cautivos* extant from the fifteenth century (dating, roughly, from 1419 to 1434) contains lengthy and, at times, rather "chatty" accounts detailing the exact time, place, and chain of events leading up to the capture of individuals who almost invariably were Granadan or North African Muslims. The bailiff general seems to view these hearings partly as an opportunity to gather army intelligence. Hence, he can often be seen here grilling captives for information regarding who was arming corsair vessels, when they were scheduled to depart, and what their intended targets were.[94] The second volume of *presentaciones* extant from the fifteenth century (dating, roughly, from 1494 to 1497) contains testimony of a markedly different character. The statements provided by the presenters, for one, are much less detailed. This was probably due to the fact that the bulk of the captives being presented were no longer subjects of rulers with whom the Crown of Aragon had direct commercial and/or diplomatic ties. The detention of Canary Islander or west African captives did not carry the same potential for compromising the Crown's economic or diplomatic interests. Thus the bailiff general was less preoccupied with pinning down the "*natio*" of every captive and investigating the circumstances of each capture.

We noted earlier how the bailiff general, at times, went to great lengths to secure a captive's "confession." In contrast with North African and Granadan *moros*, however, Canary Islander and west African *moros* spoke languages that court interpreters did not understand. Thus, in this second volume of *confessiones*, the testimony provided by captives was much more cursory. Newly arrived from the Canary Islands or the *terra de negres*, they did not speak Arabic, much less the Romance vernacular (*algemia*) spoken by Valencian Christians and Mudejars. When ten-year-old Johanico appeared before the court of the bailiff general, the scribe noted how this Wolof boy (*de Jalof*) "was not questioned since he was very uncivilized (*molt boçal*) and we could not extract any testimony from him."[95] Similarly, when seven-year-old Caterina was presented to the bailiff general, the scribe recorded that they were unable to obtain a confession from her because she was "very uncivilized (*molt boçal*)." Because she came "from other parts and regions of the Canaries," this scribe noted that even the other Canary Islander captives did not understand her.[96] Johanico's

94. For one example among many, see the bailiff general's interrogation of a group of Moorish corsairs, recorded in ARV B 193: 37v–41v.

95. "No jura com fos menor ni menys fon interroguat com fos molt boçal e nos poguesen exhigir confessions de aquell." ARV B 194: 248r–v.

96. "No jura com fos menor ni menys fonch intorroguada com fos molt boçal e nos pogues interrogar per altres catives canaries com fos de altres parts e terres de Canaria." ARV B 194: 252r.

and Caterina's cases were hardly exceptional. In this second volume of *confessiones de cautivos*, the bailiff general's scribe noted on numerous occasions that the captive in question was so *boçal* "that they were unable to extract any confessions" from them.[97] In one hearing, the scribe noted "they were unable to get any reason out of him" (*no's pogue traure raho de aquell*).[98] Such difficulties in communication presented a significant problem for the bailiff general. In the absence of corroborating testimony, the bailiff general needed to find other "evidence" in order to establish the legitimacy of their enslavement as "infidels, enemies of the Christian faith and Crown."

Most notable among the changes detectable in the records of the *presentaciones y confessiones de cautivos* dating from the last decade of the fifteenth century was an increased tendency, on the part of the bailiff general, to make reference to a captive's appearance. In stark contrast with earlier rulings, in which the bailiff general habitually cited the captive's "willing" testimony, the bailiff general now made his case by pointing to what were presented as obvious and unmistakable signs of an "infidel" character.

Thus, while the bailiff general admitted that he had been unable to extract confessions from two women from the Canary Islands "because they were *boçals*," he continued, "nonetheless it is evident by the aspect of them (*consta per lo aspecte de aquelles*) that they are from the lands and of the lineage of infidels, enemies of the holy Catholic faith and of the most high lord king."[99] Similarly, in a sentence pronouncing 119 black Africans "*catius de bona guerra*," the bailiff general maintained that even though they were unable to receive or extract testimony from them, "it is obvious and apparent by the appearance of them" (*per lo aspecte de aquelles*) that all of these "men and women, children and adults" were "infidels, from the lands and of the lineage of infidels, enemies of the holy Catholic

---

97. "Com fos molt boçal no's poguessen de aquella exhigir confessions algunes." The captives described in this way included (among others) a six-year-old girl named Ysabel, a white female from the Canaries (ARV B 194: 120r–v); a twenty-year-old black woman named Gomba, from "Mantega, land of the blacks" (ARV B 194: 150r–151r); a nine-year-old black boy named Gonbico, "natural de Jalof" (ARV B 194: 190r–v); 141 "negres . . . naturals de Jaloff," both men and women, children and adults (ARV B 194: 240r–v); and two women named Huanxa and Teroura, aged twenty-five and twenty, respectively, both "de Teneriff terra de Canaria" (ARV B 194: 387r–388r and 429r–430r).

98. "Com fos molt boçal e nos pogues traure raho de aquell." See the confession of ten-year-old Zambico, ARV B 194: 437r–438r. When an eight-year-old black boy, "natural de Jolof" and also named Zambico, appeared before the bailiff general, the scribe also noted "nos pogue traure raho de aquell." ARV B 194: 441r–442r.

99. ARV B 194: 388r. Confronted with their interpreters' inability to communicate with an eight-year-old black boy named Jalonga, the bailiff general ruled that even though "one cannot verify anything since he is 'barbarous'" (*no pot res constar com sia bosal*), nevertheless "based on his appearance it can be seen that he is of infidel lineage and from the lands of the infidels, enemies of the holy Catholic faith and most high lord king" (*ex aspectu se mostra aquell esser de linatge e terres de infels enemichs de la sancta fe catholiqua e del molt alt senyor rey*). ARV B 194: 324r.

faith and of the most high lord king."[100] What ought we to make of this change in the bailiff general's reasoning? Is it evidence that a change in thought had taken place with regard to slavery and the bases for its legitimacy?

In recent years, many scholars have situated the "birth" of modern racism and perhaps even racialized slavery in fifteenth-century Iberia, maintaining that, in the fifteenth century, ideas linking slavery with black skin color were already circulating in the peninsula.[101] In 1994, for example, Kenneth Baxter Wolf argued that statements in Zurara's account of Portuguese slaving expeditions in west Africa reflected the development of "entirely new grounds—biological ones—for enslavement." Wolf cites as evidence Zurara's observation that black Africans, though "Moors like the others," had been made "subject to all the other races of the world . . . in accordance with ancient custom, which I believe to have been because of the curse which, after the flood, Noah laid upon his son Ham(sic)."[102] In subsequent chapters, we will consider whether black Africans in fifteenth-century Valencia were, in fact, treated as individuals possessing inalterable, essentially unchanging differences that could never be erased. This book's conclusion, thus, will be a more appropriate place to assess the evidence for "racist" sentiments and the degree to which racialized thinking conditioned the experiences of black Africans and their status as slaves and freed persons. At this point, however, it is important to specify that although the bailiff general drew special attention to the physical appearance of black Africans (and Canary Islanders) in his rulings, the underlying argument justifying their enslavement remained indistinguishable from that applied to their Granadan and North African counterparts. These sentences were distinct in that they contained phrases such as "it is evident from the aspect of them" (*appar per lo aspecte de aquelles*),[103] "by the inspection of him it is made clear" (*per inspectio de aquell consta*),[104] or "having seen from the appearance of her" (*vist ex aspectu aquella*).[105] Nonetheless, black Africans ultimately were deemed enslaveable by

100. "De les dites de les quals no se son pogudes rebre ni exhigir confecions empero consta e appar per lo aspecte de aquelles et alter tots aquells esser infels e de terres e nascio de infels enemichs de la sancta fe catholiqua e del molt alt senyor rey." ARV B 194: 445r–v.

101. Most prominently, George Frederickson (2002) has argued that racism "originated in at least a prototypical form in the fourteenth and fifteenth centuries," describing late medieval Spain as "the seedbed for Western attitudes towards race." See Frederickson, *Racism*, 40. Similarly, in a special edition of the *William and Mary Quarterly* examining premodern constructions of race (1997), James Sweet also argued that the roots of American racist ideology can be traced back to the late medieval Iberian world. See Sweet, "The Iberian Roots of American Racist Thought," 143–66.

102. Wolf, "The 'Moors' of West Africa," 465. Wolf actually has misquoted Zurara here. Zurara, in fact, said that Noah had laid the curse "upon his son Cain" (*sobre seu filho Caym*). My thanks to David Brion Davis for bringing Wolf's error to my attention.

103. ARV B 194: 445v.
104. ARV B 194: 442v.
105. ARV B 194: 194v.

virtue of their presumed hostility to Christendom and the Catalan-Aragonese Crown. Hence the eight-year-old black boy named Zambico, a native of Jalof, was declared a slave not by virtue of the Hamitic curse, but because he was "a Saracen and from the land of Saracens and infidels, enemies of the holy Catholic faith and of the most high lord king."[106] He was a *catiu de bona guerra*, not racially or biologically inferior.

Unable, though, to point to statements made by black African captives affirming their lawfully captured status, the bailiff general instead pointed to outward symbols of their "infidel" identity. These outward symbols, however, were not limited to somatic or bodily differences (i.e., skin color and physiognomy). The bailiff general laid equal, if not greater, stress in his rulings on "cultural" differences—that is, differences in language and their inability to communicate with these captives. According to the logic of these rulings the distinctive appearance of black Africans and Canary Islanders merely confirmed their status as infidels and enemies of the Crown. The color of their skin did not, in and of itself, determine their status as slaves.

Regardless of whether they lost their liberty in warfare, unfree persons of all stripes were termed *catius* in fifteenth-century Valencia. Although direct capture in warfare was no longer the only, and not even the principal, source of supply, slaves would continue to be referred to as *catius de bona guerra*. Black or white, Moor or Mudejar, Greek or Canary Islander, male or female, they were deemed enslaveable because they were "enemies of the Catholic Church and Crown." According to this, perhaps only "official," understanding of slavery as revealed in notarial formulae and judicial sentences, slavery was not "natural" (or the outcome of a mythic curse); rather, it was the consequence of conscious choices and specific actions.

106. "Attenent que per inspectio de aquell consta esser sarray e de terres de sarrayns e infels e enemichs de la sancta fe catholiqua e del molt alt senyor rey." ARV B 194:

CHAPTER 2 "TALKING TOOLS"
SLAVES IN THE MARKETPLACE

In the spring of 1500, a merchant complained that his efforts to sell a white male "Moor" named Pere were being thwarted repeatedly by statements made by the slave before potential buyers. Pere's predilection for disclosing his "hidden defects" had so thoroughly compromised this merchant's ability to sell the slave that the merchant, the curator of the estate of a deceased tanner, now sought the Justícia Civil's permission to sell him at a greatly reduced price.

For the past two months and twenty days, the merchant maintained, he had made repeated attempts to find the slave a buyer, contracting the services of several brokers. These brokers had exhibited Pere "to many different households in the present city, to those of carpenters, bread makers, bakers, and other tradesmen as well." All their efforts, however, had proven in vain. For, whenever anyone expressed an interest in the slave and he was brought into their household for closer inspection, Pere invariably would announce that "by reason of a great blow he had suffered to his head, he has the affliction of being mentally disturbed." Such statements, coupled with the slave's alleged propensity toward drunkenness, precipitated Pere's hasty dismissal from each of these households, causing this exasperated merchant to lament, "because of that which the slave says no one will buy him!"[1]

Although few contracts of sale explicitly acknowledged this, in fifteenth-century Valencia slaves were often active participants in their sales.[2] A crucial part of the negotiation of any slave sale was the "interview" between the slave and his or her potential buyer. At this time, masters and mistresses relied upon their slaves to facilitate these transactions by

---

1. "Lo dit catiu de continu deya e ha dit que ell per occasio del dit gran colp del cap que ell tenia accident qu'es torbava e . . . que per occasio del que lo dit catiu deya degu nol volia comprar." ARV JCiv 935: M. 11: 4r–v.

2. As noted in the previous chapter, clauses recording a slave's "consent" to his or her sale were sometimes inserted in contracts of sale of Greek, Russian, and, occasionally, even Muslim slaves. As I will demonstrate more fully in chapter 6, "consent," seems to have been important in all slave transactions, whatever their ethnoreligious origin.

both affirming their *de bona guerra* status and responding favorably to queries concerning their health, habits, and skills. The context in which these predominantly verbal inspections took place (i.e., where they met and who was present) had a decisive impact on the sorts of responses elicited from a slave. Under ideal circumstances, their faculty of speech was exploited by their owners to effect a sale more easily and profitably, but slaves as "talking tools" also intervened in these transactions in unexpected and disruptive ways.

In this chapter I investigate how slaves were sold in the city of Valencia. In the preceding chapter I discussed the different paths by which men, women, and children of various faiths and ethnicities were enslaved and introduced into the kingdom as merchandise. In this chapter I examine how slaves were marketed after they had—at least provisionally—been incorporated into this religiously, ethnically, and culturally diverse community. I will be contrasting a captive's initial public and official sale into slavery under the bailiff general's supervision with the more private exchanges of slaves between households. Although in both instances brokers were employed, how the broker went about his business varied according to the type of merchandise he was selling. Although recently captured Moors and penally enslaved Mudejars were sold "as is" in public auctions held in city streets and squares, the resales of baptized Muslim, "eastern," and black African slaves were more complicated affairs negotiated behind closed doors. Indeed, in these latter types of exchanges, a particular class of brokers was utilized, individuals referred to as "agents of the ear" (*corredors d'orella*).

Extant court records allow us to examine the sales process in both theory and practice. First, I analyze the testimony of slave buyers, sellers, their agents, and bystanders in a series of disputed slave sales for the purposes of determining how contemporaries thought slave sales were *supposed* to work. Notarial contracts of sale are also scrutinized to determine the sorts of terms, protections, and guarantees that slave sellers typically extended. By piecing together evidence culled from both court and notarial records, I can reconstruct the steps involved in a standard slave sale: from the hiring of brokers to solicit prospective buyers to the final contraction of the sale before notary and witnesses. Other questions—such as who was buying these slaves and for what purpose—I will leave for the following chapter.

In the concluding portion of the chapter, I take a step outside the "model" slave sale to consider complaints about the subversion of the process advanced by both buyers and sellers. In suits filed before royal and municipal officials, we find not only disgruntled buyers protesting that slave sellers had deliberately concealed a slave's "hidden defects and vices" but also beleaguered sellers who attempted to refute these charges by claiming that their slaves were feigning illnesses and injuries in an effort to sabotage their resale. Thus, in this final section, the focus shifts from buyers, sellers, and their agents to examine the role of slaves in these transactions. Although slaves, as merchandise, offered the distinct advantage of being able, literally, to "sell themselves," their speech also posed significant challenges to the individuals entrusted with the task of coordinating their sales.

Public Initiation versus Private Exchange

On 20 March 1487, Pere Artus, the town crier (*trompeter*), publicized the following decree "throughout the city of Valencia and the customary places within it," accompanied by companions with horns and drums:

> Now hear this! On behalf of his majesty the most high lord king, Diego de Torre, knight, councilor, and chamberlain of the most high lord king and bailiff general of the kingdom of Valencia, makes it known to you that . . . all persons of whatever law, status, or condition in no way ought to dare or presume to buy—directly or indirectly, openly or secretly, under any pacts or conditions, either by themselves or through intermediaries—any captive, male or female, that comes from outside the kingdom[3] until the individuals transporting them have first presented them before the bailiff general and his court so that he, with the counsel of his assessor, might rule them "of good war" and that the quinto may be paid to the court of the lord king. . . . If anyone, of whatever law, status, or condition, has purchased a captive, male or female, coming from outside the kingdom that has not been presented and judged "of good war" nor the quinto paid to the court of the lord king, they are obliged to bring the captive before the bailiff general within three days. Otherwise they will be prosecuted in accordance with royal provisions. And, no less important, [he informs and notifies all that] the first sales that are made of said captives cannot be received by any notary except the scribe of the court of the bailiff general, since a certificate recording the quinto that the bailiff general is entitled to by reason of said sale must be drawn up by him. If said duty is not assessed or paid to the lord king, a fine of one hundred sous will be incurred and the contract of sale will be considered null and void. Any brokers intervening in such sales will, ipso facto, be deprived of their offices and their persons will be at the mercy of the lord king.[4]

3. "Outside the kingdom" meant outside the territories of the Crown of Aragon. These territories encompassed not only the peninsular kingdoms of Aragon and Valencia and the principality of Catalonia, but the Balearic Islands, the islands of Sardinia, Corsica, and Sicily, most of southern Italy, and a part of Greece. "Captives" being brought into the kingdom of Valencia from these territories typically did not have to be presented before the bailiff general of Valencia. Presumably they had already been ruled *de bona guerra* and the *quinto* on their sale into slavery had been assessed by Crown officials at their first port of entry in the territories of the Crown of Aragon. For an overview of the social and political history of the Crown of Aragon, see T. N. Bisson, *The Medieval Crown of Aragon: A Short History* (Oxford: Oxford University Press, 1986).

4. ARV B 1220: M. 6: 19r–20v.

Artus and his companions were hardly promulgating a new royal policy. Rather, they were reiterating the well-established procedures by which the bailiff general both prevented unlawful enslavements and assured the collection of the Crown's share in the increasing profits that trade in "war captives" generated.[5]

Thus, the only legitimate venue in which a captive could be sold into slavery in the kingdom of Valencia was in the bailiff general's court. Overseeing the transformation from captive to merchandise, the bailiff general issued the requisite license empowering individuals to sell, alienate, and trade another human being as their personal property— "*licencia e facultat . . . de vendre alienar e comerciar . . . com de cosa propria.*"[6] Although the captive's presenter could coordinate the sale, enlisting the assistance of a professional broker, once a buyer was secured, all parties involved—seller, buyer, and/or broker(s)— were obliged to return to the bailiff general's court where Crown-appointed scribes drew up the contract of sale. In this fashion, the bailiff general ensured that the tax due from the sale of all captives entering the kingdom (the *quinto*) was properly assessed and paid. Upon the arrival of "Moorish" captives in the port of Valencia, the bailiff general not only held a formal hearing to investigate the legitimacy of their seizure but also supervised their distribution and sale as slaves in what contemporaries termed public auctions.

These were not, however, public auctions in the modern sense of the term—that is, sales of an entire group of slaves occurring at a fixed time and place. Historians Rafael Cariñena i Balaguer and Andrés Díaz i Borrás have described one such public auction that was held in Valencia in 1385. As soon as the bailiff general issued his ruling pronouncing the nineteen men seized by a group of Christian corsairs "captives of good and just war," municipal authorities directed that announcements be made "in the plazas and the merchant's exchange that a public auction would be held approximately from the middle of July to the beginning of August." When the contracts of sale noted that "a legitimate auction having been held in a public place" (*facta subastatione*[7] *legitima in*

5. Vicenta Cortés, in fact, cites a similar decree, issued by the bailiff general in 1480 and "published" by the *trompeta* Joan de Luna "in the plaza and courts of Játiva" as well as "in the neighborhood of the Muslim quarter." It is transcribed in full as document #5 in her appendix, V. Cortés, *La esclavitud*, 475–77. This decree, however, does not require that the first contract of sale be drawn up by a scribe of the bailiff general, nor does it specify penalties for brokers intervening in clandestine sales. Finally, rather than giving buyers three days to hand over any captives purchased illegally, buyers in Játiva were given only one day.

6. The bailiff general typically concluded his sentences declaring captives "*de bona guerra*" with this clause empowering the presenter to sell the captive as a slave. For an example, see ARV B 195: 61r–62r.

7. The term used to denote a public auction, "*subastatio*," comes from the Latin phrase *sub hasta*, which meant "under the spear stuck in the ground at public auctions or where the tribunals of the centumviri were held, originally as a sign of booty gained in battle or of magisterial authority." See entry for "hasta" in Lewis and Short, *A Latin Dictionary* (Oxford: Clarendon Press, 1955).

encanto publico), they referred not to a specific event or one particular site where the entire lot of captives had been sold. Rather, the captives had been divvied up among "diverse brokers and agents" who offered them for sale in a number of different venues. Indeed, as Vicente Graullera Sanz has observed, a slave market in the physical sense—that is, a permanent venue assigned exclusively to the purchase and sale of slaves—did not exist in the city of Valencia.[8] Brokers exhibited captives, often individually or in small groups, wherever they thought they might encounter interested buyers: "in the plaza of the merchants, the merchant's exchange, and in other parts of the city."[9] This was one reason why the use of brokers was so important. In the absence of a central slave market, foreign merchants or corsairs unfamiliar with this community needed brokers to help them find potential buyers.

A close analysis of the contracts of sale of captives preserved in the records of the bailiff general reveals how foreign merchants and corsairs frequently enlisted the assistance of locally based brokers. In July 1484, for example, Gonçalbo Aliman, Diego Quintero, and Rodrigo Pérez, three corsairs based in Castile, came to Valencia for the purpose of selling fourteen Muslims (all males) who had been declared *catius de bona guerra* on 1 July. Although seven of these captives were destined for resale elsewhere (these three white and four black male slaves were purchased as a group by a merchant from Ibiza), the remaining seven captives were purchased individually by various residents of Valencia. A perusal of the lists of witnesses to these sales reveals that a local broker intervened in every one of them.[10]

Even if they were not sold en masse on the auction block, the sales of captives nonetheless were "public" events. Indeed, according to the language of these contracts, a crucial aspect of these transactions was the exposure of the captive in central and well-trafficked areas of the city. In the contract of sale of a thirty-year-old penally enslaved Mudejar woman named Huzeyta, special emphasis was placed on how Huzeyta had been "displayed venally and put up for auction throughout the city of Valencia." After being shown "in the customary places and for the period of time stipulated in the law code of the kingdom of Valencia," Huzeyta was sold to the highest bidder—in this instance, a Genoese merchant.[11]

---

8. Graullera, *La esclavitud*, 164.

9. "Facta subastatione legitima in encanto publico per diversos cursores sive precones in lotgia et platea mercatorum et in aliis partibus dicte civitatis." Excerpt from the contract of sale for Hamet, a North African boy captured near Bougie by a Christian galley armed by the municipality of Valencia. ARV P 2638: 28 July 1385. Transcribed and published as document #1 in the appendix of Cariñena i Balaguer and Diás i Borrás, "Corsaris valencians," 455.

10. See ARV B 217: 676r; the remaining contracts, nonpaginated, are dated 3–6 July 1484.

11. "Quam exposuimus venalem et fecimus publici subastari per civitatem Valencie locaque eius solita per tempus a foro estatutum." ARV B 217: 667v–668r.

Although explicitly put on display in an effort to solicit buyers, the public auctioning of "Moorish" captives likely performed a dual purpose. Since the plight of these captives would be visible to any passerby, they were particularly effective demonstrations of Christian dominance over infidels. Indeed, they likely were great morale boosters for the Valencian Christian community, evoking feelings of cultural, religious, and military superiority.[12] The public degradation of Granadan and North African Muslims was perhaps especially gratifying to Valencian Christians since, in some cases, immediately before their seizure, they had been terrorizing the kingdom's coastline. Between 15 and 19 February, 1424, for example, the bailiff general registered the sales of eight Muslim males, captured off the coast of Cartagena after their North African captain decided (on the advice of a Mudejar passenger from Valencia) to divert their course and engage in corsair activity against Christians. Just as the public execution of notorious Moorish corsairs was expected to "punish, terrify, and be an example to others," the public auctions of captured *moros* constituted a thinly veiled threat to Moor and Mudejar alike, graphically illustrating the consequences for resistance.[13]

The "public sale and auction" of penally enslaved Mudejars also served as an effective reminder to the kingdom's free Muslim population that, as Muslims living under Christian rule, they were a subjugated people, their continued presence within the kingdom possible only on the king's sufferance. Thus, if they committed any crime or violated the statutes restricting their movements, they too could be made "captives of the Crown," "publicly put up for sale and auctioned."[14]

In the previous chapter, I noted how in the latter half of the fifteenth century, the corsairs presenting "captives" before the bailiff general were progressively outnumbered by

---

12. The sale of Christian captives in public auctions held in Muslim-controlled territories performed much the same function, demonstrating Muslim dominance over Christian infidels. Accounts of Christian pilgrims traveling to the Holy Land during this same time period laid special emphasis on the plight of these Christian captives and expressed outrage concerning their sale to Muslim masters. Arnold von Harff, a German pilgrim who reportedly traveled through Mamluk Alexandria in the 1490s, observed "there are also sold daily Christian men and women, boys and young girls, who have been captured in Christian lands, for very little money, fifteen, twenty, or thirty ducats according as they are rated. First all their limbs are inspected, whether they are healthy, strong, sick, lame or weak, and so they buy them." Arnold von Harff, *The Pilgrimage of Arnold von Harff*, trans. M. Letts, Hakluyt Society, second series, 94 [1946]; repr. Millwood, N.J.: Kraus, 1990), 95. Cited in Olivia Remie Constable, *Housing the Stranger in the Mediterranean World: Lodging, Trade, and Travel in Late Antiquity and the Middle Ages* (Cambridge: Cambridge University Press, 2003), 273–74. Constable cautions, however, that "Von Harff's travels may be largely fictitious."

13. Cariñena i Balaguer and Díaz i Borrás, "Corsaris valencians," 449.

14. Thus, the sellers of Ali Caspi, a twenty-five-year-old Mudejar—described in his contract of sale as "condempnatus ad captivitatem et iudicatus fuit magestatie regie cum sententia nostra...certis criminibus delicitis et causis in ea contentis"—noted how "quem publice fecimus vendi et subastati." ARV B 217: 467r–468v.

merchants—entrepreneurs whom historian Vicenta Cortés categorized as slave whole-salers, "los mayoristas." The "captives" they presented often had been purchased in Castil-ian and Portuguese ports. Nevertheless, the bailiff general continued to hold hearings and oversee their distribution. Indeed, there is evidence that the bailiff general sought to attract slave traders (these mayoristas) to his kingdom by offering them reduced customs duties. In 1495, the bailiff general convinced Alfonso Sanchiz, "counselor and treasurer for the most high lord king," to bring his Canary Islander captives to Valencia rather than Barcelona by assessing the quinto owed on these fifty-six captives at the more favorable rate of fifteen lliures apiece.[15] The first sales of the black African and Canary Islander slaves entering the kingdom were duly registered in the records of the bailiff general. Black African and Canary Islander "captives" were marketed throughout the city and kingdom of Valencia just like Granadan and North African captives were. They were div-vied up among several brokers who put them up for auction in the "customary places."

There is some indication, however, that finding buyers for such sizable lots of cap-tives in the city of Valencia could occasionally pose challenges. On 28 June 1494, Benet Benavides, a merchant of Puerto de Santa Maria (acting on behalf of Alonso de Lugo, governador of the islands of Palma and Tenerife), presented forty-two captives (between the ages of six and forty years old) before the bailiff general. Benet testified that he had transported these eighteen male and twenty-four female Canary Islander from the island of Lanzalot for the purpose of selling them "in these parts, in the city of Valencia." About a week later, on 4 July 1494, however, Benet expressed concern that he would be unable to sell all forty-two captives in Valencia—especially since "due to an epidemic of the plague, he dared not bring them into the city." Although the bailiff general still required Benet to pay, up front, the quinto pertaining to the Crown on all forty-two captives in expecta-tion of their sale, he was not completely deaf to Benet's pleas. The receipt of payment contained a clause assuring Benet that he would be refunded the quinto paid for any cap-tive whom he was unable to sell in Valencia. About six months later, on 9 January 1495, Benet's fears seem to have been realized. Securing the bailiff general's permission to remove the unsold captives from the kingdom of Valencia because "he was not able to get a good enough price for them," Benet also seems to have been given a refund.[16]

Due to their sheer numbers alone, the sale of shiploads of black African and Canary Islander captives were noteworthy events in the city. During his visit to Valencia in 1494,

15. ARV B 194: 363r–364r.

16. The bailiff general promised Benavides that "los que no pots vendres seu puxa tornar." ARV B 194: 134r–137v. And, on 9 January 1495, Benavides "demana licencia de poder traure los dits catius fora de la present regne per mar com en aquelles no trobas preu competent lo qual dit noble batle general dix era content puix axi era passat entre lo dit Benavides e lo dit magnifich lochtinent del batle general segons appar dessus en lo precedent acte donant licencia per poder les s'en portar li hon plaria."

VALENTIA EDETANORUM vulgo DEL CID DELINEATA A Dⁿᵒ THOMA UINCENTIO TOSCA CONGR. ORATORIJ PRESBYTERO

The City of Valencia (an eighteenth-century map drawn by Tomás Vicente Tosca in which the fourteenth-century walls are still prominent features).

the German traveler Jeronimo Münzer was struck by the multitude of Canary Islander captives, "adults of both sexes, infants as well as children," whom he described as "beasts
in human form," awaiting sale outside a merchant's house.[17] When Muslim, African, and
Canary Islander victims of Christian corsairs were sold in the streets and plazas of Valencia, their initiation into slavery was a public spectacle, collectively witnessed and state
supervised. The Crown not only issued the requisite license to sell a captive into slavery,
it issued this license only after the legitimacy of the enslavement had been confirmed in
a court hearing. The contract of sale, moreover, would not be valid unless it had been
drawn up by the scribes of the bailiff general's court and only then if the Crown had
been given its cut of the proceeds.[18]

In fifteenth-century Valencia, a fundamental distinction was made between the sale
of a captive into slavery and the resale of a slave. Although the introduction and initial
sales of captives entering the kingdom of Valencia were strictly regulated and taxed by
the Crown, the resales and exchanges of slaves within the kingdom were private transactions, relatively immune from governmental interference since slaves (as opposed
to captives) were their master's private property—personal possessions with which
they could do as they pleased. The "public" character of the sale of "Moorish" captives
stands in stark contrast with the resales of baptized Muslim, eastern, and black African
slaves. These Christianized slaves were not exhibited and auctioned off in city streets
and squares. Instead, they were marketed primarily by word of mouth. Although buyers,
sellers, and their agents might initially come into contact with one another on the street
or at the market, the terms of sale typically were negotiated in someone's home. When
these slaves were poked and prodded by potential buyers, it happened, by and large,
behind closed doors.

Let the Buyer Beware: Selling Slaves "in Accordance
with the Usage and Customs of Valencia"

Less than twenty-four hours following her purchase, a seventeen-year-old black female
slave named Caterina died mysteriously of the plague. When the Castilian merchant who
had purchased Caterina cried foul, denouncing the seller for intentionally concealing

---

17. Jeronimo Münzer, *Viaje por España y Portugal (1494–1495)* (Madrid, 2002), 43–44.

18. Indeed, slaves who filed *demandes de libertat* on the grounds of illegitimate enslavement, habitually
cited as "proof" of the illicit character of their sale into slavery the fact that they had never been presented
before the bailiff general and declared a *catiu de bona guerra*. See, for example, ARV G 2331: M. 16: 3r–8v;
G. 2332: M. 26: 1r–4v; and ARV G 2396: M. 3: 45r, G. 2397: M. 13: 21r–24v.

her illness and refusing to pay the agreed-upon price, the slave's seller demanded his immediate payment, affirming his scrupulous observance of established sale practices. Although this seller could hardly deny that the slave had been seriously ill at the time of purchase, he insisted that "the sale had been made well, justly and legitimately, without any fraud or deception."[19]

Even if we were to take this Castilian merchant at his word and believe his allegations that this seller (Johan Draper) had deliberately conspired to sell a diseased slave "*per bona*" (as a healthy one), an analysis of Caterina's sale as depicted in the testimony of the plaintiff, defendant, and witnesses nonetheless provides us with a fairly detailed picture of how slave sales were *supposed* to work in fifteenth-century Valencia.[20] Indeed, in the process of protesting his innocence, Johan delineates the steps that were followed in a standard slave sale, steps that will be outlined using the sale of this seventeen-year-old black female as an example.

Step 1: Hiring a Broker

When a slave owner decided that she or he wanted to sell a slave, she or he typically contracted the services of an intermediary to coordinate the sale. In many cases, the seller contacted a professional broker, but in other cases a trusted acquaintance could do the job. In the case of this seventeen-year-old black female, a professional broker was hired. The broker Manuel Manblella testified that, about a week earlier, he had been contacted by a man named Johan Draper who said that he wished to sell a slave woman that was under his charge. A wool comber by trade, Johan was acting on behalf of a man named Alvaro de Poales who apparently had abandoned his long-time mistress when plague struck their household in 1450. Abandoned by her lover and struggling to sustain herself and their two daughters, Alvaro's mistress urged Johan (Alvaro's procurator) to sell this slave woman named Caterina in order to garner some much-needed income to pay for household necessities. Although all four of these women appear to have been afflicted with the disease (one of the two daughters, in fact, appears to have died), Caterina was not yet indisposed by it. Johan, thus, contracted the services of an "agent of the ear,"

---

19. "La venda de la dita sclava es feta be e justament e legitime sens alguna frau e decepcio." Thus, he continued, "lo dit comprador qui havia rebuda la dita sclava e la cosa comprada cum periculo ipsius rey e es tengut pagar lo preu de aquella lo qual es L lliures de Valencia." ARV G 2278: M. 8: 38r–v.

20. Vicente Graullera Sanz first called my attention to these disputes over sales of "defective" slaves and generously shared references to some of the cases discussed below. For some interesting comparisons, see Judith K. Schafer, " 'Guaranteed against the Vices and Maladies Prescribed by Law': Consumer Protection, the Law of Slave Sales, and the Supreme Court in Antebellum Louisiana," *American Journal of Legal History* 31, no. 4 (October 1987): 306–21, and Ariela Gross, "Pandora's Box: Slave Character on Trial in the Antebellum Deep South," *Yale Journal of Law & the Humanities* 7, no. 2 (1995): 267–316. See also Johnson, *Soul by Soul.*

telling Manuel Manblella that if he could find a buyer for this black female slave, he could broker the transaction.

Step 2: Soliciting Prospective Buyers

Now that he had been hired, Manuel Manblella immediately set about soliciting buyers for the slave primarily by word of mouth and escorted interested parties back to the household where Caterina was staying so that they could see the "merchandise." Thus, Manuel related that, about six days after he had been hired, he escorted the aforementioned Castilian merchant, Goncalbo Goncálvez, to the house where Caterina was living so that Goncalbo could "have a look at her." In contrast to the public auctioning of captives, these preliminary examinations of slaves took place in comparatively more private settings, usually within the confines of someone else's home. Thus, Manuel further testified that Goncalbo had been given an opportunity to examine Caterina inside the household where she was staying and in his presence. If the prospective buyer liked what he or she saw, the broker would arrange a meeting with the seller to negotiate the price and terms of sale.

Step 3: Reaching a Tentative Agreement

"Finding her agreeable," Goncalbo Goncálvez had asked Manuel Manblella to arrange a meeting with the slave's owner so that they could negotiate the terms of sale. These meetings also typically seem to have taken place in domestic space. Eager, perhaps, to unload this plague-stricken slave on an unwitting buyer, Johan Draper immediately went to the house where Goncalbo was staying. There, in Manblella's presence, he and Goncalbo came to a tentative agreement concerning the terms of sale: Caterina would be sold

Table 1. Average Sales Prices for Slaves Purchased in Valencia (in lliures)

	Male					Female				
Years	Average	White	Llor	Black	Canary Islander	Average	White	Llora	Black	Canary Islander
1420–1434	41.54	41.4	44	46.3	—	62.5	62.5	—	—	—
1460–1480	37.79	39.58	38.3	36	—	40.26	41.75	47.6	35.2	—
1479–1485	33.43	33.4	36.5	30	—	45.4	49	45.7	32	—
1494–1498	15.45	22.85	27	15	17	22.3	27.3	19.4	18.9	22.13

Sources: For 1420–1434, figures are drawn from contracts recording sales made in public auctions sponsored by the court of the bailiff general. ARV Bailía 193; sample size = 67. For 1460–1480, figures are drawn from sales contracts recorded in notarial registers preserved in the ARV and APPV; sample size = 252. For 1479–1485, figures are drawn from sales contracts recorded in notarial registers preserved in the ARV and APPV; sample size = 138. For 1494–1498, figures are drawn *not* from actual transactions but from estimates offered by corsairs, traders, and Crown officials of what price that particular captive would likely sell for. Such estimates were made for the purposes of assessing the *quinto* or tax levied on the sale of captives into slavery; sample size = 806.

Note: In cells in which no data are given, no sales were encountered in the sales contracts.

for the price of fifty lliures and the sale would be guaranteed "according to the usage and customs of Valencia."

Fifty lliures was a high, but not outrageous, price to pay for a black female slave in Valencia in the mid-fifteenth century. Table 1 illustrates the results of my survey of sales prices for slaves (broken down according to gender and skin color) as reported in notarial contracts of sale dating from the mid- to the late fifteenth century. Although these figures are hardly exhaustive, they indicate that female slaves typically fetched higher prices than male slaves and that as the fifteenth-century wore on, "white" slaves were valued more than "black" slaves. Although my findings could be read as evidence that skin color (as well as gender) was a key factor in determining sales prices for slaves, given the large number of other variables affecting slave prices—such as age, technical skills, perceived character and overall health, sexual attractiveness, religious and/or ethnic identity (which, in contrast, were not always noted in sales contracts)—it is difficult (if not impossible) to isolate skin color (or gender) as the definitive factor in determining sales prices.

Step 4: The Trial Period

Once a tentative agreement had been reached, the slave typically was transferred into the buyer's custody. Before the contract was finalized, the buyer was allotted a set period of time to conduct a closer and more thorough inspection of the slave. Once Goncalbo and Johan had reached an accord, Manuel explained, Johan had gone back to the household where Caterina had been staying to inform the slave of her new status. Johan told Caterina that Goncalbo was her new master and, moments later, Goncalbo arrived formally to take custody of her. Caterina, thereupon, departed from her former mistress's household and, depending on whose account you read, either followed Goncalbo back to the house where he was staying "limping and complaining" (according to the testimony of the disgruntled buyer) or "laughing and shaking hands with passersby" (according to witnesses appearing on behalf of the seller).

The duration of these "trial periods" varied greatly and it was often at this critical juncture that a slave's behavior could either make or break a sale. In Caterina's case, the trial period seems to have been very short and it appears to have elapsed without incident. Johan emphasized how Goncalbo had Caterina in his custody "for more than three hours," during which time, according to the defense, the Castilian merchant had had ample opportunity to examine and inspect the slave's condition thoroughly.

Step 5: Drawing Up the Formal Contract

That afternoon, the contract of sale for Caterina had been drawn up in the home of the notary, Gabriel Andreu. It was signed and confirmed in the presence of the notary and witnesses. Once the terms of an agreement had been affirmed formally in the presence of a notary and witnesses, the sale was considered official. Even if the sale price had not yet been paid in full, the contract was legally binding. From that time forward, any death, injury, or loss suffered by the slave was at the sole risk of the buyer. Thus, Johan noted, as soon as Goncalbo officially received this slave, he had acquired her "with all the risks associated with this thing."

Since Caterina, up until that point, had dutifully kept her mouth shut, all parties had departed from this notary's home relatively pleased. While Johan and Manuel went in one direction (perhaps congratulating one another on their salesmanship), the still unsuspecting buyer, Goncalbo Goncálvez, "headed toward the sea."

The "Agents of the Ear"

> And if you wish to be "of the ear," a discreet, prudent and expert
> intermediary, you must make contracts without commotion or rumor.[21]
>
> Passage taken from *Lo proces de les Olives e disputa dels jovens hi dels
> vells*, a collection of satirical poems published in Valencia in
> 1495/97

When Valencian nobles, professionals, and artisans required the assistance of a professional broker to help find their slaves a buyer, they typically did not turn to an auctioneer or "agent of the throat" (*corredor de coll*). Instead, they sought an "agent of the ear" (*corredor d'orellà* in Catalan or *cursor auris* in Latin).[22] Although they performed similar functions, contemporary documents distinguished sharply between these two types of brokers working in fifteenth-century Valencia. "Agents of the throat" were street hawkers, intermediaries who "worked with their throats, raising their voices" to market wares such as livestock and household articles in the streets and plazas of the city.[23] "Agents of the ear," in contrast, relied more heavily on their ears. Well connected in the city and attuned to the changing currents of the market, these brokers were in the

---

21. "Hi si desigau vos esser d'orella / discret y avisat y espert corredor, / fareu los contractes sens crits ni rumor." *Lo proces de les Olives e disputa dels jovens hi dels vells*, l. 814. Cited under the entry for "corredor," *Diccionari català-valencià-balear, inventari lexicogràfic i etimològic de la llengua catalana*, ed. Antoni M. Alcover, Francesc de B. Moll, Manuel de Sanchis Guarner, and Anna Moll Marquès (Palma de Mallorca: Editorial Moll, 1964).

22. *Corredors d'orellà* figure prominently in the witness lists for slave sales. The presence of at least one *corredor d'orellà* was noted in more than half of the slave sales whose witness lists I transcribed. Their presence is highly suggestive that they had played a part in the sale's negotiation. In her study of brokers in fourteenth-century Montpellier, Kathryn Reyerson notes that in order for a broker to collect his fee, he was required to be present at the formal contraction of the sale. Kathryn Reyerson, *The Art of the Deal: Intermediaries of Trade in Medieval Montpellier* (Boston: Brill, 2002).

23. "El qui antigament tenia per missió principal fer les subhastacions i crides relacionades amb compres i vendes . . . i per això es deien de coll, perquè treballaven amb la gargamella en alçar la veu per fer les crides i encants." *Diccionari català-valencià-balear* (Palma de Mallorca, 1964), III: 577.

business of knowing other people's business. Rather than hawk merchandise, *corredors d'orellà* listened intently and then acted discreetly, bringing parties with mutual interests together to do business.[24]

That "agents of the ear" were the brokers traditionally hired to negotiate slave transactions suggests that the resale of a slave was considered a matter requiring a certain amount of discretion. "Agents of the ear," after all, participated in the negotiation of marriage and dowry agreements and the hiring of wet nurses, servants, and apprentices.[25] Their participation in slave sales reflects how, more than simple commodities, slaves were members of their masters' households.

Although these men were hardly professional slave brokers who concentrated their efforts exclusively on trafficking slaves, "agents of the ear" were, nonetheless, considered experts concerning the local slave market. When a black slave demanding his liberation needed witnesses to confirm his claim that his many years of faithful service had more than compensated his master for his initial purchase price, the slave's legal advocate asked two "agents of the ear" to give testimony concerning the slave's market value at the time of purchase. Both Joan Castellà and Gabriel Cobrera testified that, in their professional opinion, twenty-five lliures would have been "a good price for a six-year-old 'barbaric' or 'untrained' (*boçal*) black male slave." While Johan claimed that he had sold slaves matching this description for as much as thirty lliures, Gabriel insisted that such a slave could not be sold for more than twenty-five lliures.[26]

Indeed, individuals unfamiliar with local business practices not only hired "agents of the ear" to help them ferret out potential buyers but also, on occasion, sought their advice concerning what terms to offer in the contract of sale. In a dispute regarding what was ultimately deemed an unequal slave trade, a nobleman seller disavowed his responsibility for failing to reveal his slave's "hidden defects" by claiming that he had only followed his

---

24. "El qui s'ocupava principalment de gestionar operacions de compra-venda i préstec, servint d'intermediari entre les parts contractants...per això es deien d'orella, pel caràcter privat de llurs gestions, en què, com si diguéssim, treballaven, a cau d'orella." *Diccionari català-valencià-balear*, III: 577. The two following examples foreground this distinction in function between *corredors* quite nicely. In 1471, a *corredor de coll* admitted that he had hawked publicly (literally, wore or carried around his neck—al coll) a pair of boots given to him by a black male slave. ARV JCiv 923: M. 13: 44r–48v. In 1472, a *corredor d'orella* testified that he saw a cobbler's apprentice sell a pair of stolen shoes in a public auction. ARV JCiv 924: M. 13: 19r–20r.

25. For marriage and dowry agreements, see ARV P 439 (nonpaginated): 30 July 1471. For wet nurses, see ARV P 511 (nonpaginated): 16 May 1474, and ARV P 1997 (nonpaginated) 3 October 1477. For servants and apprentices, see ARV P 511 (nonpaginated): 3 April 1474, ARV P 588 (nonpaginated): 13 September 1475, and ARV P 1995 (nonpaginated): 3 May 1475.

26. Joan Castella, a "*corredor d'orella*," testified that a "sclau de edat de sis anys negre boçal es be venut de XXV lliures poch mes o menys." Gabriel Cabrera, a "*corredor d'orella*," testified he "ha vist e praticat sclau de sis anys negre es prou venut de xxv lliures e no creu que pus s'en hagues." ARV G 2290: M. 25: 5v–6r.

broker's advice. Pleading ignorance in the ways of the Valencian marketplace, Dalmau Ferrer pinned a good share of the blame for this "miscommunication" on the "agent of the ear" he had contracted to act as his intermediary.[27]

In 1456, Dalmau had contracted the services of Pere Corella, a *corredor d'orellà*, to help him find a buyer for Jordi, his eighteen-year-old black male slave. This broker quickly informed him, however, that considering the fact that most purchasers would prefer to buy a slave that had come directly from Africa, his prospects for finding a buyer willing to pay a good price for his slave were not particularly good.[28] Pere, therefore, had advised him to consider trading Jordi for a twenty-eight-year-old Circassian female slave named Anastasia. According to Dalmau's testimony, Pere implied that this was his only real option. Trusting Pere's advice, Dalmau accompanied Pere to the house of the Circassian slave's owner, a soap seller named Vicent Valenti, to work out the details of the trade. In testimony aimed at absolving himself of liability for concealing his slave's hidden defect, Dalmau emphasized how he had deferred to this broker's superior knowledge and expertise when it became time to lay down the terms of the exchange. Indeed, when he and Vincent disagreed over the length of the trial period (Dalmau allegedly had favored a longer period, Vincent desired a more cursory one), Dalmau claimed Pere (the broker) was the one who ultimately rejected the idea of an extended trial period, stating that "it was not necessary but that the contract should be finalized as soon as possible."[29]

In most of these court cases, however, "agents of the ear" were portrayed as disinterested observers. In a dispute over the sale of a twenty-three-year-old black male slave named Andria, the broker Sancho Puig described himself simply as "the agent who brought the two parties together." When the sellers were later accused of concealing the slave's defects (the buyer claimed that Andria was a known fugitive, a drunkard, and a fool), Sancho was not in any way implicated. Rather, he was called before the governor's court merely to verify what had been said by both parties at the time of sale.[30]

A similarly nonpartisan role was attributed to the *corredor d'orella* who participated in the resale of a thirteen-year-old black male slave named Jordi infested with "worms." The owner of the slave, the Valencian tanner Berenguer Dezcortell, first discovered the slave's defect on his return to Valencia shortly after purchasing him (along with two other black male slaves) from a sailor in Barcelona. Rather than sue this sailor and file a claim in Barcelona demanding the sale's rescission—a course of action that, considering the

---

27. Dalmau Ferrer claimed that, not being a native of the kingdom of Valencia, he "ignorava la pratica e stil de la terra." ARV G 2288: M. 23: 44r.

28. Slaves brought more or less *directly* from Africa (described often as "boçal" or "uncivilized") were assumed to be more malleable and, hence, were more desirable as slaves.

29. Dalmau Ferrer insisted that Pere Corella said that "no era mester sino que tan tost se fes los contractes." ARV G 2288: M. 22: 48r–v, M. 23: 44r–45r.

30. "[El] qui concorda les dites parts de la dita venda." ARV G 2336: M. 10: 9r–12v.

fact that he had already returned to Valencia, would have required a significant amount of effort and expense—Berenquer opted instead simply to sell the slave to some unsuspecting buyer in Valencia. He hired the services of a *corredor d'orella* named Jacme Pasqual. Although Jacme initially was successful, coordinating the slave's resale to Joan Requeni, Joan soon discovered this slave's "hidden defect" and filed a claim demanding a full refund. Again, as in our prior example, there is no indication here that the "agent of the ear" was considered party to this act of deception.[31]

In all of these examples (including that of Caterina, the black female slave who died of the plague the day following her sale), there is no suggestion by either the buyer or the seller that the "agent of the ear" was cognizant of any defect. It is somewhat hard to believe, however, that the broker had been completely unaware. After all, he often had been the one exhibiting the slave to prospective buyers over the course of several days. Since it customarily was the seller who contracted a broker's services, however, it certainly was in an agent's best interests to keep quiet. Acknowledging a slave's defects, either before or after a sale, would only hurt his business. In any event, though brokers might occasionally have been willing accomplices in the "cover-up" of a slave's defects, beyond the aforementioned nobleman's halfhearted attempt to shift some of the blame onto his agent, I have come across no instance in which a broker was charged or otherwise implicated in a lawsuit concerning the deliberate concealment of a slave's defects.[32]

Ultimately, it seems that even when the individuals brokering these transactions were not professional "agents of the ear," the use of intermediaries was intended to protect the privacy of both the buyer and the seller. After all, the exchange or resale of slaves were sensitive matters. When a notary decided to rid himself of a dark-skinned slave woman named Johana "the Bearded"—the source of considerable tension between himself and his now estranged wife—he surreptitiously enlisted the help of a business acquaintance, Pere Sartre. Since this slave woman technically belonged to his wife, the transaction needed to be handled with the utmost delicacy. When Pere reported back to this notary, informing him that he had discussed the sale publicly with a potential buyer, this notary, Bernat Johan, became visibly upset. "Hearing this," Bernat reportedly "began to clasp his hands and became very distressed. He said, 'Oh lord Pere, I did not wish for you to speak of this to anyone. I cannot sell the slave. She belongs to my wife. If she finds out about this she will yell at me!" Bernat urged his agent to execute his mission with more

31. ARV JCiv 903: M. 8: 1r–3v.

32. In contrast, a *procurador* seems to have assumed at least partial liability for transactions executed on behalf of his or her principal. In a document issued in 1473, the Valencian merchant Antoni Gallent was formally released from any liability in connection with his role as *procurador* in the sale of a "defective" female slave whom he purchased and then resold on behalf of a nobleman. APPV 26815 (nonpaginated): 25 April 1473.

discretion. He instructed him to push forward with the negotiations, but asked that he first approach his wife with this proposition—without, of course, mentioning his name. He advised the broker to inquire casually what she intended to do with this slave woman and to let her know that he knew of an interested buyer. This stratagem, however, proved unsuccessful. Bernat's wife immediately suspected that her husband was behind Pere's inquiries. She threw Pere out of the house, exclaiming that her husband "had no right whatsoever in said slave nor in any other item in the household since everything had been given to her by the aforesaid Bernat Johan in restitution of her dowry."[33]

Negotiating the Terms of Sale: "Guaranteed against Hidden Vices and Defects"

Although some slaves were exchanged within the city of Valencia just as captives were, sold "as is . . . following the custom and usage of corsairs" (tal com es . . . segons costum e us de cossaris),[34] in most cases, a slave's buyer demanded and received some sort of pledge from the seller that the slave was both healthy and fit for service. The terms of these assurances would be duly noted in the contract of sale. Although sellers invariably promised that the slave had not been stolen and was lawfully captured and enslaved (affirmans dictam servam non est furatam ymo est de bona et justa guerra et ex legitimo titulo obtentam), the guarantees given concerning a slave's character and physical condition varied extensively.

Slaves sold "in accordance with the Furs de València" were covered by a sixty-day warranty covering all "hidden defects and vices" (de viciis et morbis absconsis et cohopertis).[35] If buyers discovered any "hidden" defects in the slave within sixty days of purchase, the

---

33. ARV G 2311: M. 12: 1r–17v. A dark-skinned slave girl who reputedly was of "Arab" origins, Johana was called Fatima at the time of her enslavement. Upon her arrival in Palermo, Sicily, Fatima was baptized by her new owner, who gave her the somewhat ironical name of "Bonaventura." Passing through the hands of several more owners, "Bonaventura" subsequently apostasied and reassumed her Muslim name of Fatima. When, several years later, a teenage Fatima was purchased by Bernat Johan and his wife, Beatriu, Beatriu reportedly took great pains to convert Fatima (as well as several other, unnamed "mores") to Christianity. Fatima, thus, was baptized (mistakenly) a second time in Valencia and this time she was given the name "Johana." The experiences of Johana "the Bearded" are discussed more extensively in chapter 5, see 179–81, 183–84.

34. For an example of a typical contract of sale of a captive (drawn up by the scribes of the bailiff general), see ARV Bailía 217: 522r, in which the captive was sold "tal com es e manco de la una ma o braç e lo y promet fer haver e tenir a us e costum de cosaris." For another example of a slave sold "as is . . . according to the custom of corsairs," see APPV P 11440 (nonpaginated): 4 February 1470, in which a black male slave from Guinea, twenty-seven years in age, was sold by a nobleman to a goldsmith "ad usum et consuetudinem cossariorum et no alter." See also the sale of a forty-year-old white female "Saracen" named Eretga, APPV 25217 (nonpaginated): 28 December 1473.

35. See, for example, ARV P 1997 (nonpaginated): 3 November 1477 in which a Valencian woman sold a twelve-year-old dark-skinned (llora) female to a Venetian merchant, affirming that "teneor . . . de viciis

buyer could return the slave and demand a full refund. The kingdom of Valencia's law code distinguished clearly between "hidden" (*vici amagat*) and "apparent" (*vici appareix-ent*) defects. Sellers could not be held liable for "obvious" defects such as a hunched back (*geperut*), extensive scarring (*senyals de les leges nafres*), open wounds (*nafres que encara no son sanades*), noticeable injuries or handicaps (literally, injuries that still cause pain, *nafres que se dol*), blindness (*cech*), paralysis or physical mutilation of the leg (*contret*),[36] conjunctivitis or rheumy eyes (*leganyos*), a missing hand or limb (*se perdut la ma o altre membre*), leprosy (*lebros*), or scabies or mange (*ronyos*). The failure to disclose such "hidden defects" as epilepsy, gout (*cau de gota*), chronic vomiting (*menao perdurable*), or chronic diarrhea (*jan-diflux*), in contrast, was sufficient grounds for demanding a sale's immediate rescission. Since slaves customarily were "interviewed" by buyers before the formal contraction of a sale, it is somewhat surprising to see that muteness (*mut*) and deafness (*sort*) were also classified as "hidden" defects.[37]

In addition to the "hidden" defects explicitly mentioned in the kingdom of Valencia's law code, notarial contracts of sale also admitted (or excluded) coverage for a broad array of other defects ranging from bed-wetting and incontinence[38] to the potentially more debilitating conditions of drunkenness, epilepsy, and dementia.[39] Most notably, they

---

et morbis absconsis et cohopertis secumdum forum Valencie quiquidem LX dies a foro induti volo quo incipiant currere a die presenti quibus elapsis non tenear de dicitis viciis."

36. An alternative definition for the word *contreyt* is *esguerrat* or someone who has been cut in the Achil-les tendon as a penalty for committing certain crimes. Alcover notes that fugitive slaves, trespassers, and bearers of prohibited arms were often punished in this manner. See the entry for "*esguerrar*" in the *Diccio-nari català-valencià-balear* (Palma de Mallorca, 1950).

37. *Furs de València*, ed. Colón and Garcia (Barcelona, 1999), VII: 204–5.

38. For clauses in which slave sellers stated that they would not be held liable for a slave's bed-wetting or incontinence, see, for example, APPV 499 (nonpaginated): 27 August 1476, in which the seller speci-fied that, in accordance with the *Furs de València*, she was guaranteeing this thirteen- to fourteen-year-old black male named Christofol against any hidden defects and vices, "excepto de orinar al llit." See also the sale of a thirty-year-old Russian female slave named Johana, whose seller specified that he was guaran-teeing her against hidden vices and defects "secundum forum Valencia excepto de mingendo in lecto." ARV P 2092 (nonpaginated): 9 April 1474.

39. For drunkenness, see ARV P 1996: 361v, in which a farmer guaranteed his twenty-five-year-old black male slave against the vices of "embriguesa fugidor e ladre et eciam de aliis viciis et morbis absonsis et cohopertis secundum foris Valencie." For epilepsy, see ARV P 1998 (nonpaginated): 12 January 1478, in which a merchant specified that although he was selling his thirty-year-old black male slave from Guinea named Anthony Lonch "ad usum et consuetudinem cossariorum," he was willing to guarantee the slave "de morbo vocato mal de caure de quo volo teneri ad foris Valencie." For dementia (*oradura*), see ARV P 1999 (nonpaginated): 26 October 1479, in which the seller inserted a clause stressing that he did not wish to be held liable for epilepsy, bed-wedding, or his slave's dementia. "De morbo caduco pixar al lit oradura et aliis viciis quibusvis si aliqua tenet nolo teneri aliquo modo quoniam illam vobis vendo ad usum et consuetudinem cossariorum."

included clauses concerning the slave's being a known fugitive[40] or a thief.[41] Contracts of sale for female slaves, moreover, might include clauses assuring buyers that the slave menstruated[42] or disavowing responsibility for a female slave's licentiousness. Some sellers stated that they did not wish to be held liable if the slave woman was found to be a whore (*nolo teneri de vici . . . de bagassa*)[43] or explicitly sold her "as a known prostitute" (*pro meretrice*).[44] Indicative of the other ways in which a buyer's expectations of his or her slave were gendered, contracts of sale for male slaves occasionally included clauses in which a seller refused to be held responsible for a twenty-four-year-old black male slave's excessive "arrogance" (*superbia*)[45] or a thirty-year-old black male slave's stupidity (*stultitia*).[46] Ethnic stereotypes, moreover, also may have played a role here. In 1472, Anthoni Beneyto protested to the governor that the aforementioned black male slave named Andria that Marti and Johan Castralvo had sold him was "defective." Not only was he a chronic fugitive (the slave had taken flight more than four times since entering the buyer's custody), but Andria also allegedly was "a great drunkard . . . [such] that even if he has just a bit of wine, he becomes intoxicated and is useless for doing any sort of work." Andria reportedly engaged in such bizarre behaviors that everyone in the neighborhood

40. For example, see ARV P 4301 (nonpaginated): 23 August 1474, concerning a forty-year-old "Saracen" male named Yucef Almodon, and APPV 18424 (nonpaginated): 18 November 1482, in which a seller sold a twenty-two-year-old black male slave as a known fugitive ("*pro fogidor*"). See also APPV 26674 (nonpaginated): 22 November 1477, in which thirty-three-year-old Sperancia, a former Mudejar of Aragon, was sold as a known fugitive.

41. See, for example, ARV P 2440 (nonpaginated): 22 September 1471, concerning a fourteen- or fifteen-year-old black male slave from Guinea. See also APPV 11436 (nonpaginated): 7 March 1469, in which a thirty-two-year-old Circassian female named Crespina (aka Margarita) was sold as a known thief.

42. See, for example, APPV 26674 (nonpaginated): 14 April 1478, in which a seller assured a buyer that his forty-year-old Russian female slave named Caterina "te sa purgacio." A Valencian merchant extended a similar guarantee concerning a partially manumitted forty-year-old "Saracen" slave woman named Bertomena. This merchant assured the slave's buyer (a priest named Johan Gil) that Bertomena "te de sa sporgacio segons que altres dones acostumen tenir." APPV 25214 (nonpaginated): 10 September 1470. For a dispute concerning the sale of a "defective" slave in which the buyer claimed that the eighteen-year-old slave woman he just purchased did not get her period ("no ha de sa purgacio"), see ARV JCiv 903: M. 2: 21r and ARV JCiv 904: M. 13: 31r–v.

43. See, for example, APPV 26674 (nonpaginated): 22 November 1477, concerning a thirty-three-year-old "Saracen" slave woman named Sperancia.

44. See, for example, APPV 11436 (nonpaginated): 7 March 1469, in which Crespina, alias Margarita (a thirty-two-year-old slave woman of Circassian origin), was sold "pro ladria meretrice ebria morbosa."

45. APPV 11436 (nonpaginated): 9 November 1470. The sellers (a miller and his wife) specified that, in addition to the vice of drunkenness, "de quo nullatenus volvimus vobis teneri," they also did not wish to be held responsible for his excessive pride ("*superbia*").

46. ARV P 1999 (nonpaginated): 2 January 1479. The seller (a shopkeeper) specified that "de morbo caduco stultitia et aliis quibuvis viciis nolo teneri aliquo modo." Rather, he was selling Antoni "as is," "ad usum consuetudinem cossariorum."

regarded him "a big madman and a fool."[47] Although the two merchants (a father and son) denied any prior knowledge of these alleged defects, what is noteworthy here is how they introduced a distinct standard of behavior for "blacks" (*negres*). Insisting that, while in their service, Andria had acted always in a manner suggestive that he possessed "good sense," Marti and Johan qualified their assertion by adding that as a black male slave he was "as sensible as any one of them can be, inasmuch as blacks are irredeemably vain."[48]

Consultation of notarial records dating from the latter half of the fifteenth century reveals, then, that the coverage as well as the length of the warranty given in a slave sale varied and were open to negotiation. In some instances, sellers offered extended warranties on their slaves. Some sellers vouched for the fitness and good character of their slaves for periods of up to ninety days; others accepted liability for up to four months.[49] In two separate contracts concerning the sale of teenage girls, for example, the sellers offered one-year warranties.[50] In most cases, though, sellers took pains to emphasize that this was a limited warranty. Not only did sellers often reiterate that, once the set time period had elapsed, they could no longer be held liable for any "hidden" defects found in the slave, but they also inserted special clauses limiting the applicability of the blanket sixty-day warranty by excepting certain hidden defects and/or vices from coverage. For example, in 1471 a notary indicated that he could not be held liable in the event that the buyer found that his thirty-year-old black male slave suffered chronic diarrhea.[51] Other sellers, in turn, carefully specified the defects and vices for which they were willing to assume liability. In 1479, for example, the well-known merchant Luis de Santangel guaranteed the eighteen-year-old black male slave he was selling against epilepsy, bed-wetting, and dementia. The

47. Anthoni Beneyto contended that "lo dit Andria sclau en aquests prop passats dies s'en es fogit de la casa del dit proposant per quatre ho cinch vegades," that Andria "per lo semblant es hun gran embriach es torba de vi molt sovent en manera que per poch que bega vi es torbat que nos apres aprofitar de aquell en alguna manera," and finally, that Andria "es hun gran horat e foll que en lo lo [sic] meneg e praticha de aquell los qui conexen aquell tenen per foll e orat." ARV G 2336: M. 10: 9r–12v.

48. Marti and Johan Castralbo insisted that, while in their custody, Andria "es stat ab bon seny e ab bon memoria en axi que per esser negre qui continuament son vans es stat hagut e reputat per negre de bon seny no foll ni horat ni tal que per horadura hagues inpediment algu en fer les fahenes de la casa com en aquelles donas he acostumas de dar bon recapte." ARV G 2336: M. 10: 9r–12v.

49. For examples of slave sales with a ninety-day or three-month warranty, see APPV 11380 (nonpaginated): 18 March 1477, concerning a twenty-two-year-old black female from Guinea, and ARV P 2399 (nonpaginated): 17 November 1474, concerning a twenty-five-year-old black male slave. For some examples of a four-month warranty, see ARV P 1999 (nonpaginated): 18 May 1479 (the guarantee against all hidden defects and vices, however, did except drunkenness), and APPV 25777 (nonpaginated): 13 June 1477, concerning a twenty-four- to twenty-five-year-old dark-skinned (*llora*) female, "dc linatge de moros."

50. See APPV 11436 (nonpaginated): 16 October 1473, concerning a fourteen-year-old white Russian female, and ARV P 1999 (nonpaginated): 8 July 1479, concerning a sixteen-year-old black female "de genere de Mondebarques."

51. "Excepto de morbo de exir e flux de ventre." ARV P 2396 (nonpaginated): 10 September 1471.

contract stipulated that, "concerning any other defects or vices, should he have any, I do not wish to be held responsible in any way."[52]

It was in the interests of both the buyer and the seller to have the terms of the warranty spelled out clearly. While the buyer wanted to make sure that she or he was not going to be "stuck" with damaged goods, the seller wished to avoid future lawsuits.[53] When the buyer of a twelve-year-old black male slave demanded a refund after discovering that the slave suffered from an unremitting fever, the sellers complained that the buyer's allegations concerning the slave's condition were purposefully vague. Indeed, they insinuated that the buyer's motives in filing the suit were disingenuous. The defendants alleged that the buyer had asked the court to appoint physicians to examine the slave on the assumption that the physicians were bound to find something wrong with him and then he could seize upon whatever "defect" they uncovered as grounds for the sale's rescission. This was patently unfair, the sellers insisted, "because no human body is completely healthy. No human being exists whose body does not have some defect such that every sale of a slave could be disputed." It was for this very reason, they contended, that the specific defects for which a slave sale could be rescinded had been spelled out in the Furs de València. Thus, the sellers concluded, since the defect attested to in the testimony of the physicians (a fever caused by obstructions in the liver, spleen, and belly) was not enumerated explicitly in the Furs de València as adequate grounds for a slave's rescission, the buyer's claim should be dismissed.[54]

52. "De aliis viciis si aliqua tenet nolo teneri aliquo modo." ARV P 1999 (nonpaginated): 14 September 1479. For an example of another contract in which a slave was guaranteed only against certain specified defects and vices, see APPV 25219 (nonpaginated): 22 May 1472. This parchment seller specified that he was selling his eighteen-year-old black male slave from Guinea "per specialem pactum de morbo caduco et mingendo sive de pixar al lit et non ultra."

53. Disputes over sales of defective slaves, however, could be settled out of court. If the seller was informed of the discovery of a defect within the time stipulated in the contract of sale, she or he was obliged to take the slave back and refund the sale price. For example, in a document drawn up on 30 January 1478, a buyer officially informed the seller of his intention to return the twelve- or thirteen-year-old black male slave he had just purchased because he "was unable to hold in his urine and wet the bed." ARV P 1116 (nonpaginated): 30 January 1478. If the seller contested the buyer's claims, arbitrators might be appointed in lieu of taking the dispute to court. When the widow of a silk weaver complained that the fifty-year-old black female slave she had just purchased had "moltes malaltes cubertes e visis," arbitrators were called in resolve the dispute. Although the seller, a cloth preparer, argued that the slave's two-month warranty had already elapsed, the buyer (somewhat curiously) insisted that the warranty period began on the date on which a defect was discovered. APPV 6161 (nonpaginated): 22–29 March 1471. Most contracts, however, stipulated that the warranty period began immediately, at the time of the contraction of the sale.

54. The sellers objected that the plaintiff "no es stat dit ne declarat quin ni qual es lo mal qu'es dit cubert per lo qual aquell vos rescindir o retractar la dita venda del dit sclau" and argued that "car dels coses humanals es axi que nullum corpus humanum est sumpliter sanum car no es hom que en lo seu

Indeed, just how far these clauses protected buyers and what exactly was being promised were open to interpretation and, consequently, subject to dispute. When Anthoni Beneyto demanded a refund of the price he paid for the aforementioned black male slave named Andria, a key issue in this dispute was whether the sellers (Martí and Joan Castralbo) had, at the time of sale, accepted liability for the vice of drunkenness. Although the "agent of the ear" Sancho Puig testified that, at the time of sale, the sellers told the buyer that "they knew of no hidden defect" in the slave, Sancho nevertheless did recall that during the sale's negotiation, Martí Castralbo related the following incident. A few Sundays earlier, the slave had returned home inebriated after a day spent carousing "with some others" around town in Gandia. Was this admission that, on one occasion, Martí Castralbo had discovered Andria drunk the equivalent of selling the slave as a known drunkard? Though Sancho had been produced as a witness by the sellers (who insisted that, in relating this incident, they had explicitly specified that they could not be held liable for the vice of drunkenness), this broker testified that he believed that Martí, in revealing this tidbit of information, had not presented it as a defect. Sancho quoted Martí as stating "it was not something that made him defective" (*que no era cosa que li fes mal*). Unfortunately, the civil court's ultimate ruling in this case has not survived. Thus, it remains unclear whether Martí's disclosure effectively relieved the sellers of liability with regard to this slave's propensity to drink.[55]

Even physicians appointed by the court to examine a slave might disagree over whether a slave was "defective"—that is, whether a certain physical condition constituted adequate grounds for a slave sale's rescission. In 1443, two physicians appointed by the court to examine an eighteen-year-old female slave who did not menstruate contradicted one another in their ultimate prognosis. While the physician named by the plaintiff unequivocally classified the slave's failure to menstruate as a hidden defect, indicating that she was pregnant or in danger of developing "apoplexy" (i.e., of suffering a severe stroke),[56] the physician named by the defense demurred. He testified that "according to good medicine and good philosophy," a woman who did not menstruate could still be perfectly healthy. For, he continued, "there is no doubt that the advent of the menstrual cycle in women was not always punctual, but subject to variation." Although for some women it came every seventeen days, for other women it came every thirty-five days, every forty days,

---

cors no haia qualque mal e per consequent tota venda de sclau se retardia ço que es absurdum et per ço lo fur ha volgudes declarar les malaltihes per les quals se pot la venda retardar per los dits metges no es de aquells que son per fur possades groch." ARV JCiv 904: M. 16: 27r–28v.

55. ARV G 2336: M. 10: 9r–12v.

56. The physician Pere Rossell testified that "per raho com la dita sclava no ha de sa purgacio axi com diu ella matexa que o ella sia prenyada o seria perillosa de qualque malaltia cuytada axi com es apoplexia cachecia o altra semblant que ve soptadament e per ço diu que es de oppinio que seria mal cubert." ARV JCiv 904: M. 13: 31r.

every two months, or even, "if they are hot, dry, and full of choler [yellow bile], never, and they would still be healthy."[57]

Even when disgruntled buyers were able to establish that a physical defect or vice existed in a slave and that it was covered under warranty, they faced yet a third hurdle in securing a refund: proving that this defect had been concealed deliberately. According to the Furs de València, only if a buyer could prove that the seller had knowledge of a hidden defect in the slave at the time of the sale and knowingly concealed it was the seller obliged to take the slave back into his or her custody and give the buyer a full refund.[58] The intentional concealment of a slave's "hidden defects and vices," however, was a tricky thing to prove. Indeed, rather than pursue a costly and potentially fruitless legal battle, dissatisfied buyers might first try to pawn the defective slave off on someone else. Particularly when they had ventured abroad to purchase the slave, duped buyers would attempt to recoup their losses by reselling the slave in the Valencian marketplace; hence, the Valencian tanner Berenguer Dezcortell's efforts to resell Jordi, the aforementioned black male slave he purchased in Barcelona who was infested with "worms."[59] In addition, in 1473, rather than sue the Barcelonan cloth merchant who had sold him a Circassian female slave who reputedly was "lazy, a drunkard, and a fool," a Valencian merchant tried, unsuccessfully, to resell her.[60]

57. The physician Joan Vallseguer testified that "segons bona medicina e bona philosophia la dona no haver gens de purgacio seria dupte que pora esser dit mal cubert vivint la dona en sa natural sanitat ab aquella disposicio es be fora de dupte lo adveniment de la purgacio en les dones no esser punctual ans sots alguna latitut car a algunes los ve a xvii dies a altres a xxxv e a altres a xxxx altres passen dos mesos altres son molt caldes e seques coleriques magres no han james e viven sanes. E per consequent diu ell dit testimoni que no creu verdaderament no haver purgacio les dones esser mal cubert." ARV JCiv 904: M. 13: 31r–v. As a result of these conflicting diagnoses, the court ordered that the slave be examined by two more experts: another male physician and a woman named "dona Elvira." While this physician, Bertomeu Marti, sided with the plaintiff, stating that a woman of that age who is not pregnant ought to be menstruating, the testimony of na Elvira (as well as the JCiv's ultimate sentence) unfortunately have not survived.

58. Furs de València, ed. Colón and Garcia (Barcelona, 1999), VII: 204–5.

59. According to the testimony of a local barber, this thirteen-year-old black male slave named Jordi "te una malaltia o mal . . . ço es a saber cuchs en les cames e en los pits." Indeed, one of Berenguer Dezcortell's traveling companions testified that when they stopped to eat at an inn on their way back to Valencia, he saw how Jordi, one of the three black male slaves they had just purchased, removed a worm from the sole of his foot. "Looking at said worm and then seeing how [worms] were also coming out from the other slaves' bodies, he seized one and crushed it, telling them this was how they could cure themselves of the disease." The buyer who purchased Jordi, upon Berenguer's arrival in Valencia, however, quickly discovered the slave's defect and demanded the sale's rescission. It was only then that Berenguer decided to file a complaint against the original seller, a sailor from Barcelona. ARV JCiv: 903: M. 8: 1r–3v.

60. ARV JCiv 926: M. 13: 45r–48r.

Trial Periods: Opportunities to "Observe" (Mirar)
and "Detect" (Reconexer)

In an effort to avoid such unwelcome surprises and to prevent subsequent conflicts, buyers typically were given temporary physical custody of a slave prior to the formal contraction of a sale so that they could inspect a slave more closely. Buyers held the slave "on loan" for a set period of time before the sale became legally binding. This trial period was crucial, it was argued, for two reasons. First, it gave buyers the opportunity to examine a slave more thoroughly for any physical defects outside the immediate supervision of the seller or his or her agent. Further, the trial period was designed to be of long enough duration so that any vices the slave possessed would likewise be revealed.

Indeed, sellers often refuted charges that they had deliberately concealed a slave's defects simply by affirming that they had willingly transferred the slave into the buyer's custody prior to the formalization of the sale. In a dispute over the sale of Maria, a "defective" black female slave (alleged to be, among other things, crazy, lame, and nonmenstruating), the seller, Damiata Dezlana, the widow of a nobleman, insisted that in no way could it be claimed that she had "hidden" the slave's defects. Damiata noted how she had sent Maria "to the household and into the custody of said na Ursola, where she had stayed four days or more." Damiata argued that during this period, the buyer had had ample opportunity to examine her. She affirmed that the buyer, having been given the opportunity both to look at (mirar) and detect any vices or defects that were in the slave (reconexer la dita cativa), had "deliberately" purchased the slave.[61] Damiata's testimony suggests that even if a defect was not explicitly acknowledged in the contract of sale, a seller could be released from liability for the defect simply because she had allowed the buyer to examine the slave thoroughly. Since the slave had been transferred into the buyer's custody, it became the buyer's responsibility, not the seller's, to assess the health and character of a slave.

Similarly, in the aforementioned dispute concerning the "unequal" trade of Jordi, a "defective" black male slave, for Anastasia, a "healthy" Circassian female, the owner of the black male slave, Dalmau Ferrer, dismissed charges that he deliberately concealed the fact that Jordi was "a thief, gambler, fugitive, and a drunk" by citing his offer to transfer the slave into the plaintiff's custody. Dalmau emphasized how, during the contract's negotiation, he had advocated a fairly extensive trial period of eight to fifteen days prior to the formal consummation of the sale. This, he argued, was a clear sign of his good

---

61. Thus, Damiata stressed how "tractant se la venda de la dita sclava aquella fon tramesa per la dita Damiata a la casa e poder de la dita na Ursola on stech quatre dies o mes en lo qual temps aquella compradora podia fer mirar e regonexer la dita cativa e la qual fon reconeguda per aquella e axi deliberadament la dita na Ursola compra la dita cativa." ARV G 2283: M. 3: 5r–9v and M. 4: 21r.

faith and openness. After minimizing the severity of the slave's alleged "defects," Dalmau argued that he could not possibly be accused of deliberately "concealing" them. After all, it had been the Circassian female slave's owner (Vicent Valenti) who showed discomfort with a trial period, fearing that once outside his protective custody, Anastasia would run the risk of being raped and impregnated. Indeed, even when Dalmau offered him the option of placing Anastasia in the household of a "reputable" woman during this period, Vicent still had refused.[62]

As the next and final section of this chapter will illustrate, however, when sellers released their slaves into a prospective buyer's custody, they had other things to fear besides an unwanted pregnancy. No longer under their owner's watchful eye, slaves might speak out and, possibly, scuttle the deal.

Subverting the Process

I noted in the first chapter how, in the court of the bailiff general, corsairs and Crown officials compelled captives to "confess" that they were infidels and enemies of the Church and Crown. Corsairs and Crown officials needed this testimony to substantiate claims that they could legitimately be sold into slavery. In households and inns scattered across Valencia, in contrast, slave sellers seem much more preoccupied with keeping their slaves quiet. Although prudent slave buyers wanted to question slaves thoroughly to determine their overall fitness and value, slave sellers were loath to have their merchandise speak for themselves. Indeed, the aforementioned Vicent Valenti claimed that certain individuals told him that they had overheard Dalmau Ferrer threaten his slave, cautioning the eighteen-year-old black male named Jordi that if he revealed that he was a thief, drunkard, fugitive, and a gambler, he would get a "good beating."[63] Though sellers may have verbally intimidated and/or physically abused their slaves to secure their silence, their efforts did not always succeed.

Despite the protections afforded them in the court of the bailiff general (the assistance of interpreters and the watchful presence of prominent members of the local Muslim community), when captives made their "confessions" before the bailiff general, the cards were stacked heavily against them. The customs and procedures governing this process, not to mention, in most cases, the language in which the proceedings were conducted,

---

62. The plaintiff, Vicent Valenti, of course, described this transaction very differently. Vicent claimed that Dalmau specifically had targeted him as a dupe on whom he could unload his unruly black male slave. Vicent portrays Dalmau as a smooth-talking salesman, telling Vicent that he esteemed this black male slave so highly that he would pay 120 gold florins for him. He claimed that the only reason he was offering to trade this slave was because his wife was forcing him to do so—she wanted a female slave. ARV G 2288: M. 22: 48r–v and M. 23: 44r–45r.

63. ARV G 2288: M. 22: 48r–v and M. 23: 44r–45r.

were foreign to them. Moreover, the Crown officials charged with overseeing these hearings were hardly disinterested individuals. The duty collected from the sale of captives into slavery provided significant sums for royal coffers and the bailiff general could ill afford alienating corsairs upon whom he relied for both the defense and provisioning of the kingdom. Hence, it is not terribly surprising to see that in this unfamiliar and intimidating environment, captives almost invariably "acknowledged" their slave status and gave testimony consonant with a verdict affirming their *de bona guerra* status.

With the passage of time, however, slaves living and working in the city of Valencia would have become better acclimated, learning the language and customs of their masters. Most important, they seem to have become more knowledgeable about the ins and outs of Valencia's legal system. In a later chapter, I will discuss how those who felt they had legitimate grounds for enfranchisement and could gain access to the kingdom's courts filed suits against their masters demanding their liberty. In this section, however, I will discuss how enslaved persons attempted to better their situation and exercise a bit of control over their fates by preventing or facilitating their resale. In royal and municipal courts, masters and mistresses complained that their slaves were interfering in their efforts to sell them. Indeed, they portrayed slaves as intervening in all stages of the negotiation process: soliciting certain individuals to purchase them, behaving badly toward a potential buyer to discourage a sale, and feigning illnesses and injuries to force a sale's rescission. Although in many instances these accusations were of an admittedly dubious nature, it is significant nonetheless that masters and mistresses attributed to their slaves the power to sabotage or at the very least manipulate these transactions.

Soliciting Agreeable Masters

When twenty-five-year-old Margalida (a.k.a. Melica) first arrived in the city of Valencia, she allegedly feared for her life. Her mistress, the noblewoman Yolant Centelles, suspected her of sleeping with her husband. Enraged, Yolant had packed this allegedly "free" domestic servant off with two of her squires, instructing them to dispose of her however they saw fit. Upon their arrival in Valencia, one of these squires reportedly had threatened Margalida, telling her that if she did not cooperate with their efforts to sell her (and say that she was a slave), he would slit her throat.[64] A native of "Sclavonia," Margalida insisted that, like all those from "Sclavonia," she was a free-born Christian who could not

---

64. Lorenç Jornet, a member of the Centelles's household, testified that "per quant la senyora madona Yolant tenia cells de la dita Margalida tenint oppinio que lo noble mossen Guillem Ramon Centelles se gaya carnalment ab aquella dita Margalida dix a dos scuders de la casa del dit noble mossen Guillem Ramon...que prenguessen la dita Margalida e la s'en portassen a la present ciutat...e que'n fessen de aquella lo que vols...estant en la dita present ciutat de Valencia la hu dels dits scuders appellat Nicolo...dix a la dita Margalida que renegava de son deu e crehador que si ella no deya que era cativa e sclava que ell la degollaria com ell la volia vendre." ARV G 2341: M. 9: 21r–25v.

be sold as a slave. She maintained that she went along with her sale only to avoid certain death. The defense would contend, however, that not only was Margalida of Circassian (as opposed to Slav) origins, but that she had always affirmed that she was a slave. Thus, she had freely consented to her sale, and, indeed, within the confines of the inn where she and the two squires were staying, Margalida had actively solicited potential buyers. Margalida allegedly had asked a fellow guest at the inn, Joan Frare of Segorbe, to buy her.[65]

Though the defense's contention in this particular example is somewhat suspect, considered in conjunction with other examples of slaves depicted as approaching individuals in an effort to get them to buy them suggests that slaves could attempt to improve their living situation by asking men and women whom they deemed to be more preferable as masters (or mistresses) to purchase them.[66] Such a tactic might not only better their material conditions, it might also heighten their chances for winning their liberty. Thus, in 1464, a widow advised a pregnant dark-skinned (llora) slave woman (the aforementioned Johana "the Bearded") to inform the child's father (a court chaplain) of her predicament. For, she explained, "if this chaplain has any responsibility in this, for the love of the child, he will buy you and then make you free."[67]

Asserting Different Ethnicities, Claiming Free Status

In contrast to the hearings held in the bailiff general's court, slaves reportedly were more outspoken in the interviews between buyers and sellers in households and inns. Though surely still nerve-wracking and intimidating experiences, these perhaps were more open-ended exchanges occurring in more informal spaces. When a prospective buyer came by the inn where the aforementioned slave named Margalida (a.k.a. Melica) was staying, Margalida allegedly attempted to discourage him from purchasing her (or, at the very least, improve her chances for an only temporary period of enslavement) by asserting she was a free-born Christian. The prospective buyer testified that when he

65. The defense contended that Margalida "dient e afermant aquella esser sclava e encara pregat al honorable en Johan Frare ciutada de Segorbe que la compras aquella afermant tot temps e dient que era sclava." ARV G 2343: M. 1: 17r.

66. ARV G 2345: M. 6: 7r–11v.

67. This widow testified that about two years ago, Johana had come to her house, "as she was accustomed to," extremely upset, nearly crying. When the widow asked her why she was upset, Johana had responded, "O wretchedness! I have been living immorally so I fear that I am pregnant. If it is true, if I am pregnant, my master and mistress will make my life miserable!" When Johana told her that the child's father was a court chaplain, this widow said she had responded, "Calm down! God will help you as He helps all women in trouble. If this chaplain has any responsibility in this, for the love of the child, he will buy you and then make you free." ARV G 2311: M. 12: 1r–17v. A few days later, however, this widow continued, Johana came back to her house with the "happy" news that she had gotten her period. Johana "the Bearded," as portrayed in contemporary court records, was a notorious femme fatale and reportedly was infamous in her community for her sexual proclivities. For more on this, see chapter 5, pp. 179–81.

questioned Margalida concerning her status, she claimed that she was of Russian (hence Orthodox Christian) origin. This witness, however, claimed that he immediately saw through Margalida's ruse. He strongly rebuked her, stating, "You've lied to me. You look more like a Circassian, not at all like a Russian."[68]

The efforts made by a fifteen-year-old black male to prevent his sale were reputedly even more brazen. In 1493, Nicholau Marquo foiled a broker's repeated attempts to negotiate his sale by proclaiming before all prospective buyers, "Don't buy me. I am free. I cannot be sold." After Nicholau did this several times, the broker allegedly beat the slave severely, rebuking him for his insolent behavior, demanding "Why did you say that?"[69]

Sabotaging a Sale: Slaves Behaving Badly

Somewhat more open to interpretation were the actions taken by another female Circassian slave named Magdalena, twenty-five to thirty years in age. In 1473, the merchant Salvador Bernau purchased Magdalena in Barcelona from a Sicilian merchant, presumably intending to resell her in Valencia. After transporting Magdalena to Valencia by sea, however, "he discovered strange and hidden defects in her." Bernau alleged that not only was she dangerous and violent,[70] but she was also a drunkard (*grandissima embriaga*) and a fool (*molt folla*). Rather than incur the expense of a risky long-distance lawsuit, the merchant (as noted earlier) first tried to dump the defective slave on some unsuspecting Valencian. Although Bernau portrayed the slave woman here as a raving lunatic, one cannot help but suspect that perhaps there was a method to Magdalena's madness.

Luys Gepter, a Majorcan merchant who happened to be staying at the same inn as Bernau and Magdalena, stated that he saw Bernau entrust Magdalena to "many different

---

68. Johan Frare testified that, about two-and-a-half years earlier, while he was staying in the hostel managed by Berthomeu Guinovart, some people approached him to ask whether he was interested in purchasing a slave woman owned by a nobleman. When he replied that he might be interested, someone came and brought the slave woman to the hostel for him to examine. Thus, "afronte ab la dita sclava present en Guinovart e en lo hostal de aquell e interrogat ell dit testimoni a la dita sclava li demana de quina nacio era o si era sclava e aquella li dix e respos que era rosa e sclava e ell dit testimoni li dix que deya falsia que ella mes tenia paria de xarquesa que no de rosa." ARV G 2343: M. 1: 17r, M. 7: 12r–15v.

69. The *corredor d'orellà*, however, did eventually manage to find Nicholau a buyer: the baker Antoni Stheve. Stheve was Nicholau's master at the time when he filed a successful *demanda de libertat* claiming that he had been kidnapped and unlawfully sold into slavery after he fled Tunis for Sicily to convert to Christianity. ARV G 2396: M. 3: 45r and ARV G 2397: M. 13: 21r–24v. For more on Nicholau and the *demanda de libertat* he filed in 1493, see chapter 6, pp. 211–12.

70. Magdalena allegedly bit the arm of an innkeeper's wife after her master, frustrated by her alleged laziness, roused her from her slumbers by giving her a good lashing. The bite wound this innkeeper's wife received was reportedly so severe that, eight to ten days later, it still had not healed. The innkeeper's wife protested that Magdalena had directed her anger at the wrong target. She testified that she had just wrested the whip from her master's hands in order to prevent him from hurting her ("per que lo dit son amo no la maltractas"). ARV JCiv 926: M. 13: 45r–48r.

brokers of the city of Valencia" who "carted her around town in order to sell her." On some occasions, these brokers seem to have made some headway, leaving Magdalena "on temporary loan" with interested buyers. But inevitably, Luys continued, "due to the bad defects that she has, they [eventually] returned her. [These brokers] were unable to find anyone who would give one dinar for her!"[71] Joan Vinet, a Valencian bookseller who often had business dealings with Salvador Bernau, testified that on one of the many visits he made to the inn during this period, he encountered a very frustrated "agent of the ear," Luys Ramon. Having returned from yet another unsuccessful attempt to find Magdalena a buyer, the broker regaled Vinet with a description of the slave's latest antics. Ramon's most recent prospect, Luis Vives, ended up refusing to buy her because, almost immediately upon entering his house, "Magdalena had raised her skirts and defecated [literally, purged her stomach] in the front entranceway." In addition, "no sooner had she gone upstairs than did she demand some bread and cheese, all the while acting like a demented person."[72] One could argue that Magdalena's behavior, rather than the actions of a "demented fool and drunkard" (as Salvador Bernau alleged), were deliberate and calculated acts of resistance, specifically aimed at scaring off prospective buyers. It is altogether possible that Magdalena was "feigning" madness in an attempt to prevent her resale to an unknown and perhaps less benign master in a new city. Perhaps Magdalena hoped that her strange behavior would force Bernau to return her to Barcelona, where she presumably had friends and family.[73]

Securing a Sale's Rescission: Feigned Illnesses and Self-Inflicted Injuries

Such testimony suggests that slaves not only absorbed Valencian culture in its most obvious forms (religion, food, dress, sports, and other pastimes), they also became conversant with its laws and legal procedures. That slaves themselves were (or at the very least were considered by others to be) aware of the consumer protection clauses contained in their contracts of sale is revealed in accusations made by individuals (both interested and

---

71. Luys Gepter testified that he saw how "diversos corredors de la dita ciutat han portat la dita sclava per vendre aquella lexant aquella a sobre alt e tostemps per los mals vicis que te la s'en ha tornada que no troben qui hi do hun diner." ARV JCiv 926: M. 13: 45r–48r.

72. Joan Vinet testified that the broker Luys Ramon had told him "com entrant en una casa de hun home que ha nom Luys Vines a la qual la havia portada per que si la volien comprar com fonch dins en la entrada de la dita casa se alca les faldes e aqui purga son ventre e no comenca de aco com fonch dalt en la dita casa de fet demana pa e formatge e tot aco ab continenca de persona incensada." ARV Justícia Civil 26: M. 13: 45r–48r.

73. Contemporary testimony suggests that one of a slave's greatest fears was resale. In addition to uprooting a slave, distancing him or her from all that was familiar and cutting him or her off from any support network she or he may have assembled, resale to a new owner would likely endanger, if not completely undermine, any progress a slave had made toward regaining his or her freedom.

disinterested parties in these disputes) that slaves were feigning illnesses and injuries in an attempt to force the sales' rescission. Consider, for instance, the testimony of a witness in the dispute over the sale of the aforementioned black female slave named Caterina who was suffering from the plague. Upon first hearing the slave complain about her condition (while seated on a bench outside the house where she and her new owner were staying), the tailor Gabriel Torella's immediate presumption had been that Caterina was faking the illness in an attempt to reverse her sale. Observing how a young boy had been taunting Caterina, trying to get her to open her mouth so that, like a horse, he could examine her teeth to determine her age, Gabriel overhead Caterina tell the boy to "leave her alone because she had a massive headache." The tailor testified that, after hearing this, he had approached Caterina and said to her, "Perhaps you are pretending to be ill since you do not wish to be sold. Perhaps you were in a good household and you do not want to leave." According to Gabriel's telling, Caterina appeared offended by the accusation, replying rather firmly that "she was not joking. She was ill with the plague." She added, moreover, that the mistress with whom she had been staying had threatened her, telling her that if she dared to limp or walk hunched over, she would beat her severely."[74]

Some slaves, moreover, were accused of taking even more extreme measures to sabotage a sale. The merchant and notary Martí Andrés, for example, tried to convince a pair of court-appointed physicians that, hardly a preexisting defect, the drippy nose and excessive congestion his thirty-year-old Circassian female slave were experiencing were the consequence of her having stuck a sewing needle up her nose. Martí argued that his slave named Margarita had injured herself deliberately in a desperate attempt to repeal her sale. The physician Ramon de Monçó, alias Porter, testified that the day before he was to see Margarita, Martí had come to see him. Martí informed him that Margarita was "malicious" and that "out of malice" she had punctured herself in the nasal passages so that he would be obliged to recover her from her new master's custody. The physician Joan Barbera likewise testified that two days before he was to examine the slave, Martí had appeared at his home, telling him that Margarita had scratched her nose up "really well" with a sewing needle and that this puncture wound in her nasal passages had become infected. Unimpressed with this seller's explanation, however, both physicians insisted

---

74. ARV G 2278: M. 7: 16r–19v; M. 8: 38r–v. Gabriel Torella's testimony was echoed by that of his wife, Caterina, who recounted how her husband had confronted the slave woman and said to her, "That which you are saying, that your head hurts, are you not saying this in order that they do not sell you? By chance, is this because you are in a good household and you do not wish to depart?" (Tu aço que dius que't fa mal lo cap non dius sino per ço que no't venen car per ventura stas en bona casa e non voldries exir). Caterina reportedly had responded "that she was not joking but that she was ill with the plague and that the woman with whom she was living was menacing her, telling her that if she walked like a crippled person that she would wear her down with beatings" (que no fahia burlant sino que era ferida de granola e que al dona ab qui stava la havia menacada dient li que si la dita sclava anava coxa que ella fartaria de bastonades).

that, based both on the nature and progression of Margarita's ailment, it was clear that her symptoms were neither the consequence of a self-inflicted puncture wound nor of a recent injury. Rather, their diagnosis was that she suffered from a malady called *ypolit* or an ulcerated nasal polyps and that, in their expert opinion, she had had this medical condition for at least a year.[75]

Preventive Measures

Ultimately, the fear that slaves might speak or act out provoked masters to take preventive measures. Such measures principally took the form of threats of physical violence such as Dalmau Ferrer's warning to his eighteen-year-old black slave named Jordi that if he said anything that would jeopardize his sale "he would give him, or see to it that he was given, an excessively severe beating."[76] Indeed, statements attributed to Caterina, the plague-stricken slave with whom we began this chapter, serve as good illustrations of how, in most instances, slave sellers effectively managed to control their slave's speech. After witnessing Caterina's sale to Goncalbo Goncálvez, the Castilian merchant who was boarding in his household, the Valencian merchant Gabriel Andreu came home to find this seventeen-year-old black female lying in his house with her head down. Immediately suspecting that she was stricken with the plague, Gabriel testified:

> He asked her what was wrong and she responded that she was ill. She had an inflammation on her hip and her head hurt her very much. He asked her how long she had been ill, and she replied, "since yesterday." He then asked her why she had not told them this and she responded that the reason why she had not said this was ... that her mistress where she was staying, knowing that she too had caught the illness, had threatened her, [telling her] that if she said that she was ill with the disease that she would give her a very bad beating. For this reason she had kept quiet and had not wished to say anything of it until this moment.[77]

75. ARV JCiv 903: M. 2: 7r and ARV JCiv 904: M. 13: 18r. Although the buyer's original complaint was that Margarita had an excessively runny nose, two months later this same buyer protested that the seller had also failed to disclose that Margarita had leprosy. The buyer contended that if his earlier complaint regarding an alleged "hidden defect" had been insufficient grounds to demand the sale's rescission, surely the fact that Margarita had leprosy constituted more than adequate grounds. Although the JCiv ultimately ruled in favor of the buyer, Martí immediately filed an appeal.

76. The plaintiff contended that, wishing to rid himself of the slave, Dalmau "said and was overheard to say to said black captive that he better not reveal that he was a thief, drunkard, fugitive, and excessive gambler, that otherwise, he would personally administer or have someone else give him a major whipping." ARV G 2288: M. 22: 44r–v; M. 23: 44r–45v.

77. "Demana a la dita sclava que havia. E aquella respos li que stava mal car tenia vertola en lo angonal e que doli alli molt lo cap. Et el testimoni demana li que quant temps havia que'n havia e aquella respos li

Not particularly sympathetic to this slave woman's plight (more concerned, perhaps, with protecting his own household against infection), Gabriel's immediate response to Caterina's revelation was to expel both slave and owner from his home. That very evening, he sent both of them to a house in the *converso* (Jewish converts to Christianity) quarter of the city.

What is especially revealing of the ways in which slaves were manipulated as "talking tools"—how their faculty of speech was either exploited or suppressed according to their owner's best interests—is how the following day the slave's seller, Johan Draper (who previously was concerned only with silencing the slave) now anxiously sought Caterina's testimony. Upon hearing news of the discovery of Caterina's illness by her buyer, Johan had hurried over to the house where Caterina had been sent in order to extract testimony from her that would relieve him of liability. Finding her lying on her side in a room inside the house, Johan questioned Caterina thoroughly concerning when exactly she had contracted the illness—in particular, Johan sought testimony specifying whether she became ill before or after she entered Goncalbo's custody.

Conveniently enough, Joan Capata, the "porter of the lord king," was among those individuals hastily assembled to witness this crucial exchange.[78] Joan was there "on official business," commissioned by the governor (at Johan Draper's insistence) to arrest Goncalbo Goncálvez. Fearing that Goncalbo, upon learning that Caterina had the plague, would try to renege on the deal, that very morning Johan had filed a suit against Goncalbo for nonpayment of the slave's sale price. After all, according to the Furs de València, a slave sale was considered "perfected" as soon as the seller stated formally that he was willing to hand over the slave and the buyer stated that he would pay the agreed-upon sales price. In the interim, during the period between this formal statement of intent and the actual payment of the sales price, if the slave was lost or damaged, this would be at the buyer's risk.[79] Hence, in Johan Draper's estimation, even if Caterina died, Goncalbo Goncálvez still had to pay the previously agreed-upon price.

Unless, that is, Johan reasoned, Goncalbo could prove that he had deliberately concealed the slave's illness from him. As added insurance against such a possibility, Johan now interrogated Caterina concerning when she first contracted the plague. Most obligingly, Caterina—who died that very day—provided Johan Draper with the

---

que del dia passat llavors el dit testimoni dix li que per que non havia dit e aquella respos li que per co non havia dit per tal com huna fadrina era morta en la casa on aquella dita sclava stava e que ni havia huna alter malalta e que la dona on la dita sclava stava sabent que la havia presa el mal la havia menacada que si ella dehia que fos ferida del mal que la fartaria de bastonades e que per aquella raho la dita sclava havia callat fins en aquella hora que non havia volgut dir res." ARV G 2278: M. 7: 16r–19v and M. 8: 38r–v.

78. In addition to Joan Capata, "porter of the lord king," Luys Cic, a *corredor d'orellà*, was also in attendance. ARV G 2278: M. 7: 16r–19v and M. 8: 38r–v.

79. Furs de València, ed. Colón and Garcia (Barcelona, 1999), VII: 204–5.

testimony he needed to relieve him of liability. Joan Capata described the exchange as follows:

> [Johan Draper said to her], "What ails you?" and she responded that her head hurt her very much. Draper then said to her, "How long has your head been hurting you?" and she responded, "I have not been feeling well and my head has been hurting me since last night, when I was brought into this house, and up until this very moment." Draper then said to her, "Tell us, when you left your mistress's household, did anything at all ail you?" She responded, "Nothing at all bothered me when I left the household of my mistress, but rather [it began only after], when I was in said household where I have been brought."[80]

Whether or not Caterina actually made any of these statements is perhaps less significant than the fact that both parties in this dispute felt compelled to buttress their claims regarding this slave's condition with statements purported to come from the mouth of Caterina herself.

As soon as they had been proclaimed "*catius de bona guerra*," enslaved men, women, and children (be they black or white, Muslim or Christian) became commodities to be exchanged: resold, inherited, or mortgaged for debts. Slaves, however, unlike other commodities, were expected to help market themselves. Not only were they obliged to make their bodies available to potential buyers to be poked and prodded, but they were also expected to respond politely to inquiries concerning their place of origin, overall health, and skills. Although I have demonstrated how the "process of marketing," to a certain extent, gave slaves latitude to shape their own sales, claiming a different ethnic identity or drawing attention to a physical defect in an attempt to manipulate or resist a sale posed real dangers. Thus, as historian Edward Baptist has cautioned (citing the testimony of the ex-slave William Wells Brown, who reported that it was not uncommon for traders in the antebellum South to force slaves to dance and sing "to make them appear cheerful and happy"), "one must be careful not to place far more emancipatory hopes on the process of marketing than the evidence will bear.[81] As the frequency of references to owners

---

80. "Lo dit en Johan Draper interroga dient li Caterina que't fa mal e aquella respos que lo cap li fahia gran mal. Et lo dit en Draper dix li que de quant enca li faya mal lo cap. Et aquella respos que de la nit passada que fon menada a la dita casa fins en aquella hora li dolia e li feya mal lo cap. Et lo dit en Draper torna li dir digues e com ixques de casa de ca dona fahiat res mal e aquella respos que lavors no li fahia res mal quant ixque de casa de la dita casa dona mas com fonch en la dita casa on fon menada e per el testimoni aqui vista allis senti molt mal e dolor de cap." ARV G 2278: M. 7: 16r–19v and M. 8: 38r–v.

81. Edward E. Baptist, " 'Cuffy,' 'Fancy Maids,' and 'One-Eyed Men': Rape, Commodification, and the Domestic Slave Trade in the United States," *American Historical Review* 106, no. 5 (December 2001): 1634–35.

threatening and/or physically beating their slaves into submission makes clear, most slaves were sold to owners not of their own choosing. Although some enslaved men and women were no doubt aware that divulging a preexisting medical condition could result in the rescission of their sale, in the majority of breach of warranty cases presented before the Justícia Civil we see sellers attempting to deflect responsibility for their own shady selling practices onto their slaves. Rather than admit that they knowingly concealed their slaves' injuries, it was far more convenient to insist that slaves were feigning illnesses in an effort to defraud their masters.

CHAPTER 3 SLAVE LABORS

In 1466, two sisters, Johana and Ursola, filed a wrongful enslavement suit against their master (a Valencian merchant) demanding that, in addition to their immediate liberation, they receive back salary for the more than fifteen years of service they provided "as slaves even though they were free." Kidnapped from their Castilian Mudejar parents at the ages, respectively, of three and five, Johana and Ursola detailed how, both in their master's household in the city and on his rural properties located near the village of Paiporta, they had "worked with all their might," providing "as much service as slaves can and are obliged to do." Within the household, their daily chores included making bread (*pastar*), cooking (*cuinar*), cleaning (*scurar*), sweeping (*agranar*), and doing the laundry. This last chore, according to their testimony, was especially taxing, requiring them both to soak the dirty clothing in boiling hot water (*fer bugades*) and scrub them with soap (*ençabonar*). No less significant, however, were the contributions Johana and Ursola made to the merchant's income by their labors *outside* the household: picking fruit and selling it in city markets (*collir fruyta e vendre aquella*) and pitching in, when needed, in the maintenance of his agricultural holdings. Thus they had gone out to work on their master's rural properties "at the time of the wine harvest" (*en lo veremar*), "at the time of the harvesting of cereals" (*en lo meses*), and "at the time of the production of olive oil" (*en fer oli*).[1]

Johana and Ursola's demand for payment of back salary hinged upon the recognition of their contemporaries that slaves were more than mere status symbols; they were highly valued for their productive capacities. Indeed, slaves in fifteenth-century Valencia participated in a broad range of economic activities. Their contributions were not limited

---

1. "Axi com a sclaves fahent tant servitut com sclaves fer poden e deuen iatsia fosen franques axi en la present ciutat com en la alqueria de aquell treballant per tot son poder en pastar cuynar scurar agranar fer bugades ençabonar collir fruyts e vendre aquella ajudar en lo veremar e en les meses e en fer oli e altres fahenes." ARV G 4583: M. 1: 22r and ARV G 2318: M. 12: 6r. For more on the sisters Johana and Ursola, see chapter 4, pp. 136–37.

to domestic service but encompassed agricultural as well as artisanal production.[2] The job description for a twenty-two-year-old male slave purchased by a carpenter, however, differed substantively from that for a twenty-two-year-old female slave owned by an inn-keeper. Male and female slaves were subject to disparate demands and, as we shall see, endured distinctive indignities. Gender, along with age and the owner's socioeconomic status, were important determinants in a slave's living and working conditions.

In this chapter I consider how work distinguished the slave experience. Were some tasks considered so demeaning as to be "fit" only for slaves? Were slaves, in turn, barred from exercising certain (i.e., skilled) trades? Examination of the extant source material reveals that slaves, by and large, worked side by side with free laborers in the house-hold, field, and artisan's workshop.[3] As a title for this chapter, then, the term "slave la-bors" is somewhat misleading. Certainly, whenever possible, tasks considered especially distasteful were consigned to slaves. In general, however, the tasks performed by slaves roughly paralleled those performed by free workers. Ultimately, what distinguished the slave experience in fifteenth-century Valencia was not the type of work performed, but the conditions under which they labored.

The Crown placed few restrictions on a master's or mistress's ability to exploit a slave's labor capacity. The most significant restrictions affected only Jewish and Muslim mas-ters, who technically could not own or even hire temporarily the services of Christian slaves.[4] The only limitations imposed on all (including Christian) masters and mistresses were that they could not ask their slaves to work on Christian holidays and feast days[5] nor could they "force" their female slaves to prostitute their bodies, particularly if they were Muslim or lived outside the precincts of the municipally regulated red-light district.[6]

Sources often are frustratingly silent concerning the actual functions performed by slaves. In the absence of explicit statements detailing their daily activities, historians have argued that we can approximate their work assignments by looking at who their buyers were.[7] For example, if a carpenter purchased a slave, it is more than likely that the slave as-sisted him in his workshop, sawing, sanding, and hauling wood. Examination of notarial

2. Aurelia Martín reached similar conclusions in her study of slavery in sixteenth-century Granada. See Aurelia Martín Casares, *La esclavitud en Granada del siglo XVI: Género, raza, y religión* (Granada: Universi-dad de Granada y Diputación Provincial de Granada, 2000), esp. 321–27.

3. This seems to have been characteristic of slave-holding societies throughout the late medieval Medi-terranean world. In his study of black slaves and freedmen in Portugal, for instance, A. C. de C. M. Saun-ders notes the "coexistence of slaves and free labourers in various sectors of the economy," affirming that "no occupation was exclusively associated with slaves." Saunders, *Black Slaves and Freedmen*, 84–85.

4. Nor, for that matter, could Jews or Muslims employ Christians as domestic servants or wet nurses. *Furs de València*, ed. Colon and Garcia (Barcelona: Editorial Barcino, 1974), II: 81.

5. *Furs de València*, II: 81–82.

6. *Furs de València*, II: 85.

7. See, for example, Meyerson, "Slavery and Solidarity," 298.

contracts of sale dating roughly from 1450 to 1500 reveals that slave buyers came from all walks of life in late medieval Valencia. Slave owners were not limited to members of the nobility or urban elite—farmers, tanners, and even cobblers possessed slaves. Among the most prominent slaveholders in fifteenth-century Valencia were carpenters (*fusters*), bread bakers (*flaquers*), and those connected with the textile industry.[8] Since a significant proportion of slave buyers came from these trades, it is likely that slaves were extensively employed in these industries. Indeed, if we take into account the fact that masters and mistresses coming from the nobility and urban elite frequently contracted out their slaves' services to less well-to-do artisans, the number of slaves engaged in artisanal production was likely even higher. Owners profited from their slaves' productive capacities in a variety of different ways, both directly (putting them to work in their own households, fields, and workshops) and indirectly: renting out the services of their slaves to third parties in exchange for payment of a "salary."

Domestic Service

Independent of whatever trades their masters or mistresses may have practiced, a good proportion of the slaves working in fifteenth-century Valencia were purchased for the purposes of providing domestic service. Indeed, in the estimation of many scholars, slave was synonymous with domestic in the late medieval Mediterranean world.[9]

"Domestic," of course, is a vague job title. As the testimony of the sisters Johana and Ursola informs us, a female domestic's role was hardly circumscribed within the walls of her master's household. The upkeep and management of a household, after all, involved not only cooking, cleaning, laundry, and child care, but also making daily trips to the local market, grain mill, and oven. A slave woman's work responsibilities also typically included fieldwork on their master's or mistress's agricultural holdings (usually located outside the city walls, in Valencia's surrounding agricultural hinterland or *huerta*)[10]

---

8. Although roughly a quarter of slave buyers were merchants, shopkeepers, or brokers, 8 percent were members of the nobility and 8 percent were urban professionals (i.e., notaries, lawyers, and doctors), 11 percent worked in the textile industry, 5 percent were carpenters or otherwise involved in construction, and 4 percent were bread bakers. These figures derive from my analysis of 317 slave sales, taken from a random sample body of notarial records dating from 1460 to 1480 and found in the ARV and the APPV.

9. Heers, *Esclavos*, 138.

10. In contrast with the field work performed by men, the field work performed by women seems to have been more seasonal in nature, centered around the gathering and processing of crops rather than on their cultivation. Although Johana and Ursola's testimony does not provide us with any more detailed information, contemporary gender divisions suggest that their "assistance" at the time of the wine harvest meant that they stomped on the grapes, their assistance at the time of the wheat harvest meant that they threshed the wheat, and that their assistance in the production of olive oil meant that they helped operate the olive presses. For a detailed description of a female domestic servant's chores in late medieval

and selling fruit gathered in their master's orchards (or pilfered from neighboring properties) in city markets. A slave woman named Jordia, for example, was working in her master's vineyard when she allegedly was assaulted by another slave woman who, in conjunction with her master, threw stones at her and then punched her in the face and eyes.[11] Slave women also appear frequently in the records of the Justícia de 300 Sueldos (Valencia's small-claims court) accused (often in conjunction with free persons) of stealing fruit and other items associated with agricultural production. Over the course of two years, for example, one slave woman was charged with stealing, respectively, the stakes used to support vines from a neighboring vineyard, a basket of figs, an entire grape harvest, and some alfalfa.[12] Similarly, in 1478 a black slave woman was charged with stealing and then selling a neighbor's entire grape harvest.[13]

In addition, slave women often participated in local textile production by spinning raw fibers (flax, wool, hemp, cotton, and silk) into skeins of yarn or thread in between doing their other chores. In the last will and testament of Manuel Muncada, a Valencian merchant, for example, Manuel instructed his executors to reimburse his former slave woman Damiata (whom he had freed about four years previously) "for whatever sums of money he had collected on her behalf for the thread she had spun."[14]

Thus, as Bernard Vincent has argued, "We ought once and for all to dispense with the prevailing view of 'domestic' slaves . . . [as] individuals who were well-treated by their masters and did only light housework." "Domestic" slaves, in fact, worked outside the household as well as within it. In Vincent's view, what distinguished "domestic" slaves from slaves who worked "on the plantations of Madeira, the Canary Islands, or the New World" was the "polyvalent" character of their work assignments. In addition, while the latter group of slaves lived and worked together in "gangs" numbering into the dozens, "domestic" slaves worked individually, in relative isolation from other slaves, under the direct authority of an all-powerful *dominus* (master). In Vincent's perspective, the classification of a slave as a "domestic" has more to do with his or her living and working conditions than with the type of work she or he performed.[15]

Tuscany, see Christiane Klapisch-Zuber, "Women Servants in Florence during the Fourteenth and Fifteenth Centuries," in *Women and Work in Preindustrial Europe*, ed. Barbara A. Hanawalt (Bloomington: Indiana University Press, 1986), 60.

11. ARV JCrim 23: M. 4 (Clams): 26 August 1449 (nonpaginated).

12. ARV Justícia de 300 Sueldos 1092 (Manifests): 27 February 1473 (nonpaginated) and 8 October 1473; ARV Justícia de 300 Sueldos 1093 (Manifests): 30 August 1480 and 22 May 1480 (nonpaginated).

13. ARV Justícia de 300 Sueldos 1092 (Clams): 16 November 1478 (nonpaginated).

14. "Per la filaça que aquella ha feta e fara fins al dia de la mia mort." APPV 22551 (nonpaginated): 29 March 1477.

15. Bernard Vincent, "L'esclavage en milieu rural espagnol au XVIIe siècle: L'exemple de la région d'Alméria," in *Figures de l'esclave au Moyen-Age et dans le monde moderne*, ed. Henri Bresc (Paris: Editions L'Hartmattan, 1996), 176.

Predominantly (but not exclusively) female, domestic servants performed tasks that were essential to the local economy. Contracting the services of a free female servant, however, was a much more widespread practice than purchasing a slave. One need only page through a few volumes of contemporary notarial registers to get a sense of the frequency with which parents put their young daughters and sons (ranging in age, generally, from four to seventeen) into service. The salary and length of service expected were recorded in a contract of service (an *afermament*). *Afermaments* rarely specified the nature of the work required. Rather, the contracts usually featured blanket statements such as "serving you and your household in all things licit and honest" (*ad serviendum vobis et familie vestre in omnibus licitis et honestis*).[16] Nonetheless, we can piece together a rough picture of the work free female domestics typically performed from incidental references in notarial and court records. For example, when the legal guardian of a fifteen- to sixteen-year-old girl declared his charge, Caterina, "unfit" for household service, he noted how Caterina's previous employer, the notary Berthomeu Matoses, had "justly" canceled her *afermament* because Caterina's shortsightedness (*curta de vista*) caused her to break dishes and spill oil on the ground when she filled the lanterns. Caterina's guardian complained that, despite his most diligent efforts, he could not find the teenage girl a new employer; even her aunt and cousin had refused to take her. Nevertheless, he acknowledged that, since entering his service, Caterina had performed chores requiring less hand-eye coordination, such as "sweeping and scouring."[17] Incidental references in notarial and court records also reveal free female domestics doing fieldwork, picking (and stealing) fruit to sell in local markets,[18] and spinning raw fibers into thread. In a salary dispute between a free servant and her former mistress, the mistress cited as "proof" that the young girl

16. Excerpt from the *afermament* of the six-year-old daughter of a cloth preparer. She was contracted to serve the wife of a tailor for a period of three years. APPV 14399 (nonpaginated): 14 April 1477. Carmen García Herrero notes that contracts in fifteenth-century Zaragoza feature similarly nondescriptive statements regarding work assignments. María del Carmen García Herrero, *Las mujeres en Zaragoza en el siglo XV*, vol. 2, *Cuadernos de Zaragoza* (Zaragoza: Ayuntamiento de Zaragoza, 1990), 2: 58. In her study of female domestics in fifteenth-century Málaga, María Teresa López Beltrán notes how "in no contract does there appear any specifics with respect to their duties." Indeed, she continues, the clause typically employed was so vague that it enabled some masters to direct their servants to perform tasks that their parents would not have expected or intended. In consequence, López Beltrán argues, concerned parents began inserting protective clauses, "directed towards preventing the potential abuses that could occur." María Teresa López Beltrán, "La accesibilidad de la mujer al mundo laboral: El servicio domestico en Málaga a finales de la edad media," in *Estudios historicos y literarios sobre la mujer medieval* (Málaga: Diputación Provincial de Málaga, 1990), 133–34.

17. ARV JCiv 924: M. 14: 1r–2r.

18. In 1474, a merchant's widow collected twenty-five lliures in salary "pro laboribus in colligendo fructus et redditus in Alcocer per me sustentis." APPV 14399 (nonpaginated): 24 September 1474. In 1478, a black male slave apprehended a married woman who was caught trespassing on his mistress's property with a "skirt's worth" of cherries. ARV Justícia de 300 Sueldos 1092: Clams: 18 May 1478. Also in 1478,

had never been in her service the fact that she had never "spun any thread, either or linen, cotton, wool, or any other material for her."[19]

On the surface, then, free female domestics had much in common with their enslaved counterparts. They not only lived under the same roof, they also performed many of the same chores. Indeed, I encountered no clear preference for a free or slave domestic in the itemized requests filed by widows demanding an allowance to cover household expenses during the one-year mourning period (any de plor) before they could recover their dowry. Rather, slave and free domestics were presented as interchangeable, suggestive that they were considered to execute the same chores and perform roughly the same functions.[20] Free servants and slaves, moreover, were both household dependents. Masters and mistresses were empowered to compel—by force, if necessary—both groups to do their bidding.[21] When parents put their daughters "into service," they not only sold their daughters' labor, they also relinquished custody and, by extension, paternal authority over their children for considerable periods of time. It was not unusual to see terms of service of twelve years. Masters and mistresses were empowered to discipline and even to "recapture" these freeborn children in the event that they took flight.[22]

---

a group of six free women were apprehended by a female slave and a male servant stealing pomengranates from their master's orchard. ARV Justícia de 300 Sueldos 1092: Clams: 28 September 1478.

19. "Que nunqua la dita Catarina en lo temps que ella dita proposant stech ab son marit fila filaça alguna de lli de coto ni de llana ni de alguna manera de filaça per la qual se pogues mostrar que aquella fos de la dita na Johana." ARV G 2278: M. 10: 44r and ARV G 2279: M. 12: 25r–26v; 33r–35r.

20. For one example among many, see ARV JCiv 930: M. 10: 46r–48v.

21. The authority of the pater familias was, at least in theory, nearly absolute. They had the authority to punish their children, their younger brothers, their wives, as well as their apprentices, servants, and slaves. Herlihy, Medieval Households, 114–15. Indeed, according to the kingdom's legal code, "Furts o rapines o injuries domestiques, ço es, que seran fetes per persones que seran de sa casa, sien castigats per aquells senyors o per los meestres ab qui estaran. Enaxí que no sien tenguts de respondre a nós ne a la cort, ne aqueles persones no sien hoÿdes per nós e per la cort d'aquel castigament que sia feit." Nevertheless, the statute continues, there were limits to "paternal" authority. They could not impose corporal punishments that would result in the loss of a limb or permanent physical disfigurement—that is, cut off the hand, the foot, the nose, ears, or poke out eyes. Furs de València, ed. Colon and Garcia (Barcelona, 1990), V: 104–5. Moreover, in practice, we find heads of households also requesting licenses from the Justícia Criminal to administer certain corporal punishments on their relatives and free household dependents— that is, to put them in irons. For one example among many, see the following record in which the Justícia Criminal granted permission to a silk weaver to put his son in irons, for however long he saw fit, "without incurring any penalty." ARV JCrim 24: (Cedules) 30 July 1456 (nonpaginated): "Lo honorable justicia criminal dona licencia e facultat an Bernabeu Tafaya seder de la ciutat de Valencia que sens encorriment de penes algunes puxa metre cep o ferra'l e desferrar an Anthoni Tafaya fill seu al lur coneguda la qual licencia li dona per lo temps que a ell sera ben vist dins lo present any e no pus." Such licenses, of course, would not have been necessary if the household dependent in question was a slave.

22. For one example among many, see ARV P 2440: 2 August 1471, in which a parent granted their child's new master "facultatem et plenum posse et auctoritatem quod possitis et valeatis absque licencia

The most obvious differences between free and enslaved female domestics were that for a free female domestic, the term of service was fixed rather than indefinite and that, upon completion of this set term of service, she would be paid a "salary" (*soldada*) and customarily would be given a new set of clothes.[23] Slaves, in contrast, were not entitled to collect any compensation for their labor. For, as was stated in the kingdom's law code, "for however long he [she] is in his [her] master's power, [a slave] can have nothing that is his [her] own."[24]

In weighing the relative merits of securing a slave versus a free domestic servant, one important factor was no doubt financial. In both cases, masters and mistresses would be obliged to supply the basic necessities of food, clothing, and shelter. Judging from the aforementioned allowance requests, the cost of maintaining a female slave was considered roughly equivalent to that of a female servant. Purchasing a slave, nevertheless, required a sizable capital outlay. Depending on her age, physical attributes, and skills, a female slave typically cost anywhere from thirty to sixty lliures, with an average cost of forty lliures (see table 1 in chapter 1). Contracts of service (*afermaments*) dating from the same time period, however, reveal free female servants being promised salaries (a *soldada* or *mercede*) of between fourteen and twenty-five lliures, payable upon completion of terms ranging from four to twelve years. Thus, while a female slave generally cost upward of thirty lliures, the salary demanded by a free female servant seldom surpassed twenty-five lliures.[25]

Masters and mistresses, however, also had to take into consideration the number of years of labor he or she expected to get from a slave. Since buying a female slave could cost as much as twice as much as hiring the services of a free female domestic for twelve years of service, if a master, for example, intended to follow papal injunctions and free his Greek slave gratis after seven or eight years of service, then contracting the services of a female servant might be more cost effective. If, however, a master expected to retain a

---

alicuius iudicis seu officialis sed vestra propria auctoritate ipsum Ferdinandum inquacumque loco eum repereritis capere seu capi facere et in vestri servitutem reducere et tornare et hoc tociens quociens dictus Ferdinandus a servicio et posse vestris recedere contigerit."

23. For example, see ARV P 2182: 8 October 1477.

24. "Si servu qui serà d'alcú guaanyarà alcuna cosa per alcun contract o per alcuna mercaderia o per alcun cas de sa bona ventura, tot allò que guanyarà ne haurà guanyat serà del senyor car, com ell sia en poder de son senyor, no pot haver alcuna cosa que sia sua própria." *Furs de València*, ed. Colon and Garcia (Editorial Barcino, Barcelona, 1999), VII: 185.

25. Most servant girls began their term of service between the ages of nine and eleven, and completed it upon reaching "marrying age" (generally, it seems, eighteen to twenty years in age). The salaries that they earned (on average between fourteen and twenty-five lliures) typically were earmarked for their dowries. For a detailed set of salary figures for male and female domestics dating from the sixteenth century, see Miguel Lop, *Un aspecto económico de la Valencia del siglo XVI: Los salarios* (Valencia: Ayuntamiento de Valencia, 1972), 231–34.

slave in his service for the bulk of her productive life—say, twenty or even thirty years—purchasing a female slave could become the wiser investment. Furthermore, many masters perhaps hoped to recoup and even profit from their investments by either contracting their slave's services out to third parties in exchange for a salary or by offering the slave woman the opportunity to purchase her freedom and setting the redemption fee at an amount equivalent to or even greater than her initial purchase price.

"Honest" Work

Social and cultural norms no doubt also factored into these decisions. The similar work assignments given to slave and free domestics should not blind us to the fact that slave and free members of a household were regarded and treated differently. The language employed in every contract of *afermament* is instructive here. When placing their daughters, granddaughters, and nieces into service, parents and relatives routinely specified that they could only be asked to perform "respectable" duties. Such clauses—"for the purposes of serving you and your family in all things licit and honest" (*ad serviendum vobis et familie vestre in omnibus licitis et honestis*)[26] and "for the purposes of accomplishing all of your licit and honest directives both night and day" (*ad faciendum vestra mandata licit et honesta tam de die quam de nocte*)[27]—suggest an important distinction in how contemporaries regarded "free" domestics: most notably, their "honor." Though these clauses admittedly were formulaic in character, they reveal a concern with protecting free women against sexual exploitation. While free girls had mothers, fathers, brothers, and/or uncles who could demand that their duties be restricted to those of an "honorable" character, slave girls lacked legally recognized parents and/or guardians who could advocate for them, much less ensure that their "honor" was protected.

Contemporaries, in contrast, recognized that it was a master's prerogative to have sex with his slave women. In 1484, an enslaved woman named Beatriu noted how her master, Francesc de Cas, "lay with her carnally many different times, especially at those times when [his] wife was away for several days, at the rural property that they owned, located between Santa Anna and Torrent."[28] Although the money changer Gabriel Torregrossa vehemently denied the accusation that he was the father of his slave's child, he

---

26. Excerpt from an *afermament* in which the six-year-old daughter of a cloth preparer was put in the service of a tailor's wife for a period of "at least" three years. APPV 14399 (nonpaginated): 14 April 1477.

27. Excerpt from the *afermament* of the fifteen-year-old daughter of farmer from Alboraya. The girl was placed in the service of a Valencian notary for a period of six years. ARV P 438 (nonpaginated): 28 March 1464.

28. "Se jague moltes e diverses vegades carnalment ab aquella e senyaladament en aquell temps que la muller del dit mestre Francesch de Cas stava per alguns dies en la alqueria que tenien tunch temporis los dits conjuges situada entre Senta Anna e lo loch de Torrent." ARV G 2371: M. 3: 14r and ARV G 2372: M. 13: 38r–42r.

nevertheless admitted that he had, on several occasions, availed himself of his Russian slave woman's sexual services.[29] Finally, an enslaved black woman named Leonor described her initiation into her master's household as a brutal sexual assault. "Seeing himself as her lord and seeing that she could not contradict him, he took 'love' from her whenever he willed, knowing her carnally one and many times."[30] Such statements—particularly since they were expressed casually and matter-of-factly—reflect a generalized conviction that an enslaved woman's body was at the complete disposal of her master.[31]

It was quite another matter, however, for a master or mistress to make their slave women's bodies available, for a fee, to the general public—particularly if she or he lived outside the boundaries of Valencia's municipally regulated red-light district (the *bordel* or *la Pobla*).[32] From the date of the kingdom of Valencia's foundation, masters were prohibited from prostituting their Muslim slave women. The *Furs de València* stipulated that "no one who has a Saracen female can hold her as a prostitute nor collect earnings from her. If anyone should do this, he shall lose her and she will be confiscated by us [i.e., for the Crown]."[33] By the end of the fifteenth century, "forcibly" prostituting a slave woman (literally, "making her lie carnally with men and collecting a fee for this") could be cited as grounds for her immediate liberation.[34] Masters who participated in such activities were condemned not only because their behavior clashed with the paternalistic

29. Gabriel Torregrossa admitted that "algunes vegades se jague ab aquella." ARV G 2351: M. 15: 1r–4v.

30. "Vent se senyor de la dita Leonor e vent que aquella no li podia contradir a sa voluntat pres amor ab aquella e coneguda aquella carnalment per una e moltes vegades." ARV G 2403: M. 2: 12r and ARV G 2405: M. 28: 46r–52r. For more on this black slave woman named Leonor (aka Elionor), see chapters 4 and 5, pp. xx and xx.

31. For a groundbreaking analysis of how sexual exploitation and reproductive work shaped and distinguished the experiences of enslaved women in the Atlantic world, see Jennifer L. Morgan, *Laboring Women: Reproduction and Gender in New World Slavery* (Philadelphia: University of Pennsylvania Press, 2004).

32. In a series of royal privileges reissued in 1515, Fernando II ordered that "no woman...be she slave or free...be admitted in a hostel or tavern outside the city's red-light district, be it in the city or its suburbs, for the purposes of prostituting her body to travelers or other men." Both the prostitute and her client were to be punished. In addition to being whipped naked through the streets, they were to be fined twenty *morabatins* for each offense. If, moreover, it could be shown that the slave prostitute had been doing so on her owner's orders, she or he, too, would be punished. She or he would forfeit custody of the slave and the slave woman (after being whipped publicly) would be freed. *Aureum Opus Regalium Privilegiorum Civitatis et Regni Valentie*, ed. Luis Alanya, Textos Medievales, 33 (Valencia, [1515] 1972), 521.

33. Rather than marking an end to a life of prostitution, however, an enslaved Muslim woman's confiscation by the Crown sometimes meant that she would be put to work in royal brothels. See Mark D. Meyerson, "Prostitution of Muslim Women in the Kingdom of Valencia," in *The Medieval Mediterranean: Cross-Cultural Contacts*, ed. M. Chiat and K. Reyerson (St. Cloud, Minn.: North Star Press, 1988), 87–96. For the relevant statute, see *Furs de València*, ed. Colon and Garcia (Barcelona, 1974), II: 85.

34. For one example, see the *demanda de libertat* filed by a slave woman demanding her immediate liberation on the grounds of "forced carnality" (*forçada de carnalitat*). ARV G 4848: M. 1: 17v and ARV G 2305: M. 16: 5v–7v. Witnesses cited a statute in the *Furs* prohibiting "la qis diu forçada de carnalitat."

ideology bolstering slavery's legitimacy—masters, after all, were supposed to be teaching their slave women the virtues of chastity—but also because, by "publicly exposing" their slave women, by forcing them to practice "the evil art," they had provoked others to sin as well, encouraging "the public sin of carnality."[35] Indeed, from the perspective of royal and ecclesiastical officials, such activities threatened the kingdom's security. Inasmuch as such acts were a great "offense to God," they must be banned in order to prevent "divine retribution" in the form of "epidemics, wars, famines, droughts, earthquakes, and other evils."[36]

Despite the moralizing of preachers and public officials, however, innkeepers working in the city's red-light district purchased slaves (almost invariably females between the ages of twenty and thirty), many of whom were likely employed as prostitutes.[37] On 13 June 1477, Caterina Borreguera, an innkeeper in Valencia's bordel, purchased a twenty-four- to twenty-five-year-old llora (dark-skinned) slave woman named Yolans.[38] Similarly, in the autumn of 1476 the innkeeper Joan Bardaxi sold Maria, a baptized black African slave woman, to the wife of Bertomeu Gualindo, also an innkeeper "en lo bordel."[39] Slave masters and mistresses living outside Valencia's bordel also appear in municipal court records accused of purchasing slave women "for the purposes of illicit gain" (tenir la a guany illicit). Indeed, for at least one slave mistress, this reputedly constituted her principal source of income. Ursola Vinader, aka Na Rotlana, was the widow of the innkeeper Dalmau Rotla. Though she lived outside the precincts of Valencia's bordel, in the parish of San Andreu, she had achieved local notoriety in the 1460s as the "madam" of a group of slave prostitutes. Operating her household "as if she had been in the bordel," Ursola forced her slave women to have sex "with all men who came [to them], the good as well as the bad

35. This language is taken from two separate demandes de libertat filed, respectively, in 1462 and 1464, by enslaved women claiming they had been forcibly prostituted. ARV G 4848: M. 1: 17v; G. 2305: M. 16: 5v–6v and ARV G 2304: M 2: 31v; M. 8: 48r–v; G. 2310: M. 3: 41r; G. 2311: M. 13: 7r–38r.

36. See the royal privileges issued in 1515, in which Fernando II demanded stronger enforcement of laws prohibiting gambling, unlicensed prostitution, and usury. Aureum Opus Regalium Privilegiorum Civitatis et Regni Valentie, ed. Luis Alanya, Textos Medievales, 33 (Valencia, 1972), 521. On attitudes toward prostitution in general during this period, see Jacques Rossiaud, Medieval Prostitution, trans. Lydia G. Cochrane (New York: Blackwell, 1988), and Ruth Mazo Karras, Common Women: Prostitution and Sexuality in Medieval England (Oxford: Oxford University Press, 1998).

37. Repeated efforts to prosecute slave owners who prostituted their slave women suggest that it was a recurring problem. In his discussion of illicit sexual activity in fourteenth- and early fifteenth-century Valencia, Rafael Narbona cites charges leveled against an innkeeper who had two slave women, Johaneta and Caterina, who, with this innkeeper's encouragement, had carnal relations with all sorts of men, living openly as "àvols fembres ab consentiment de dit llur amo." Rafael Narbona, Pueblo, Poder y Sexo: Valencia Medieval (1306–1420) (Valencia: Història Local 10, Diputació de València, 1991), 135.

38. APPV 25777 (nonpaginated): 13 June 1477.

39. APPV 16894 (nonpaginated): 19 September 1476.

and the criminal, the young as well as the old."[40] Guillem Gostanc, a male servant living in her household, testified that it was common knowledge that Ursola bought female slaves for the purpose of prostituting them. He recounted how, on one occasion, he overheard Ursola browbeat a less than enthusiastic enslaved sex worker, "Come here, Johana! Earn! Advance! Work hard, for I cannot live except on what you earn!"[41] On at least two separate occasions, Ursola was hauled before the court of the governor on charges that she was forcibly prostituting her female slaves. In 1462, a Russian slave woman named Caterina charged Ursola, her mistress, with "repeatedly exposing her for illicit gain and to the sin of carnality." Literally living off the wages of her slave's sin, Ursola allegedly forced Caterina "to lie with more than one thousand men." Describing Ursola as her *entrevenidora* or her pimp, Caterina recounted how her mistress "negotiated with those who wished to sleep with her, telling them, 'My girl is a sweet roll. She has such [a great] body that it is a great delight not only to have sex with her but also to touch and fondle her.'"[42]

Two years later, in 1464, another slave of Ursola's, a white woman named Johana, came forward to accuse her mistress of forcible prostitution. Johana, however, recounted a considerably more harrowing tale. When, shortly following her purchase, Johana proved less than compliant in obeying her new mistress's orders, Ursola complained to the slave's seller, contending that he had sold her a "defective" slave. The notary appointed to arbitrate this dispute reported how Johana said that while she was "content" to have sex with "some man of honor, or a merchant," she was not willing to have sex with "all men."[43] Complaining that Johana "does not wish to do that for which she had been purchased," Ursola demanded that the seller, Luys Vinader, exchange Johana for a slave woman better suited for the trade and, if possible, one "more beautiful in body" (*que es pus bell cors de dona*). When Luys protested that "no one would be willing to do this work," Ursola

40. "La feya jaure publicament ab tots los homens que y venien axi bons com dolents e criminals chichs e grans axi propiament com si stigues en lo bordell." ARV G 2310: M. 3: 41r and ARV G 2311: M. 13: 7r–38r.

41. Guillem Gostanc testified that "esser ver que ell dit testimoni hoy dir moltes vegades a la dita na Rotlana dient a la dita Johana vine açi Johana. Guanya e avança e treballa be que yo no puch viure sino de ço que tu guanyes." ARV G 2310: M. 3: 41r and ARV G 2311: M. 13: 7r–38r.

42. Ursola, allegedly, "una e moltes e mes de M. vegades ha exposada a guany illicit e a peccat carnalitat la dita sclava sua faent la jaure ab mes de mil persones e ella dita na Rotlana prenent preu e loguer del peccat de la dita Caterina e vivint del quest illicit e damnat guany de la dita Caterina.... Essent ella entrevenidora ab aquells qui volen jaure ab ella e dient de la dita Caterina la mia borda es un rollet de pasta que unes carns te que es un gran delit no solament de usar ab ella solament lo toquar la o menejar la." ARV G 4848: M. 17: 17v and ARV G 2305: M. 16: 5v–7v.

43. This notary testified that "la dita sclava responia que de algu home de be o mercader ella era contenta de fer ho que de tot hom no so volia fer." Hearing this, the notary himself said that he replied, "Bear in mind, Johana, that your mistress purchased you to do this sort of work (and that if you cooperate) she will be very good to you and grant you freedom" (*guardat Johana que la senyora per aquesta fahena t'a comprada e ella't fara molt de be e fara francha*). ARV G 2310: M. 3: 41r and ARV G 2311: M. 13: 7r–38r.

reportedly had retorted, "[my dear] nephew, prostitution (*quest*) is a career for many!"[44] Since Luys had no other slave woman to offer her, a compromise was reached whereby the buyer and seller essentially joined forces to bully Johana into submission. The slave seller took the matter, literally, into his own hands. Luys brought Johana home with him; they both got undressed, and then, as one witness recounted, "he put her in his bed and took a 'nap' (*sesta*) with her." Ten to twelve days later, Ursola retrieved Johana and the "problem," apparently, had been resolved.[45]

Johana herself, not surprisingly, told a different story. Over a period of fifteen days, she was beaten, whipped, and forcibly induced "to commit sins." Thus, Johana, recounted, over the course of this two-week period, Luys Vinader wore her down physically and "taught her how to do shameful things with men."[46] Johana, moreover, insisted that even after this initial period, she had continued to resist whenever she was asked to perform sexual favors—especially on religious holidays. For this reason, the aforementioned servant, Guillem Gostanc, was called in, "on Good Friday and the vigils of the Virgin Mary," to whip and beat her into submission. Indeed, by Guillem's own admission, he forced Johana to sleep with men "against her will."[47]

In her defense, Ursola tapped into contemporary prejudices concerning the supposed natural carnality of slave women. She denied any part in either encouraging or forcing this illicit behavior. As her slave's mistress, however, she insisted that it was entirely within her rights to claim for herself any money given to her slave in exchange for the slave "willingly" prostituting her body. Ursola, therefore, countered Caterina's charges by making a seemingly dubious distinction between the private exchange of sexual favors in "open" areas and what went on in public brothels. Since she did not keep her slave "in some brothel or public place," Ursola insisted, she could not be accused of "forcibly"

44. This notary testified that "la dita na Rotlana trames per lo dit en Luys Vinader clamant se de aquell que la dita sclava no volia fer ço que ella la havia comprada.... E lo dit en Luys Vinader li deya deguna per que no volia fer aquesta fahena. E la dita na Rotlana deya al dit en Luys Vinader nebot quest es carrer de molt." ARV G 2310: M. 3: 41r and ARV G 2311: M. 13: 7r–38r.

45. This notary related that "lo dit en Luys Vinader prenia la ma e porten la a la seu e despullas ab ella e metia la en lo llit e tenia la sesta ab ella. E aço dura per los dits deu o dotze dies e a cap del dit temps la dita na Rotlana traure ella e present lo dit en Luys Vinader foren de acort que ab tot." ARV G 2310: M. 3: 41r and ARV G 2311: M. 13: 7r–38r.

46. Johana insisted that Ursola "la feu metre en lo peccat e qu'es jagues ab los homens carnalment. E ella dita responent non volia fer car mes de XV li dura de induhir la al pecat encara la feya batre de açots an Gostanc e son fill que ta la aperellaven e la lexaven de açots que mal goig feya. E lo dit en Luys Vinader venia en la sesta e tenia la sesta ab ella e mostrava li com havia de fer la taquanyeria ab los homens induhint la a fer ho." ARV G 2310: M. 3: 41r and ARV G 2311: M. 13: 7r–38r.

47. Guillem Gostanc acknowledged that Ursola "feya gitar carnalment ab homens tot l'any specialment lo divendres sant o en les vigiles de la Verge Maria ultra voluntat de la dita Johana e si aquella no volia fer la feya açotar e batre per la dita raho e la feu açota a ell dit testimoni." ARV G 2310: M. 3: 41r and ARV G 2311: M. 13: 7r–38r.

prostituting her slave. Although it was certainly possible that Caterina had carnal rela-tions with many men, these encounters took place in her mistress's home, "a private house with open doors. Any time that said Caterina was in said house...she had been able to go and do whatever she liked." Thus, Ursola's advocate concluded, "however many men who had lain carnally with her had lain with her of her own free will and with her permission, not by force. Her mistress did not force or constrain her to do so."[48] Finally, Ursola's advocate added, if Caterina was being compelled to sleep with all these men, she should have immediately filed a complaint before the appropriate authorities. These authorities, after all, would have been extremely receptive to her complaint since Ursola did not live within the precincts of the bordel. Thus, Ursola's advocate argued, "it is not plausible that [Caterina] was forced or compelled [to prostitute her body] because in a city such as Valencia, where you, the most magnificent lieutenant governor and a great number of officials are, it is inconceivable that, if force were being employed, she would not have filed a complaint."[49]

In spite of the grandiose claims Ursola's advocate makes here regarding slave agency and the protections available to slave women against sexual exploitation, it is difficult to deny that, within the household, slaves—as dishonored and natally alien-ated persons—enjoyed fewer safeguards than free servants. Consider, for example, the following request filed before the Justícia Civil by a concerned father. On 20 February 1461, Bernat Nadal, a farmer from Torrent asked that the afermament of his daughter in the household of the hosier Leonard d'Arago be canceled. Noting how Leonard's wife re-cently had died, leaving the thirteen-year-old girl alone with her master, Bernat success-fully sought the Justícia's assistance in dissolving this contract since "it would be a very dangerous thing for such a grown-up young girl to stay with a man who, at present, does not have a wife."[50] It is difficult to imagine a similar action being taken on behalf of a female slave.

48. Ursola denied that she "la expusta e deliurada e distinctament a carnalitat la dita Caterina...ni que aquella aia forçada o necessitada a carnaliter en algun bordell o loch publich e publicament e si aquella ha usat carnalment ab alguns homens en casa de la dita sua principal la dita casa es casa privada e portes ubertes e tota hora que la dita Caterina era en la dita casa que diu cassava ab los homens s'en podia hanar e fer ço qu'es volgues e quants se jagueren carnalment ab aquella se jagueren ab aquella ab gran voler e beniplacit de aquella e no per força ni que la dita sua principal la'n forcas o instruingues." ARV G 2310: M. 3: 41r and ARV G 2311: M. 13: 7r–38r.

49. "No es versemblant sia stada forçada o necessitada car en tal ciutat com Valencia hon son vos molt magnifich lochtinent de governador he a copia de officials no es presumidor esser feta e alguna força tal que nos puga clamar e ja per fur es statuhit a la dita quis diu forçada de carnalitat." ARV G 2310: M. 3: 41r and ARV G 2311: M. 13: 7r–38r.

50. "Sera cosa perillosa una fadrina tant gran star ab lo home que a present no te muller." Bernat Nadal sought not only to recover custody of his daughter but also to collect the salary she had earned in the past year and a half in this widower's service. ARV JCiv 920: M. 1: 38r; M. 7: 32v.

In light of this parental concern with safeguarding the honor of their daughters, female slaves possibly were an especially valued (if not essential) addition to a household because, as natally alienated individuals who lacked personal honor, they (theoretically) could be compelled to perform "dishonest" and disagreeable chores without raising a fuss. Consider in this regard the respective fates of an enslaved woman named Caterina and a free female servant named Berthomena. In 1464, while the town of Lleida was under siege, a baptized Muslim slave woman named Caterina was sent on an errand: delivering meat to her master's servants who were stationed in a tower located outside the city's walls. Traveling unaccompanied through what essentially was a war zone, Caterina was captured and subsequently raped by Crown forces. It bears noting that we learn of her rape and capture not because anyone had ever bothered to send out a search party to find and rescue her (perhaps she was presumed dead), but because now, several years later, Caterina had filed a lawsuit demanding her freedom based on a promise made by her original master in Lleida shortly before she was captured by Crown forces.[51] Although it is certainly true that free female servants too could be sent out on dangerous errands, a master was more likely to think twice before doing so given the fact that he could be faced with complaints, if not lawsuits, from the free servant's family members. On 21 November 1441, for instance, the brother and guardian of an eighteen-year-old girl named Berthomena filed a formal complaint in the court of the Justícia Criminal after his sister, a domestic servant (mancipa), was kidnapped while harvesting grass to feed livestock in a field her master owned, located in Alboraya (a village located just north of Valencia).[52]

"In This World, Some Make Bread and Others Go to the Bakery"[53]

Female honor, however, was tied to more than sexual chastity. It also was reflected in the sort of work women performed—or, rather, in the sort of work that women would

---

51. Caterina's present owner, however, insisted that rather than being kidnapped while performing an errand for her master, Caterina (along with all the women in the city) had been cast out "due to the great food shortages the city was suffering." Inasmuch as Caterina thereby had been *forfeited* by her master, her present owner insisted that any promise he had made to her was null and void, particularly since, in the course of the civil war between Juan II and the principality of Catalonia (1462–72), Caterina had been recaptured and put up for sale "com a sclava de enemichs e rebelles de la dita real maiestat." ARV G 2331: M. 19: 28r–30v; 35v; 41v; 45r–v; 47v and ARV G 2332: M. 25: 17r–19v; 27r–28r. For more on the Catalonian civil war, see Teofilo F. Ruíz, *Spain's Centuries of Crisis, 1300–1474* (Oxford: Blackwell, 2007), esp. 108–9, and Santiago Sobrequés i Vidal and Jaume Sobrequés i Callicó, *La guerra civil catalana del segle XV: Estudis sobre la crisi social i econòmica de la baixa Edat Mitjana*, 2 vols. (Barcelona: Edicions 62, 1987).

52. ARV JCrim 104 (Denunciacions): 21 November 1441 (nonpaginated).

53. "En este món, uns pasten i altres van al forn." Cited as an old adage under the entry for "pastar" in Alcover, *Diccionari català-valencià-balear*.

not perform. According to the kingdom's legal code, an "honorable" widow was defined as one who, in addition to being chaste, "does not do work with her hands."[54] In her discussion of the status of working women in fifteenth-century Saragossa, María del Carmen García Herrero cites a thirteenth-century Provençal adage in which a "noble" woman was defined as a woman who did not go to the mill, oven, or washhouse.[55] Thus, as Christiane Klapisch-Zuber has observed, women often entrusted the execution of the most disagreeable chores to "those persons brought perforce into the family." Who exactly performed these services—be they free working women, impoverished widows, freedwomen, or slaves—depended on an individual household's demographic composition and the demographic and economic conditions of the period. In her study of female servants in fourteenth- and fifteenth-century Florence, for example, Klapisch-Zuber found that free female domestic laborers were in an exceptionally good bargaining position. Many of the contracts she encountered contained clauses exempting a female servant from performing disagreeable tasks. One of the tasks that free female servants in fifteenth-century Florence were refusing to perform was doing the laundry.[56] Slave women and freedwomen, of course, were in a comparatively worse bargaining position. Thus, it is not all that surprising to see them performing this task that fifteenth-century Valencians also regarded with particular disdain: doing the laundry (*fer bugades*). A partially manumitted freed woman named Johana, for instance, earned pocket money by taking in extra laundry. Likewise, the master of an enslaved black woman named Ursola was confident that she could raise the forty lliures needed to pay her redemption fee by doing other people's washing. Given permission to "go wherever she willed to earn the money," Ursola's master considered her most viable employment options to be contracting her services out as a domestic servant or working as a laundress.[57]

Suggestive that bread making was another domestic chore that was universally detested, Ursola's master, the mason Francesc Martínez (alias Francesch "the Hot-head"), would later declare her contract of manumission null and void since she had refused to continue coming to his house every day to make bread. Francese claimed that, according to the terms of their agreement, Ursola's manumission was conditioned not only upon her payment of forty lliures but also upon her coming to his household every day to make

54. "Que no faça faena de ses mans." *Furs de València*, ed. Colon and Garcia (Barcelona: Editorial Barcino, 1999), VII: 29.

55. García Herrero, *Las mujeres*, 58.

56. Klapisch-Zuber, "Women Servants in Florence," 61–68.

57. Note, however, this master's stipulation that Ursola earn the sum "honestly." Another obvious way a partially freed slave woman might have earned money toward her redemption fee was prostitution. Thus, this mason specified that Ursola "pogues anar hon se volgues a guanyar ves a soldada guanyant ab alguna persona o a fer bugades vel alter honestament." ARV G 2348: M. 7: 1r–2v; 36r–v.

and knead bread dough (pastar), take it to the oven, and then, return to his household "bearing however many loaves of baked bread as she had [initially] taken from it."[58]

The research of María del Carmen García Herrero and María Teresa López Beltrán suggests that household chores such as doing the laundry and making bread were disdained by free woman not only because they were "hard" but also because they were "dishonorable." They suggest that since washhouses and ovens were often the sites of brawls and licentious behavior, they were as disreputable places as taverns and bathhouses. In her study of female domestics in fifteenth-century Málaga, López Beltrán notes how fathers preoccupied with safeguarding their daughters' reputations inserted special clauses in their contracts of service forbidding masters from sending them to such places. In so doing, López Beltrán argues, parents were attempting to distinguish their daughters from "other" female domestics, that is, girls of lower social status and slave women. While one father specified that his daughter could only be required to provide service within the walls of the household (literally, "from the doors leading to the street inside"), other parents specified, variously, that their daughters could not be sent to taverns, inns, butcher shops, fish markets, the central plaza, or even neighboring households.[59] García Herrero's research reveals similar preoccupations in fifteenth-century Saragossa, with parents inserting clauses specifying that their daughters could not be sent on errands to ovens, mills, and riverbanks.[60]

Considered collectively, this evidence suggests that although slave and free domestics performed many of the same services, significant distinctions existed between them with respect to their relative "honor" and perceived suitability to perform certain errands. Such distinctions—in addition to financial considerations—clearly factored into a master's or mistress's decision making in choosing one type of worker over another.

Men at Work: Slaves in the Field

So far I have been discussing the working lives of female domestic slaves, the "prototypical" slave in most discussions of late medieval Mediterranean slavery. In fifteenth-century Valencia, however, male slaves can be found in equally significant numbers. Although some of these male slaves were also employed as household servants (male

58. "Que li pastaria tot lo pa de casa tant temps com duraria lo temps del rescat e que tornaria lo pa a compte axi com lo trauria de casa." ARV G 2348: M. 7: 1r–2v; 36r–v. I will discuss Ursola's experiences in greater detail in chapter 6, see pp. 202–6.

59. The first contract further specified that if, by chance, she had to work outside the confines of said household, "She was to be [treated] like the daughter or niece of the said Alonso." López Beltrán, "La accesibilidad de la mujer al mundo laboral," 133–34.

60. In 1432, for instance, a father directed that his daughter "no vaya por agua al rio d'Ebro ni vaya a moler de la farina." Garcia Herrero, Las mujeres, 58.

slaves, for instance, occasionally were referred to as cooks), their experiences as laborers were, nevertheless, distinct. Male slaves were employed more extensively in artisanal and industrial production and many were engaged full time in the cultivation of crops, rather than simply lending a hand at the time of their harvesting or processing. In most circumstances, then, it seems that tasks we might refer to today as "housework" were subsidiary to enslaved men's primary vocations. Thus, though a black male slave named Johan Viscaya[61] boasted that he was renowned for "his knowledge of the art of bread making," his primary responsibility (like that of many enslaved black African men) was to farm and cultivate his master's agricultural holdings, located, usually, outside the city's walls and a fair distance from his master's principal household.[62]

In his article "Aspects quantitatifs de l'esclavage méditerranéen au Bas Moyen Âge," Charles Verlinden contended that, after 1457, and especially in the 1480s, large numbers of black slaves in the kingdom of Valencia were engaged in agricultural production.[63] Mark Meyerson, in a footnote to his article "Slavery and Solidarity," however, questioned Verlinden's claim, arguing that, since the reality was that "in most cases" agricultural work was performed by free Mudejar vassals, "images of gangs of foreign Muslim slaves, or even black Africans, toiling in the fields of Christian lords do not correspond to the reality of late medieval Valencia."[64] Although my evidence hardly contradicts Meyerson's assessment, it does, nevertheless, significantly qualify it. For, it seems that for some male slaves, particularly black Africans, agricultural production was their primary function.

When the aforementioned Johan Viscaya outlined the services he had provided to his master, a merchant, over the course of nearly twenty years, almost all were associated

61. Captured along with his mother and brother by a band of corsairs raiding the coast of Cartagena, Johan was only about five years old when he entered the service of the Valencian merchant Johan Ferrer. Ferrer had received these three black African captives in payment of a debt owed by one of the corsairs, a Basque merchant. Johan, his mother, and his one-year-old brother (also named Johan) remained in Ferrer's service for more than twenty years. In his last will and testament, Ferrer promised all three members of Johan's family their freedom. However, although this merchant specified that Johan's little brother would be freed automatically and expressed an interest in teaching him to read and write so he could be an "artist" or an urban professional (i.e., a notary, pharmacist, or barber), the elder Johan and his mother Johana, in contrast, would have to "earn" their freedom. He and his mother would be liberated if and only when they provided service that was equivalent in value to their initial purchase price.

62. To bolster his claim that he had provided his mistress with more than enough service to "purchase" his freedom, Johan Viscaya noted how, during an epidemic of the plague, his mistress had come to stay with him on their alqueria (rural estate), during which time he had served her and her daughters "in the kitchen and in the household, doing anything they needed and everything they ordered." Nevertheless, Johan put most stress on how "he was such a good farmer and tiller of the soil, knowing also the art of farming and cultivating." ARV G 2290: M. 22: 27r–29v; M. 25: 32r–33v.

63. Charles Verlinden, "Aspects quantitatifs de l'esclavage méditerranéen au Bas Moyen Âge," Anuario de Estudios Medievales 10 (1980): 777.

64. Meyerson, "Slavery and Solidarity," 298.

with agricultural production. "Being able and disposed to serve" from the age of nine, Johan began his career on his master's rural estate looking after his master's mule, feeding the other livestock, and lending assistance at harvest time. As he grew older, Johan was instructed in the art of cultivation. It bears emphasis that Johan's mentor and instructor in the art of cultivation was a former slave, the freedman Antoni Feliu, aka Sinali. Antoni testified that, when Johan was about twelve, he began teaching him how to dig and excavate the soil (cavar). Under this freed slave's tutelage, Johan also developed into a "good pruner." Soon Johan was managing the cultivation of his master's property on his own, hoeing, weeding, and even plowing. Thus, Johan claimed, by the age of fifteen he was executing "all the tasks normally assigned to the tiller or cultivator of a farmstead"; and, by the age of nineteen, Johan contended, "he was so knowledgeable in the arts of farming" that when his mistress negotiated the sale of her deceased husband's rural estate, the nobleman purchasing the property wanted to retain Johan's services.[65]

The labor contributions of male slaves to the Valencian economy, then, were hardly limited to the urban context of the nobleman's household or the artisan's workshop. Although Johan, no doubt, was exaggerating the value of his services, there is ample evidence that other male slaves were also engaged in agricultural production. In the last will and testament of a farmer from Chivella, the farmer named his former slave and namesake, the black freedman Pere Guillem, as his principal beneficiary. Expressing gratitude for his former slave's loyal service, especially during times of famine and extreme grain shortages (when he himself was too ill to work), this farmer affirmed that "if it had not been for said Pere Guillem I would have perished from hunger."[66] Indeed, slaves were hardly unfamiliar figures in the rural countryside. They turn up frequently in the testimony of farmers, plowmen, and shepherds appearing before royal and municipal courts. In his testimony before the court of the governor in 1484, for example, the laborer Lorenç Periç recalled how a black male slave named Cristofòl told him that his master promised to free him if his mistress gave birth to a baby boy "while he [Cristofòl] was digging in the vineyard of Joan Cirial."[67] In August 1480, a black male slave was cited on two sepa-

65. Johan contended that he was such a "bon laurador bon cavador podador magencador e conreador de una gran alqueria e possesio que ja en lo temps que la dita madona Damiata vene la dita alqueria al honorable mossen Luis Gras ja aquel dit mossen Luis sabent la dita bona industrea del dit Johan de Viscaya e com era gran e bon treballador no volgue comprar la dita alqueria sens aquell." ARV G 2290: M. 22: 27r–29v; M. 25: 1r–9v; M. 27: 32r–33v. I will discuss Johan Viscaya's efforts to secure his freedom in greater depth in chapter 6, pp. 217–19.

66. "Si no per lo dit Pere Guillem yo fora perit de fam com yo fos indispost e no pogues treballar e senyaladament en lo temps de la fam e fretura de forment yo en fora perit sino per ell." ARV P 817 (nonpaginated): 2 March 1478. I will discuss this in greater detail in chapter 4, see pp. 151–52.

67. ARV G 2371: M. 4: 11v and ARV G 2372: M. 18: 1r–8v. For more on the promise made to this black male slave named Cristofòl, see chapter 4, p. 149.

rate occasions by the Justícia de 300 Sueldos for permitting his master's livestock—more than one hundred sheep and goats—to trespass into neighboring fields, trampling delicate plants and destroying, most notably, a melon patch.[68]

Farmers, in fact, were relatively prominent among the buyers and sellers of slaves appearing in contemporary notarial records. Although some lived in the city itself, others came from small rural communities located in Valencia's *huerta*. In 1477, Joan Marcho, a farmer and citizen of Valencia, purchased a twenty-six-year-old black male slave named Orlando.[69] In 1474, a farmer from Burgassot (a village just north of Valencia) purchased an eight-year-old black male slave named Çamba.[70] Farmers, moreover, like artisans, hired the services of slaves as temporary workers. In 1449, a black male slave contracted out to a local farmer as a temporary laborer was detained by the Justícia Criminal for committing an unspecified crime.[71]

It is important to note, moreover, that nobles as well as merchants, notaries, lawyers, physicians, and well-to-do artisans also owned rural properties in Valencia's *huerta*. It is more than likely, then, that the slaves owned by these nobles, artisans, and urban professionals were also engaged, at least part-time, in agricultural production. Thus, Anthoni, a Tartar slave owned by a Valencian notary, testified (in 1470) that, for the past seventeen years, he had served his master "well and loyally... performing all the tasks associated with the art of farming."[72] Either exclusively or in addition to their duties in the household and/or workshop, male (and female) slaves worked on their masters' and mistresses' rural estates (*alquerias*): harvesting crops (*collir*), digging and excavating the soil (*cavar*), and even plowing the fields (*laurar*). Such evidence well supports Bernard Vincent's conviction that we need to seriously question the received wisdom that slavery in the Iberian Peninsula was an exclusively "urban" phenomenon. After all, Vincent reminds us,

68. In one of these instances, the black male slave was described as acting alone; in the other, he had a partner in crime who was described as a free older male servant. ARV Justícia de 300 Sueldos 1093: (Manifest): 4 August 1480 (nonpaginated).

69. APPV 24369: 8 May 1477 (nonpaginated). In my analysis of a random sample of notarial records dating from 1460 to 1480, 11 out of a total of 317 slave sales or transactions involved farmers as either the buyer or the seller. Although they did not appear in these records nearly as frequently as merchants (134 instances) or nobles (101), in comparison with other urban professionals and artisans, farmers were a significant, if not equally as prominent, group of slave owners. Twenty-seven of the sales involved notaries, 23 featured carpenters, and bakers, lawyers, and cloth preparers figured, respectively, in 12 sales apiece.

70. ARV P 2350 (nonpaginated): 28 December 1474. For some other examples, see ARV P 2165 (non-paginated): 20 March 1480; ARV P 9954 (nonpaginated): 28 February 1471; ARV P 1996 (nonpaginated): 9 December 1476; ARV P 2092 (nonpaginated): 25 June 1475; ARV P 2400 (nonpaginated): 23 February 1476; APPV 18424 (nonpaginated): 30 October 1472; and APPV 28485 (nonpaginated): 9 February 1478.

71. ARV JCrim 23: M. 5 (Clams): 17 October 1449 (nonpaginated).

72. ARV G 2331: M. 20: 41r–42v; ARV G 2332: M. 27: 3r–12v.

many of the towns and cities of late medieval Iberia could more accurately be described as "agro-villes."[73]

As had been the case with female domestics, slave and free male agricultural laborers seem to have performed roughly the same tasks. The laborer Mateu Pelegri testified that on the many occasions when the Tartar slave named Anthoni took flight, his master hired free workers (moços) to do his chores—that is, digging in the vineyards (cavar).[74] In addition to digging, however, Anthoni had also been entrusted with the responsibilities of managing his master's draft animals at work in the field and leading heavily laden pack animals over uneven terrain. Free laborers, somewhat self-interestedly, portrayed the employment of a slave in such positions of responsibility as a misguided and ultimately costly decision. The aforementioned laborer, Mateu Pelegri, for example, testified that "on many occasions" he saw Anthoni "abuse the livestock." He related how, one time, he "saw how, after placing the plowshare in the ground and tying the beasts of burden to the beam," Anthoni gave the horses "many blows with a stick, beating them very cruelly on both the face and sides."[75] A free laborer named Miquel Garcia also recalled incidents when Anthoni's disciplining of his master's livestock got out of hand. On one occasion, his excessive thrashing resulted in a horse losing an eye, and on another the horse died.[76] The underlying implication in both Mateu's and Miquel's testimony was that the placement of slaves in such positions of authority went against the natural order. After all, slaves (in the contemporary imaginary) were themselves brute animals in need of constant discipline.[77]

Further exacerbating this apparent rivalry between slave and free laborers was the fact that male (and, occasionally, female) slaves often worked as security guards on their masters' and mistresses' rural estates. Slaves protected their masters' property from unwanted intruders—be they animal or human. Human trespassers included other slaves as well as free laborers accused of swiping fruit, agricultural implements, vines, branches,

73. Vincent, "L'esclavage en milieu rural espagnol," 165–76.

74. ARV G 2331: M. 20: 41r–42v and ARV G 2332: M. 27: 3r–12v.

75. "Moltes vegades veya com lo dit Anthoni laurant en terres del dit son amo maltractava les besties que lauraven e veya com ficava lo ladre en terra e ligava les besties al timo e pegava'ls bastonades per cap e per costats molt bravament." ARV G 2331: M. 20: 41r–42v and ARV G 2332: M. 27: 3r–12v.

76. Mateu Pelegri, for example, told a harrowing tale of how Anthoni allegedly had sadistically tortured his master's ass, tying up his legs and beating him repeatedly. When Mateu confronted Anthoni and asked him why he was deliberately trying to kill this ass, Antoni reportedly swore "by the ass of Our Lord" that he was willing to do whatever it took to get it to cross over this irrigation ditch. ARV G 2331: M. 20: 41r–42v and ARV G 2332: M. 27: 3r–12v.

77. See Paul Freedman, Images of the Medieval Peasant (Stanford: Stanford University Press, 1999), 86–104, and, for similar types of imagery being applied to serfs and vilains, 133–75.

and even mounds of the animal dung (*fem*) that was used as fertilizer.[78] Thus, one Friday afternoon in July, a black male slave chased off a horse belonging to a Valencian resident that was eating his master's alfalfa.[79] Similarly, at around ten o'clock one evening, when a black male slave saw an unfamiliar figure walk across his master's alfalfa field "carrying a bundle of alfalfa grass on his head," he shouted, "Hey! You have stolen the grass of my master," and promptly got into a scuffle with him.[80]

Reflective of their role as guardians of their master's rural properties, slaves (particularly black males) also frequently appeared in the records of the Justícia de 300 Sueldos as witnesses to petty thefts. Defending their masters' fields, vineyards, and orchards, slaves chased away trespassers and, in some instances, even apprehended thieves. In early August 1480 a black male slave belonging to a butcher chased a man carrying a basketful of apples from his master's orchard.[81] If the slave managed to apprehend the offender, she or he customarily was entitled to seize some object of value (a weapon, a basket, or a piece of clothing) as a security deposit, to make sure that the offender would compensate his master for any damages. Thus, in June 1473 a black male slave seized a lance in pledge from the shepherd responsible for allowing the more than forty goats he supervised to run rampant over his mistress's vineyard, "tearing down and trampling the vines laden with grapes."[82]

Given the slave's degraded status—and the fact that many of these confrontations occurred at night and in relatively deserted areas—it is not terribly surprising to learn that free persons frequently resisted the authority of slave guardians. Indeed, they often responded by verbally abusing or beating them for their "impudent" behavior toward free persons. In November 1473 a black male slave belonging to a farmer discovered a flock of sheep and goats devouring his master's mulberry bushes. When the slave tried to seize a goat in pledge for payment of his master's damages, the shepherd attacked him

---

78. For one example among many of servants being charged with manure theft, see ARV Justícia de 300 Sueldos 1092: Manifests (nonpaginated): 24 April 1478. In his defense, the servant stated that "his master ordered him to do it." In one of the most sizable "manure heists" encountered, a servant named Simonet and an unspecified accomplice were caught stealing more than thirty *carregues* (or "beast-loads") of manure. ARV Justícia de 300 Sueldos 1092: Manifests (nonpaginated): 4 June 1478. According to Alcover's *Diccionari català-valència-balear*, a "carrèga" is a unit of measurement that can have different values depending on the geographical region as well as the object that is being measured; however, in general, it refers to the amount one pack animal can carry.

79. ARV Justícia de 300 Sueldos 1091: Clams (nonpaginated): 5 July 1473.

80. The "negre" (unnamed) testified that he cried out, "A furtau la erba de mon amo!" and then "abrassas ab aquell." The accused thief reportedly responded, "Don't you see, crazy one, that this alfalfa grass does not belong to your master? I harvested it from the field belonging to *en* Lluna and am bringing it to him!" ARV Justícia de 300 Sueldos 1093: Clams (nonpaginated): 24 September 1480.

81. ARV Justícia de 300 Sueldos 1091: Clams (nonpaginated): 8 August 1480.

82. ARV Justícia de 300 Sueldos 1091: Clams (nonpaginated): 2 June 1473.

with a knife.[83] Similarly, on 2 September 1473, a shepherd attacked the black male slave who tried to apprehend him after he had allowed a herd of cattle to pasture in a rice field belonging to the slave's master. One witness recounted that the shepherd attacked him with his lance "because the black male slave had made them leave the field."[84] Finally, in October 1473, when a black male slave seized and slit the throat of one of the sheep who had trampled a newly planted vineyard, the shepherd, rather than accept the action as the legitimate execution of a slave's duty to defend his master's property, "beat up [the] black male slave."[85]

Artisan Owners: Slaves in the Workshop

Although well-to-do artisans may have purchased slaves because they wanted to employ them as domestic servants and field hands, male slaves were also highly valued by artisans as extra laborers in their workshops. In my analysis of slave sales encountered in notarial registers dating from 1450 to 1480, artisans figured in about 40 percent of the transactions. Considering the many alternative mechanisms (besides outright purchase) for acquiring a slave's services, the number of artisans employing slave laborers in their workshops was likely even higher than this figure indicates.[86]

Those for whom it was simply too expensive to purchase and support a slave independently sometimes opted to buy a slave jointly, sharing the costs and burdens of slave ownership with a partner. The carpenters Jacme Lombart Sr. and Rodrigo Alegret, for example, pooled their resources to purchase a forty-year-old Muslim slave named

83. The slave's owner subsequently filed a complaint against this shepherd before the city's small-claims court, protesting that "lo negre dell clamant les hi troba e pres una cabra e lo pastor attacava lo negre ab hun punyal." ARV Justícia de 300 Sueldos 1091: Clams (nonpaginated): 17 November 1473.

84. Perot Garcia, who witnessed the attack, testified that "per que lo negre los feya exir del camp lo dit pastor ab la lanca volgue li donar [hun colp?]." The remainder of this witness's testimony, unfortunately, is missing. ARV Justícia de 300 Sueldos 1091: Clams (nonpaginated): 2 September 1473.

85. The slave's master subsequently filed a complaint, protesting that "li han abastonejat lo seu negre per que'l degolla una ovella." ARV Justícia de 300 Sueldos 1091: Clams (nonpaginated): 25 October 1473.

86. In his analysis of slave purchasers at public auctions supervised by the bailiff general between 1410 and 1434, José Hinojosa Montalvo found that 63 percent of the buyers were artisans. José Hinojosa Montalvo, "Tácticas de apresamiento de cautivos y su distribución en el mercado valenciano (1410–1434)," Qüestions Valencianes 1 (1979): 32–35. Mark Meyerson, in contrast, found that only about 35 percent of the 583 "foreign" Muslim captives sold under the bailiff general's supervision between 1479 and 1503 were purchased by artisans. Meyerson argues that "the discrepancy between my findings and those of Hinojosa can be explained in part by the fact that 128 of the sales . . . were to merchants. Many of these merchants probably bought slaves with the intention of retailing them elsewhere, perhaps to artisans." Thus, Meyerson posits that a figure of some 44 percent of all purchasers being artisans might be more accurate. Meyerson, "Slavery and Solidarity," 298–99.

Natarachi.[87] Similarly, in 1453, the governor appointed arbitrators to resolve a dispute between two carpenters, Miquel Garcia and Miquel Johan, concerning the male slave they had purchased jointly "to saw wood and do the other chores of carpenters."[88]

One of the most inexpensive ways for an artisan to augment his labor force was to bail out (capllevar) or assume temporary custody of a slave being detained by royal or municipal officials. In most cases, these slaves were fugitives, detained by local authorities until their owners could be found and arrangements made for their recovery. In exchange for taking responsibility for guarding, feeding, and sheltering the fugitive, the capllevador acquired temporary use of his or her services. In 1479, a carpenter assumed temporary custody of a black male fugitive who had been arrested by Valencian authorities. Holding the slave "in comenda," on behalf of the bailiff general, this carpenter, however, also assumed personal liability in the case of a repeated attempt at flight. Thus, when the slave ran off a second time, this carpenter was obliged to compensate his owner by paying him a sum equivalent to the slave's original purchase price.[89]

More commonly, artisans who could not afford to buy a slave of their own (or perhaps needed their services only temporarily) borrowed or rented someone else's—be it a slave belonging to a fellow artisan, nobleman, or merchant.[90] Jacques Heers does not seem to have fully appreciated the pervasiveness of this practice, arguing that the rental of slave laborers was strictly occasional and had little impact on the labor market in the late medieval Mediterranean world. Based on his analysis of slave rental contracts encountered in notarial archives in Genoa and Barcelona, Heers suggested that the only people contracting their slave's services out to third parties were impoverished masters or their widows.[91] As the examples cited below illustrates, however, in fifteenth-century Valencia contracting out the services of slave laborers seems to have been a fairly widespread practice, particularly in trades such as carpentry and bread baking. In 1476, for example, the carpenter Marc Bonanat hired the services of Joan, the merchant Bernat Climent's black male slave, for one year.[92] Similarly, on 21 November 1449, the carpenter Francesch Selva

87. ARV G 4581: M. 7: 15r–17v.

88. ARV JCiv 917: M. 17: 2r–v.

89. ARV G 2352: M. 21: 1r–2r. For a discussion of the terms of more "typical" commenda agreements, facilitating long-distance trade in slaves and other types of merchandise, see Robert S. Lopez, Irving Raymond, and O. R. Constable, Medieval Trade in the Mediterranean World: Illustrative Documents (New York: Columbia University Press, 2001), 174–84.

90. Seigneurial lords also contracted the services of their free Mudejar vassals out to third parties—including bakers. See ARV P 1998 (nonpaginated): 15 May 1478.

91. Heers, Esclavos, 92.

92. In payment for his slave's services ("pro precio seu logerio"), Bernat Climent would receive twelve lliures. According to the terms of this contract, the sum would be paid in installments of forty sous every two months, with a penalty of five sous for each late payment. Moreover, in the event that the slave took flight while in his custody, Bonanat was obliged to pay Climent forty lliures in compensation for his

hired the services of Bernat, a dark-skinned (llor) slave owned by his neighbor and fellow carpenter Francesch Gomiz. According to the terms of the contract, Bernat, a thirty-year-old baptized Muslim, would "saw wood and work as a day laborer alongside the slave that said Francesch Selva himself held and possessed."[93] In his testimony before the court of the governor, Francesch Selva explained that "practice and custom was and has been for a long time in the present city... that those who have slaves share them with others, [in some instances] lending them freely, [in other instances] in return for comparable labor, and [in other instances] for a fee."[94] Francesch Gomiz's daughter also affirmed that her father and Francesch Selva "were accustomed to lend or share between themselves [the labor services of] their slaves—[the slaves] sometimes sawing wood for the profit of the former, and other times for the profit of the latter."[95] Francesch Selva, moreover, testified that he not only had occasion to lend the services of his male slave to Francesch Gomiz, but also contracted the slave's services out "to others."

Such cooperative ventures between artisans, however, could quickly devolve into acrimony in the event that the "borrowed" slave took advantage of the inevitable confusion associated with supervising a slave who was commuting between households and took flight. Indeed, we only learn of the arrangement between Francesch Gomiz and Francesch Selva because Gomiz's daughter subsequently filed a lawsuit against Selva demanding financial compensation for the fact that, some twelve years before(!), Bernat had run away while in Selva's custody.[96] To forestall such disputes, however, most contracts specified who was to be held responsible in the case of the slave's flight. When the

---

loss—"cum hoc pacto quod si intus dictum annum dictus Joannes abierit tali [sic—in tali casu] quod vos dictus Marchus Bonanat teneamini mich dare xxxx libras dicte monete pro fugita illius etc." APPV 9636 (nonpaginated): 25 June 1476.

93. Francesch Selva stated that he had hired the slave "per a serrar e torna jornal per a que serras ab altres sclaus que lo dit en Franesch Selva tenia e possehia." ARV G 2300: 157r–v and ARV G 2302: M. 29: 11r–25v.

94. "Pratica e costuma estada e es stada e es de gran temps ença en la present ciutat e altres parts que los que tenen sclaus se ampren los huns als altres els se presten volunteres e atorguen a torna jornal e a cert loguer e axi com se concorden." ARV G 2300: 157r–v and ARV G 2302: M. 29: 11r–25v.

95. "Los dits en Francesch Gomiz e en Francesch Selva acostumaven de atorgar o prestar entre si los sclaus de aquells e serraven hun temps al hu e a profit de aquell e altre temps a profit del altre." ARV G 2300: 157r–v and ARV G 2302: M. 29: 11r–25v.

96. Similarly, in September 1475, when a black male slave owned by a merchant took flight while in the custody of the carpenter who had temporarily contracted his services, the merchant sued the carpenter for damages. Since the rental contract had not specified liability in case of flight, the carpenter and merchant appealed to the Justícia Civil for assistance in determining (1) who should be held liable for the slave's flight; (2) the slave's replacement value; (3) the amount of back salary this carpenter owed the merchant for the slave's services; and (4) who was responsible for paying the expenses incurred in the fugitive slave's recovery (i.e., for the search parties that reportedly had been sent into the kingdom of Castile). ARV P 1086 (nonpaginated): 20–28 September 1475.

carpenter Francisco Balagari hired Zuleyman, a thirty-year-old white Muslim owned by a baker, Balagari promised that he would compensate this baker for any losses he would sustain if Zuleyman took flight while in his custody.[97] On 22 April 1477, when the Valencian carpenter Joan Cucala hired the services of Joan, a baptized Muslim, the carpenter promised the slave's owner, a notary, that he would pay him forty lliures in the event that Joan (described as "dark-skinned" or llor) took flight.[98] Finally, when the carpenter Sthefan Castell contracted the services of Martí, a thirty-year-old black male slave "de Guinea," the contract specified that he was holding Martí "at your own risk, namely of flight. If, by chance, said captive should take flight during said period, and you are unable to recover him, you will have to give me thirty-five lliures for said captive immediately."[99]

Beyond appreciating their value as laborers, however, artisans were also quick to recognize the potential profit they could gain from purchasing and then ransoming Muslim captives. Bakers, carpenters, cloth preparers, and other artisans seem to have played an especially prominent role as middle-men in Muslim redemptionist activity. Acquiring them in public auctions supervised by the bailiff general, artisans temporarily employed these Muslim captives as laborers in their workshops while they sought out coreligionists willing to put up money for their ransoms. In most instances, the ransoms collected from members of the local Muslim community were higher than the initial purchase price. For example, in 1452, the baker Jaume Spunyes collected sixty lliures from Abrafim Xayt, a Muslim dyer and jurat of the morería of Valencia. That was the redemption price for a thirty-five-year-old white Muslim from the kingdom of Fez.[100] A Valencian carpenter who appears to have been especially active in this "trade" was Jacme Lombart.[101] Purchasing Muslim captives at prices ranging from thirty-seven to forty-five lliures apiece, Jacme subsequently ransomed them to their coreligionists for sums as high as eighty lliures.[102] The speculative character of Jacme's activities is made apparent by the following example.

97. ARV P 9986 (nonpaginated): 20 February 1461.

98. APPV 20619 (nonpaginated): 22 April 1477.

99. "Ad vestri riscum scilicet de fugita et si forte dictus captivus infra dictum tempus fugierit et illum recuperare non poteritis quod pro dicto captivo habeatis michi dare triginta quinque libras monete regalium Valencie in continenti." ARV P 1994 (nonpaginated): 26 November 1474

100. ARV P 436 (nonpaginated): 27 June 1452. Less than one month before, Abrafim Xayt seems to have played a similar role in raising the redemption prices for a forty-year-old Muslim captive owned by a baker. He promised this baker that if the slave took flight while in his custody, he would pay him fifty lliures or however much he had paid for him. ARV P 436 (nonpaginated): 11 May 1452.

101. In Crown and notarial records from between 1471 and 1486, Lombart appears as a participant in dozens of transactions involving the purchase, sale, rental, and redemption of Muslim captives, almost all of whom were men. See, for example, ARV P 2785 (nonpaginated): 26 November 1474; ARV P 443 (nonpaginated): 31 July 1481; ARV P 445 (nonpaginated): 7 February 1486; ARV P 443 (nonpaginated): 31 January 1480; ARV P 444 (nonpaginated): 29 April 1484.

102. ARV P 444 (nonpaginated): 21 November 1483.

On 26 February 1485, in a public auction supervised by the bailiff general, Jacme Lombart purchased two white Muslim slaves of North African origin—both of whom had been declared slaves of the Crown for begging without a license. The two captives were purchased by Jacme for the combined price of 63.5 lliures.[103] Less than four months later, on 16 June 1485, Jacme collected forty-five lliures from a group of Mudejars from the Vall de Uxó in payment of the redemption price for just one of these captives, a thirty-six-year-old man named Muça al-Medini.[104]

Whether purchasing them outright (compra), borrowing (se ampra or se presta) or hiring (loca ad tempus or loga) slaves owned by others, Valencian artisans exploited slaves as a fairly dependable and financially accessible source of labor. Jacques Heers (and others) have portrayed the slaves working in artisanal workshops as a relatively privileged group. In contrast with their companions toiling in fields and mines, these were "men with trades," endowed with skills that supposedly not only increased their market value but afforded them special opportunities to "buy back" their freedom. In support of this assertion, Heers cites the high demand for Muslim captives following the conquests of Islamic-controlled territories such as Lucera (in southern Italy) and Granada due to their renowned skills as master armorers, carpenters, cobblers, masons, and silk workers.[105] Evidence encountered in Valencian archives, however, reveals that the artisans purchasing slaves in the greatest numbers were not engaged in the production of luxury articles. Rather, it was bakers and carpenters who predominated.[106] Although I did come across many carpenters and silk workers who employed Muslim slaves in their workshops, they generally did not seem to have been interested in any technical skills they may have possessed. Instead, they seem more keen on exploiting these slave laborers' brute force. By and large they seem to have been acquired for the purposes of executing tasks that were considered harsh, tedious, and/or dangerous by the general populace. Contracts of sale, of course, rarely specified the purposes for which a slave had been purchased. Contracts of service, however, where a slave's services were hired for a set period of time, typically

103. ARV B 218: 56v–57v.

104. ARV P 444 (nonpaginated): 16 June 1485.

105. Heers, Esclavos, 134–35. The Muslim colony of Lucera was founded in northern Apulia by Emperor Frederick II, who deported an estimated twenty thousand Sicilian Muslims there as a way to "resolve" the Muslim problem in Sicily. The colony was dissolved in 1300 on the orders of the Angevin king Charles II. For a recent discussion of the Muslim community of Lucera, highlighting its diversified economy and the skills of its local craftsmen, see Julie Taylor, Muslims in Medieval Italy: The Colony at Lucera (Lanham, Md.: Lexington Books, 2003).

106. Mark Meyerson has already noted the preponderance of bakers and carpenters among those purchasing foreign Muslim captives and penally enslaved Mudejars in fifteenth-century Valencia. Citing J. Hinojosa Montalvo's study, Meyerson notes that between 1410 and 1434, 25 percent of slave buyers were bakers and 19 percent were carpenters; between 1479 and 1503, Meyerson found that 29 percent of slave buyers were bakers and 17 percent were carpenters. Meyerson, "Slavery and Solidarity," 299.

would contain clauses explicitly outlining the nature of work to be provided. Such clauses (taken in conjunction with references to slave workers in court records) shed valuable light on the participation of slaves in local industries.

Carpentry and Construction Work

Carpenters were not only prominent among artisans in terms of slave ownership, they were also among the most oft-cited categories of slave owners overall. Thus, when a pharmacist's widow needed assistance moving furniture and other bulky household items to be put up for public auction, she immediately thought of her neighbor, the carpenter Joan Montesino and "his male slaves."[107] In a random sample of slave sales dating from 1460 to 1480, carpentry was the third most-reported occupation of slave owners (after merchants and members of the nobility).[108] The primary task assigned to these slaves— almost always male and, in many instances, nonbaptized Muslims[109]—was sawing wood. In a dispute between two carpenters concerning the use and earnings of the slave they held jointly, the plaintiff noted how he and the defendant had purchased the slave "for the purposes of sawing and doing the chores associated with carpentry" (per obs de serrar e fer faena de fusteria).[110] Similarly, when carpenters temporarily contracted the services of a slave, it was almost invariably specified that he was being hired "for the purposes of sawing wood" (ad serrandum fusta sive serrar fusta). Thus, when Ysabel, the wife of the aforementioned carpenter Joan Montesino, contracted the services of her black male slave out to her husband, it was specified that he was hiring the slave "for the purposes of serving you in your trade and for the task of sawing wood."[111]

Carpenters of greater means employed slave laborers not only to cut wood for their own use but also to saw and distribute cut wood to others. In the dispute regarding the aforementioned dark-skinned slave named Bernat, a fugitive slave belonging to the carpenter Francesch Selva, witnesses noted that, immediately before Bernat had taken flight he had been seen delivering wood to another carpenter, Bernat Portales. Portales recalled

---

107. ARV JCiv 923: M. 15: 41r–v.

108. As noted earlier, while merchants appeared as either the buyer or seller in 134 slave sales, members of the nobility appeared 101 times, carpenters appeared in these records as often as notaries did, on 27 separate occasions. These figures are based on my random sample of slave sales dating from 1460 to 1480 encountered in notarial records preserved at the ARV and APPV.

109. See, for example, ARV P 2464 (nonpaginated): 19 December 1469 and ARV P 2092 (nonpaginated): 9 August 1474.

110. ARV JCiv 917: M. 17: 2r–v.

111. "Ad serviendum vobis ad officium vestrum et ad oppus de serrar fusta." ARV P 816 (nonpaginated): 21 December 1470. See also APPV 16703 (nonpaginated): 28 April 1477 and APPV 19071 (nonpaginated): 12 March 1477.

that he had given "a certain amount of wood to Francesch Selva that the slave of said Francesch Selva and [the slave] of said Francesch Gomiz chopped." Portales testified that on the evening of Bernat's flight, "around the hour of prayers," Bernat, along with another slave, had showed up at his household to deliver the wood they had cut for him, unloading it from the back of a goat.[112]

That slaves were closely associated with saws is also reflected in the inventories post-mortem of the possessions belonging to the carpenters Jacme Lombart Sr. and Bernat Climent. Among the many tools found in Jacme's workshop were "two saws for cutting wood for the use of slaves."[113] Similarly, among the items encountered in the home and workshop of the carpenter Bernat Climent were four slaves—Yça, a thirty-year-old white Muslim; Joanet, a twenty-two-year-old black male from Guinea; Andreu, a sixty-year-old black male, also from Guinea; and Allena, a forty-five-year-old white female—along with two large saws, and a *verduc*, or an extremely long saw that required two men, one at each end, to manipulate it.[114]

There are some indications, however, that, beyond sawing and hauling wood, some slaves were trained to perform more "skilled" tasks associated with carpentry. In 1498, a carpenter specified in his last will and testament that he would grant his slave named Johan his freedom as soon as he completed "a certain project" he was building. This carpenter, moreover, had also instructed his executor that when he finally issued Johan his charter of freedom, he should also give him any tools he may need "so that he could support himself" (*per que vixques*), presumably as a carpenter.[115] Likewise, when the widow of a cabinetmaker (*coffrener*) sought the bailiff general's assistance in recovering two white Muslim male fugitives, she described the elder of the two slaves as a "carpenter" (*fuster*). The two slaves, both named Mahomat, seem, in fact, to have worked as a team. While the

---

112. ARV G 2300: 157r–v and ARV G 2302: M. 29: 11r–25v.

113. "Dues serres de serrar per als catius." ARV G 4581: M. 7: 15r–17v. Jacme's workshop was located in the plaza in front of the Portal de Serrans. A number of carpenters seem to have lived there, perhaps due to its close proximity to the Turia River, which Valencian encyclopedist Marcos Antonio de Orellana described as the natural conduit through which "the wood comes every year from the pine forests of Moya." Upon their arrival in Valencia, these logs were "arranged and prepared outside the Portal dels Serrans . . . for use and employment in construction." Orellana, moreover, also claimed that the Portal de Serrans was so called because it looks out "on the wooded areas (*serrania*) of Daroca, Teruel, Albarracin, etc." Orellana, *Valencia Antigua y Moderna*, 538–44.

114. Suggestive that slave laborers did not always perform these tasks willingly, the executors also noted a pair of leg irons with four ankle rings and "a long chain for holding captives." APPV 9636 (non-paginated): 24 January 1476.

115. A leather worker testified that the executor of this carpenter's will told him that he would issue the slave his charter of freedom as soon as he "acabasa certa obra que restava en casa." In addition, he told the witness "que si algunes ayna de la botigua haver mester que les hi donarien per amor de deu per que vixques." ARV G 2403: M. 2: 27v; M. 9: 25r–30r.

elder Mahomat (fifty years in age) built wooden coffers, the younger Mahomat (thirty-five years in age) painted them.[116]

These two examples, however, seem to have been the exception rather than the rule. Slaves were in high demand among carpenters not because of any presumed technical expertise they possessed, but because they could more readily be coerced to execute such physically demanding tasks as sawing and hauling wood. These seem to have been the principal functions of slaves working in the service of carpenters.

Bread Baking

Bakers (*flaquers*) and oven owners (*forners*) were also prominent among slave owners in fifteenth-century Valencia.[117] The two *sindichs* (syndics) and *procuradors* of an association formed to represent the interests of the principal slave owners in the city of Valencia (an association, reportedly, of more than one hundred members) were (in 1466) both bakers: Luis Borraç and Martí de Sant Martí. In their capacity as spokesmen for this organization, the two bakers asked the governor to convoke a more general assembly of slave owners to publicize and discuss the enforcement of a royal privilege specifying that slaves who rebelled against their owners and seriously injured them or any other member of the household were to be executed at the collective expense of the city's slave owners.[118] The threat of slave resistance likely was of especial concern to bakers because, like carpenters, they often employed several slaves at one time. In the course of one year, the baker Guillem Boix purchased four captives in the public auctions sponsored by the bailiff general. Five months after he purchased a thirty-five-year-old white Muslim (seized, along with forty-two others by the nobleman/corsair Francesc de Bellvis), Guillem purchased three more Muslim captives (seized, along with six others, by the Majorcan corsair Marti de Eviça).[119] Likewise, in the inventory postmortem of the estate of the baker Francesch Curca, his executors recorded his ownership of five slaves: Joan, a thirty-year-old

116. "Lo hu dels quals es fuster e ha apres l'offici de fuster o de fer coffrens de fusta e lo altra ha apres lo offici de pintor ço es de pintar coffrens . . . lo hu fent coffrens de fust e l'altre pintar los." ARV JCiv 926: M. 15: 28r–30r.

117. Though in court and notarial records, the occupational labels of *flaquer* and *forner* seem to be used fairly interchangeably, Juan Vicente García Marsilla, in his study of food production and consumption in medieval Valencia, distinguishes sharply between *forners* and *flaquers*. While a *forner* simply owned an oven—a place where people came to bake bread they made themselves in exchange for a fee—a *flaquer* made and baked bread commercially, selling his bread publicly. Juan Vicente García Marsilla, *La jerarquía de la mesa: Los sistemas alimentarios en la Valencia bajomedieval* (Valencia: Historía Local/13—Diputació de Valencia, 1993), 110–11.

118. ARV G 2272: M. 1: 15r–v. Miguel Gual Camarena has discussed as well as transcribed the royal privilege that these two bakers seem to be referring to (issued in 1445 by Queen Maria, wife and lieutenant general of Alfonso V). Miguel Gual Camarena, "Un seguro contra crímenes de esclavos en el siglo XV," *Anuario de Historia del Derecho Español* 23 (1953): 247–58.

119. Other bakers who purchased Muslim captives in these public auctions supervised by the bailiff general included Jacme Moreno (who purchased a thirty-year-old white male Muslim), Francesc Canals

baptized white Christian from the Nasrid Sultanate of Granada; Alfonço Quasqual, a six-ty-year-old white baptized Christian "of Arab lineage," formerly of Portugal; Barchh, a forty-five-year-old black Muslim from Fes (also described as "of Arab lineage"); Marti-net, a twenty-year-old black baptized Christian from Guinea; and an unnamed seventy-year-old dark-skinned female of "Moorish" origin.[120] The baker Joan Domingo owned at least three slaves: Caet, a twenty-six-year-old white Muslim; Pere, a twenty-two-year-old black baptized Christian; and Margarita, a baptized Christian.[121]

Bakers, like carpenters, seem to have valued slaves for their productive capacities. When the baker Joan Malo sued his colleague, Domingo de Sales, accusing Domingo's slave Sal-vador of aiding and abetting his slave, Miquel, in an attempted flight,[122] Joan demanded monetary compensation not only for the expenses incurred in securing Miquel's recovery but also for the loss of Miquel's labor. In addition to the two hundred sous he sought in compensation for what he spent on "sending men out to look for said slave, on horseback and on foot, broadcasting [the slave's flight] throughout the city and other places, renting pack animals for himself and another horseman to go and collect the slave [after he had been captured]," Joan also sought fifty additional sous for "the many damages and ex-penses he sustained" in the fifteen days Miquel was absent from his service, "during which time the slave would have earned a salary or otherwise brought profit to his master."[123]

(who purchased a twenty-two-year-old white Muslim), and the *former* Martí Ferrandez (who purchased a twenty-seven-year-old white Muslim). See ARV B 193: 60r–78v; 97v–104v.

120. APPV 09653 (nonpaginated): 18 June 1473.

121. Joan Domingo purchased Caet from another baker, Dominic Sales (aka Domingo de Sales, men-tioned below). APPV 21819 (nonpaginated): 18 January 1476. See also APPV 11245 (nonpaginated): 14 November 1477 and APPV 21819 (nonpaginated): 14 July 1474.

122. Domingo de Sales, in turn, charged that Joan Malo's slave, Miquel, was the instigator. He in-sisted that his slave, Salvador, was too simple and ignorant to plot an escape. Though no reference is made here to either Salvador's or Miquel's ethnic origins, Domingo seems to indicate here that Salvador was a black African slave, while Miquel (perhaps) was a *moro*. Domingo, notably, described Salvador as both *boçal* (uncivilized) and *bestia* (bestial). Furthermore, he stressed how Salvador (presumably unlike Miquel) "knew no other slaves in Valencia." Thus, he lacked the necessary local connections to coordi-nate a successful flight. Miquel, in contrast, was, in Domingo's estimate, a notorious fugitive, publicly reputed to be a "corruptor" of slaves. On several previous occasions, this "astute," "very experienced and accomplished" fugitive "persuaded" and "induced" other slaves to take flight. Miquel had been impli-cated in the flight of the slaves belonging to bakers Joan Gil and Pasqual Verdego. Both of these bakers' slaves subsequently were discovered in the cave where, reportedly, Miquel had hidden them. Miquel's em-ployment in his master's bakery, moreover, allegedly gave him access to the food supplies necessary for sustaining them while they were in hiding. Domingo suggests that Miquel had been stockpiling biscuits in preparation for their escape. ARV G 2315: M. 15: 12v and ARV G 2316: M. 26: 24r–38r.

123. "Que lo dit en Johan Malo per la fuyta del dit sclau ha sostengut molts dans e despeses com haia vagat lo dit sclau del jorn que fogi de la casa de aquell fins al jorn que torna quinze jorns en los quals lo dit sclau hauria guanyat o de fet de proffit a son amo." ARV G 2315: M. 15: 12v and ARV G 2316: M. 26: 24r–38r. In addition, Joan Malo sought compensation for the ten *timbres* (unit of currency) he had given to an un-specified individual as a finder's fee.

Most slaves in the service of bakers worked in their ovens, doing what contemporaries referred to as *palegant*: "putting in or taking out loaves of bread from the hot oven with a *pala*," or a "wooden shovel with a very long handle."[124] In 1449, when Mahomat, another slave owned by the baker Joan Domingo, was charged with assaulting and fatally injuring a fellow slave woman, the weapon Mahomat allegedly used was precisely this implement. Thus, the complaint specified, in the course of a heated argument, Mahomat grabbed the tool that was most handy, ramming the handle of the wooden shovel he used to take bread in and out of the oven (*la pala del forn*) into Marta's face, stabbing her just above her right eye.[125]

In 1488, when Floristany, the son of a free father and a slave mother, appeared before the governor, he demanded not only recognition of his freeborn status but also back salary for the more than four years he spent working (*palegant*) in his master's oven. Contending that free men typically earned some sixteen lliures annually for performing this labor, Floristany sought compensation both for the four years he spent working in the ovens of his master, the baker Joan Salvaterra, and the six months his services had been contracted out by his master for the purposes of *palegant* in the oven belonging to the baker Joan Gorguera.[126] As Floristany's complaint indicates, free men, as well as slaves, toiled in hot ovens. Indeed, in 1499, Miquel Assensi, the former slave of the oven owner (*forner*) Jaume Assensi, adduced as proof of his freed status the fact that he had contracted out his own labor to the baker (*flaquer*) Frances Ribert, whom he served *palegant* in his oven.[127]

Although *palegant* in a hot oven seems to have been what most slaves (and freedmen) in the service of bakers did, occasionally they may have been trained to execute more "skilled" tasks as well. Suggestive that slaves in the service of bakers might have received some form of vocational training is the example of the freedman Joan Verdecho, who had been in the service of the bakers Pasqual Verdecho and Pere Livello. After securing his liberation, Joan is described in notarial registers, variously, as a miller (*pistor*), a bread maker (*pastador*), and a baker (*flaquer*).[128] Moreover, when bakers hired the services of someone

124. See the relevant entries ("palejar" and "pala") in Alcover, *Diccionari català-valencià-balear*. A "pala" might also be used to shovel coal in and out of hot ovens. Thus, slaves might (alternatively) have been employed for the purposes of stoking the fires heating the ovens.

125. "Barallant se li dona en la coha de la pala del forn . . . hun colp prop l'ull dret a part deius." ARV JCrim 23: M. 5: (Clams) 12 September 1449 (nonpaginated).

126. ARV G 2385: M. 2: 47r and ARV G 2387: M. 29: 18r–36r.

127. ARV G 2406: M. 1: 25v; M. 8: 5r–6v.

128. See APPV 21593 (nonpaginated): 24 January 1476 and APPV 21593 (nonpaginated): 17 April 1476. For another reference to a slave being described as a miller, see a letter from Valencia's city councilmen (*jurats*) reporting, in 1423, the flight of a Russian slave named Jacomet (which took place, not coincidentally, on a feast day, Maundy Tuesday). Not only was Jacomet described as "white," nineteen to twenty-one years in age, of average height, with an athletic build, "not wearing any chains" (*no porta ferres alguns*), and dressed in a dark gray tunic "of the local style" and a green jacket, but the Russian fugitive was also

else's slaves, they occasionally promised to teach the slave their trade in addition to paying for the slave's services (the *logerio*). On 8 May 1459 the baker Joan Valls hired the services of Jerónimo, the thirty-year-old black slave and baptized Christian owned by the priest Vicent Tarasquo. In exchange for the use of Jerónimo's services for the next four years, Joan paid the priest 15.5 lliures. In addition, Joan promised to take Jerónimo on as his apprentice—said Joan "being obliged to instruct him in your trade [of being a baker]." Even within the same household, however, a slave's working and living conditions could vary significantly. About a month later, this same priest put another slave of his in Joan Valls's custody. This time, however, the baker did not seem to be taking on Jeorgy, a thirty-year-old black Ethiopian, as his apprentice. Thus, we see here how all slaves did not share the same opportunities for vocational training and socioeconomic advancement.[129]

Silk Production

The Valencian silk industry experienced a period of tremendous growth in the latter half of the fifteenth century. A key development contributing to this industry's expansion was the influx of Genoese immigrants highly skilled in the art of silk weaving. Germán Navarro has shown that the arrival of these Genoese artisans prompted significant changes in both the technology and techniques used to spin raw silk fibers into thread. In place of the more traditional practice of spinning silk either by hand or with crude and simple wheels, Valencian silk weavers increasingly began to employ wheels (*tornos*) of greater circumference and with multiple spindles.[130] Though elsewhere in the Mediterranean these wheels were being powered entirely by hydraulic energy, in fifteenth-century Valencia these wheels of between 94 to 192 spindles were turned primarily by animal and human power. As Navarro affirms, "the growth of the urban textile industry [in Valencia] was founded on wheels driven by human energy or animal traction."[131]

Though, in 1465, the newly established guild of silk workers issued ordinances explicitly prohibiting the use of slave laborers in silk production,[132] analysis of notarial records reveals that throughout the second half of the fifteenth century, slaves were purchased by silk merchants (*seders*) and other artisans linked to the silk industry. Above all else, these

---

described as a "miller" (*moliner*). See document #144 in Agustín Rubio Vela, ed., *Epistolari de la València Medieval II* (València/Barcelona: Institut Interuniversitari de Filologia Valenciana, 1998), 356.

129. "Ad officium vestrum de flaquerio et teneamini ipsum in dicto officio instruere ad tempus quatuor annorum continue." ARV P 1099 (nonpaginated): 8 May 1459.

130. Germán Navarro Espinach, *El despegue de la industria sedera en la Valencia del siglo XV* (Valencia: Consell Valencià de Cultura, 1992), esp. 151. See also the description of Valencia's silk industry in Guiral-Hadziiossif, *Valence*, 383–86.

131. Navarro notes that though there were a few hydraulically powered silk mills (*molinos de sede*) in Valencia's *huerta*, they were not in widespread use in the kingdom of Valencia. Navarro Espinach, *El despegue*, 89.

132. Navarro Espinach, *El despegue*, 45.

slaves seem to have been employed as manual laborers, given the task of driving the wheels equipped with multiple spindles used for spinning the raw silk fibers into thread (*menar lo torn de seda*). Thus, when the bedspread maker Manuel Soler contracted the services of Carolus, a fifty-year-old black male slave owned by a notary, the contract stated that this baptized Christian slave was being hired "for the task of steering the wheel for spinning silk" (*ad officium de menar lo torn de seda*) as well as for providing general household service.[133] Indeed, so close was the linkage between slaves and silk spinning in the minds of some Valencians that on 30 October 1478 the merchant Fernando Dandugar sold his thirty-five-year-old white Muslim slave named Ali along with "a wheel for twisting silk" (*torn per a tòrcer seda*). The slave's purchaser, a silk weaver named Fernando de Blanes, purchased Ali and this wheel as a package, paying forty-five lliures for both.[134] Members of the nobility were also interested in profiting from Valencia's burgeoning silk industry. Thus, they too had wheels for twisting silk in their households. In 1487, a former notary was charged with inducing Mayniques, a black male slave, to steal silk thread that had been spun on the wheel that he steered in the household of his master, a nobleman with the surname Torris.[135]

Since the silk industry in Valencia had Islamic antecedents, one might expect to find that Muslim slaves were in particularly high demand among Christian masters for their technical skills as silk workers. Indeed, in a few of the contracts I encountered, Muslim slave laborers were promised higher salaries.[136] For example, although the black male slave named Carolus had been promised a salary (*precio seu verius mercede*) of seven lliures for a three-year term of service, when the merchant Jaume Roig contracted out the services of his Muslim slaves to two different silk merchants, he was promised, respectively, eight lliures thirteen sous and ten lliures for just a one-year term. Nevertheless, rather than perform more specialized tasks, such as weaving or dyeing silk, both of these Muslims— Mahomat, a forty-five-year-old originally from Malaga, and Ali ben Moli (aka "the Ox"—*le Bou*), a thirty-five-year-old—were hired, respectively, "for the purpose of driving a wheel used to spin silk"[137] and "to steer a wheel used for [twisting] silk."[138]

---

133. APPV 6161 (nonpaginated): 1 August 1477.

134. ARV P 1998 (nonpaginated): 30 October 1478.

135. ARV JCrim 25: Denunciaciones: M. 2: 15r–16v.

136. For example, on 14 July 1475, the German merchants Jacme Vizlant and Miquael Rolabux contracted out the services of their twenty-five-year-old white Muslim slave named Abdurramen to the silk twister (*torcetor sericis*) Bernabeu Tafoya. Hiring Abdurramen's services on a month-to-month basis, Bernabeu Tafoya agreed to pay the slave's owner, Miquael Rolabux, twelve sous monthly and assumed full liability for the slave in case of flight, promising, in such an event, to pay Rolabux twenty lliures. ARV P 1995 (nonpaginated): 14 July 1475.

137. "Causa menandi unum torn de torcie seda." APPV 16073 (nonpaginated): 26 August 1477.

138. "Causa menandi unum torn de seda." APPV 16073 (nonpaginated): 26 August 1477.

Metal, Leather, and Textile Production

In addition to the carpenters, bakers, and silk weavers just mentioned, artisans from almost every trade practiced in the city can be found (at least occasionally) employing slave laborers. Thus, one encounters slaves working for masons,[139] cloth preparers, cobblers,[140] and mattress makers,[141] as well as armorers, saddle makers, and tanners. Given the fact that many of the city's most famous architectural landmarks—the Torres de Quart, the Torres de Serrans, the Lonja, and the Batlia—were constructed during the fifteenth century, it seems more than likely that at least some slaves were conscripted to work on these massive building projects. A statute in the kingdom's law code suggests that slave laborers were commonly employed in construction. In a section of the Furs de València discussing liability for damages to property that had been loaned or entrusted to third parties, we find the following statute concerning the "borrowed" slave who fell while working at a construction site:

"If I loaned him to you for doing this specific task—that is, that he work at this height and on this particular project—you, to whom I loaned him, are not to be held liable. If, however, I loaned him to you with the understanding that he would work on the ground, and you employ him for another purpose, that is, to work at a height, and he, consequently, falls down from this height—either as a result of something you did or for some other reason, be it scaffolding that was old or support ropes that were poorly tied—you will be held liable for any damages to the slave you have taken here and are obliged to compensate me financially for what I loaned to you.[142]

Slave laborers were also employed by metalworkers. In 1417, for example, the cuirass maker and armorer Joan de Vilalba reported the flight of the no fewer than three slaves who, at that time, had been in his service. Two of the three were his own slaves and the third was a Muslim fugitive he was holding in "comenda" from the bailiff general.[143] Though we do not

---

139. For one example, see ARV P 4301 (nonpaginated): 23 August 1474, in which a mason purchased a forty-year-old Muslim male.

140. For one example, see ARV G 2374: M. 4: 39r.

141. The mattress maker (matalafer) Bernat Cortilles, for example, was a frequent customer at the bailiff general's public auctions. In 1481, he purchased three slaves: Muça, a thirty-year-old white Muslim male; Macot, a twenty-eight-year-old "dark-skinned" (llor) Muslim; and Ali, a twenty-two-year-old black Muslim. ARV B 217: 391r–v; 423r.

142. "Si a aquella cosa-l te presté, que en aquella altea obràs. Mas si-l te presté que en pla obràs o feés obra e tu lo fist obrar en alt e d'aquella altea és caegut per colpa de tu, o d'altra manera per vellea de les pertxes o de les cordes car mal fossen ligades, lo dan que-l servu haurà pres aquí m'és tengut de retre tu a qui-l presté." Furs de València, ed. Colon and Garcia (Barcelona: Editorial Barcino, 1983), IV: 116.

143. ARV B 1430: M. 1: 35r–44r; M. 2: 4r–v.

have explicit statements concerning the sort of work they performed, it seems likely that at least part of their workday was devoted to assisting this armorer in his workshop.

Artisans from the leather industry, namely curriers (*assaonadors*) and tanners (*blanquers*), also employed slaves in their workshops.[144] On 8 May 1473, the tanner Joan Ruvio hired the services of Salvador, a conditionally manumitted thirty-year-old black Christian convert. In exchange for a five-year-term of service, Joan paid the slave's owners, the merchants and brothers Francesc and Gil Garcia, twenty-nine lliures and five sous.[145] Some indication of the sort of work performed by slave laborers in the leather industry can be deduced from the terms of service imposed on three slaves conditionally freed in the last will and testament of the tanner Garcia d'Agramunt. Garcia specified that his slaves, Francesc, Pere, and Jordi, were required to serve his wife for at least two years following his death, during which time they would be expected to perform the distasteful chore of cleaning (literally, extracting blood from) animal hides. Garcia emphasized that only those slaves who agreed to fulfill this obligation would win their freedom. If any of the slaves took flight or otherwise failed to carry out their responsibilities, they would immediately be reenslaved and, possibly, resold.[146]

One further occupational group that appears to have regarded slaves as valuable laborers were wool clothiers or cloth preparers (*perayres* or *panni parators*). Although both enslaved and freed men can be found working in this industry,[147] women also seem to have been prominent participants in textile production. Several of the slaves owned by wool clothiers (encountered in notarial records dating from 1460 to 1480) were women. Although some, if not all, of these women might have been purchased to provide domestic service, it seems likely that they also helped out with cloth production.[148]

144. For some examples, see ARV G 4854: M. 21: 34r–38v and ARV P 1996 (nonpaginated): 24 May 1476.

145. It was not until some eight years later, however, that Joan Ruvio stated that he was "content" with the service provided and proclaimed Salvador "free." ARV P 1913 (nonpaginated): 8 May 1473, and the appended note, dated 22 October 1481.

146. ARV P 442 (nonpaginated): 23 July 1476.

147. For some references to male slaves owned by cloth preparers, see ARV P 9986 (nonpaginated): 12 May 1461, APPV 752 (nonpaginated): 22 October 1477, and ARV P 1998 (nonpaginated): 2 September 1478. I also came across references to two black freedmen who, after being awarded their freedom, took up the trade of *panni parator*. On 16 January 1472, a black freedman (*libertinus*) named Joan entered into a three-year contract of apprenticeship with the Valencian *panni parator* Joan Fandos, "ad adiscipicendum officium vestrum laniffici seu panniparatorie." ARV P 822 (nonpaginated): 16 January 1472. Similarly, in a document dated 4 April 1478, a black freedman named Joan Maroma described himself as a *parator pannorum*. ARV P 1998 (nonpaginated): 4 April 1478.

148. For some references to female slaves employed by cloth preparers, see ARV P 1253 (nonpaginated): 3 June 1474; ARV P 1999 (nonpaginated): 17 May 1479; APPV 25217 (nonpaginated): 19 December 1473; APPV 23837 (nonpaginated): 18 August 1467; APPV 23837 (nonpaginated): 29 May 1467; and APPV 9636 (nonpaginated): 12 December 1477.

As previously noted, enslaved and freed women were frequently described as spinning raw fibers into thread. For example, when her alleged lover, a servant named Domingo, needed some new shirts, a freedwoman named Johana Amalrich reportedly spun the raw flax her lover gave her into thread. Once spun, Domingo entrusted this thread to a local weaver who in turn wove it into a piece of cloth. An acquaintance of this freedwoman's recalled how Johana's lover, Domingo, subsequently brought the piece of woven cloth back to her, saying, "Look, Johana! See how the flax you spun turned out?"[149]

As this last example indicates, although it was not uncommon to find free female servants placed in contracts of apprenticeships for the purpose of learning more "skilled" female occupations such as weaving,[150] dressmaking,[151] embroidery,[152] or making veils,[153] slave women do not seem to have been trained to perform these more specialized (and better compensated) activities. Casual statements in court testimony suggest that slave women were expected to be able to do basic mending. When a merchant solicited his mother-in-law's opinion about a black female slave he was interested in buying, for example, the widow asked the slave woman (the aforementioned plague-stricken Caterina) to thread a needle.[154] When more complicated needlework was required, it seems, slave women turned to a professional tailor (*sartor*) or seamstress (*costurera*). The aforementioned freedwoman named Johana, for example, was accused of contracting the services of a seamstress under false pretenses. Tricking the seamstress into thinking she was acting on her master's behalf, Johana reportedly handed the piece of woven cloth

149. A female boarder (*estagera*) who lived in the same household as Johana testified that the freedwoman showed her the flax she was spinning on at least two separate occasions, saying, "*Madona* Maria, look at what Domingo has brought for me to spin for his shirts!" Later on, she continued, she observed how Domingo brought the cloth back to her after it had been woven into a piece of cloth, saying, "Mirau Johana quin es exit lo lli que vos haveu fillat." ARV G 2346: M. 6: 25r–39v and ARV G 2347: M. 14: 1r–2v; 6r–v. I will discuss Johana Amalrich's experiences as a freedwoman in greater depth in chapter 7.

150. In 1471, Margarita, the nine-year-old daughter of a merchant, entered the service of a Valencian pharmacist and his wife for a six-year term, during which time she would be taught "to weave silk, cotton, as well as silk-blend threads." APPV 11436 (nonpaginated): 22 April 1471.

151. In 1477, the eleven-year-old daughter of a farmer was put in a contract of service with a Valencian couple "ad addicendum (sic) artem costurie sive de tallar e cosir." APPV 6161 (nonpaginated): 14 October 1477.

152. In 1479, a widow and her daughter put themselves in a contract of service with another widow "to do for you as much sewing and embroidery work as you should wish, free of charge, up to the sum of said seven lliures" (the amount of a debt they owed her). ARV P 1999 (nonpaginated): 29 July 1479.

153. In 1475, Maria, the eleven-year-old daughter of a leather worker was put in a contract of service for a six-and-a-half-year term, during which time "teneamini demonstrare…officium vestrum faciendi vetas sive vetos." APPV 6486 (nonpaginated): 27 August 1475.

154. His mother-in-law did this because she suspected that this slave woman had problems with her eyesight. ARV G 2278: M. 7: 16r–19v; M. 8: 38r–v.

Domingo had given to her over to the seamstress and asked her to make shirts for her lover (Domingo) with it.[155]

Hardly a privileged group of men (and women) "with trades," the slaves working in Valencia's artisanal workshops performed distasteful and arduous tasks such as sawing wood, shoveling loaves of bread into and out of hot ovens, driving the large wheels used to twist raw silk, and cleaning animal hides. In stark contrast to previous scholars' rather rosy depiction of the position of "artisanal" slaves in the medieval Mediterranean work-force, we see that the vast majority of these slaves were engaged to perform menial and physically demanding labors.

The living and working conditions of these slaves, moreover, were hardly enviable. Among the most evocative items noted in the inventory postmortem of the carpenter Ber-nat Climent's workshop were the tools used by Bernat and others to control and discipline his slaves. Next to the saws and other assorted carpentry tools were a pair of leg irons with four ankle rings, each weighing an *arova* (roughly 25 U.S. pounds), and the "long chain used for holding slaves." Similarly, in this carpenter's kitchen was something termed a "*ballesta*," or what seems to have been some sort of cage with two chains or stirrups (*gambla*) used "for detaining slaves."[156] Bernat's household, moreover, does not seem to have terribly unique in this respect. In the dispute between the daughter of the carpenter Francesch Gomiz and the carpenter Francesch Selva concerning their relative liability in the flight of Gomiz's dark-skinned (llor) slave Bernat, Gomiz's daughter complained that Selva had been criminally negligent with respect to his responsibility to guard the slave. Arguing that the defendant had been derelict in his supervision of the slave, Francesch Gomiz's daughter emphasized how "at night [her father] had been accustomed to keep the said slave shut up in the *ballesta* with a lock and key." Indeed, an apprentice who had worked in the Gomiz household testified that one of his most important responsibilities had been to lock the slave up in the *ballesta* each night and release him from this cage every morning so that he could go to work.[157] Similarly, in the carpenter Jacme Lombart's household, his executors found two wooden *ballestes* or cages equipped with ropes (rather than metal stirrups) for restraining "unruly" slaves. Indicative, moreover, that the food given to slaves owned by artisans was strictly rationed, these same executors noted that in the dining room of Lombart's home they found two pine boxes used "for holding the bread of the slaves." Each of these two boxes had its own key and padlock. The bread

155. ARV G 2346: M. 1: 10r; M. 6: 25r–39v and ARV G 2347: M. 14: 1r–2v, 6r–v.
156. Found in this carpenter's workshop (*botiga*) were "un parel de camals ab quatre anelles que pessen una arova grosa e dues lliures. Item una cadena larga de tenir catius." In the kitchen, the executors found "una ballesta de ferre de tenir catius ab dos gambla." APPV 9636 (nonpaginated): 24 January 1476.
157. Francesch Gomiz, reportedly, "tenia e havia acostumat tenir de nit lo dit sclau en la ballesta e tancat ab clau." Thus his apprentice, the carpenter Pere Remangossa, testified that "tanquava de nit lo dit sclau en la balesta e de mati lo'n trahia." ARV G 2300: 157r–v and ARV G 2303: M. 29: 11r–25v.

slaves were served also seems to have been of an inferior quality. For, in the bread-making room (*pastador*), executors noted the presence of two large wooden bowls for making bread dough (*pasteres*), each with its own cover. While one had been used for making bread "for the slaves," the other was earmarked for making the bread "of the master."[158]

Although some, more privileged, slaves appear to have been trained to perform "skilled" occupations in the construction, leather, metal, and textile industries,[159] such practices were controversial and provoked the resentment of free laborers. Concern over the competition posed by slave laborers can be detected both in municipal ordinances and guild statutes restricting their employment. Heers observes how some contemporaries were concerned about the competition posed by slave laborers. He notes, for example, how in Barcelona the members of the gold and silver worker' guilds issued statutes imposing quotas on the number of slaves a master craftsmen could employ in his workshop. He also cites a decree issued by municipal authorities limiting the number of slaves artisans working with semiprecious stones (*fabricantes de objetos de coral, joyas o botones*) could employ in their workshops. According to this decree, they could employ just two, only one of whom could be male.[160] This statute likewise dictated that they could not teach their art to a slave unless they first tried (unsuccessfully) to find a free or freed person to be their apprentice.[161]

This last example reveals how measures were enacted in Barcelona not only to limit the number of slave laborers working in individual workshops but also to ban the training of slaves in certain trades. Jacqueline Guiral-Hadziiossif, Mark Meyerson, and Manuel Benítez Bolorinos have all shown how, in Valencia, over the course of the fifteenth century, there was a proliferation of such ordinances, forbidding the employment and training of slaves

---

158. In the dining room, Lombart's executors found "dos artibanchs de pi lo hu ab dox caxons ab sos panys e claus per tenir pa per als sclaus buyts" and "dos ballestes de fust ab ses cordes." In the "pastador" they found "dues pasteres de fust ab ses cubertes per a pastar la una per als catius e l'altre per al senyor." ARV G 4581: M. 7: 15r–17v.

159. For example, in Caterina de la Nana's last will and testament, she left twenty lliures to her former slave, Johanot Agosti, so that he could finish his apprenticeship with a local cloth preparer (*perayre*). ARV P 9956 (nonpaginated): 19 September 1489. Similarly, the attorney Pere Valcanell specified in his last will and testament that, if his black male slave Johan was "good," he would give him money to help him set up a workshop so that he could support himself as a cap maker (*barreter*). "Que si aquell volra mirar a be e usar lo offici de barreter e viure com a bon home que li sien donades de mos bens x lliures en subvencio de son offici." ARV P 10251 (nonpaginated): 29 August 1501.

160. Pierre Bonnassie notes how, in 1490, the quota for slave laborers was increased to two males. Pierre Bonnassie, *La organización del trabajo en Barcelona a fines de siglo XV* (Barcelona: Consejo Superior de Investigaciones Científicas, 1975), 97–103.

161. Heers, *Esclavos*, 135–36. Heers does acknowledge that these trade regulations were sometimes ignored. He cites a document from 1457 in which a master *coralero* (maker of coral jewelry) employed no fewer than four slaves, three of whom were male.

in trades such as carpentry,[162] silversmithing, and belt making.[163] In 1465, for example, the guild of silk weavers issued ordinances explicitly prohibiting the use of slave laborers.[164] Some of these restrictions possibly had fourteenth-century antecedents. In 1374, a Valencian weaver protested that his son Miquel—an apprentice with another weaver in neighboring Villena—had been the victim of a cruel "joke." His rival apprentices were alleging, falsely, that he was a Tartar and a fugitive slave, thus ineligible for employment as the weaver's apprentice. After Miquel was arrested and thrown into prison as a suspected fugitive, his father sent a strongly worded missive to the marquis of Villena in which he insisted that though his son, admittedly, had some Tartarlike features (i.e., he was somewhat short in stature and had a round and flat face), he, nonetheless, was a freeborn Christian who could legitimately be placed in a contract of apprenticeship. Indeed, Miquel's father insisted, before entering this weaver's workshop in Villena, he had been put in a contract of apprenticeship with a weaver in Xativa. Thus he not only demanded his son's immediate release from the local prison but that he also be allowed to resume his apprenticeship.[165]

That free laborers considered slaves and freed men as competitors is also reflected in a contract of manumission drawn up in 1473 by the saddle maker (çeller) Martín Vilalba. Vilalba made the emancipation of his thirty-year-old black male slave named Fernando (a baptized Christian) contingent not only upon Fernando providing nine more years of unpaid service but also on Fernando's promise that he would never work in a rival saddle-maker's workshop.[166]

A close reading of the Valencian evidence suggests that these restrictive measures were motivated by something more than just fear of economic competition from a potentially much cheaper labor source. Master craftsmen and municipal officials seem equally preoccupied with protecting the "honor" and "reputability" of their professions. Among the ordinances confirmed by Alfonso V for the confraternity of the silversmiths of Valencia was the following:

> Likewise, to avoid the frauds that, by infidels, could be committed in the practice of said trade—which, principally, ought to be taught to natives, loyal subjects of the

---

162. Guiral-Hadziiossif, *Valence*, 379, and Meyerson, "Slavery and Solidarity," 300.

163. Manuel Benítez Bolorinos, *Las cofradías medievales en el reino de Valencia (1329–1458)* (Alicante: Universidad de Alicante, 1998), 200–201.

164. Navarro Espinach, *El despegue*, 45.

165. Noting how his son's rivals "per joch o per deveres, affermassen que és tartre e catiu fuyt de qualque senyor," this father affirmed that his son Miquel, "de pocha estatura ab la cara queacom grossa e plana, quasi semblant a disposició de faç tartaresca," was *not* a slave. See document #111 in Agustín Rubio Vela, ed., *Epistolari de la València Medieval* (Valencia: Institut de Filologia Valenciana, 1985), 286.

166. If, upon winning his freedom, Fernando decided to stay in Valencia, he could remain in his former master's service as a salaried worker. ARV P 1913 (nonpaginated): 3 February 1473.

lord king (as there are many here who travel the entire kingdom)—we ordain that, henceforth, no silversmith dare himself teach or permit someone else to teach said trade of silversmithing to any Jew or Moor—be he free or slave—or to any other man of any nation that can be subjected to slavery. He who countermands this decree will pay, for each offense, a fine of 10 lliures.... The *majorals* [leaders of this confraternity or guild] hereby request that any silversmith [employing a Jew or Moor or some such other person] should immediately eject him from his workshop and pay the said fine. In this group, however, are not to be included Sard or Greek apprentices, since they are natural-born Christians, nor are sons of Catalan fathers who have been redeemed [from captivity].[167]

An even more marked example of "status anxiety" is discernible in the guild regulations for cobblers. In 1597, the guild of cobblers (*lo offici de cabaters*) reaffirmed an ordinance that initially had been issued in "the book of old statutes," ca. 1458–84, whereby:

No master of said guild of cobblers should dare, presume, or be able to receive, accept, or welcome as an apprentice—by means of an agreement or in any other manner— in his household, or outside of it, a black man nor a man the color of quince jelly, a former slave, nor the son of slaves of a similar color, nor a Moor. Nor [should he dare, presume, or otherwise be able] to instruct them in said trade of cobblers.[168]

What was particularly noteworthy about this statue, however, were the reasons given to justify its promulgation:

And this is so that these ones should not walk intermixed with the masters and journeymen of said guild in processions or in any public acts due to the great commotion

167. "Ítem, per squivar fraus qui per persones infels se porren seguir en lo dit offici, lo qual principalment deu ésser aprés per persones leals e naturals del senyor rey, com molt hi vaja a tota la terra, ordenam que d'açí avant algun argenter no gosa ne deja mostrar lo dit offici d'argentaria a algun juheu, ni moro ffranch ne sclau, ne a negun altrell de nació qui sia sotsmessa a cativage. E qui contrafarà pach de pena cascuna vegada deu liures, qui sien partides per terç axí com damunt és dit. E que lo dit argenter request per los dits majorals deja encontinent gitar de son obrador lo dit juheu o moro a altre axí com dit és e pagar no res menys la dita pena. En açí emperò no són mosos sarts, ni grechs, per tal són christians de natura, ne encara hi són enceses [sic] neguns que sien fills de cathalà que sien reemuts." In addition, under penalty of one hundred sous for each offense, another statute prohibited any freed person from opening a silversmithing workshop or stall in the city. Benítez Bolorinos, *Las cofradía medievales*, 264–68.

168. "Se había determinat, statuhit e ordenat que ningún Mestre confrare del dit Offici de çabaters pogués tenir ni tingués en sa casa ningún aprenent que fos aquell sclau, ni negre, ni de color de codony cuit, ni fills d'esclaus de semblant color, ni moro." This document has been transcribed and published in the appendix of Leopoldo Piles Ros, *Estudios sobre el gremio de zapateros* (Valencia: Ayuntamiento de Valencia, 1959), 169–70.

that said black slaves and the children of slaves or Moors would cause and also due to the inconveniences that would follow by having these ones walking in public entries and in general and private ceremonies due to the laughter and mockery it would incite among the people and the brawls and disputes it would provoke between members of said trade and other individuals. Therefore, to avoid such inconveniences, it has been determined—with heavy penalties [in cases of its violation]—that the masters of said trade ought not dare nor endeavor to welcome or receive apprentices of this type into their households.[169]

In 1597, on the occasion of these statutes' confirmation, we see these arguments not just restated but amplified. Thus, the guild of cobblers explained that it was issuing this statute,

in order to avoid the damages and inconveniences referred to above that might result and occur to members of the confraternity and guild of cobblers and similar such persons: the infamy and mockery that seeing either a slave, the son of a black slave, a slave the color of quince jelly, or a Moor walking in processions, general and private ceremonies, and/or other public acts would and could incite among the populace, the commotion and disturbances that would and could result as a consequence of having those ones walking among and intermixed with the honorable and well-dressed members of the said guild.[170]

The *primary* reason cited by Valencian cobblers for barring slaves, freedmen, and individuals of African and Muslim descent from admittance into their ranks, then, was to protect their status, to prevent themselves from becoming the targets of ridicule and scorn. In addition, the administrators of the cobblers' guild stated that they were doing this because "other guilds in the present city of Valencia have [issued] this same ordinance."[171]

169. "E açó perque en profesóns ni en altres actes públichs no anassen aquells mesclats entre los Mestres y Jovens del dit Offici, per la molta inquietut que y hauría portant als dits negres esclaus y fills d'esclaus o moros y també per los inconvenients qu'es seguiríen en anar aquells en entrades públiques y mostres generals y particulars, per la risa y burla que la gent feya de aquells y les ocasions que y hauría de bregues y questions per dita causa entre los particulars de dit Offici y altres persones particulars, per evitar los quals inconvenients se havía determinat ab groses penes que los Mestres de dit Offici no gosasen ni emprenguessen a rebre ni acollir en ses cases semblants aprendisos." Piles Ros, *Estudios*, 169–70.

170. "E açó per evitar los dits danys e ynconvenients desús referits qu'es poden seguir y haver entre los cofrares çabaters del dit Offici y les tals persones e per la ynfamia y burla que causaría y pot causar al poblat en veure anar en profesons, mostres generals y particulars y en altres actes publichs, un esclau o fill de sclau negre o de color de codony cuyt o moro, per la ynquietut y desasosiego que y'ha y poria haver anant aquell entre persones honrrades y ben vestides mesclats del dit Offici." Piles Ros, *Estudios*, 170.

171. "E principalment havent hi esta mateixa ordinació en los altres officis de la present Ciutat de Valencia." Piles Ros, *Estudios*, 170.

Although slaves, both male and female, performed many of the same tasks and worked closely alongside free laborers, their opportunities for socioeconomic advancement and integration were limited by a concurrent concern with preserving social hierarchies. Precisely because they were working so closely together in the household, workshop, and field, the slave/free distinction took on added significance.

CHAPTER 4 ENEMIES OR EXTENDED

FAMILY?

SLAVES IN THE HOUSEHOLD

In 1453, the nobleman Luis de Castellar sued Castelleta, the wife of another nobleman, for custody of Ventura, the daughter of his white slave woman. Though Luis possessed documentation recording how he had purchased Ventura as a fetus, buying Ventura's mother when she was seven months' pregnant, this nobleman did not simply brandish the duly notarized contract of sale and leave it at that. In order to more conclusively establish his rights, Luis detailed how he had raised Ventura from infancy. Thus, Luis stressed how, within the first few weeks of Ventura's birth, he had seen to it that she was baptized and given a Christian name; throughout her infancy and early childhood he had provided her with food and clothing; and, finally, when Ventura reached the age of six, he saw to it that she was properly educated, transferring her into the custody of an elderly couple "so that she might learn some handicrafts, such as sewing and tailoring." In recounting his efforts, Luis enunciated a claim over Ventura that was twofold in nature: "the young slave girl ought not stay in any other household besides his own since she is his slave, purchased and nurtured (nodrida) by him."[1]

What was at stake in this dispute between two nobles, it seems, was something more than just control over this slave woman's labor. Ventura, after all, had not been living or providing service in Luis's household for many years. Rather, what seems to have spurred Luis into action was the fact that Castelleta was arranging Ventura's marriage. Not only had Castelleta retained the young girl "and even today holds her, by force, against the will of said mossen Luis," but she also "wishes to give the said Ventura a husband," usurping Luis's paternal authority.[2]

1. "La dita fadrina e sclava no deu esser en altra casa sino en la sua com sia sclava sua per ell dit responent comprada e nodrida." ARV JCiv 916: M. 18: 17r–28v; 45r–v.

2. "Ha retenguda la dita fadrina e huy en dia la te contra voluntat del dit en Luis en tant que la noble na Castelleta muller del dit noble mossen Pere Centelles vol dar marit a la dita Ventura." ARV JCiv 916: M. 18: 17r–28v; 45r–v.

For her part, Castelleta, having no formal claim over the girl either as her owner or as her legal guardian, contended that Ventura was a free person who was legally competent to direct her own affairs. Thus, Castelleta reasoned, Ventura "could not be constrained or forced to be in the household of said Luis de Castellar but rather [pertains to] the household in which she wants to be and live."[3] The voice of Ventura herself, however, was conspicuously absent from these proceedings. Rather than produce testimony from Ventura herself affirming a desire to continue living in her household, Castelleta, somewhat dubiously, spoke for her, proclaiming simply that Ventura "did not wish to leave."

Although Luis and Castelleta disagreed about Ventura's true status, they used similar arguments to bolster their claims over this daughter of a slave woman. Both parties contended that they had "raised" (criada) the now twenty-year-old Ventura from a young age. Their parallel claims are revealing of how masters and mistresses presented themselves as bound to their slaves by "ties analogous to kinship."[4] Just as slave and free dependents were expected to honor and respect their masters "like their parents," masters and mistresses not infrequently professed that they looked after their slaves "like their children."[5] Thus, Castelleta adopted a similar posture of paternal solicitude. Countering that she and her husband had been the ones feeding, clothing, and caring for Ventura for the past twenty years, Castelleta maintained that it was perfectly within her rights to see to it that Ventura was married off "well and honorably." Indeed, she suggested, it was their responsibility. Declaring that she could not "be forced or constrained to return the said young girl to the said en Luis de Castellar," Castelleta avowed that Ventura would not be leaving her household "except with a husband."[6]

Unfortunately, we do not know the Justícia Civil's ultimate ruling in this case. Nevertheless, this dispute between two nobles highlights an important facet of the master-slave relationship. Although their enslavement may have been justified (in contracts of sale and sentences issued by the bailiff general) by labeling them "enemies of the Catholic faith and Crown," once they entered the households of their masters and mistresses, slaves became "familiars." Though masters were under no statutory obligation to ensure their slaves' physical or spiritual well-being (as would be the case with their legitimate

---

3. In the kingdom of Valencia, the age of majority was twenty years old. Furs de València, ed. Colón and Garcia (Barcelona, 1974), II: 215.

4. I am borrowing this phrase from Sally McKee, who observed in her study of households in fourteenth-century Venetian Crete that "however unequal members in a household might be, the slaves were bound to the free members of the household by ties analogous to kinship." Sally McKee, "Households in Fourteenth-Century Venetian Crete," Speculum 70 (1995): 27–60.

5. See, for example, the last will and testament of Miquel Valero, in which he directed his wife to treat his two slaves, Lucia and Angelina, "like daughters" (com a filles). APPV 09653 (nonpaginated): 11 October 1472.

6. "No vol exir sino ab marit." ARV JCiv 916: M. 18: 17r–28v; 45r–v.

children), testimony in civil and criminal court records, as well as testamentary clauses, reveals a widespread conviction that masters and mistresses had "paternal" responsibilities with respect to their slaves—particularly if she or he was a *bort* or *borda*—a child (often illegitimate) born in their household. As *pater familias*, Luis was expected to attend to the material and spiritual needs of all of his dependents—both slave and free.[7] A master's authority over his slave, then, was established not only by the single act of purchase but also (if he wished to retain honor and status within the community) through the performance of his paternal obligations.

In this chapter I examine how (and the degree to which) slaves were incorporated into their masters' and mistresses' households. Baptism, naming, marriage, and testamentary practices reflect how masters and mistresses, to a certain extent, conceived and treated slaves as members of their extended family. Admittedly, such practices were self-serving; they helped naturalize, and thus, legitimate, their authority. Masters and mistresses, however, did more than pay mere lip service to their paternal obligations. In last wills and testaments, they bequeathed significant sums of money and even landed property to their former slaves. As Sally McKee has observed (with regard to fourteenth-century Venetian Crete), slaves not only formed part of the family patrimony, they also could lay claim to it.[8]

Slavery and Paternalism: Master as Provider

According to the kingdom's legal code, parents were obliged to provide their children with "those things necessary to one's body," that is, adequate food, drink, clothing, footwear, and shelter for "however long as they shall live, even into adulthood if they should lack sufficient means."[9] Requests for allowances filed by widows and legal guardians (*curators*) of orphans reveal that the obligation to care for one's children customarily was extended to cover all "domestic persons" living in the household, including squires, ladies-in-waiting, wet nurses, male and female servants, and slaves. In an itemized list

7. The *pater familias* "was master not only of the family property but of all family members." This included his wife and children as well as anyone (that is servants, slaves, and other dependants) living under his roof. Not only were all household members subject to his *potestas* (authority) and "obliged to show him the proper obedience and respect," but he, in turn, "was responsible for assuring their material and spiritual well-being." David Herlihy, *Medieval Households* (Cambridge: Harvard University Press, 1985), 3, 114–15. According to the kingdom of Valencia's law code, "Persones domestiques son appellades muller, servuus, homens qui staran a loguer, nebots, dexebles, scolans e tots homens e fembres qui son de la companyia d'alcu." *Furs de València*, ed. Colón and Garcia (Barcelona, 1990), V: 105.

8. McKee, "Households in Fourteenth-Century Venetian Crete," 27–60; and, McKee, "Greek Women in Latin Households of Fourteenth-Century Venetian Crete," *Journal of Medieval History* 19 (1993): 229–49.

9. *Furs de València*, ed. Colon and Garcia (Barcelona, 1990), V: 173. Children also were obliged to support their parents when they were no longer able to support themselves.

of the expenses "necessary" to maintain her household, a pharmacist's widow requested that approximately one *real* a day be set aside to cover the costs of providing "food, drink, footwear and other necessities" (*aliments*) to each member of her household, including three pharmacist's apprentices, a slave woman, and an unspecified number of "other companions."[10]

Though distinctions were clearly made here, with respect to what constituted "adequate" sustenance, between blood relatives and other household dependents, the sums allotted for supporting slaves were roughly equivalent to those allotted for free servants. In 1478, Johana, the widow of the merchant Alfonso de Santangel, requested an allowance to cover, among other things, the expenses of feeding and supporting a female domestic to care for her two ten-year-old sons. Regardless of whether Johana retained a slave or a free domestic, the amount budgeted for her support was ten lliures for the year.[11] Similarly, in 1450 the curator of the estate of the nobleman Joan Tolsà requested twenty lliures to cover the annual expenses of supporting a salaried female servant and a female slave at a rate of ten lliures apiece, or about one *real* a day. Indeed, he noted, "such is the practice in the city of Valencia that ten lliures [is a sufficient amount] for providing food and drink for one person for one year, especially a person who serves."[12]

With respect to slave children born in their masters' households, contemporary testimony suggests that they were treated (at least initially) very similarly to any freeborn children living there. When a white woman named Ursola found her freeborn status contested upon reaching the age of majority, her advocate categorically rejected several witnesses' claims that they had seen how Ursola had been raised "as a slave" (*com a sclava*). Noting how during her early childhood "it could not be said whether they treated her as a slave or as a free person," he insisted that "at that age" there would have been no discernible difference.[13]

In addition to providing food, drink, and clothing for their slaves, masters and mistresses also gave them shelter. Inventories postmortem constitute some of the best sources available for getting a sense of the material conditions under which slaves in fifteenth-century Valencia lived. In compiling these official, itemized accounts of the deceased's worldly possessions, the executors of the estate typically went through the deceased's house and/or workshop room by room and described each chamber's contents. If the deceased had been a slave owner, they often identified a room as the place where

---

10. ARV JCiv 923: M. 15: 30r–48r.

11. ARV JCiv 930: M. 10: 46v–48v.

12. "Tal pratica sia en la present ciutat de alimentar de menjar e beure una persona deu lliures l'any specialment persona qui servex." ARV JCiv 915: M. 16: 15r–19v; M. 16: 25r.

13. "No era de tal edat ni tal qu'es pogues dir si la tenien per sclava o per franqua." ARV G 2304: M. 3: 45r, ARV G 2305: M. 11: 8r–23v; M. 20: 13r–21v and ARV G 2306: M. 25: 16r–17v; M. 26: 36r–37v; 42r–43v; M. 29: 19r–v.

a certain slave of the household slept. For example, in the inventory postmortem of the possessions formerly belonging to the French-born merchant Franch Guanot, his executors noted that "in the room where Maria, [a slave] whom the deceased just freed, slept," they found "a four-poster bed, with its wooden planks," "two mattresses, stuffed with poor-quality wool," "two blankets, already old," and "a set of three sheets made of hemp, each one very used."[14] In another room, "where the [fourteen-year-old] black male slave [named Johanico] slept," the executors found "two mattresses of poor quality on [a bed] with five[?] posts and their supports," a sheet made of hemp, a "Moorish" bedspread, described as "thin and of little value," a "Castilian" floor covering, and a long feather pillow. Also in "Johanico's room" were "a big frying pan and two other cooking pots."[15] In the deceased merchant's study, moreover, the executors noted how, inside a certain chest, they found "four suits belonging to the black slave of the household, of different colors, already used, along with a belt."[16]

Although the quality of the furnishings itemized in these inventories postmortem clearly was not the finest, they indicate that it was not uncommon for masters and mistresses to provide slaves with their own personal space to sleep inside their homes, a bed furnished with linens and blankets, and occasionally even a feather pillow. In the inventory postmortem of the possessions belonging to the wool merchant Llupe Rodriguez, his executors noted how in the room where the deceased's black male slave, Andrenot, slept (*en la cambra del negre*), they found a bed with four posts, one mattress, two sheets, three blankets, described as very used, a cloak, also "used," and a black tunic, again, "used."[17]

References in the last wills and testaments of slave owners similarly indicate that slaves had their own beds, linens, and articles of clothing. In 1480, Orfresina d'Anyo, the widow of Marti Sayes, specified in her last will and testament that, subsequent to her death, her slave woman Elena should be freed as well as given "her" bed, "such as it is," along with

---

14. "Item en huna cambra hon dormia Maria la qual a dexat franqua lo dit defunt fon atrobat hun llit de posts ab quatre pots ab sos petges e dos matalafs sotils plens de llana sotill. Item dos flacades cardades ja velles. Item hun parell de llancols de canem de tres teles cascu molt usats.... Item sinch tovaloles de lli les dos bones les tres sotills. Item set cubertes de xoins de cap de lli entre bones e sotills." APPV 11248 (nonpaginated): 4 January 1478.

15. "Item en huna altra cambra on dormia lo dit negre fon atrobat dos matalafs sobre cinch posts sotils e sos petges. Item hun llancoll de canem e hun cubertor morisch sotils e de pocha valor. Item huna catifa castelana forradada. Item huna paella gran e dos ferros de cuynar. Item hun travesser de ffluxell." APPV 11248 (nonpaginated): 4 January 1478.

16. "Quatre sayos del negre de casa de diverses colors ja hussats e hun cint." APPV 11248 (nonpaginated): 4 January 1478.

17. "Item en la cambra del negre fon atrobat hun llit ab quatre posts. Item hun matalaf. Item dos llencols. Item tres flacades de borra ja molt ussades. Item una manta ja usada del dit defunt. Item una clocha negra del dit defunt ja ussada." APPV 19281 (nonpaginated): 9 February 1497.

"her coffer where she [Elena] keeps all her things."[18] Ysabel, the widow of the lawyer Pere Marti, specified in her last will and testament that, subsequent to her death, her slave woman Barbera was to be freed and given "the bed with three[?] posts where she sleeps," along with the one mattress, two blankets, and the two sheets "that it has today." Additionally, Ysabel instructed her executors to give Barbera "all the clothing that, at the time of my death, can be shown to have been hers."[19]

As Orfresina's and Ysabel's last wills and testaments demonstrate, in addition to pro-viding food, clothing, and shelter for their slaves during their lifetimes, masters and mistresses occasionally took pains to ensure their former slaves were properly cared for even beyond the grave. In the last will and testament of the nobleman Berenguer Vives de Boyl, he directed that his former slave woman, Cathelina, be given a yearly allowance of one hundred sous for the duration of her life.[20] Similarly, in the last will and testament of Johana, the widow of the surgeon Guillem Barcelona, Johana directed her executor to make sure that her former slave, Margalida, always had sufficient food, drink, clothing, and shoes. Although Margalida, now freed, would be expected to support herself with the money she earned contracting out her own labor, Johana specified that "if that which she is able to earn is not sufficient, the remainder [needed] for her sustenance . . . will be provided by the said mestre Raffel (her executor)."[21]

Though, slaves, of course, unlike wives and children, had no legal recourse in the event that their masters (or mistresses) failed to provide them with adequate food and clothing, Vicente Graullera Sanz has pointed out that slaves could and did express dissatisfaction

18. "Item vull e man que Elena sclava mia servexscha a la dita na Orfesina filla e herena mia de tota la vida de aquella. E apres obte de de la [sic] dita filla mia si la dita Elena viva sera en tal cars ara per llavors faz franqua aquella de tota servitut e en tal cars leix a aquella cent solidos. Item hun llit seu com esta e hun cofre seu on aquella te la sua roba a fer ne a ses voluntats." ARV P 443 (nonpaginated): 17 February 1480. See also the last will and testament of Maria "la Galleta," in which she granted her black or dark-skinned slave woman Luisa freedom as well as "lo lit on aquella jau e tota la roba de aquell." ARV P 2240 (nonpaginated): 21 March 1477.

19. "Item vull e man que la mia esclava nomenada Barbera del dia de la mia mort en anant sia liberta e no sia mes cativa a la qual deixe tota la roba sua de vestir que al temps de la mia mort se mostrara esser sua ensemps ab hun llit de tres posts hon aquella jau hun matalaff dos flacades e dos lancols que huy te en lo dit llit." ARV P 3105 (nonpaginated): 1 March 1501. See also the last will and testament of a lawyer who, in addition to freeing his slave woman Angela (effective upon his wife's death), promised her "totes les robes de vestir que aquella en lo dit temps tendra." ARV P 2771 (nonpaginated): 18 March 1508.

20. APPV 26629 (nonpaginated): 3 August 1477.

21. "Item jaquesch franqua de tot jou de servitut a Margalida cativa que era del dit marit meu e ara mia. E que lo dit mestre Raffel li dos sos obs de la vida de aquella los quals aga per les mans de aquell ço es mengar beure vestir e calçar . . . deduhit empero lo que aquella pora guanyar. . . . Vull li servisqua per a la dita sustenacio e sino li bastava lo que aquella poria guanyar lo restant per a la dita sustenacio segons dit es li sia donat per lo dit mestre Raffel com aquella es mester sia rogida per alguna e per ço vull e man se regescha ab lo consell del dit mestre Raffel." ARV P 1914 (nonpaginated): 12 October 1475.

with their material living conditions by taking flight. Graullera found that the most oft-cited reason given by fugitive slaves questioned by Crown officials in sixteenth-century Valencia concerning why they took flight (besides physical abuse) was insufficient food and/or clothing. "Certainly," Graullera acknowledges, "we cannot take these declarations at face value, since the slave, in each case, was interested in exonerating himself of responsibility and justifying his flight."[22] Nevertheless, the fact that fugitives felt that they could use such arguments to excuse their actions suggests that contemporaries expected owners to provide their slaves with a minimum level of care. Indeed, a statute in the kingdom of Valencia's legal code stipulated that masters were legally obligated to reimburse third parties who, in a slave owner's absence, covered the expenses "necessary" (covinent) to feed a slave or cure them of a certain physical ailment or illness. If the slave's owner should refuse to compensate this third party for his or her medical expenses, the slave was considered forfeit and automatically became the property of the individual(s) who had seen to it that the slave received proper care.[23]

Baptism: Appointing Godparents

Just as parents were expected to raise their children to be good Christians, masters, as paters familias, were responsible for promoting their slaves' spiritual well-being. Charles Verlinden has noted how, in 1327, Philip of Majorca, the tutor to Jaume III of Majorca, instructed confessors to urge their slave-owning penitents "that, out of reverence for God and for the benefit of their souls, as well as that of their slaves, they freely permit and support the baptism of slave children as well as any other [adult slaves] they might have."[24] Although in earlier centuries such initiatives might have been met with strong resistance by slave owners concerned with protecting their property rights, both André Vauchez and Benjamin Z. Kedar have traced how, from about the thirteenth century onward, canonists, clerics, and secular authorities worked out a new understanding concerning the impact baptism had on an enslaved person's legal status. Although initially slaves were generally thought to acquire freedom automatically upon receipt of baptism—on the basis of the teaching that among Christians "there is no longer slave or free...we are all one in Christ" [Galatians 3:28]—, with the expansion of missionizing in the thirteenth century

22. Graullera Sanz, La esclavitud, 148 (my translation).

23. Furs de València, ed. Colon and Garcia (Barcelona, 1974), II: 202. For an example of a physician suing the mistress of a male slave for nonpayment of a doctor's bill (some 125 reals), see ARV G 2279: M. 11: 44r–45v. The physician, Nicolau Thomas, claimed that he had visited the slave named Martí daily for a period of two months to treat, and ultimately cure, him of the plague (glanola).

24. "Quod ob reverentiam Dei et animarum suarum et captivorum suorum salutem, gratis permittant et sustineant batizari pueros captivos, et alios quos havent, absque praeiudicio iuris eorundem quod habent in captivis eisdem: cum iuri per ipsum babtismum et servituti ipsis dominis praeiudicium nullum fiat." Cited in Verlinden, L'esclavage, 458.

there developed a mounting concern that slaves in increasing numbers would embrace baptism as a tool for social promotion. Missionizing among slaves thus came to be regarded as a threat to the social order. To assuage the fears and protect the interests of slave owners, therefore, both ecclesiastical and secular officials introduced restrictions limiting the "liberating effects" of baptisms.[25] Thus, in the Furs de València (ca. 1238), we see a distinction being made between slaves converting with or without their masters' approval. Only those slaves who converted at their masters' prompting were entitled to an automatic manumission. Slaves accepting baptism without their masters' permission, in contrast, "would remain in that self-same servitude in which they had been prior to their conversion." In 1271 an amendment was added specifying that the act of baptism in and of itself could no longer effect a slave's manumission. For slaves to win their freedom, the act of baptism henceforth had to be accompanied by a second, separate ritual of manumission. The statute reads, "In whatever guise, whether baptized with or without their masters' permission, [a baptized slave] shall remain the captive or slave of his lord in perpetuity unless his lord explicitly frees them."[26]

With the concerns of slave owners' satisfied, by the fifteenth century the practice of baptizing slaves had become widespread and even—save for Muslim captives—customary among Valencian masters. Most slaves living in Christian households in fifteenth-century Valencia had been baptized. In the several hundred slave sales I collected dating from 1460 to 1480, at least 89 percent of the slaves exchanged between Christians either were explicitly described as "Christian" (xristià) or bore "Christian" names.

Indeed, the pendulum had swung so far in the other direction that Christian masters occasionally seem to have used baptism as a tool to strengthen their authority over a slave. In 1465 Francesc Ferrer reportedly believed that the most effective way to secure his claim over two kidnapped and unlawfully enslaved Mudejar girls was to have them baptized. His brother testified that, since the two girls were not catius de bona guerra, Francesc, "being in great fear that they [the two Mudejar sisters, subsequently called Johana

---

25. Vauchez observes how, in the Crusader states, where a Christian minority struggled to survive amid a majority Muslim population, granting Muslim slaves freedom upon their conversion to Christianity made sense on both a theological and tactical level. Thus, the twelfth-century Assises de la cour des bourgeois had stipulated that a slave who converted to Christianity was freed upon receipt of baptism. The power dynamics in late medieval Valencia, of course, were dramatically different. André Vauchez, "Note sure l'esclavage et le changement de religion en Terre Sainte au XIIIe siècle," in Figures de l'esclave au moyen age et dans le monde moderne (Paris: Editions L'Harmattan, 1996), 91–96. See also Benjamin Kedar, Crusade and Mission: European Approaches to Muslims (Princeton: Princeton University Press, 1984), 76, 152.

26. "E si sens volentat del senyor se batejarà, que romangue al senyor en aytal servitut con era e-l temps que no era batejat e pusque aquel vendre o en altra manera alienar a christians. En aquest fur enadex lo senyor rey que en qualque guisa, se bateig ab volentat o sens volentat del senyor, que tota hora romanga catiu e servu del senyor seu, si doncs lo senyor espressament no l'enfranquirà." Furs de València, ed. Colon and Garcia (Barcelona, 1990), V: 106.

and Ursola] would be taken away from him . . . made haste to make them Christians."
Francesc reportedly reasoned that the bailiff general would be less likely to return these
two girls to the custody of their Muslim parents if they had been baptized and converted
to Christianity.[27]

In baptizing their slaves, masters were assuming a responsibility that technically was
their biological fathers'. In fact, the Furs de València specified that if a Christian man slept
with someone else's slave woman and impregnated her, it was the man who had impregnated the slave, rather than the slave's owner, who was responsible for coordinating
the infant's baptism.[28] Testimony encountered in contemporary court records, however,
indicates an expectation that masters saw to it that all persons born in their household
were baptized and received a proper Christian upbringing. When a twenty-one-year-old
slave woman named Ysabel contended that her master's participation in her daughter's
baptism constituted an acknowledgement of paternity, the executors of his estate rejected
this argument out of hand:

> If said Alfonso de la Barreda had solicited godparents to participate in the baptism
> of Ysabel's children . . . he would have done so not because the child was his, but be-
> cause, whoever the child's father was, since Ysabel had given birth in his household,
> he had no choice but to see to it that the infant was baptized. Every master of a slave
> woman who gives birth in his household is obliged to make sure that the child is
> baptized.[29]

Nevertheless, no matter how common the practice was, this disparity between statutory
law and customary practice provoked a considerable amount of confusion. The numerous paternity suits that ensued, nonetheless, provide us with detailed accounts of slave
children's baptisms. Friends, neighbors, godparents, and midwives typically were called
upon to testify concerning their knowledge of the circumstances surrounding an infant's birth. Not infrequently they provided eyewitness testimony concerning the festivities connected with the child's baptism, ceremonies that they attended and sometimes
even participated in.

---

27. "Com aquelles no fossen de bona guerra . . . ab molta por que no les hi levassen car si algu hi
hagues hagut qu'en hagues dit al dit batle general de Valencia que les hi hagueren llevades. E per la dita
raho cuyta de fer les xristianes a les quals a la una posa nom Johana e a l'altra Ursola." ARV G 2318:
M. 12: 6r–12r.

28. Furs de València, ed. Colon and Garcia (Barcelona, 1990), V: 110.

29. "Que si lo dit en Alfonso de la Barreda ha convidat los compares per bateiar les criatures o criatura
que la dita Ysabel ha parit en sa casa ja per ço nos seguex que la criatura que aquella pari fos sua car fos
de quis vulla puix la dita Ysabel paria en casa sua forçadament havia fer bateiar com cascun senyor de
sclava que pareixca en casa sua la fa bateiar." ARV G 2395: M. 11: 37r–46v.

In 1498, a group of wives from the town of Alginet individually recalled how their neighbor, Luis Almenara, celebrated the baptism of the child born of his black slave woman named Leonor (aka Elionor). Beatriu, the wife of the laborer Jacme Fuster, for instance, noted how Luis had the child baptized "with as much festivity as was customarily done for legitimately born children. Many women and men attended; good and honorable godparents (compares) were appointed; he served sweets and he threw a great party."[30] While Yolant, the local midwife (the wife of the laborer Pere Martínez) described how she had carried the infant to the church for the baptism ceremony, Beatriu, the widow of another local laborer, remarked that Luis had had his black slave woman's daughter baptized "as if she were the daughter of his wife."[31]

Such statements indicate that it was not uncommon for masters to name godparents for their slave women's children. In the testimony he provided in support of a paternity suit filed in 1462, the weaver Guillem Guimera testified that after a slave woman named Maria gave birth to a baby girl named Yolant (aka Ursola),[32] her master, the nobleman Jofré d'Anyo, approached him to ask if he was willing to be the child's godfather (padri or compare). As was customary in the baptism of all infants—free or slave—three adult males and one female participated in the ceremony at the church of Torrent, none of whom was supposed to be a blood relative of the infant. In addition to the aforementioned weaver, two notaries were appointed as Yolant's (aka Ursola's) godparents.[33]

Typically, the midwife who delivered the infant was appointed as the child's godmother. The aforementioned Yolant, for example, testified that not only was she the midwife (madrina) who, at the time of the child's birth, "lifted the infant" from her mother's (Leonor's) womb (li leva la criatura), but she was also the child's godmother (padrina), who carried the baby girl to the parish church for the baptismal ceremony (la porta a la

30. "Lo dit en Luis Almenara feu batejar la dita sua filla ab tanta festa com se acostmava fer en les legitimes e anaren moltes dones e molts gents e ague bons compares e honrats e y dara confit e y feu bona festa segons als ledesmes acostuma fer." ARV G 2403: M. 2: 12r and ARV G 2405: M. 28: 46r–52r. We first met Leonor (aka Elionor) in chapter 3, p. 88.

31. "Veu ella testimoni que lo dit en Luis Almenara la feu batejar ab tanta festa que si fos filla de sa muller e convida als compares." ARV G 2403: M. 2: 12r and ARV G 2405: M. 28: 46r–52r.

32. The fourth child of this Russian slave woman named Maria, Yolant/Ursola claimed that she was the biological daughter of her mother's master, the nobleman Jofré d'Anyo. This slave woman named Maria had arrived in Valencia eight months' pregnant, accompanying her master Jofré and his wife Francesqua, who was also expecting. Maria subsequently gave birth to Ursola/Yolant on Jofré's rural property (alqueria) in Picanya (near Torrent). Though Maria claimed that her master, Jofré, was the child's father, others insisted that Ursola's father was a Sardinian slave or a Sardinian merchant. I will discuss the lawsuit Ursola/Yolant filed, demanding her freedom, in chapter 5, see pp. 177–78, 184–89.

33. ARV G 2304: M. 3: 45r and ARV G 2305: M. 11: 8r–23v; M. 20: 13r–21v and ARV G 2306: M. 25: 16r–17v; M. 26: 36r–37v; 42r–43v; M. 29: 19r–v.

sglesia a batejar).[34] When it came to selecting the child's godfathers (*padrins*), however, greater attention seems to have been paid to their social condition. The aforementioned slave woman Maria maintained that the high status of the men her master selected to be her daughter's godfathers constituted further evidence that the nobleman considered her daughter as his own. "Wishing that they [the child's *padrins*] were men of honor and notable just as he was," Jofré selected "the most honorable men who could be found at the time of Ursoleta's (aka Yolant's) birth": a weaver and two notaries.[35]

Admittedly these descriptions of elaborate baptismal festivities for slave children were designed to substantiate allegations that a slave woman had given birth to her master's child (and that the master, in turn, had acknowledged this child as his own). The advocate representing the interests of the slave woman Ysabel, for instance, affirmed that the baker Alfonso de la Barreda "retained *compares* and *comare* to baptize her and had her baptized," because he "knew and was completely certain that the baby girl to whom said Ysabel had given birth was his."[36] Hence, these celebrations were not necessarily representative of the experiences of most slave children. As the following set of examples will illustrate, however, baptism was, nevertheless, considered a crucial part of any slave's integration into a household—even for those acquired as adults through purchase and/ or conquest.

Only a small proportion of the more than one thousand "captives" entering the port of Valencia between 1494 and 1498 were already baptized at the time of their presentation before the bailiff general. About half of these baptized "captives" (some twenty-eight of fifty-five) were either long-time slaves who, in contrast with the more recently captured, had been born into slavery (four of the twenty-eight) or had been living in servitude in Castile,

---

34. In addition to being the "madrina e la anas a vesitar e apres li leva la criatura," Yolant described how "la porta a la esglesia a batejar e y feu tanta festa com si fos sa filla de sa muller que confits ydona e tot lo qu'es acostuma esta." ARV G 2405: M. 28: 46r–52r. Though she ultimately gave birth to only one child, Leonor, incidentally, appears to have been pregnant with twins. The midwife testified that they had opted to delay the first-born daughter's baptism a few days "in order to wait and see if the other child would arrive since a bump (*bony*) had remained in her stomach and they waited for her to give birth with great pleasure."

In 1492, Ursola Felip stated that she was both "the midwife who 'lifted' (*leva*) the infant when the said Ysabel gave birth" as well as the "*comare*" (godmother) who, along with the godfathers, "lifted" (*leva*) the infant from the baptismal font. ARV G 2395: M. 11: 37r–46v.

35. "Volgue que fossen homens de be de notables segons que ell era. E axi ampra lo discret en Berthomeu Queralt notari e en ... [blank] Guimera e en ... [blank] e que eren e son homens notables o de la condicio del dit en Anyo o los pus honrats homens que en lo temps de la nativitat de la dita Ursoleta se trobaren." ARV G 2304: M. 3: 45r; ARV G 2305: M. 11: 8r–23v; M. 20: 13r–21v; and ARV G 2306: M. 25: 16r–17v; M. 26: 36r–37v; 42r–43r; M. 29: 19r–v.

36. "Lo dit en Alfonso de la Barreda sabent e essent be cert que la dita filla que la dita Ysabel havia parit era de aquell hague los compares e comare per a bategar la e feu bategar aquella." ARV G 2395: M. 11: 37r–46v.

Portugal, or Italy.[37] A twelve-year-old baptized Muslim named Johanet, for instance, testified that, before his arrival in Valencia, he had been living as a slave in Genoa.[38] A baptized black slave named Johan, originally from "Galoff," testified that he had been living as a slave in Portugal for more than twenty years.[39]

The testimony of these baptized Christian "captives" coming from Italy, Castile, and Portugal frequently indicated that their baptisms had been part and parcel of their incorporation into their former master's household—taking place either simultaneously with or shortly after their entry. A thirty-year-old baptized Canary Islander woman named Magdalena ("formerly called Chabo") testified that, although she was originally from the island of Tenerife, before her arrival in Valencia she had lived in Seville as the slave of a Castilian merchant named Juan Sánchez. Magdalena explained that after being captured by the governor of Canaria, she had been brought to Seville, where "she was introduced into the household of said Juan Sánchez . . . who made her Christian."[40] Similarly, on 21 January 1494, Francisco, a twenty-year-old "native of Jaloff, land of the blacks," testified that after being captured by "the king of Jaloff," he had been sold to the Portuguese, who brought him to Lisbon where he was purchased by a friar named Johan "who made him a Christian."[41] Similarly, on 30 April 1495, a twenty-year-old black male named Johan recounted how he had been captured as a youth in the kingdom of "Jaloff" and then brought to the town of Tomar in the kingdom of Portugal, where he was purchased by Rui de Goiz, "in the power of whom he was raised and who baptized him."[42] Finally, Catalina, a thirty-year-old white female of Muslim descent, testified that shortly following

---

37. Though the remaining twenty-seven baptized captives were described as coming to Valencia directly from the Canary Islands or the west African coast, most had made intermediary stops in either Santa María del Puerto, Cadíz, or Jerez de la Frontera (if they were coming from the Canary Islands), or in the port of Lisbon (if they were coming from west Africa). See map 2.

38. Johanet testified that, although he did not know this for certain, he had been told that he was originally from Granada. After being captured during the fall of the Nasrid Sultanate, Johanet was brought to the Castilian port of Cadíz where he was purchased by a Genoese merchant. Johanet now accompanied this Genoese merchant who was relocating to Valencia. Indeed, this merchant swore that rather than bringing Johanet to Valencia for the purposes of resale, he intended to retain the slave in his personal service. ARV B 194: 260r–v.

39. Joan, nevertheless, had been sold and resold several times. After accompanying one of his Portuguese masters to Granada, Joan went on to serve masters living in Málaga and then Puçol before coming to Valencia. ARV B 194: 230v–231v.

40. Magdalena testified that she "fon portada a la casa del dit en Johan Sanchez lo qual dit Johan Sanchez la feu xristiana." ARV B 194: 379r–381r. Although Magdalena stated that she was a Christian, she did not swear an oath before giving her testimony—reportedly "because she is very boçal."

41. When asked if he was a Christian, Francisco replied affirmatively, adding that "en Lisbona lo feu crestia frare Johan del qual era catiu." ARV B 194: 391r–392r.

42. "Que l'an bategat en una terra que dihen Tomar del Realme de Portogal. . . . e hun home qui dihen Rui de Goiz en poder del qual s'es criat e lo bategat." ARV B 194: 226r–227r.

her capture during the conquest of Granada, she had been taken to Seville where, after
being enslaved (*feta cativa*), she was "made Christian" (*feta crestiana*).[43]

Equally prominent among captives who had been Christianized before their arrival in
Valencia were Canary Islanders who were baptized in what appear to have been mass ceremonies performed on their native soil.[44] According to the testimony of many of these Canary
Islanders, baptism was one of their very first experiences as slaves. In her testimony before the bailiff general on 6 March 1497, a thirteen-year-old girl named Cathalina, formerly
known as "Magarznay," affirmed that she was a Christian, that in Tenerife, after she was
captured, she was made a Christian by a bishop.[45] Likewise, when Francisco, a twelve-year-
old boy from Tenerife, was asked when and where he became a Christian, he replied, "over
there, in his homeland, after being captured by Christians."[46] Those Canary Islanders not
baptized "in their homeland" immediately after their capture typically seem to have been
baptized upon their arrival in Puerto de Santa María, Castile—a veritable clearinghouse for
Canary Islander captives. Thus, when the Valencian merchant Domingo Pere Andreu presented a group of Canary Islander captives before the bailiff general, he noted that all four of
them (between the ages of nine and eighteen) had been baptized in Puerto de Santa María.[47]

The black African captives, in contrast, generally were "not yet baptized" at the time
of their arrival in the port of Valencia.[48] It is likely, however, that most would have been
baptized by the time they entered their new owner's household. To take just one example,
while in her testimony before the bailiff general, a twenty-five-year-old Wolof woman
called herself "Gomba," in the contract of sale drawn up the very same day recording her
purchase by a local merchant, "Gomba" was referred to as "Maria." Although no explicit
mention was made here of her baptism, the name change indicates that Christianization
constituted an important first step toward this black African slave's incorporation into
her master's household.[49]

43. ARV B 194: 465r–466r.

44. For this reason (perhaps), some masters felt it necessary to rebaptize their slaves. In 1502, Martí,
a thirteen-year-old boy from Tenerife, testified that he had been baptized twice. The first time was immediately after his capture in the Canary Islands. The second baptism occurred in connection with his sale
to his first Christian master in Seville. ARV B 195: 97r–98r.

45. "Dix que es xristiana e que en Theneriff hun bisbe la feu xristiana apres que fonch presa." ARV B
194: 379r–381r.

46. "Fonch interrogat hon se feu xristia. E dix allà en la sua terra apres que fonch pres per xristians."
ARV B 194: 395r–396r.

47. Ysabel, an eighteen-year-old Canary Islander, the only one (of the four she was presented with)
with whom they were able to communicate, testified that she was "presta per xristians ab altres e fon
portada en Senta Maria del Puerto e alli la batejaren." ARV B 194: 477r–478r.

48. With the exception of the aforementioned thirteen black African captives who had been living
for a period of time in Castile and/or Portugal.

49. In the contract of sale she was described as "una negra de hedat de XXV anys poch mes o menys
olim appellada Gomba e ara Maria natural de Jaloff." ARV B 194: 194r–v.

The rate of baptism, nonetheless, was not uniform for all slaves. It varied, to a significant degree, according to the slave's ethnic and/or religious identity. Slaves of Canary Islander or west African origins were almost unilaterally baptized.[50] Slaves of "Saracen" origin, in contrast, often, though not always, appear to have persevered in their Muslim faith. Of the 141 Muslim captives sold under the bailiff general's supervision between 1479 and 1486, 128 were not baptized at the time of purchase. Although it would be difficult to trace the subsequent history of each one of these captives, it seems fairly likely that, given the extensive Muslim redemptionist activity during this period, a substantial number of them were ransomed by their coreligionists.

Moreover, in stark contrast with their black African and Canary Islander counterparts, whose baptisms seem almost to have been reflexive, baptism was hardly automatic or an obligatory part of the process of integrating a Muslim slave into a Christian household.[51] Out of the 228 slaves being purchased by Christian masters who were described in their contracts of sale as "baptized Christians" or who had "Christian" names, only about 16 percent (thirty-seven) were converts of explicitly Muslim origin (described as "de genere sarracenorum," "de genere agarenorum," or "de genere de Alarps"). In contrast, about 65 percent (seventy) of the 107 slaves described as being "of Saracen origin" bought or sold by Christian masters (or mistresses) retained their "Muslim" names.[52]

Jacques Heers has similarly observed that "in the regions of the Crown of Aragon, the majority of Moorish captives were not baptized and continued bearing their 'Arab' names from Africa or Andalucia, especially those tied to seigneurial lands in the Balearics or in the kingdom of Valencia." Attributing this low rate of baptism, "without a doubt," to a "refusal" and a "strong resistance" on the part of Muslim slaves, he reasons that, given the relative proximity of Muslim territories and the survival, in Christian lands, of powerful Muslim communities dating from before the Reconquest, Muslim slaves harbored a realistic expectation of regaining their freedom. "For these [Moorish] captives violently removed from their homelands, the dream of returning home remained alive, thanks to the [practices of] exchanging and ransoming captives or else taking flight and being reunited with friends and relatives."[53] Although there is certainly much truth to

50. Some black African slaves being introduced into the kingdom of Valencia during this time period, however, were Muslims at the time of entry.

51. Some Muslim captives, of course, were baptized. In 1433, a Majorcan merchant brought a white male Muslim, originally from One, to Valencia for the purposes of selling him. Although in his presentation before the bailiff general he was referred to as "Ali Benmahomat," in the contract of sale drawn up the following day he was referred to as "Anthony." ARV B 193: 85r–88r.

52. My research findings are consistent with the evidence (dating from a slightly later period) discussed in Mark Meyerson's article, "Slavery and Solidarity." In this article, Meyerson argued that since "foreign Muslim" captives could rely on the assistance of their free coreligionists to negotiate their redemption, they were much less likely to accept baptism and convert to Christianity. Meyerson, "Slavery and Solidarity," 304.

53. Heers, Esclavos, 94 (my translation).

this argument, it nevertheless seems to attribute to slaves an inflated degree of agency. It fails to take into consideration an equally important factor: a master's (or mistress's) relative interests in promoting their slave's Christianization. Although some nonbaptized Muslim slaves were purchased by Christians for their own personal use, many were subsequently redeemed, and, in fact, the majority of the buyers of nonbaptized Muslim slaves were their Muslim coreligionists. Of the seventy contracts of sale concerning slaves who were referred to by Muslim names, over half (at least forty-six) were "purchased" (i.e., ransomed) by a fellow Muslim. Since the redemption price was, in many cases, significantly higher than the initial purchase price, it seems likely that Christian masters purchasing Muslim captives were perhaps not as interested in baptizing them because they eventually intended to ransom them among their coreligionists. Thus, rather than attributing the substantially lower baptism rate among Muslim slaves solely to Muslim obstinacy, one ought also take into account the possibility that a master's greed occasionally might have outweighed his zeal to spread the truth of Christianity. Although black African slaves had comparatively dimmer prospects for returning to their homeland and such hopelessness perhaps made them more receptive to Christianity,[54] given the nature of the source materials available, the issue of desire, motives, and consent with respect to slave baptisms must be approached with a great deal of circumspection.

These accounts of Muslim slaves being baptized, of course, were written from a Christian perspective. Significantly, they present baptism as a privilege Christians granted cautiously—and selectively—only *after* the sincerity of the Muslim slave's convictions had been tested. Thus, although the aforementioned Francesch Ferrer reportedly had "made haste" to see to it that the two kidnapped Mudejar girls in his service were made Christians, the girls' advocate in this case took pains to emphasize that the rite was performed in the parish church of Santa Caterina only after the two girls—the sisters Johana and Ursola—"were of legitimate age and possessed discretion."[55] Although, as noted earlier, quick action on the part of Francesch Ferrer seems to have been necessary here to forestall any action by the bailiff general to return the children to their biological, Muslim parents, in 1466, more than a dozen years later, Johana and Ursola's advocate had a very different agenda in recounting the baptisms of these two Mudejar girls. His aim was to convince the court that Johana and Ursola were sincere Christians who deserved an immediate liberation. Stressing how these two Mudejar girls would not have been permitted

54. Noting how some of the black African captives entering the kingdom of Valencia were Muslims, Mark Meyerson has speculated that black African Muslims were perhaps more receptive to Christianity. Inasmuch as these black African Muslims had been slaves in Islamic territories, Meyerson has posited that this "discriminatory treatment at the hands of white Muslims in North Africa" possibly "dampened their enthusiasm for Islam." See Meyerson, "Slavery and Solidarity," 329–31.

55. "De continent que les dites moratelles foren de legittima edat e agueren discrecio feu bategar aquelles ab voluntat de elles mateixes e imposa nom a aquelles." ARV G 2318: M. 12: 6r–12r.

to receive the rite of baptism unless they could formally avow and intellectually compre-hend the Catholic faith, his description of Johana's and Ursola's baptisms stands in stark contrast to contemporary descriptions of the baptisms of Canary Islander slaves. Indeed, the majority (58 percent) of Canary Islander converts were children who did not speak the language. Thus, when Crown officials asked Caterina, a ten-year-old girl from the island of Tenerife, if she was a Christian, she reportedly replied, "I do not understand."[56] Similarly, when Crown officials asked Perico, a seven-year-old boy from Tenerife, if he was Christian, he seemed confused, reportedly responding, "not yet."[57]

The court documents describing the baptism of Fatima, the daughter of a free Mudejar vassal of Novelda, in contrast, laid emphasis on the strength and sincerity of her Chris-tian convictions. In 1475, Fatima was put in the service of the Christian lord of Orihuela, pledged in surety for the repayment of her father's debts. When the girl's father, Yuçeff Ajavent, and his wife returned to Orihuela to redeem Fatima from captivity, the daughter, reportedly, refused to accompany them:

> Seeing that her father was leading her back to the place of Novelda to live among Mus-lims, moved or called by the Holy Spirit, wishing to be a Christian, to come to the true and most holy faith of Christianity, which is the way and path to Paradise and the door-way to heaven, Fatima broke away from her father's grasp, the said Yuçeff Ajavent. Run-ning into the collegiate church of Santa María of Orihuela, with great cries of 'Baptize me!' she demanded baptism and stated her desire to convert to Christianity.[58]

Despite Fatima's sense of urgency, she was not granted an immediate baptism. Even after her parents had been sent away, empty-handed, the canons of this church reportedly felt it prudent to carefully examine this young woman's motives and intentions. It was only four or five days later,[59] with Fatima not having changed her opinion, that she was "per-mitted" to receive the holy sacrament and was baptized Johana."[60]

56. "Fonch interrogada si es crestiana e dix que no entens." ARV B 194: 128r–130r.

57. "Fonch interrogat si era xristian. E dix que no encara." ARV B 194: 286r–287r.

58. "Vehent que lo dit son pare la s'en portava o menava al dit loch de Novelda entre moros moguda o vocada per lo sant sperit volent esser crestiana e venir a la vera e sanctissima fe xristiana la qual es via e carrera de paradis e porta del cel fogint de les mans del dit Yucef Ajavent pare seu s'en entra corrent dins la esglesia cridan ab gran crits batisme demanant que volia esser xristiana." ARV G 2392: M. 4: 27v and ARV G 2393: M. 11: 14r–26r.

59. According to the *Code de Tortosa*, if a Muslim slave took refuge in a church and declared his wish to be a Christian, he had to remain in the church for at least three days to prove his conviction before he could receive baptism. Any time thereafter, however, no one could prevent him from receiving baptism. Once baptized, of course, the slave would be returned to his master and his master was enjoined not to treat the baptized slave any worse than he had treated him before. Cited in Verlinden, *L'esclavage*, 292.

60. One of Johana/Fatima's godfathers recalled how, following her parents' departure, "Fatima resta en la esglesia e los canonges delli delliberaren de acomanar la en casa del governador... e alli stech per

Obviously, one ought not accept these conversion narratives at face value. Such descriptions of young Muslim girls defying their Muslim fathers and beseeching male Christian clerics to grant them the gift of baptism belie a reality in which Muslim girls were doubly subjugated: subject both to the authority of their Muslim fathers and Christian overlords. Beneath their high-flown rhetoric, these accounts were only thinly veiled efforts of Christian men to secure and exercise control over Mudejar women. Through the "holy rite of baptism," Christian lords might effectively trump the claims of Muslim parents to custody over their own children. Indeed, what prompted the lord of Orihuela to recount Fatima's/Johana's dramatic conversion was, in fact, a desire to regain custody of his former "captive" or pledge. Through the intervention of an unnamed Christian official, Yuçeff apparently had managed to regain custody of his daughter. Rather than reembracing his daughter into the family, however, Yuçeff reportedly had sold his daughter to another Christian master. In emphasizing the role he played in Fatima's/Johana's conversion, the lord of Orihuela aimed to outstrip the rival claims of both Fatima's father and her new master.

What motivated masters to baptize their slaves? Two countervailing forces conditioned relations between masters and their slaves: the desire to assimilate and the desire to differentiate. As the above examples indicate, the intensity of the owner's efforts to "Christianize" his or her slave (and the enslaved person's willingness to be assimilated) varied significantly according to the age, ethnic identity, gender, and/or parentage of the slave. Irrespective of a convert's age, gender, or ethnic identity (paternity was a separate issue), however, baptism conferred upon slaves the benefit only of "spiritual" equality before God. It did not bring about any change in their legal status. Although some might (for this reason) discount the significance of a slave's conversion, Jacques Heers has insisted that even though in the eyes of their authorities they remained slaves, by joining "the community of the faithful" they "perhaps felt less foreign, better recognized, and even comforted by the solidarity instilled by prayer and the spiritual assistance of priests. . . . They practiced the same religion as their masters and often even in the same churches. These were hardly insignificant things."[61]

Slaves did attend Mass and hear the divine offices in the company of their masters in fifteenth-century Valencia. In 1473, for instance, witnesses testified that they knew that a black slave named Jaume was Christian because they had seen him "perform Christian acts such as kneeling and praying."[62] In 1471, a surgeon testified that he saw how

---

quatre o cinch jorns per veure si's remouria de sa oppinio. E vehent que aquella stava ferma hun dia la portaren a la seu e bategaren la." ARV G 2392: M. 4: 27v and ARV G 2393: M. 11: 14r–26r.

61. Heers, *Esclavos*, 99 (my translation).

62. One merchant testified that he considered Jaume "per cristia e al qual havia vist fer actes de cristia ço es a genollar se e fer horacio e que tal lo ha tengut e tenia ell dit testimoni e que james havia sabut lo contrari." ARV JCiv 926: M. 15: 21r–v.

the white slave named Pedro de Mena regularly "went to hear Mass and the divine offices with his master, Johan Ferrandiz." Other witnesses also attested that they had seen the white slave, always in the company of his master, attend religious services in churches scattered all over the city: at the parish church of Sant Joan del Mercat, the church of the Innocents, the Mercedarian and Franciscan convents, as well as many other churches in Valencia. Since Mass was a very public event, masters desirous of displaying their status naturally would have wanted their slaves to accompany them. Any conclusions regarding the religious beliefs or piety of slaves based on this type of evidence, however, would be extremely tenuous. A closer reading of this evidence, in fact, offers an important corrective. The reputedly "pious" and "sincere Christian" slave Pedro de Mena, for example, subsequently took flight, abandoning his Catholic faith seemingly as quickly as he had abandoned his master's household. Though Pedro had been baptized, attended the divine offices, and met regularly with a confessor (the friar Joan Pugades, a lecturer in theology and conventual of the Franciscan convent of Valencia),[63] as soon as he escaped his master's custody, he renounced Christianity in favor of his native Islam. When, several months later, the fugitive was discovered living in the town of Lorca (Castile), he was calling himself Ali.

Naming

At the time of their baptism, slaves were given a Christian name. Along with baptism, the assumption of this new, Christian name symbolized their induction into the broader Christian commonwealth. Reflective of a desire to assimilate them into the Christian community, four of the most common names given to slave women were figures of popular religious devotion: Maria (for the Virgin Mary), Magdalena (for Mary Magdalene), Caterina (for St. Catherine of Alexandria), and Lucia (for St. Lucia of Syracuse).

Jacques Heers has argued, however, that the names assigned to slaves at the time of their baptism reveal "a deliberate will to mark or indicate the servile condition." Based on a comparative analysis of the names assigned to baptized slave women with those given to freeborn women across the Christian Mediterranean, Heers found that while there was some evidence of overlap (e.g., with the name Caterina), the names most

---

63. A local barber testified that "sab que lo dit Pedro de Mena era xristia. E aço per quant ell testimoni vehia anar ab lo dit en Johan Ferrandiz amo de aquell a hoir missa e los officis divinals axi en les sglesies de sent Johan del Mercat de la present ciutat de Valencia com als Ignocents e en altres sglesies de la dita ciutat." Similarly, a blanket-maker testified that he saw Pedro de Mena (aka Ali) go with his master to attend Mass, "axi a sent Johan del Mercat com al monestir de la Merce e en altres parts e esglesies hon lo dit en Johan Ferrandiz amo de aquell anava." Finally, the friar Johan Pugades, "lector en sachra theologia e conventual del monestir de frares menors de la ciutat de Valencia," testified that "lo dit Pedro se confessa de ell." ARV JCiv 923: M. 16: 31r–33v. For more on Pedro de Mena's subsequent flight to Lorca, Castile, where he reputedly reembraced Islam, see chapter 6, p. 224.

frequently assigned to slave women, regardless of ethnic origin, were Lucia, Marta, and Margarita. These were not among the names characteristically assigned to the daughters of merchants and nobles. Inasmuch as masters and mistresses from Marseilles to Genoa displayed "the same tastes and preferences," baptismal naming patterns were reflective, in Heers's view, of a desire "to impose on all of them the same label" and should be re-garded as "a type of segregation."[64]

Though evidence culled from Valencian notarial archives reveals similar "tastes and preferences" in slave names, it is far from clear whether this reflected "a deliberate will to mark or indicate the servile condition." Out of the 215 baptized slave or freed women whose names were noted in notarial records dating from 1458 to 1480, 60 percent bore one of six names: Caterina, Johana, Lucia, Margarita, Maria, and Magdalena. Indeed, about one out of every five were called Caterina. Similar to the pattern Heers observed in Genoa and Marseilles, these names seem to have been given irrespective of a slave's eth-nic origin or previous religious identity. Slave women named Caterina included Tartars, Russians, baptized Muslims, as well as black and dark-skinned slave women described as "de Mont de Barques," "de Guinea," "de Jalof," and "de Borno." The remaining 40 percent of the slave women encountered, however, were assigned names coming from a signifi-cantly broader pool. I came across at least thirty-eight different variants, none of which seems to have been any more popular than the other.

Reviewing the names assigned to baptized male slaves, we also see that certain names enjoyed special popularity. Sixty percent of the 193 baptized male slaves named in notarial records dating between 1458 and 1480 were given one of five names: Joan, Martí, Pere, Jordi, or Antoni. More than one out of every three were called Joan. As had been the case with baptized slave women, there seems to be no correlation between the name given and a slave's ethnic origin or prior religious affiliation. Male slaves called Joan included black Africans ("de Guinea," "de Volos," and "de terra de Ahan"), "dark-skinned people" ("de terra de Alarps" and "de Montdebarques"), as well as "whites," both baptized Russians and Tar-tars and baptized Muslims ("de genere agarenorum," "de genere sarracenorum," and "de linatge de moros").

Though the naming patterns among the baptized slave population in fifteenth-century Valencia seems to conform with that encountered by Heers in Genoa and Marseilles (i.e., the preponderance of slave women named Caterina, Lucia, and Margarita), the names assigned to baptized slaves in Valencia were not noticeably distinct from those given to freeborn Christians. In fact, it was not uncommon for masters and mistresses to make their slaves their namesakes. Thus, both a farmer from Chilvella and his black male slave answered to the name of Pere Guillem[65] and a slave belonging to Joan Navarro was also

---

64. Heers, Esclaves, 97–98 (my translation).
65. ARV P 810 (nonpaginated): 3 March 1478. I discussed Pere Guillem earlier, in chapter 3.

called Joan Navarro.[66] Although a much broader sample would be needed to reach a definitive conclusion, judging from the names of slave mistresses encountered in notarial records dating between 1460 and 1480, slave women frequently shared the same names as their mistresses or their masters' and mistresses' daughters. The six most common names among these 168 slave mistresses were Ysabel, Johana, Beatriu, Elionor, Caterina, and Yolans. As can be noted above, all six of these names could be found among members of the slave population. Indeed, a mistress reportedly changed her slave's name from Yolant to Ursola because her daughter was also called Yolant and she wanted to prevent any further confusion and miscommunication. Beatriu Valleriola thus testified that she had changed the slave's name from Yolant to Ursola, since "when she called for one, the other would respond."[67]

We see in these last few examples that while slaves frequently shared the same names as their mistresses and other free persons, unlike free persons, their names could be changed at their master's or mistress's whim, to suit their own personal needs. In 1459, a noblewoman decided to rename her slave woman Ysabel because "the name of Eulalia was strange to her." Thus, she explained, she "imposed upon her" the name Ysabel "because it was more familiar to her."[68]

Education

In addition to supervising their slaves' spiritual upbringing, masters and mistresses also assumed the "paternal" responsibility of supervising their education. At the most basic level, this meant seeing to it that their slaves learned the local (vernacular) language. Although all slaves had to learn *català* in order to communicate with their owners and the broader community, those born in Valencia were much more likely to become fluent. In a notice reporting the flight of a twenty-year-old Tartar slave named Johan in 1400, Valencia's city councilmen (*jurats*) took pains to stress how this Tartar fugitive, since he had been born and reared in Valencia, spoke *català* like a native. By implication, these

66. ARV JCiv 929: M. 16: 35r–v.

67. "E per com ella dita responent tenia una filla que havia nom Yolant e com cridava lo una, responia l'altra. E feu fe la confermat la dita Yolant e muda li nom Ursola." ARV G 2304: M. 3: 45r; ARV G 2305: M. 11: 8r–23v; M. 20: 13r–21v and ARV G 2306: M. 25: 16r–17r; M. 26: 36r–37v; 42r–43v; M. 29: 19r–v. Yolant/Ursola was the biological daughter of the aforementioned slave woman named Maria, owned by the nobleman Jofré d'Anyo.

68. "Vehent que lo nom de Eulalia li era strany . . . li imposa lo nom de Ysabel per que li era molt notori." Ysabel/Eulalia herself, however, portrayed her mistress's motives in much more sinister terms. The twenty-three-year-old contended that she did so "in order to defraud her of her liberty." Born in Majorca, Ysabel/Eulalia allegedly was packed off to Valencia because everyone in Majorca knew that she was the daughter of a free man and, thus, could not be sold into slavery. As an added insurance measure, her mistress changed her name to Ysabel "so that she would not be recognized" ("per ço que no pogues esser coneguda"). ARV G 2295: M. 12: 40r; M. 18: 16r–17v and ARV G 2296: M. 21: 39r–41r.

councilmen suggest here that most Tartar slaves, particularly those who arrived in Valencia as adults, were not fluent.[69]

Masters and mistresses, moreover, occasionally supervised their slaves' vocational training. If they were male, this might mean that they were apprenticed with artisans so that they could learn a trade. If they were female, they could be put into service in another household to learn more specialized "feminine" skills such as sewing or dressmaking. Thus we already saw how the aforementioned Ventura was, at the age of six, put into service in another household so that she might learn how "to tailor, sew, and work."[70] Most atypical was the mistress who taught her dark-skinned slave woman her trade of midwifery.[71] As noted in the last chapter, however, the vast majority of slaves seem to have worked as unskilled laborers. Indeed, those masters who did place their slaves in contracts of apprenticeships with artisans often seem to have done so in preparation for their liberation. They wanted to see to it that their slaves acquired marketable skills so that, upon winning their freedom, they could support themselves and lead an independent existence. We noted in the previous chapter, for example, how in Caterina de la Nana's last will and testament, she directed that her slave, Johanot Agosti, not only be freed, effective immediately upon her death, but that he also be given forty lliures to complete his apprenticeship with a wool comber (per acaba'll de son ofici).[72] The attorney Pere Valcanell similarly instructed his executors to set aside ten lliures for the education of his black slave Johan in the trade of hat making (en subvencio de son offici).[73] Pere had specified, however, that this grant of freedom and money to learn a trade was contingent upon Johan making a conscious decision to improve his conduct and live honorably (si aquell volra mirar a be... viure com a bon home). Two months later, in fact, Pere would revoke this bequest, proclaiming his efforts to "educate" this slave a failure. Noting how he made the bequest to Johan "not because he deserved it, for he has always been disobedient and ungrateful toward me, but... in the hope that it would encourage him to mend his ways," Pere complained that "as far as he could tell," Johan "has only behaved worse and has become even more disobedient."[74]

69. "Sia fuyt pochs dies ha un catiu de linyatge de tartres, emperò batejat e apellat Johan, de edat de .XX. anys poch més o menys, e paladí en son parlar català, com de poquea a ença se sia nodrit ací." See document #110 in Agustín Rubio Vela, ed., Epistolari de la València Medieval (Valencia: Institut de Filologia Valenciana, 1985), 285.

70. "Per aprendre de tallar cosir e obrar." JCiv 916: M. 18: 17r–28v; 45r–v.

71. ARV G 2308: M. 4: 44r and ARV G 2309: M. 15: 22r–34v.

72. ARV P 9956 (nonpaginated): 19 September 1489.

73. ARV P 10251 (nonpaginated): 29 August 1501.

74. "Les quals coses yo feya no per que aquell ho mereixques com tostemps me sia estat desobedient e ingrat. E per yo fer li tal gracia crehent aquell se esmenaria, es tornat pijor y pus mal per los effects que en aquell he vist." ARV P 10251 (nonpaginated): 31 October 1501.

Marriage

Also suggestive that masters and mistresses adopted slaves as members of their extended family was their assumption of the role traditionally ascribed to the bride's father: selecting or approving their former slave women's marriage partners. Thus, on 17 April 1476, a forty-six-year-old Russian woman named Anna, the former slave of the merchant Galceran Martí, contracted marriage with the baker Joan Verdecho, also a former slave.[75] In the place where the consent of the bride's father customarily would be noted, here we find Luis Martí, the son of Galceran Martí, Anna's former master (now deceased), "praising, approving, and agreeing to these arrangements, which were made not only with his consent and approval, but also in his presence." Affirming that she acted "with the express will and consent" of her "legitimate administrator" (her former master's son and heir), Anna "gave herself" in marriage. In addition, at the very base of this document we see Luis's "signature" alongside hers and her fiancé's, endorsing the transfer of twenty lliures in dowry.[76]

Masters and mistresses also took steps to ensure that their former slave women were married off "honorably" by leaving their slave women sums of money explicitly earmarked to go toward their dowries in their last wills and testaments. These monetary bequests were often given in tandem with grants of freedom. In the last will and testament of Beatrix, the wife of Pere Boïl, the lord of Manises, for example, this noblewoman left fifty-five lliures to her black slave girl, Blanquina, now just twelve years in age, "in contemplation of her marriage."[77] The sums granted ranged widely, from as little as ten lliures[78] to as much as sixty lliures, depending on the socioeconomic status of the legator, the intimacy of the relationship between legator and legatee, and the social status of the prospective groom. In the last will and testament of Brianda Pere Carroça de Mur, the wife of the viceroy of Cerdagne, she specified that, subsequent to her death, her two female slaves, Luisa and Lorençeta, were to be given (in addition to their freedom) fifteen and twenty

75. I discussed the freedman Joan Verdecho's skills as a baker earlier, in chapter 3, see p. 110.

76. "Anna olim serva honorable Galcerandi Marti mercatoris civitatis Valencie civis nunc vero libera et franqua ex certa sciencia et consulte de expressis voluntate et consensu honorable Lodovici Marti mercatoris Valentinae eiusdem Galcerandi fratris et procuratoris collocando me ipsam in matrimonium vobiscum Johanne Verdecho flaquerio olim servo honorable Pasquasi Verdecho flaquerii dicte civitatis vicini nunc vero libertino et civitatis predicte vicino." Similarly, the document records how "Lodovicus Marti nomine meo proprio et tanquam procurator dicti Galcerandi Marti fratris mei instrumenta nubcialia huiusmodi tanquam de meis voluntate et consensu et in mei presencia facta laudo et aprobo atque eisdem consencio." Finally, at the base of the agreement, we find, "Signum mei Anne Marti. Signum mei Johannis Verdecho. Signum mei Lodovici Marti predictorum qui predicta omnia et singula singulis referendo laudamus concedimus et firmamus." APPV 21593 (nonpaginated): 17 April 1476.

77. "Les quals li sien donades en contemplacio de matrimoni." ARV P 1915 (nonpaginated): 7 September 1477.

78. APPV 09653 (nonpaginated): 11 October 1472.

lliures, respectively, "for a husband" (per a marit).[79] Alternatively, in the last will and testament of the deacon and cathedral canon Pere de Vilarasa, Pere bequeathed to his former slave woman Honesta the substantial sum of sixty lliures, all of which was to go toward her dowry. We know that Honesta subsequently collected this legacy, for in August 1478, some time subsequent to this cathedral canon's death, Pere's executors, in accordance with Pere's last wishes, transferred said sixty lliures to Honesta's betrothed, a freed black named Mathias Cardona, in dowry. Mathias, for his part, was the former slave of the attorney Mathias Cardona (now deceased), his namesake.[80]

Masters and mistresses, however, did not seem to play a role in the marriages of their former male slaves. Although the aforementioned groom, Joan Verdecho, too, was a former slave, he—in contrast with Anna, his betrothed—did not seem to have needed the approval of his former master, the baker Pasqual Verdecho. Neither Pasqual's consent nor his participation in the marriage negotiations was recorded anywhere in the document. Similarly, we do not see masters and mistresses leaving bequests to help their male slaves get married—that is, to help pay the traditional sum the groom offered to the bride (the creix or augmentum sive donacionem propter nubcias, originally given in recognition of her virginity), a sum that customarily was roughly equivalent to about half the value of the bride's dowry.[81]

In the last will and testament of Miquel Spital, a priest beneficed in the diocese of Valencia, we once again see a master taking charge of the arrangement of his slave girl's marriage. Miquel instructed his executors that, subsequent to his death, they should see to it that his slave girl Anna was placed in a contract of service "with an honorable person" for however long and for whatever salary they saw fit. He also empowered his executors to collect any salary Anna earned for the purposes of marrying her off "to the person that they wished and selected." Though Anna, at the time of her marriage, would be granted her freedom as well as a dowry, it is important to note that Anna's liberation was contingent upon her marrying a spouse of his executors' choosing. Until, or rather, unless Anna found a "suitable" husband, she would remain a slave "subject to every order and directive issued by his heir."[82] Similarly, in the last will and testament of Elvira de

79. APPV 22731 (nonpaginated): 16 October 1467.

80. ARV P 2067 (nonpaginated): 30 August 1478.

81. The promise made by Didacus de Torres, the bailiff general of the kingdom of Valencia, to give his freedman Johannes de Castilla, an eighteen-year-old black male, twenty lliures at the time of his marriage seems to have been exceptional. ARV P 10440 (nonpaginated): 22 March 1491. For a recent discussion of the customs and laws regulating marriage in Valencia at this time, see Dolores Guillot Aliaga, El regimen económico del matrimonio en la Valencia foral (Valencia: Biblioteca Valenciana, 2002), esp. 50–65, 73–135, and 179–93.

82. Miquel granted his executors the "facultat e poder de pendre la dita Anna e aquella posar e affermar a soldada ab alguna bona persona a tant temps com aquells volran e prenguen e reben la soldada que aquella guanyara e tenint ab que la puixen casar de la dita soldada aquells dits mon hereu e mossen Johan Huguart casen e donen marit a la dita Anna ab aquella persona que ells volran e eligiran e en lo dit

Ribelles, the wife of the lord of Alcudia, she made her gift of freedom and fifteen lliures in dowry to her black slave girl named Margarida (the daughter of another black slave woman of hers named Caterina), contingent upon her marrying a husband handpicked for her by Elvira's daughter, Beatric. Elvira specified that Margarida would be freed and could collect the aforementioned sum earmarked for her dowry only "*ab marit,*" when Beatric "gave her [Margarida] a husband."[83]

Granting their consent, and, occasionally, as we have just seen, even choosing their slave's spouse, masters and mistresses also joined in the celebration of their former slaves' marriages. Thus, in 1459 the marriage of the freed persons Magdalena and Jordi Daries was contracted "in the presence and with the consent and permission" of their former mistress, Ysabel, the widow of Joan Daries, an espadrille maker.[84] In some instances, the ceremonies took place in their former master's and mistress's households. Sometime in the 1430s, the neighbors of the widow Ysabel Puig attended the wedding of her former slaves Luisa and Marti Bossa, both of whom had been freed in her husband's last will and testament. The priest who officiated at the ceremony, Marti Dalfambra, later confirmed that he had married Luisa and Marti, not only "with the consent of the aforementioned honorable Ysabel, the widow of the honorable Pere Puig," but also "in the household of the said honorable Ysabel Puig," which was located near Denia.[85] Indeed, one of Ysabel's next-door neighbors (who does not seem to have been invited to the festivities) recalled how "while standing in his doorway, he saw a great crowd of people, including the vicar Marti Dalfambra. They were following a small cart departing from the household of Ysabel Puig, the widow of Pere Puig." When he asked a bystander what all the commotion was about and who was riding in the cart, the man had replied, "Lucia, of the en Puig household, who wishes to get married, the vicar who will marry them, and Marti."[86] The priest,

---

cas la dita Anna sia franca e liberta e no en altra manera ans la dita Anna fins sia casada haia a estar a tota ordinacio e manament de la herena mia e casar se ab voluntat de aquella segons dit ha e fent lo contrari sia e reste sclava e cativa de la dita mia herena." APPV 20123 (nonpaginated): 16 September 1487.

83. APPV 18557 (nonpaginated): 15 December 1477.

84. See the contract of *fraternitatem et germaniam* (a type of marriage contract in which spouses pooled their resources, holding them jointly and in common) between Magdalena and the espadrille maker Jordi Daries "servi qui eratus Johannis Daries tapinerii civitatis Valencie de consen presencia et voluntate dicti Johannis Daries et Ysabelis uxoris eius contemplacione matrimoni deo dicte inter nos fiendi." ARV P 436 (nonpaginated): 3 July 1459.

85. This priest testified that he "los sposa abduy los dits Marti e Lucia ... de voluntat de la dita honorable Ysabel muller del dit honorable en Pere Puig quondam feren e fermaren lo dit lur matrimoni. Interrogat de loch e dix que en la vila de Denia en casa de la dita honorable na Ysabel Puig." ARV G 2290: M. 21: 34r.

86. Johan Canemac testified that "stant a la sua porta veu exir de casa de la honorable na Ysabel ... com seguen tots en hun carruc gran gent e mossen Marti Dalfambra vicari de Denia. E ell dit testimoni que era e digueren Lucia d'en Puig quis vol marir e lo vicari als sposats aquells e a Marti." ARV G 2290: M. 21: 36r.

moreover, noted that not only had Ysabel, their former mistress, hosted and participated in this wedding but, after the ceremony, she had publicly expressed her great affection for the couple. After she congratulated the newlyweds, Ysabel reportedly told them "you can either remain in my household or go elsewhere. Either way, I would be happy. Do what you wish with my blessing."[87]

The affection that masters and mistresses reportedly had for their slaves, however, could prove disappointingly fleeting. Marti Bossa would later protest that a short time after she had hosted their wedding (after his bride, Lucia, had fallen ill and died), Ysabel "threw him out of her household." "Seeing that he was old and no longer of any use," she allegedly told him "that he must leave, that she no longer wanted him in her household, that he was free and that he would have to look after himself."[88] And now, Marti protested, after years of scrounging for work and sustenance in the towns of Denia and Ruzafa, Ysabel, to add insult to injury, was suddenly denying that Marti had ever been freed. Since Ysabel, it seems, had fallen on some hard economic times, she was threatening Marti with reenslavement in a desperate effort to extract some meager profit from him.[89]

Thus, although one could present a master's or mistress's participation in a former slave's marriage as evidence of their enduring "affection," one ought not to assume that this was their primary motive or that such a display of "affection" was welcomed by their former slaves. Rather, their participation likely served to underscore the enduring power and influence that they wished to exercise over their former slaves' lives. A slave woman's liberation, as we have seen, was often made contingent upon her contracting marriage with a groom approved of by her former master or mistress. When a silk weaver named Joan Despuig promised Maria, his Circassian slave woman, her freedom, he specified that until a satisfactory suitor was found, she would remain under his power and dominion, obliged to continue providing service to him without receiving any compensation in return.[90] Indeed, a slave woman named Soffia would protest that her master's so-called paternal concern that she find a "good" husband was nothing but a pretense to keep her in servitude. In 1458, Soffia appeared before the court of the governor complaining that

87. "La dita na Guisabel dix al dit Marti si voleu star en casa mia yo so contenta e si voleu star fora casa axi mateix fes lo qu'es placia de tot ço contenta." ARV G 2289: M. 18: 42r.

88. "Com lo dit Marci fos vell e no goyas res…la dita na Guissabell lança aquell de casa sua dient aquell que se anas de casa sua que no'l volia tenir en casa que franch era e qu'es donas recapte." ARV G 2289: M. 18: 42r.

89. For a transcript of the entire trial, see ARV G 2289: M. 18: 42r–46v; M. 20: 28r–v and ARV G 2290: M. 21: 34r–38v. I discuss this case further in chapter 7.

90. "Volo te dictam Mariam presentem franquam liberam et alforram omni ora et quando fueris matrimonio collocata quod matrimonium facere tenearis de meis expressis licencia consensu e voluntate…imposicione itacumque interim id est donech fueris matrimonio collocata ut superdixi sis et remaneas in dominio potestate et servicio meis absque aliquo salario." ARV P 10310 (nonpaginated): 5 August 1471.

her liberation was being delayed unduly because her master was being unreasonable; he was rejecting each and every one of her suitors. Although she technically was already "freed" as a consequence of having given birth to her master's child, Soffia had consented to being placed in a contract of service so that she could earn enough money to put together a good dowry. Soffia acknowledged that her master, at least initially, might have had good intentions. Fearing that if he freed her right away, she would be too poor to find a husband and end up prostituting her body, he placed her in a contract of service. Later on, however, Soffia had protested that she had earned enough money "to get a husband and be good." Soffia's master, however, continued to "search out ways to postpone [her emancipation]." He did so, Soffia contended, by deliberately finding fault with every one of her prospective partners. Though friends and other "notable persons" had intervened on Soffia's behalf, her master steadfastly refused to hand over Soffia's dowry, insisting that he would not do so until he was presented with "a good, rich, and young laborer so that she would not have to live in misery or prostitute herself."[91]

The intervention of masters and mistresses in their former slaves' marriages, then, reinforced their "paternalistic" self-image. Soffia's master, after all, protested that he was acting in Soffia's best interests. Yet one more example of how slaves were presented as members of their extended family, masters and mistresses arranged their slaves' marriages—just as they had provided them with food, clothing, and shelter, coordinated their baptisms, and/or provided them with an education. In the perspective of slave women like Soffia, however, such "paternal" oversight regarding their choice of marriage partners was but one more tool masters and mistresses wielded to extend, indefinitely, their subjugation.

Slaves as Parents and Patrons

In his study of households in fifteenth- and sixteenth-century Venice, Dennis Romano noted that the extraordinary "mix of generations within households" meant that familial relations between masters and slaves could take a variety of different forms.[92] Although the conventional image was that slaves fit into their masters' households like children, slaves also, on occasion, assumed positions of authority over their masters and mistresses. There is ample evidence, for instance, that enslaved women breast-fed their

91. Soffia contended that "foren parlats alguns matrimonis a la dita Sofia e venint al cloure no vingue be al dit mossen Johan nengun matremoni dient al hu que era pobre e cercant algunes dilacions." When "algunes notables persones amichs del dit mossen Johan de Bonastres" intervened on Soffia's behalf, Johan replied "que ell be veia content que la dita Soffia prengues marit pero volia que fos algun bon laurador rich e jove per que ella no vixques ab miseria e que agues anar per mal cap." ARV G 2291: M. 4: 9v and ARV G 2293: M. 21: 30r–31v.

92. Dennis Romano, Housecraft and Statecraft, 202–3.

master's children.[93] In 1472, a slave woman named Juliana filed a demand for liberty based on a promise that her master and milk-son, Miquel de Natera (now a butcher), allegedly had made her in gratitude for having breast-fed him from infancy. Such relationships, of course, were not without their tensions. If we accept Juliana's story at face value, Miquel was an especially manipulative and ungrateful "child." After drawing up a contract in which he promised to free her within the next two years, Miquel attempted to trick Juliana into giving the contract back to him, disingenuously promising that he would immediately issue her a new one granting her freedom after only one year of service. When she refused to comply with this request, Miquel broke into the coffer where she kept all her possessions, purportedly with the intention of finding and then destroying the document.[94]

Male as well as female slaves occasionally assumed the roles of nursemaids. In 1468, for example, a black slave named Joan de Loric demanded his liberty, citing his mistress's promise that on the occasion of her daughter's nuptials she would free Joan in gratitude for having "raised their children from a young age." A notary named Ausias Monfort confirmed that Joan's master and mistress loved him "very much." They loved him not only because "they [his master and mistress] had raised him [Joan] from a young age," but also because he, in turn, "had raised their children."[95] Though Joan, subsequently, ran away and, at the time of his master's death, was living as a free man in the kingdom of Castile, he reputedly, upon learning of his death, came back to Valencia, jeopardizing his security and sacrificing his freedom "out of love for [his master's and mistress'] children." One witness, impressed by the selflessness of Joan's act, recounted how he had urged Joan's mistress to free him, pleading with her, "By my faith, my lady, Joanet has shown you great kindness. . . . Out of love for his [master's] children and for you he has returned from Castile, coming back into your power and, once again, providing you good company."[96]

Romano has also noted that the homilies of late medieval and early modern preachers—"that the poor were closer to God than the rich"—appear to have inspired other types

93. For a discussion of the use of slave women as wet nurses in thirteenth-century Perpignan, see Rebecca Lynn Winer, *Women, Wealth, and Community in Perpignan, c. 1250–1300: Christians, Jews, and Enslaved Muslims in a Medieval Mediterranean Town* (Aldershot: Ashgate, 2006), 148–55.

94. Miquel reportedly had promised to grant his milk-mother her freedom, "per los bons servis que la dita Juliana li feya e havia fets en haver lo criat de chich de mamella." ARV G 2336: M. 1: 37v; M. 6: 21r–22r. For his part, Miquel denied all of Juliana's allegations and said that he never would have made Juliana such a promise because she was not his to begin with.

95. "Per ço que'l havien criat de chich e aquell los havia criat sos fills lo amava molt lo dit mossen Johan de Loriç e muller de aquell." ARV G 2324: M. 5: 27r; ARV G 2326: M. 22: 36r–40v, and ARV G 2327: M. 31: 2r.

96. "Per ma fe senyora gran bondat ha feta Johanet que sabent que mossen Johan de Loriç era mort per amor de sos fills e de vos es vengut de Castella e tornat en vestre poder e vos li de nou fer bona companya." ARV G 2326: M. 22: 36r–40v and ARV G 2327: M. 31: 2r.

of role reversals as well. As a consequence of their abject poverty, slaves were thought to enjoy a "privileged moral position." Thus slaves, on occasion, became "the patrons and matrons of their masters and mistresses, pleading for intervention on behalf of their souls."[97] Indeed, in 1484, Cristòfol, a black slave belonging to the merchant Andreu Albert, recounted how his master and mistress, desperate to have a child, had asked him to pray for them. "Anxious to have a son or daughter since they did not yet have one," Andreu reportedly "said to his slave Cristòfol such or similar words, 'Cristòfol, ask God to give us a son or a daughter. If God gives us one, I will immediately make you free.'" Andreu's wife subsequently gave birth to both a son and a daughter and though Cristòfol claimed that this was due (at least partly) to his prayers, his master and mistress refused to honor their agreement. Thus, Cristòfol subsequently filed a lawsuit demanding his freedom on the grounds that his master and mistress "owed" him because they had conceived a child through his spiritual intervention.[98] Unfortunately, we do not have the governor's ruling in this case. Nevertheless, even though all of the aforementioned "slave patrons" wound up in court, the very fact that they demanded recognition for providing reciprocal services for their masters served but to emphasize contemporary notions that masters and slaves formed a "family" linked by mutual obligations.

Slaves as Heirs

In her study of households in fourteenth-century Venetian Crete, Sally McKee has emphasized that "each member of the household, whether kin or nonkin, stood in a particular relationship with the property, or patrimony, that formed the basis of the household." Slaves, in McKee's view, were no exception. Though such property relations "were shaped by law or convention," McKee observes that "there was also movement of property unchoreographed by law, from member to member or out of the household altogether, in response to ties of familiarity existing between the members [both slave and free] of the household." Although, according to law, family members "controlled or used the patrimony in the interests of the lineage," servants "absorbed property through their wages,"

---

97. Romano, *Housecraft and Statecraft*, 202–3.

98. Cristòfol contended that "los sobre dits en Andreu Albert e muller de aquell desajosts de haver fill o filla com no tinguessen en aquell temps digueren al dit Christofol tunch catiu tals o semblants paraules Christofol prega a deu que us done fill o filla si deus ne dona tantost te fare franch." Cristòfol's advocate continued, and now, "attest e considerat que apres de la dita promesa los dits conjuges de llur matrimoni han hauts fill e filla a la oracio de aquells e del dit en Christofol es stada hoyda e la dita promesa resta pura. E pux s'es seguit que los dits conjuges han hauts e procreats los dits fill e filla lo dit Christofol seria e es franch e quiti de tot jou de servitut e a obtesa per virtut de la promesa plena libertat." ARV G 2371: M. 4: 11v and ARV G 2372: M. 18: 1r–8v. I discussed Cristòfol's role as an agricultural laborer earlier in chapter 3, see p. 97.

and slaves generally were considered only to have formed part of the property, McKee found that slaves, like free members of the household, were also often the beneficiaries of testamentary bequests. McKee is careful to recognize that these practices were not necessarily motivated by affection. She explains, "By ties of familiarity, I mean bonds whose substance was not necessarily sentimental. Ties of familiarity were feelings of duty and obligation which in a group of people living together were fostered by daily, intimate contact and intercourse as well as by blood relations and marriage ties. Affection could be, but was not always, a consequence of such ties."[99]

McKee's observations, based on her analysis of last wills and testaments drawn up in fourteenth-century Venetian Crete, describe equally well the testamentary practices of masters and mistresses living in fifteenth-century Valencia. Examination of evidence found in Valencian archives reveals the widespread practice of masters and mistresses leaving substantial legacies to their slaves. It bears emphasis, however, that the fact that slaves appeared as beneficiaries in wills and testaments of masters and mistresses in fifteenth-century Valencia (as McKee also has observed) "neither [contradicts] modern perceptions of slavery as an inherently brutal phenomenon nor [implies] that conditions under which slaves lived were comfortable."[100]

Bequests made by masters to their slaves in last wills and testaments ranged widely. At one end of the spectrum, masters and mistresses simply lumped slaves together with all other household dependents as beneficiaries of sets of mourning clothes.[101] In the last will and testament of Caterina, the widow of Bernat Serra, for example, Caterina left her slave woman, also named Caterina, a set of mourning clothes.[102] Similarly, in the will of the notary Pau Agosti, aka "de Beses," Pau directed that his slaves—a black woman, a dark-skinned woman and her infant son (bort)—be given "black mourning cloth."[103] Finally, in the last will and testament of Caterina, the wife of the pharmacist Bernat Fulleda, she directed her executors to outfit her female slave Lucia (as well as Lucia's two children, Catina and Johanot) with a set of mourning clothes.[104]

At the other end of the spectrum, slaves were the beneficiaries of more substantial legacies: the "gift" of freedom coupled with sizable grants of money, household articles,

---

99. McKee, "Households in Fourteenth-Century Venetian Crete," 28.

100. McKee, "Households in Fourteenth-Century Venetian Crete," 64.

101. That slaves and freed persons, in turn, freely disposed of the property bequeathed to them is revealed by a reference in an inventory postmortem to a set of mourning clothes that a slave woman had offered in surety for repayment of a loan. "Item hun mantell negre qu'es diu que es penyora de la sclava d'en Folch per sis reals." ARV P 442 (nonpaginated): 22 August 1475.

102. ARV P 3148 (nonpaginated): 9 March 1474.

103. ARV P 10310 (nonpaginated): 12 September 1471.

104. APPV 22731 (nonpaginated): 7 November 1471.

and/or real estate. Masters and mistresses invariably presented these gifts as expressions of what might be described as paternalistic concern—to help them live independently and to aid them in setting up their own households. As we have seen, in addition to sums of money earmarked for their dowries, female slaves were given legacies of beds, linens, clothing, furniture, and other articles deemed essential for setting up a household. In some instances, they were granted usufruct of a room or even an entire house. In the last will and testament of Johana, the widow of the surgeon Johan Barcelo, Johana's former slave, Margalida, was granted usufruct of their former stable (in exchange for an annual rent of four sous six *diners*) and some assorted household furnishings: a dining room table, a bed with its linens, a chest, and "as many things, such as kitchen utensils and other items, as would be necessary for her to set up her own home."[105] Occasionally, male slaves were given tools of their chosen trade. A tanner acting on behalf of a freedman, for instance, demanded that the executors of his former master's estate honor the last wishes of the deceased (the carpenter Johan Tarrago) by not only issuing Johan a "*carta de libertat*" but also giving him "some tools from the workshop . . . [namely,] those he would need to make a living."[106]

Not all slaves living in the same household shared equally in their master's or mistress's patrimony. In the last will and testament of the aforementioned Caterina de la Nana, for example, she directed that "after her death, as soon as he has his own household," her male slave Johanot Agosti (now freed) would be given a bedspread, a linen canopy, six towels, some napkins, three sets of sheets, some linen and burlap cloth, a big pot and a small cloth, as well as "some properties that I own and possess in the present city of Valencia in the parish of San Lorenc." Caterina's generosity with respect to Johanot Agosti, however, contrasted starkly with her treatment of another one of the slaves living in her household. Caterina specified that her black slave woman, Ysabel, would remain in servitude after her death. Upon her death, Ysabel would not only be cast out from her household and resold but, worse still, she would be separated from her daughter—a dark-skinned (llora) slave girl named Johanota. Directing that Ysabel be put up for sale on the island of Ibiza "and no other place," Caterina directed that the revenues garnered from Ysabel's sale be used to subsidize Johanot Agosti's apprenticeship with a wool comber as well as to commission an altarpiece dedicated to the Virgin Mary "de Albuxech." Ysabel's daughter, the dark-skinned (llora) girl named Johanota, in turn, was granted freedom, effective immediately upon Caterina's death, and a legacy of ten lliures.[107]

In an admittedly more exceptional example, in 1478 a farmer from Chilvella named Pere Guillem, "a black man, who used to be my slave," his universal heir. In recognition,

105. ARV P 1914 (nonpaginated): 3 September 1474.
106. ARV G 2403: M. 2: 27v; M. 9: 25r–30r. See the earlier discussion of this case in chapter 3.
107. ARV P 9956 (nonpaginated): 19 September 1489.

perhaps, of the extraordinary character of this bequest, this farmer felt obliged to offer some sort of explanation. Thus, he affirmed:

> [Pere] has been good and faithful to me. If it was not for said Pere Guillem, I would have perished from hunger when I was ill and unable to work. Most notably, during the period of famine and grain shortage, I most surely would have died if it had not been for him. Although I made him free he never departed from me or my service. Rather, he has continually served me even though he was and is free.[108]

Although it appears that this farmer did not have any direct surviving male descendants, it is nevertheless striking that he left his biological daughter Bernarda only a set of mourning clothes and his adopted son, Joanot Guillem (the son of his female servant, Ursola, the widow of a Portuguese tailor), a single plot of land, just over two acres in size. Everything else, "all my other goods, rights, and actions that I have or should have by any title, cause, manner or reason," went to this black man, his former slave and namesake.[109] Five months later, in the presence of a notary and witnesses, this black freedman "gratefully accepted" his legacy.

Considered in conjunction with the participation of masters and mistresses in slave baptisms and marriages, such testamentary bequests buttress Sally McKee's assertion that "however unequal members in a household might be, the slaves were bound to the free members of the household by ties analogous to kinship." Indeed, what is particularly remarkable about this document, reflective of the durability of ties between masters and slaves, is the fact that we find appended to Pere Guillem's last will and testament a notation recording how, some twenty-eight years later, on 12 July 1508, this black freedman's daughter, Ysabel Otto, the wife of Joan Martí, a laborer of Ruzafa, inherited Pere Guillem's legacy and acknowledged receipt of the property originally granted to her father by his former master.[110]

Nevertheless, though they occasionally may have been embraced by their masters as surrogate children or beloved family members, slaves, unlike other kin relations, could

---

108. "Lo qual me es stat bo e fel e sino per lo dit Pere Guillem yo fora perit de fam com yo fos indispost e no pogues treballar e senyaladament en lo temps de la fam e fretura de forment yo'm fora perit sino per ell e jatsia yo'l hagues fet franch ell may se es partit de mi ne de mon servey ans continuament me ha servit jatsia fos e sia franch." ARV P 810 (nonpaginated): 3 March 1478. I discussed Pere Guillem's skills as a farmer earlier, in chapter 3. See p. 97.

109. "Tots los altres bens meus drets e actions que hara ha e de aci anant haure per qualsevol titol causa manera o raho do e leix al dit Pere Guillem negre criat meu lo qual solia esser catiu meu e aquell dit Pere Guillem negre vull que sia hereu de tots los dits bens meus drets e actions mies a fer dels dits bens meus a totes ses planes voluntats." ARV P 810 (nonpaginated): 3 March 1478.

110. Appended to this document was a notation dated 12 July 1508. Ysabel Otto, "muller de Johan Marti laurador del loch de Ruceffa" received "la herencia al dit en Pere Guillem negre pare de aquella dexala per lo dit en Pere Guillem olim amo de aquell." ARV P 810 (nonpaginated): 3 March 1478.

be sold off. Indeed, to balance the impression left by Pere Guillem's last will and testament, we ought to consider one final example.

On a summer afternoon toward the end of the fourteenth century, a baptized Christian slave named Miquel, a Tartar in origin, seized a knife and stabbed his mistress repeatedly in the back while she was kneading dough. His mistress (Sibilia) dying instantly, Miquel went on to attack his master, Guillem Ros. Miquel stabbed his master "only" twice, but he allegedly did so with such force that the wounds were deemed fatal. Taken into custody and asked why he had murdered his mistress and attacked his master, Miquel replied that "he had become very angry and felt betrayed upon learning for certain that said Guillem Ros, whom he had served for six or seven years, had decided to sell him, and that said Sibilia had taken part in this decision."[111] Hardly a mutinous attack by an unruly other, Miquel would like us to believe that this violent outburst stemmed from the legitimate frustrations of a devoted familiar.

In many ways, then, the ties binding masters, mistresses, and their slaves were likened to the bonds linking parents to their children. Miquel protested, however, that despite all his efforts to win acceptance, despite his conversion to Christianity and his many years of faithful service, in the end his master and mistress had forsaken him, expelling him from their household and putting him up for resale.

---

111. "Interrogat... per que havia morta la dita na Sibilia senyora sua. Et dix per tal com era fort irat et despagat com havia sabut de cert que lo dit en Guillem Ros volia vendre o havia venut a ell dit confessant a qui havia servit sis o set anys et que us tenia loch la dita na Sibilia." ARV JCrim 44: M. 8: 13r–15v.

CHAPTER 5 SEX AND SWORDPLAY
SLAVERY AND HONOR

In 1471, a nobleman appeared before the court of the Justícia Civil protesting that Johan, the partially manumitted black male slave he inherited from his brother, had put him and his household "in great peril." To avoid "the dangers and scandals that the slave caused and would continue to cause him," he insisted that he had no choice but to sell the slave—despite the clause in his brother's will promising Johan freedom after completing a ten-year term of service.[1]

Six witnesses appearing on this nobleman's behalf corroborated his assessment, describing Johan as "a big disgrace," "extremely arrogant," "despicable," and disobedient to everyone.[2] The household cook, for instance, complained that Johan was never content with the bread he was given; invariably, the black male slave demanded meat, tuna, "and other delicacies." Indeed, she continued, Johan had no compunction about raiding his master's wine cellar. He allegedly uncorked and drank so many bottles of white wine that his mistress had been forced to put a lock on the cellar door.

Much more serious, however, were the allegations made by the remaining witnesses. A female servant recounted an incident in which the black male slave burst into his master's bedchamber "with his hand on the sword that he possessed" and accused the nobleman of spousal abuse. A priest was scandalized by how Johan continually "menaced" his master, "holding him in great contempt."[3] A local shopkeeper overheard Johan proclaim that "he would rather be [the slave] of a Jew" and serve him in perpetuity than serve this nobleman for the remainder of his ten-year term of service. Johan, moreover,

1. "En tant que ell dit proposant te la sua casa en molt perill lo que li es molt dampnos e axi de necessitat per fugir als perills e vergonyes que lo dit sclau li fa e pot fer com sia tant vicios dellibera vendre aquell." ARV JCiv 923: M. 13: 44r.

2. A shopkeeper testified that he considered the black male slave "hun gran tacany e gran ladre e molt ultratgos e superbios e molt deshobedient al dit magniffich en Johan de Corella amo de aquell." ARV JCiv 923: M. 13: 44r–48v.

3. "Ha vist ell dit testimoni com lo dit negre menacava al dit magniffich en Johan Roic de Corela amo de aquell... tenint lo en gran menyspreu menacant lo tots temps." ARV JCiv 923: M. 13: 48r–v.

had even boasted that he would kill this nobleman if he refused to resell him to a new master.[4]

These charges, admittedly, had been carefully crafted; they were designed to provoke indignation against this black male slave who (allegedly) had so flagrantly flouted established norms of behavior. To secure the court's permission to sell this partially freed black man back into slavery, this nobleman needed to convince the Justícia Civil that Johan had forfeited his claim to freedom. Nevertheless, as calculated as these charges might have been, they expose a very real anxiety felt by many masters and mistresses in this honor-conscious society: their inability to control their slaves' behavior and the impact this might have on their reputation in the community. It is this nobleman's contention, after all, that his own status had been seriously compromised by his slave's misbehavior. Indeed, each one of these witnesses stressed how they had seen and/or overheard Johan insult and challenge his master publicly. They recounted these incidents, moreover, not matter-of-factly but with an air of concern. The shopkeeper, for example, testified that, upon hearing these statements, he was so shocked that he felt compelled to confront the slave, saying, "Aren't you ashamed for saying what you said?"[5]

In the previous chapter I noted how the bonds linking masters, mistresses, and their slaves were often likened to those between parents and children. Slaves were supposed to be the grateful beneficiaries of their masters' and mistresses' paternal attention. A less secure picture of the masters' and mistresses' position emerges, however, from the testimony offered (respectively) by this nobleman, priest, shopkeeper, and female servant. Not only do we learn that masters and mistresses *need* their slaves to honor and obey them, but slaves could undermine as well as enhance their reputation in the community.[6]

---

4. The shopkeeper testified that he heard Johan say that "mes amaria esser de hun juheu que no del dit magniffich en Johan Roic de Corella. E que si ell nol venia que ell lo mataria." ARV JCiv 923: M. 13: 45r.

5. "E ell dit testimoni li deya no has vergonya de dir lo que dius." ARV JCiv 923: M. 13: 46r.

6. What we see here, perhaps, is an expression of what Hegel termed the socio-psychological dependency of the master on the slave. Noting how "the master depends upon the slave for recognition, or what [Orlando] Patterson analyzes in terms of the timocratic value of honor, and what we also call 'deference,'" Cynthia Willett has observed how "entangled at the very core of the dialectic of master and slave lies a double irony. The first irony is that the master finds himself dependent upon the slave—not simply as chattel or other instrument of desire—but for recognition. This mode of intersubjectivity, asymmetrical as it is, would be no problem except for the second irony. The master finds himself recognized not by another person but by a mere slave, someone who is dependent and not independent of the will of the master, and therefore someone whose recognition does not count. In truth, Hegel argues, the master is no better than the slave upon whom he depends for a sense of self." See Cynthia Willett, "The Master-Slave Dialectic: Hegel vs. Douglass," in *Subjugation and Bondage: Critical Essays on Slavery*, ed. Tommy Lee Lott (Lanham, Md.: Rowman and Littlefield, 1998), 155–60. For Hegel's master-slave dialectic, see G. W. F. Hegel, *Phenomenology of the Spirit*, trans. A. V. Miller (Oxford: Oxford University Press, 1977). See also Orlando Patterson, *Slavery and Social Death*, 2 and 99.

Through an analysis of contemporary court records concerning slaves who bore their masters' swords or bore their masters' children, in this chapter I expose the tensions inherent in the master-slave relationship and how persons reputedly without honor figured prominently in contests over status and precedence in this society.[7]

Living "Honorably" in Fifteenth-Century Valencia

In 1450, a recently widowed noblewoman filed a petition before the Justícia Civil requesting an allowance in excess of three hundred gold florins to sustain her and her household (*familia e servents*) during the mandatory one-year mourning period (*any de plor*) before she could recover her dowry. In her petition, this noblewoman, Margarita Tolsà, demanded funds not only to defray the costs connected with her own personal sustenance but also to feed, clothe, and shelter two "ladies" (*dones*), a female servant, a squire, and her female slave. When the curator of her husband's estate objected, arguing that Margarita would be well enough served by a more modest household staff of two attendants (an "elderly" male servant and her female slave), the widow's advocate maintained that an entire retinue of household attendants was essential to the preservation of her honor. For, he insisted, Margarita's husband, Joan Tolsà, had been "a knight and landed gentry man who was accustomed to having a household well outfitted with squires, ladies, male and female slaves, and beasts of burden" such that his wife had "at all times been well attended and served in the household." Furthermore, the widow's advocate continued, Margarita was herself "a woman of lineage." When she contracted marriage with Joan Tolsà she possessed "over fifty thousand sous in patrimony and was recognized publicly as a lady of honor and of lineage." Given the status, lineage, and patrimony of both Joan and Margarita, he concluded, "it is clear, and one cannot deny, that according to justice, she should be given said three hundred gold florins as they are very necessary to her."[8]

This view, that maintaining a "suitable" number of household dependents was essential to upholding one's status in the community, was not restricted to members of the nobility. It penetrated down into the ranks of well-to-do artisans and urban professionals

---

7. I am inspired here by the essays by Richard Boyer, Lyman Johnson, Sonya Lipsett-Rivera, and Sandra Lauderdale Graham in *The Faces of Honor: Sex, Shame, and Violence in Colonial Latin America* (Albuquerque: University of New Mexico Press, 1998).

8. "Car deu se considerar que mossen Johan Tolsa era cavaller e be heretat e acostumave de tenir casa sua ben acompanyada de scuders dones sclaus e sclaves e basties [sic] en axi que la muller del dit mossen Johan Tolsa tots temps stava ben acompanyada e servida en la casa. E com exia de la casa anava ben acompanyada de scuders e de dones.... Apar donchs que nos pot impugnar de justicie que nos deuen tatxar los dits CCC florins a la dita dona car son molt necessariis a aquella aquells e molt mes attes e considerat le stat linyatge e patrimoni del dit mossen Johan Tolsa e de la dita madona Margarita." ARV JCiv 915: M. 16: 15r–19v.

as well. When a pharmacist named Pere Martí died in 1460, for example, his widow, Ursola, professed a "need" for maintaining a household of at least ten dependents. Having lived, prior to her husband's death, "very honorably, having in their household between thirteen and fourteen dependents [literally "eaters" or *menjadors*]," Ursola struggled to continue living in the style to which she had become accustomed. In addition to supporting the three young apprentices who worked in her husband's pharmacy, Ursola fed, sheltered, and clothed a young girl who was a distant relative of her husband's, a salaried female servant, a young male servant, a slave woman and her ten-year-old son, an orphan girl taken in from a local hospital, as well as several other of her husband's relatives, "who never left."[9]

Margarita and Ursola were hardly unique among well-to-do widows in affirming the necessity of earmarking a significant portion of their allowances for the support of multiple slaves and servants. In fifteenth-century Valencia, a slave, beyond being a source of labor, was a source of honor.[10] Contemporaries viewed slaves as essential adornments for the household of any man or woman "of honor" (*de be*). An important component of living honorably in fifteenth-century Valencia was "having a household well outfitted with squires, ladies, male and female slaves, and beasts of burden."[11]

As has already been noted, an analysis of the documentation recording the individuals buying and selling slaves in fifteenth-century Valencia reveals that men and women of a broad range of occupations and socioeconomic conditions owned slaves. In addition to nobles and urban professionals (merchants, lawyers, notaries, and physicians), artisans such as tanners, cobblers, bakers, and carpenters were also prominent among slave owners, not to mention many farmers. In fifteenth-century Valencia, slave owners included men and women, members of the clergy[12] as well as members of the laity, and, though

9. "Aquell vivia molt honradament tenint en casa sua tretze o quatorze menjadors." ARV JCiv 923: M. 15: 30r–48r.

10. Social anthropologists such as Julian A. Pitt-Rivers, J. G. Peristiany, and Julio Caro Baroja have long maintained that the "Mediterranean" notion of honor is an "honor of precedence" whereby the ability to dominate others is a major attribute of prestige. See Julian A. Pitt-Rivers, "Honour and Social Status," in *Honour and Shame: The Values of Mediterranean Society*, ed. J. G. Peristiany, (London: Weidenfeld and Nicholson, 1965), 19–78. More recently, Christian Giordano has argued that we should envision honor not as an archaic moral code but rather as "a hierarchizing principle" and "an instrument of social differentiation." See Christian Giordano, "Mediterranean Honour Reconsidered: Anthropological Fiction or Actual Action Strategy?" *Anthropological Journal on European Cultures* 10, no. 1 (2001): 39–58. Also instructive, however, is Michael Herzfeld, "The Horns of the Mediterraneanist Dilemma," *American Ethnologist* 11, no. 3 (1984): 439–54.

11. Taken from the aforementioned petition filed on behalf of Margarita Tolsà. The text is transcribed in footnote 8. ARV JCiv 915: M. 16: 15r–19v.

12. Among the many male clerics who owned slaves (both male and female, both Muslim and Christian) was Pere de Vilarasa, a deacon at the cathedral of Valencia, who possessed at least four. Three were

subject to certain restrictions, Muslims and Jews[13] in addition to Christians. Although bakers and tanners perhaps were not under the same societal pressures as members of the nobility to have an impressive retinue of slaves and servants, the very pervasiveness of slave-holding in fifteenth-century Valencian society hints at the broader importance that such displays of power might have had in this honor-conscious, religiously and ethnically plural-istic society.[14] Indeed, as Orlando Patterson has noted, what is universal about the master-slave relationship is that, while the experience of enslavement produces feelings of shame and humiliation, the experience of mastership produces an inflated sense of honor.[15]

Defending Their Masters' Honor? The Role of Slaves in Feuds between Households

In their peregrinations around the city, Valencian noblemen customarily were escorted by a male slave bearing a sword. In a suit filed in 1454 against a squire accused of assault-ing a nobleman, the nobleman's wife insisted that her husband had done nothing to pro-voke the attack. She stressed that her husband carried "no arms whatsoever with him."

---

male slaves (including a twelve-year-old Muslim named Azmet) and the fourth was a woman named Honesta. See APPV 25217 (nonpaginated): 2 July 1473, APPV 10927 (nonpaginated): 23 January 1477 and ARV P 2067 (nonpaginated): 30 August 1478. See also APPV 25214 (nonpaginated): 10 September 1470, ARV P 2440 (nonpaginated): 27 June 1471, ARV P 2667 (nonpaginated):28 April 1472, ARV P 2863 (non-paginated): 4 June 1474, and ARV B 217: 1 February 1480. For examples of female religious who owned slaves, see APPV 25217 (nonpaginated): 28 December 1474 and ARV P 1997 (nonpaginated): 4 November 1477.

13. According to the kingdom of Valencia's legal code, "Jews and Muslims ought not and cannot buy any slave that is Christian; nor can they come into possession of them by receiving them in donation or in any other manner." Furs de València, Colon and Garcia, eds. (Barcelona, 1974), II: 81. In addition, the Furs specified that any slave owned by a Jew who subsequently converted to Christianity was entitled to an automatic manumission. Furs de València, Colon and Garcia, eds. (Barcelona, 1990), V: 107. Though no mention was made here about Jews or Muslims owning Muslim, Jewish, or pagan slaves, there is evidence that, on occasion, restrictions on Muslim and Jewish slave-owning extended to these groups as well. See Cortés, La esclavitud, 134; Verlinden, L'esclavage, 343–44, 459, 534–535; and Meyerson, "Slavery and Solidarity," 331–32.

14. For historical studies investigating the importance of honor in late medieval Valencian society, see Rafael Narbona Vizcaíno, Pueblo, Poder, y Sexo: Valencia Medieval (1306–1420) (Valencia: Diputació de València, 1991), esp. 125–44; Pablo Pérez Garcia, La comparsa de los malhechores: Valencia 1479–1518 (Valen-cia: Diputació de València, 1990), and Mark Meyerson, The Muslims of Valencia, esp. 225–70. Also useful is David Nirenberg, Communities of Violence: Persecution of Minorities in the Middle Ages (Princeton: Princeton University Press, 1996), esp. 186–200.

15. Patterson, Slavery and Social Death, 11. See also Kenneth S. Greenberg, Honor and Slavery: Lies, Duels, Noses, Masks, Dressing as a Woman, Gifts, Strangers, Death, Humanitarianism, Slave Rebellions, the Pro-Slavery Argument, Baseball, Hunting and Gambling in the Old South (Princeton: Princeton University Press, 1996), esp. 33–39.

Rather, "as is customary among men of honor of the present city," he had his male slave, who traveled in his company, carry his sword for him.[16] Although the obligation was not always taken so literally, the expectation that slaves would "bear their masters' swords" was broadly recognized in fifteenth-century Valencian society.

Interpreting and fulfilling this duty in a variety of different ways, female slaves as well as male slaves were expected to come to their master's defense. When a rival of her master's son showed up at the doorway of his house and hurled insults at them, the female slave of the nobleman Francesc de Vilanova shouted down at him from an upper-story window, "You aren't man enough to speak against the home of Francesc de Vilanova!"[17] Besides using their tongues, slave women might also employ common household objects as weapons in defense of their master's honor. In the fall of 1464 a shopkeeper charged that "because of the dispute that is between him and the priest Joan Vidal," a member of this priest's household who was on the upper story terrace, possibly a slave woman, had dumped a bedpan full of animal or human excrement on him while he was standing in the street below.[18]

Social anthropologists have long maintained that violence is a natural by-product of cultures that believe honor is established and gained through the domination of others. As J. G. Peristiany has observed, "honor-precedence promotes touchy aggressiveness."[19] Although not entirely discounting the valuable contributions of scholars such as Julian Pitt-Rivers and Peristiany, historians like Rafael Narbona Vizcaíno and Pablo Pérez García have resisted accepting unicausal cultural explanations for these violent outbursts. Instead, in addition to the so-called Mediterranean culture of honor, they attribute the intense feuding (bandositats) characteristic of fourteenth- and fifteenth-century Valencia to a combination of socioeconomic changes. Pérez García argues that a dramatic increase in Valencia's population during the fifteenth century, brought on largely by immigration,

16. Damiata Pardo claimed that her husband, the nobleman Tristany Pardo, "de la casta cavaller... acostuma anar pacificament per la present ciutat de Valencia axi a cavall com a peu sens portar armes algunes ab si sino tant com a vegades lo seu sclau li porta una spasa segons es costum entre homes de be de la present ciutat." ARV JCrim 52: Denunciacions: M. 1: 28v.

17. To which her target (Joan Nadal) reportedly had responded, "Shut up, you drunk, this is none of your business!" ARV JCrim 99: Denunciacions (nonpaginated): 27 May 1441. "E ladonchs la sclava del dit en Francesch de Vilanova de la finestra dix... vos no sou hom per parlar de casa d'en Francesch de Vilanova. Et el dit confesant dix callau vos na enbriaga que vos non haveu aconexer."

18. Francesch Miro charged that some unspecified members of this priest's household "li lancaren de la terrat de la casa del dit mossen Vidal huna mongeta plena de fem e merda e per la differencia que es entre ell clamant e lo dit mossen Vidal." ARV JCrim 36: Clams (nonpaginated): 16 September 1464.

19. Peristiany, Honour and Shame, 189–90. Christian Giordano has also stressed how honor should be seen as "a competitive conduct," producing "fierce feelings of rivalry, with respect to status, between groups and persons." Christian Giordano, "Mediterranean Honor and Beyond: The Social Management of Reputation in the Public Sphere," Sociologija: Mintis ir veikmas 1 (2005): 44–45.

aggravated an already mounting economic crisis, "provoking an intensification of social exchanges and, consequently, the exacerbation of conflicts."[20] Not only nobles but also urban professionals, artisans, and even slaves became embroiled in these disputes for social status and political power. Whether their participation was forced or voluntary, it reflected how, in the eyes of their contemporaries, slaves were considered members of their master's household. Literally fighting their master's battles, this was simply one more distasteful task that masters entrusted to their slaves.[21] In addition to doing the cooking, cleaning, and washing, slave women might taunt, slander, and verbally degrade their master's enemies. Just as they were ordered to saw wood, prune vineyards, and stoke the fires of their ovens, male slaves bludgeoned, gashed, and otherwise debased their master's enemies.

Analysis of what essentially constituted the local police blotter—the registers of the Justícia Criminal devoted to reporting suspicious deaths, serious injuries, and preliminary oral complaints (clams y cedules)—reveals that (contrary to their owners' fears) slaves were implicated most frequently not in attacks perpetrated against their masters[22] but in acts of violence executed on their masters' behalf and directed against their masters' enemies. Intermixed with the often tedious setting of court dates, citations, and orders releasing prisoners on bail bonds were allegations of physical assault and verbal abuse in which slaves not infrequently were implicated. These records reveal that slaves were deeply embroiled in the feuds and rivalries of their masters. The following entry, taken from these registers (and dated 31 July 1464), is but one of many:

Na Ursola, the daughter of en Guillem Liniat, deceased, makes a complaint before the magnificent Justícia against the black male slave belonging to mossen Melchior de Vilanova, who is called Anthoni, and against said mossen Melchior, affirming that today, after midday, the said black male, on the orders of his master, beat her with diverse

20. Pérez Garcia, La comparsa de los malhechores, 267–68. Narbona Vizcaíno, Malhechores, Violencia y Justicia Ciudadana en la Valencia Bajomedieval (Valencia: Ayuntamiento de Valencia, 1990), 108–20. See also Ernest Belenguer Cebrià, València en la crisi del segle XV (Barcelona: Edicions 62, 1976).

21. Some masters and mistresses also ordered their slaves to steal for them. Vicente Graullera cites a case in which a thirty-year-old black male slave named Domingo attempted to justify his flight by protesting that his master, the baker Francesc Gil of Alcira, not only treated him poorly but also sent him out in the middle of the night to pilfer the wood needed to heat his oven. Graullera, La esclavitud, 138. Domingo's testimony is transcribed as document #18 in the appendix, 209.

22. Such attacks, however, certainly, were not unheard of. In 1445, Mahomat, a slave owned by the baker Domingo Rubert, allegedly went on a rampage, attacking not only his master's wife, Johana, and two female servants but even going after his master's two-year-old son named Onoffre. After beating his mistress and one of the servant girls with his fists, punching them repeatedly in the head, neck, back, and stomach, Mahomat attacked two-year-old Onoffre and the other servant girl with a knife, stabbing them, respectively, in the arm and hand. ARV JCrim 22: Clams: M. 6: (nonpaginated): 2 October 1445.

blows that have left her completely bruised in her person. Requesting that they be arrested and that she be granted justice.[23]

What ought we to make of these reports of slaves beating up men and women "on the
orders of their masters"? Were these persons without honor[24] defending their master's
honor by harassing, insulting, and assaulting members of rival households? Dennis Romano has argued that such incidents suggest that slaves identified with and internalized
the values of their masters.[25] But ought we to interpret their involvement in these violent
crimes as evidence that slaves considered the battles of their masters (and mistresses)
their own? A close reading of the available evidence in fifteenth-century Valencia, raises
serious problems with this assumption, particularly when we consider the roles that traditionally were assigned to slaves and how they were prosecuted for their participation
in these crimes. The fact that the slave perpetrators we encounter in fifteenth-century
Valencian court records were almost exclusively black males, moreover, seems more than
coincidental.

In his work *Regiment de la cosa pública*, the Franciscan moralist Francesc Eiximenis exhorted servants "to defend their lords and stand up for them whenever needed, even if
they are not ordinarily required to prove their fidelity in battle."[26] Although it was expressly
the duty of knightly retainers to come to their master's military aid when called upon, in
certain circumstances heads of households mobilized as many individuals as they could
muster, including slaves. Thus, although in many of the complaints filed against slaves
encountered in the records of the Justícia Criminal, slaves (their masters' henchmen)
acted "alone" (that is, they went unaccompanied to perpetrate violence), in other instances

23. "Na Ursola filla d'en Guillem Liniat quondam se clama al magnifich justicia de hun sclau negre de
mossen Melchior de Vilanova appellat Anthoni e del dit mossen Melchior afermant que en lo dia de huy
apres mig jorn lo dit negre de manament del dit son amo li ha pegat diversses bastonades de les quals la
ha tota magnada en la persona. Requirent esser presos esser li feta justicia." ARV JCrim 36: Clams (nonpaginated): 31 July 1464.

24. Legislation from the period suggests a generalized view of the slave as a person without honor.
According to the *Furs de València*, a physical injury suffered by a slave could not be the subject of a judicial
complaint unless it affected the slave's owner. The perpetrator could only be prosecuted if the slave suffered an injury (i.e., a broken bone or loss of limb) rendering him or her incapable of providing service,
or if the slave's owner felt the attack was directed against himself or herself. Moreover, only the slave's
owner, not the slave himself or herself, could claim injury. Finally, this statute specified that a verbal attack ("injurious words") against a slave could not be subject to prosecution. *Furs de València*, Colón and
Garcia, eds. (Barcelona, 1999), VII: 47.

25. Romano, *Housecraft and Statecraft*, 205–6.

26. "Aquests aitals serviçials son tenguts de defendre llurs senyors e d'ensenyar-se per ells quan es
hora, jatsia que per ells no sien tenguts de posar fe en brega ordenariament, ne de fer res per ells que
es contra Deu, ne contra llurs animes." Francesc Eiximenis, *Regiment de la cosa pública* (Barcelona, 1972).
Cited in Jill Webster, ed., *La societat catalana al segle XIV* (Barcelona: Edicions 62, 1980), 60–61.

they simply joined the fray. In such incidents, slaves acted alongside their master's sons, younger siblings, and/or domestic servants, all seemingly engaged in a common mission.

Slaves—particularly a single black male slave—were stock figures in these rather unchivalric contests targeting unarmed and unsuspecting rivals. In 1441, for example, Johan de Fababux, a harness maker, and his wife Anthonia filed a formal denunciation alleging that, in violation of a truce agreement, their rivals, the harness maker Matheu de Straborech and his wife Johana, had directed a group of armed men, including their son Berthomeu and their "Moorish" slave named Mahomat, to launch a surprise, unprovoked attack against their household one Sunday. Mahomat's master and mistress were accused not only of instigating the attack but also of not so surreptitiously participating in it. Matheu and Johana allegedly threw bars and sticks of wood at them from their upper story window as well as shouted down words of encouragement to their henchmen, such as "Kill him! Eliminate him!"[27] In 1464, a laborer filed a similar complaint against a group of four men associated with the household of the nobleman Gizbert Valleriola. The four men—two laborers, a squire, and a black male slave—had come and attacked him in his house the previous evening, "without any just cause . . . and with the lance (ballesta) unsheathed as well as other arms."[28]

These were hardly fraternal bands of men whose shared experiences forged bonds of solidarity crossing boundaries of status, race, and religion. Not exactly fighting side by side, slaves, within these larger groups, were given a distinct role and performed a special function. In his account of the most noteworthy events of the reign of Alfonso V the Magnanimous, the court chaplain Melchior Miralles recounted the "very cruel" slaying perpetrated by a group of armed men, including a black male slave. On that particular late autumn afternoon, the victim was on his way home after a day's hunt. Riding well ahead of the rest of his companions, he was intercepted by a band of armed men in a heavily wooded portion of the road. This was not a random assault by a group of road bandits. The victim's attackers included the sons of several prominent Valencians as well as this one black male slave. What is remarkable about Miralles's account is that, although the black male slave was but one of several assailants, he was set off from the rest of the attackers by his mode of transit, his weaponry, and his apparent function. Though they were all of one party, the black male slave traveled "on foot" while the rest were "astride fine horses." When the attackers burst forth from their hiding place, stabbing the victim

27. Mahomat, for his part, denied having any knowledge of the incident. He insisted that his master and mistress were "good persons," not the sort who provoked fights and brawls. Johan and Anthonia subsequently withdrew their complaint. They offered little in the way of explanation, stating cryptically that they were dropping the charges because now "they knew the truth of the matter." ARV JCrim 99: Denunciacions (nonpaginated): 14 March 1441.

28. ARV JCrim 36: Clams (nonpaginated): 14 December 1464.

with their lances, the black male slave remained behind, not participating in this initial assault. Rather, the black male slave was called upon only afterward—charged with performing the more brutal task of delivering the death blow. Miralles noted that "they had the black man slit his throat."[29]

A similar division of labor is evident in Miralles's description of yet another assault involving a black male slave that was perpetrated against the gardener of a monastery. Once again, although it was a free person who initiated the attack—the provost of the same monastery—it was the black male slave who ended it. Once the slave's master had grabbed the victim by the hair, the black male slave stepped in, seized the gardener's sickle, and stabbed him with it between his shoulders. The slave thereupon gave the victim's pregnant wife—described as "only a few days from giving birth"—a few whacks on the back of the neck with the sickle's handle for good measure. While the gardener died a couple of weeks later, we aren't told what became of his wife or her baby. Miralles does inform us, however, that the provost and his slave continued to walk the streets of Valencia with impunity. He reports that "so little mention was made of what happened that it was as if [only] a chicken had been killed!"[30]

Certainly masters entrusted these tasks to their slaves because they were gruesome and dangerous. Nevertheless, there seems to have been more going on here than a simple aversion among masters for getting their hands dirty. Closer examination of discussions of slave hit men in court cases that were actually prosecuted makes it clear that masters delegated these tasks to their slaves for two additional reasons: in order that they might subject their rivals to even greater humiliation and in order that they might more easily displace the blame for the violent act off themselves.

Literally adding insult to injury, masters aimed to compound the shame of these assaults by entrusting the task to a "vile" or ignoble person. Indeed, in a denunciation filed before the Justícia Criminal, a physician's wife contended that the pharmacist's apprentice who threatened her husband's life merited the death penalty since "according to the dispositions of the Furs of the most high king and according to ancient practice, when a vile and lowly person harms or otherwise injures a man of honor, he ought to be condemned to death."[31] In a dispute between siblings over their father's inheritance, one of the more far-fetched accusations Johana Blasco leveled against her brother (Bernat

29. "E feren-lo degollar al negre." Melchior Miralles, *Dietari del Capella d'Alfons el Magnànim*, ed. Vicent-Josep Escarti (Valencia: Edicions Alfons el Magnànim, 1988), 106.

30. "E lo pabordr[e] lo pres per lo cabells, e lo negre li donà la llançada. Tan poca menció se n'és feta com si fos mort un poll: paborde e negre van per València com si no haguessen fet res." Melchior Miralles, *Dietari del Capella d'Alfon el Magnanim*, 212–13.

31. "Segons disposicio de fur del alt Rey...e segons pratica antiquada quant hun vila e menestra aminuara e dona de fet carrech a hun hom de be deu esser condempnar a pena de mort." ARV JCrim 53: Denunciacions: M. 3: 6v–10v.

Coll, a pharmacist) was that he had purchased a black male slave named Mayniques for the sole purpose of employing him as his hit man, assassinating his siblings one by one so that he, the sole surviving heir, would not have to share their father's estate with anyone.[32] By specifically commissioning a black male slave to do the deed, Johana contended that her brother meant to vilify as well as eliminate his rivals. Thus, she claimed that Bernat Coll had menaced her husband, telling him that he would endure an especially shameful and undignified death: murdered "by the most contemptible black male slave in his household."[33] Whether proved or disproved, Johana Blasco's accusation suggests both that fifteenth-century Valencians could not conceive of an individual of baser social status than a black male slave[34] and that it was not unheard of for a master to capitalize on his slave's low social status in order to humiliate as well as disable his enemies. Using his slave, in essence, as a double-edged sword, a master could augment his own sense of honor by having his "most contemptible" slave maim, injure, or butcher his enemies.

Although slaves were expected to do their master's bidding, the black male slave named Mayniques reportedly had thwarted this pharmacist's "cruel plot" by impudently refusing to serve as his assassin. Although such willfulness on the part of a slave would likely irk or antagonize his or her master,[35] in other circumstances—that is, when a master sought to avoid liability for a crime—a slave's possession of free will could come in rather handy.

Though slaves did not possess a full juridical personality—they could neither testify for (or against) their masters in a criminal court nor file charges against their masters[36]— slaves could be prosecuted for certain crimes. The kingdom's legal code stipulated that although a court of law normally could not impose a corporal or pecuniary penalty on a slave, this was "to be understood to apply only with regard to a civil, not a criminal, action."[37] Whereas a master would ultimately be held responsible for any purchases or

---

32. "Lo dit en Bernat Coll . . . compra hun negre appellat Mayniques al qual comprat hague dix davant moltes e diverses persones que aquell negre havia comprat per matas an Sobrevero o alguna de ses jermanes per husurparse los bens de la herencia de son pare per que nols haguessen aquells." ARV JCrim 25: Denunciacions: M. 2: 18r–22v.

33. "Que ell lo faria matar e castigar ab lo pus rohin negre de casa sua." ARV JCrim 25: Denunciacions: M. 2: 18r–22v.

34. Vicente Graullera draws a similar conclusion in his study of slavery in Valencia during the sixteenth and seventeenth centuries. See Graullera, La esclavitud, 142–43.

35. According to Johana's denunciacion, Mayniques's refusal to comply with his master's orders infuriated her brother so much that "seeing that said black slave did not wish to do this, he placed him in irons and put him in the serra" (a contraption akin to the aforementioned ballesta, that was used both to detain and discipline unruly slaves). ARV JCrim 25: Denunciacions: M. 2: 18r–22v.

36. Furs de València, Colon and Garcia, eds. (Barcelona, 1974), II: 129.

37. "Servu en juhii ne en pleit no pot ésser, ne condempnatió que sie feita en persona d'ell, no estie ni haja valor. En aquest fur adobà lo senyor rey que sie entès en pleit civil e no en criminal." Furs de València, Colon and Garcia, eds. (Barcelona, 1978), III: 5.

debts made by their slaves (any contract negotiated by a slave was assumed to have been made on behalf of his master),[38] with regard to a slave's criminal acts, the issue of a master's liability was considerably more complex. Key mitigating factors were whether the offense had been perpetrated without their master's permission and/or whether, given the opportunity, the master could have prevented the slave from committing the crime. The relevant statute read that

> if a slave belonging to a certain master causes injury or harms another person (with or without his master's knowledge) and the master could not prevent it, that master is obliged only to surrender the slave to the person who suffered harm—even if the injury [inflicted by the slave] is greater in value than that of the slave. However, if the slave should harm another person and the master not only knew about it but did not wish to prevent it, even though he could have prevented it, [the master] is obligated to compensate the injured party for *all* the damages inflicted by his slave. He [the master] is not delivered or absolved of any further liability [simply] by surrendering his slave [to the injured party to compensate him] for the injury and/or damages that the slave inflicted and/or caused.[39]

Masters, thus, could evade responsibility for their slaves' crimes by either professing ignorance or bewailing their powerlessness: protesting their inability to control their slaves' violent impulses.[40] Just as slaves themselves were bartered, sold, and exchanged by their masters, their crimes also could be renounced, disavowed, and repudiated. Thus, one further motive that might have prompted Valencian masters to employ slaves as their hit men was the prospect that they could more easily avoid responsibility for the crime. By surrendering the slave, masters, technically, could walk off scot-free.

In late August, 1456, a band of at least twelve men, including a black male slave, was charged with stabbing, beating, and bruising a laborer's wife named Caterina. In the

---

38. *Furs de València*, Colon and Garcia, eds. (Barcelona, 1974), II: 245.

39. Emphasis added. "Si catiu d'alcú donarà o farà mal o dan a alcuna persona, lo senyor, sabén o no sabén, e no-u podie vedar, aquel senyor no és tengut sinó que dó aquel catiu a aquel qui-l dan haurà sufert e pres, jasia ço que més sia el dan que no val lo catiu. Emperò si el catiu darà dan a alcú, e el senyor seu ó sabé e no-u volch vedar com ó pogués vedar, és tengut tot lo dan a restituir que aquel catiu haurà feit; ne és deliurat ne absolt si volrrà dar aquell catiu per lo mal ne el dan que haurà feit ne donat. E si aquel catiu qui haurà feit dan o mal, lo senyor sabén o no sabén, e no volch vedar com vedar ó pogués, vendrà en poder d'altre novell senyor per compra o per altra justa rahó, aquel novell senyor serà tengut tan solament a liurar aquel catiu per lo mal e per lo dan que haurà feit enans que vingués en son poder, car la malafeyta seguex aquel qui feita la haurà." *Furs de València*, Colon and Garcia, eds. (Barcelona, 1978), III: 254–55.

40. In some instances, though, masters were not able to deflect responsibility for their crimes onto their slaves. For an example in which a slave and his master were both convicted for theft and sentenced, jointly, to the death penalty (though *in absentia*), see ARV G 2351: M. 16: 1r–2r.

initial denunciation filed before the Justícia Criminal, Caterina noted how "for some time now" Bernat Noguera and his brother-in-law, Perot, had conceived "great hatred, rancor, and bad will" toward her. In an effort to satisfy these feelings of anger and resentment, Bernat and Perot allegedly had assembled an entire gang of men who had lain in wait for her one night on a deserted stretch of the royal highway. Upon seeing Caterina approach, the band of men reportedly shouted "Kill! Kill!" and then burst out of their hiding place with swords and lances unsheathed. Caterina's two young male escorts immediately took flight, leaving this woman completely defenseless as the assembled throng descended on her. Stabbing her with their lances, they wounded her in the back and the right leg; "beating her with diverse blows," they gave her multiple bruises on her head and face as well as all over her body. Indeed, she claimed, "there was such a great effusion of blood" from said wounds, "that if Our Lord had not helped her, she surely would have died."[41]

In this, her initial denunciation, Caterina demanded that her attackers be punished with the harshest and most severe penalties. Noting that because the attack had been committed on the royal highway and involved more than twelve men attacking one woman, she contended that surely at least ten of them merited the death penalty.[42] She also stressed that

> the aforementioned criminals and those accused along with them are all very much of one company, such that if one of them is offended, they take pleasure in collectively— all ten, twelve, fifteen, or twenty of them—wreaking vengeance on that person. Such is their practice and thus they are accustomed to band together to attack houses, households, rural estates, as well as inflict injuries in the streets. They are men of bad reputation, of bad morals and customs (*homens de mala fama vida e conversacio*). This is how they are considered and that is their reputation among those who know them.[43]

41. "Sabent que la dita Caterina era en lo dit loch e s'en deuia anar la dita nit aquells ensemps ab los dessus dits Luis Maria Bernat Bosch Maria Polo Nalfonso Alvarez en Johan Guimera Anthoni Marti en Jacme Marti fill de aquell se meteren e lo dit negre del dit Bernat Noguera com dit es en lo dit aguayt... tots de companyia armats de diverses armes mort acordada sortiren del dit aguayt e cami real e cridant ab les espases e broguers arranquats a mort a mort irruhien vers e contra la dita na Caterina." ARV JCrim 53: Denunciacions: M. 3: 24r–26v.

42. The *denunciacion* concluded, "Los dits delats e denunciats per esser exits en lo cami real a la dita na Caterina e haver naffrada aquella e haver fet ajust entre aquells de XII homens en sus poch mes o menys serien X son encorreguts en pena de mort e altres grans penes." ARV JCrim 53: Denunciacions: M. 3: 24r–26v.

43. "Que los dits delats e denunciats ab altres son molts de una companyia. En axi que si al hu de aquells fan enuig atroba plaer de dampnificar a alguna persona se ajustament comunament X XII XV o XX e tal es lur practhica e aquells en la dita forma son anats de fer ajusts e combatre cases alberchs e alqueries

There is a highly interesting postscript to this case. Three days later, Caterina appeared before the Justícia Criminal stating that she would like to renounce and formally with-draw her denunciation because she now "knew and it was certain that the injury or inju-ries done to her person had been and were committed by Jordi, the black male slave of Bernat Noguera's father, *for his own motives and at his own risk*" (emphasis added).[44] In a startling reversal, Caterina dropped the charges against the ten or twelve other assailants and held the black male slave named Jordi solely responsible for this assault.

Caterina's sudden "realization" strikes the reader as an all too convenient resolution to this dispute. It seems likely that a compromise had been negotiated between Cateri-na's husband and Bernat Noguera in an effort to preserve both households' sense of honor. The demands of the injured party (Caterina and her husband) for justice would be met inasmuch as someone was being held accountable. And yet by pinning the blame entirely on the black male slave, Bernat did not have to admit or assume any real culpa-bility for the crime. Rather, he was incriminated only incidentally, as the son of the black male slave's beleaguered master. Being able to lay blame on someone other than the two principals in the disputes, especially on a marginalized figure like a black male slave, likely made it easier for the feuding parties to make peace. Indeed, Caterina states here that she was also willing to renounce her claim against Jordi, the black male slave. She explained that she had decided to withdraw her charges against "the aforementioned ac-cused and also the black male slave largely because this seems to her to be the right thing to do and to say inasmuch as it redounds to the utility of the aforementioned accused, to each one of them, as well as to the black male slave."[45] Thus, she requested that both parties make a pact to proclaim a truce with respect to this matter. Although it seems fairly likely that Caterina and her husband received some form of monetary compensa-tion, there is no record made of it here. Rather, Caterina assured the court that she was not withdrawing her charges because she had been bribed or threatened but "only out of reverence for God, to clear her conscience, and to make sure that she did not unjustly trouble anyone."[46]

---

e naffrar per camins e finalment son homens de mala fama vida e conversacio e per tals son hauts tenguts e reputats per los conexents aquells." ARV JCrim 53: Denunciacions: M. 3: 24r–26v.

44. "E ella proposant regonexent sa consciencia com sapia e sia certa que la naffra o naffres en sa persona fetes hauria e ha fetes Jordi sclau negre del pare del dit Bernat Noguera per son propri motiu e atreniment." ARV JCrim 53: Denunciacions: M. 3: 24r–26v.

45. "De sa certa sciencia los absol e diffeneix axi los dits denunciants com eciam lo dit sclau negre largament segons que mils fer e dir se puixa a sa e bon enteniment e a tota utilitat dels dits denunciats e de cascun de aquells e del dit sclau negre." ARV JCrim 53: Denunciacions: M. 3: 24r–26v.

46. "Per la dita raho e offir vos jurar que no posa la present abolicio per dines menaces ne per altra raho sino solament per reverencia de deu e per descarrech de sa consciencia com no vulla injustament vexar algun." ARV JCrim 53: Denunciacions: M. 3: 24r–26v.

Although slaves certainly might have taken up arms out of a sense of affinity for their masters, further analysis of the extant sources belies a straightforward reading of these incidents as unequivocal evidence of a slave's integration. Slaves, it seems, might have been the preferred agents in these assaults precisely because they were liminal and marginalized figures. Masters ordered their slaves to ridicule, assault, and batter their enemies because their debased status rendered the indignity more degrading. In addition, it would seem that, by enlisting slaves to perform these tasks, they hoped to evade censure for crimes executed on their behalf and at their instigation.[47] It was easier for a master to renounce responsibility for an attack perpetrated by a slave because, in comparison with other household dependents, slaves (perhaps black males in particular) were more readily assumed to be violent and uncontrollable. Indeed, it could be argued that by entrusting these brutal and bloody tasks to their black male slaves, masters perpetuated an image of the black male slave as a dangerous and sadistic other. Slaves thus become the scapegoats for the violence that disturbed the peace and threatened the stability of the community.

By their own testimony, however, masters and mistresses were not always in control; while purchasing a slave might have offered them an efficient and convenient way to humiliate their enemies, it also gave rise to new vulnerabilities. According to the internal logic of the master-slave relationship any injury suffered by a slave would be felt by a master. Thus their rivals now had an additional target.

Not always the "aggressors," slaves often found themselves caught in the cross fire; indeed, they seem to have been relatively easy marks in feuds between neighbors and rival artisans. In the spring of 1452 a butcher named Luis Martí (and his wife) allegedly directed their servant, Francesquet, to attack Caterina, a slave woman owned by his enemy, the baker Johan Pascual (aka Johan the "Double-Chinned"). In the verbal complaint filed before the Justícia Criminal, the slave woman's master, the baker Johan, presented the attack against his slave woman as but a preliminary to this butcher's direct assault against his kin. After Francesquet came to his household armed with a butcher's hammer and "deliberately" gave Caterina two blows in her left arm ("having been incited by and on the orders of said Luis Martí and his wife"), Luis himself came over the following evening, a Sunday. He attacked Johan's wife and mother-in-law while they were on their way to

47. Suggestive that this was a common tactic utilized by masters, Dennis Romano has posited that noblemen in Renaissance Venice often "made their servants take the blame for certain crimes." Though he does not make the same observation with respect to slaves, in a footnote Romano cites a case in which Niccolò Saraceno, the slave of the nobleman Marino de Garzoni, was blamed for the death of a twelve-year-old boy named Giovanni (a boy who, Romano reasons, "in all likelihood was another of Garzoni's servants"). The most incriminating testimony presented against Niccolò came from the nobleman's son. See Romano, *Housecraft and Statecraft*, 296.

church to attend vespers, hitting them repeatedly with a bat.[48] Similarly, in 1445 a textile worker attacked Ali, a Muslim slave owned by a rival textile worker, slapping him several times in the face, pulling his beard, and then grabbing a big stick and threatening to beat him with it.[49] In 1449, finally, Gabriel de Sentacilia complained that a black slave of his named Domingo had been attacked and beaten "without cause" by a laborer from Almacera working on an adjacent plot of land.[50]

"Shameful Acts": Sex and Honor

Extant court records, thus, amply demonstrate how masters and mistresses considered attacks against their slaves as personal assaults. In lieu of an open confrontation in the street, however, a fifteenth-century Valencian might also injure his rival by the decidedly more covert means of seducing his slave woman.

Contemporary testimony indicates that honor in fifteenth-century Valencia was measured (at least partly) by a man's ability to protect and control the women of his household—including his slave women. In 1492, a slave woman named Ysabel refuted charges leveled against her chastity by emphasizing how her master kept her (as well as all his other slave women) "very well guarded."[51] The nobleman Johan Ros reportedly

---

48. "Affermant que dissabte prop passat lo dit Francesquet a tracte e giny e de manament dels dits Luis Marti e muller d'aquell vench ab una clavilla de carniceria o basto a la casa d'ells dits clamants e acordadament dona a Caterina sclava del dit en Johan Pascual dues bastonades en lo braz squerre." ARV JCrim 102: Cedes: M. 2 (nonpaginated): 6 March 1452. A week and a half later, Pascual and his wife (Berthomena) dropped the charges. Unfortunately, they did not give a reason.

49. ARV JCrim 22: Clams: M. 6: (nonpaginated): 4 December 1445. In this instance, however, although his master's name was also given, Ali himself (as opposed to his master) lodged this claim.

50. Domingo allegedly had suffered at least two grave injuries: his left arm was severely broken and he was in danger of dying from the injury he suffered as a result of being hit with a stick on the left side of his head. According to the testimony of the court-appointed physicians, however, the black slave was on the road to recovery and no longer was in any danger of dying—that is, if he followed his doctor's advice. ARV JCrim 23: Clams: M. 4: (nonpaginated) 29 August 1449.

51. Ysabel testified that her former master, Alfonso de la Barreda, a baker (now deceased), "tenia les sclaves molt guardades." ARV G 2395: M. 11: 39r. At the time when Alfonso acquired her, Ysabel reportedly was only eleven years old. Escorted from an unspecified marketplace in Castile to Valencia by Joan, a black male slave of Alfonso's, Ysabel insisted that she entered this baker's household as a virgin. Her master, however, she contended, subsequently "took" her virginity and impregnated her with his child. The three other slaves living in Alfonso's household (Joan, Pere Andreu, and Sperança, who also had had sexual relations with Alfonso) all confirmed that they had seen Ysabel and Alfonso have sex "many different times," both "during the day and at nighttime," in Alfonso's chamber as well as elsewhere in the house. Suggestive that these goings-on were well known throughout the community, when a neighbor bumped into Alfonso's mother-in-law at the local oven, she chided her, "Good woman, how can it be that your daughter [speaking of Alfonso's wife] is still in love with her husband? Oh, unfortunate one! If all

ejected a Castilian squire from his household because he suspected him of impregnating Margalida, his slave woman.[52] Moreover, according to the kingdom's law code, a man guilty of impregnating another person's slave woman was to be punished with a fine of twenty-five lliures, payable to the slave's owner. If he was unable to pay this fine, the "impregnator" (emprenyador) would be forced "to run completely naked through the city and given a good lashing."[53] The impregnation of someone else's slave woman was considered a crime not only because it compromised her value as a piece of property—the pregnancy would temporarily reduce her productivity and imperil her health (she could die in childbirth)[54]—but also because it damaged her master's reputation, exposing his weakness or failure to protect his slave women. Impregnating someone else's slave woman was considered a particularly heinous offense when the guilty party was a "familiar" or a member of the household. In 1458, when a physician accused his former servant, Pascual Vilanova, of impregnating Pavaria, his Russian slave woman, he emphasized how, at the time of the offense, Pascual had been "eating his bread and drinking his wine." Likening the violation of his slave woman's chastity to sedition, the physician insisted that his former servant "incur the punishment and other penalties stipulated in the kingdom's law code for treason."[55] Rather than turn to the courts for redress, when the nobleman Galceran Castellar de Borga learned that his squire had impregnated his slave woman Luqua, he, in contrast, reportedly chased him out of his house with a knife.[56]

Such testimony suggests that "the logic of honor" functioned in fifteenth-century Valencia in ways similar to those encountered by social anthropologists doing field work in twentieth century Mediterranean societies.[57] When, as David Gilmore observes, "male honor" is "insecurely dependent" on the control of female chastity,

---

three of them [Alfonso's wife and his two slave women] were to become pregnant, how will it be possible to find Madona Loba [ostensibly, the local midwife]?"

52. ARV G 2314: M. 9: 36r–43v.

53. In exchange for payment of said fine, "if he wished" the impregnator of the slave woman could take possession of the child, who, if he himself was of free status, had technically been born free. Furs de València, Colon and Garcia, eds. (Barcelona, 1990), V: 111–12.

54. If the slave woman died in labor, the "impregnator" was obliged to compensate the slave's owner, "paying him the price of the slave." Furs de València, Colon and Garcia, eds. (Barcelona, 1990), V: 111–12.

55. Pascual "menjant e estant en casa e prenent soldada s'es jagut carnalment ab la dita Pavaria e la ha emprenyada e per consequent es encorregut en pena de traydor e altres penes en furs e privileges statuhides." ARV JCrim 54: M. 1: 1r; M. 2: 1r–5v; 48r–v. Pascual, however, managed to escape before his former master could file charges. Although the Justícia Criminal condemned Pascual to death, it bears noting that he was sentenced in absentia.

56. "Aquell lo corregue ab hun punyal per casa." ARV G 2294: 330r.

57. Arguing that "the logic of honor" is "a transcultural phenomenon that goes beyond the historical context as well as the ethnographic and geographic ones," Christian Giordano argues that "honor is not so much a moral code as a language and a set of rational social strategies whose purpose is the skilful

sexuality becomes a form of social power. Sex is a competitive idiom by which men jockey for control over women both as objects to achieve narcissistic gratification and to attain dominance over other men.... Successful claims on a woman entail domination of other men, both from the point of view of the husband, who jealously guards his wife, and of the adulterer, who shows himself to be more powerful than the husband.[58]

Although Gilmore presents this as a competition between men, in fifteenth-century Valencia maintaining the honor of a household—and, by extension, monitoring the sexual behavior of its female members—was not exclusively a male concern. Slave mistresses displayed a similar interest in controlling their slave women's chastity. In 1456, for example, a woman filed charges against a cobbler for impregnating her slave woman, Anna.[59] The ratio of slave mistresses to slave masters filing complaints against slave "impregnators," in fact, was considerably larger than the ratio of female to male slave owners overall—suggesting that mistresses had to be especially vigilant in this regard. Although women acting independently generally accounted for only about 11 percent of slave buyers and sellers overall, two of the five plaintiffs encountered in contemporary court records filing this type of claim were women.[60]

Irrespective of whether the impregnated slave's owner was male or female, however, the impregnation of a slave woman was often linked to theft. The aforementioned physician, for example, contended that the seduction of his slave woman Pavaria was part and parcel of Pascual's elaborate scheme to despoil him of his possessions. Eyeing his "rich and opulent" household, Pascual allegedly reasoned that "there was no better way to accomplish so great a theft than to sleep with a slave woman of the household named Pavaria." Promising the Russian slave woman that he would "take her away with him," Pascual reputedly wooed Pavaria for the sole purpose of making her his accomplice. Convinced by Pascual to betray her master, Pavaria reportedly stole (on his behalf) items worth twenty lliures.[61]

---

management of one's individual and group reputation by trying to avoid being publicly discredited and humiliated." Giordano, "Mediterranean Honor and Beyond," 40.

58. David D. Gilmore, "The Shame of Dishonor," in *Honor and Shame and the Unity of the Mediterranean*, ed. David Gilmore (Washington, D.C.: American Anthropological Association, 1987), 7. See also Giordano, "Mediterranean Honor and Beyond," 42–43.

59. ARV JCrim 24: Clams (nonpaginated): 26 April 1454.

60. Only sixty-seven of the 608 slave buyers and sellers encountered in notarial records dating from 1460 to 1480 were women acting alone. In contrast, almost half of the slave owners who filed formal complaints charging that their slave women had been impregnated by third parties were women.

61. Pascual de Vilanova "vehent e sabent que la dita casa del dit mestre Gabriel era riqua e oppulent...vehent...que bonament no podia fer gran furt si ja aquell nos jahia ab la sclava de casa appellada Pavaria induhit del esperit malign e la temor de deu e de la senyoria real apart posada...s'es jagut carnalment ab la dita Pavaria e la ha emprenyada....Jahent se ab la dita sclava induhit aquella que robas totes

Similarly, in 1472 a slave owner named Riqua contended that in addition to impregnating her slave woman, Elena, her former servant, Francesc Rosques, had stolen items worth more than fifty lliures from her household—presumably with Elena's connivance.[62] The testimony of these plaintiffs suggests that it was conventional wisdom that the success of a robbery hinged on the cooperation and complicity of the household's slave woman. In 1454, a Valencian dyer named Pere Dolesa cited the fact that his apprentice, Arnau Ribes, was sleeping with (and ultimately impregnated) his slave woman, Lucia, as "proof" that Arnau was stealing from him. Pere stated that he suspected his apprentice not only because it was rumored that he was a thief but also "because during said period [when the thefts occurred], he had been sleeping with his slave woman."[63]

As the cases just outlined indicate, "impregnated" slave women were not always viewed as innocent victims. Indeed, in the next set of court cases we will examine, masters and mistresses portrayed their slave women as willfully promiscuous. Given the slave woman's position of extreme powerlessness and vulnerability, the degree of agency masters and mistresses attributed to their slave women merits further exploration and discussion.

Bearing Their Masters' Child: Sex, Lies, and Paternity Suits

Since, as suggested earlier, "the measure of a man's honor is [at least in part] the shame of his women,"[64] it is not surprising to discover that slave owners viewed the sexual activities of their slave women with special anxiety. Although they might have actively defended their masters' honor with their tongues and bedpans, slave women could significantly tarnish the reputation of their household by committing "shameful acts" (tacanyería) within its confines. Illustrative of how contemporaries believed dishonor "was contagious through women"[65] and that slave women, in particular, were " 'weak links'

que pogues de aquella e que lo y donas prometent li que la s'en portaria en altres parts." ARV JCrim 54: M. 1: 1r; M. 2: 1r–5v; 48r–v.

62. Accused of behaving like a fox in a henhouse (in more ways than one), Francesc was also charged with swiping twenty of Riqua's chickens. Convicted "in abstentia," Francesc was sentenced to death. ARV G 4261: M. 5: 39r–40v.

63. "E fon sospita e encara fama que lo dit Arnau hi auria çabut. E axiu deu esser presumit per raho com aquell en lo dit temps se jahia ab la dita sclava segons que en apres se es mostrat." ARV JCrim 52: Denunciacions: M. 1: 7r; M. 2: 33r–35r.

64. An observation of Julian A. Pitt-Rivers, quoted in John Davis, People of the Mediterranean (London: Routledge, 1977), 160.

65. Davis, People of the Mediterranean, 160. Mary Douglas has also shown how anxieties concerning group identity have been expressed through corporeal metaphors and how fears of pollution, penetration, and corruption have tended to focus on the female body. Mary Douglas, Natural Symbols: Explorations

in the chain of masculine virtue,"[66] sexual licentiousness (vicio de bagassa) was one of the "hidden defects and vices" that could be cited as grounds for the immediate rescission of a slave woman's sale. When a Valencian tanner negotiated the sale of his slave woman named Sperancia, he warned the slave's buyer (the daughter of a pharmacist) that the thirty-five-year-old baptized Muslim was "whorish." Though the sale would still be covered by the standard sixty-day blanket warranty against "any hidden vices and defects," the seller insisted that he could not be held liable if it should be found that Sperancia has either a proclivity to run away or a predilection for having sex with many men (vicio de fugitive et de bagasa).[67] Although masters and mistresses clearly condemned slave women for being "unchaste," what happened when the slave woman's sexual partner was her master? Was sex between a master and his slave woman regarded as "shameful" behavior?

Nowhere is the ambivalent character of the master-slave relationship more conspicuous than in the sexual interaction between masters and their female slaves. Sexual relations between masters and their female slaves considerably blurred distinctions between enemy and familiar, free and slave. When a Russian slave woman named Anna described her relationship with her master, she noted how for the past ten years they had slept together in the same bed each night "as if she was his wife" (com si fos sa muller).[68] Likewise, pointing out how she and her master "ate together at one table" and "slept together in one bed," another Russian slave woman named Rosa contended that she was "more properly speaking" her master's concubine than his slave.[69] The pregnancies that not so infrequently resulted from these relationships confused distinctions between kin and

---

in Cosmology (New York: Pantheon Books, 1970), and, Douglas, Purity and Danger: An Analysis of the Concepts of Pollution and Taboo (London: Routledge, 1966), 122–28. For a discussion of how fifteenth-century Iberian authors attributed the outbreak of epidemic diseases to woman's "sinfulness, excessive behavior or demonic and diabolical acts," see Michael Solomon, The Literature of Misogyny in Medieval Spain: The Archipreste de Talavera and the Spill (Cambridge: Cambridge University Press, 1997), esp. 67–93.

66. Gilmore, "The Shame of Dishonor," 12.

67. APPV 26674 (nonpaginated): 22 November 1477.

68. "Se ha jagut carnalment ab la dita Anna olim sclava d'aquell e jahia cascuna nit ab aquella en hun llit com si fos sa muller e la emprenya de la dita filla." ARV G 2317: 234r–235v.

69. "Menjava ab aquella en una taula e dormia en hun llit e jahent se carnalment ab aquella axi propriament com si fos una concubina sua hoc en tant que li tenia una sclava que la servia." ARV G 2344: M. 12: 9r. The notary Arnau Castello purchased Rosa when she was eighteen years old. At the time, he was a bachelor living in the newly conquered kingdom of Naples and she "a pretty, white and young" slave woman. Noting how Arnau already had another slave woman who did the chores, Rosa claimed that she enjoyed a privileged position in the household. Indeed, shortly after she started living in Arnau's household, she got pregnant and gave birth to their first child, a daughter named Lucrecia. Though Lucrecia died while still in infancy, Arnau reportedly embraced her as his daughter and, when he subsequently moved back to Valencia, though he was married now to a noblewoman named Ursola, Arnau brought Rosa along with him. In Valencia, moreover, he and Rosa reputedly maintained the same "friendship" as before.

stranger further still. As a consequence of giving birth to her master's child, the slave woman and her owner were now linked together by blood ties. In such circumstances, a master was faced with a dilemma: How should he treat this slave woman who had given birth to his child? What was the "honorable" thing to do, particularly in the event that a slave's pregnancy provoked tensions between the master and his wife? Could a master, in good conscience, sell a former lover and the mother of his children?

We saw in the previous chapter how likening the master-slave relationship to that between a parent and a child served to naturalize the relationship. However, doing so simultaneously imposed limits on the slave owner's authority. Masters and mistresses could be criticized for a failure to live up to their responsibilities towards their "kin." In contrast with other Christian slave-holding societies in the late medieval Mediterranean world, slave women who bore their master's child in the kingdom of Valencia were entitled to an automatic manumission. According to the *Furs de València*, a master who impregnated his slave woman was obliged not only to acknowledge the child's freeborn status and see to it that the child was properly baptized but also to free the child's mother. The statute reads, "If any Christian lies with his slave woman, and a son or daughter is produced from this union . . . both the mother and the son or daughter shall be free."[70]

Historians of slavery quite rightly have pointed to sexual exploitation as a distinguishing feature of the enslaved woman's experience. In the paragraphs that follow, however, I will be examining court records that portray slave women as exploiting their sexuality as a tool to secure their liberation. Bearing their masters' children offered slave women a path to freedom not available to their male counterparts. Thus, when the aforementioned Russian slave woman named Anna informed her master that she was pregnant with his child, he reportedly advised her, "Take good care of the fetus, for through it you will have good fortune."[71]

In the event, however, that a master opted to deny his own child, slave women (like any other slave alleging wrongful detainment) had recourse to the kingdom's courts. My research in the court records of the kingdom of Valencia has brought to light the efforts of slave women of a variety of different ethnic origins to win their freedom (as well as that of their children) by filing what were, in essence, paternity suits against their masters. Winning recognition of their freed status on the basis of such claims was an admittedly

---

70. "Tot chrestià qui jaurà ab cativa sua e n'haurà fill o filla, que aquell fill o filla sia tantost batejat e que sien franchs la mare e-l fill o la filla." *Furs de València*, Colon and Garcia, eds. (Barcelona, 1990), V: 110.

71. "Puxs est prenyada de mi guarda lo prenyat que per aquell hauras be." ARV G 2317: 234r–235v. Her master, ultimately, however, did not honor his commitment to her. Anna protested that even though her master knew very well that she had given birth to his child, he flouted the kingdom's laws and tried to re-sell her, all because he wanted to use the proceeds to purchase a black male slave to work in his vineyards. I discuss Anna's *demanda de libertat* in chapter 6, see pp. 215–16.

problematic endeavor—much trickier, we will see, for instance, than confirming their fulfillment of the terms of a contract of manumission or a clause promising freedom in their master's (or mistress's) last will and testament. In the absence of DNA testing, to secure their freedom slave women had to establish not only that they had had a sexual relationship with their master but also that their master had recognized their children as their own. In the most ideal circumstances, they produced witnesses who could testify that they had heard the master explicitly confess that the child was his, but even if the master never acknowledged his paternity in words, these enslaved women's advocates contended that he had done so through his actions.

What is particularly noteworthy about these court records is how, in their efforts to protect and/or advance their interests, enslaved women adopted the rhetorical strategies of their masters. Hardly rejecting their masters' paternalistic pretensions, slaves turned the ideology that justified their subjugation to their own advantage. Emphasizing how their masters celebrated their children's births and coordinated their infants' baptisms, slave women interpreted such actions as expressions of affinity. No longer nameless *testes* ("heads"—the term used to describe shiploads of captives when they arrived in Valencia's *grau*), they were their mistresses' beloved stepdaughters or their masters' faithful concubines. As intimates, not enemies or objects, honor dictated that they could not be cast aside.

In 1461, a slave woman named Margalida gave birth to a baby boy whom she insisted was her master's son. In a lawsuit filed on her behalf some four years later, Margalida noted how, at the time of the child's birth, her master readily had acknowledged, if not embraced, her son Michalet as his own, coordinating the infant's baptism, contracting the services of a wet nurse, and "doing those things which a father does for his child."[72] As soon as the infant was entrusted to the care of the wet nurse, however, Margalida complained, she had been cruelly and faithlessly repudiated. In flagrant disregard of her newly won "freed" status as the mother of her master's child, Margalida was cast out from her master's household, dispatched secretly to the town of Lucena, where she was sold, illicitly, to a new master.[73]

For his part, Margalida's master, the nobleman Johan Ros, protested that, hardly greeting the news of his slave's pregnancy with joyful anticipation, he considered the slave's

72. "Que lo dit honorable mossen Johan Ros tantost que fon nat lo dit Michalet lo feu lo feu [sic] donar a criar a una dida de la vila d'Onda e paga a aquella la soldada o la let del dit Michalet axi com a fill d'aquell.... tots temps ... ha fet e fa vers aquell ço que pare fa envers fill.... Que lo dit mossen Johan Ros ha portat vestit lo dit Michalet axi com a fill tenint aquell per fill e mostrant li amor de fill." ARV G 2314: 41v; 44or.

73. "Lo dit honorable mossen Johan Ros sabent que la dita Margalida per ley de la terra attes que havia parits de aquell era franqua vene la fora la ciutat de Valencia ço es en la vila de Lucena." ARV G 2314: 44or.

condition an affront to the honor of his household. In response to Margalida's allegations, Johan not only denied paternity but represented his slave's pregnancy as an act of
rebellion.[74] In stark contrast to Margalida's description of a proud father caring for his
son, Johan's account emphasized how, immediately after the infant's birth, he beat Margalida as punishment for this "shameful act" that she had committed in his household.[75]
Fearful that beating alone was not a sufficient enough chastisement, Johan maintained
that it was necessary and that he was completely within his rights to expel the unruly slave
from his household. Indeed, "in order to cause her even greater distress," he intended to
see to it that she would never again see her son and threatened to pack her off to the island
of Ibiza.[76] Thus, in opposition to Margalida's assertions that her resale was legally invalid
and morally reprehensible, Johan vigorously asserted the authority of a master over his
slave woman: Johan, "being lord of the said slave woman Margalida . . . decided to sell her
for having committed such an act in his power."[77]

In what is a very well-documented pattern, masters attempted to refute paternity allegations by distancing themselves both morally and physically from slaves and their
purported offspring. Rationalizing the repudiation of these slave women by portraying
them as devious and ungrateful others, masters and mistresses recast their pregnancies
as acts of rebellion. Thus, after affirming his own good reputation, Johan Ros denounced
Margalida as a slut who was "accustomed to have many lovers . . . for which reason she
became pregnant."[78]

These slave women plaintiffs, in contrast, professed enjoying a special intimacy with
their masters. Recounting how their masters recognized, and occasionally even fulfilled, their obligations to them as both their concubines and the mothers of their children, they portrayed themselves as bound to their masters by feelings of kinship. Thus,

74. Margalida was described repeatedly as a "dona molt fort," "viciosa," and possessing a "mala
lengua," not only by Johan Ros but by several witnesses testifying on his behalf. ARV G 2314: 41v;
440r–447v.

75. "De continent que la dita sclava hague parit se congoxa molt ab aquella batent la e menacant la
vendre a Eviça." Similarly, Johan stressed how he had ejected a Castilian squire from his household, the
"true" culprit responsible for impregnating his slave woman. Thus, Johan insisted, "James en lo criar
que ha fet fer de la dita criatura nos pot dir lo haia fet criar en forma de fill sino com a sclau ans lo dit
mossen Ros ne ha mostrat molta congoxa e enug que la dita sclava li havia parit en casa." ARV G 2314:
441r–443v.

76. "E de fet per donar li maior congoxa per lo cas que havia fet en la casa sua li leva la criatura e no
volgue la crias. . . . Per que la dita sclava no hagues causa de veure la feu criar en la vila d'Onda en poder de
una dona qui la criava sens que nos cura pus de aquella." ARV G 2314: 443v.

77. "Essent senyor de la dita Margalida sclava . . . e per haver comes tal acte en poder seu ell dellibera
de vendre aquella." ARV G 2314: 443v.

78. "Es molt viciosa fort e acostumada de tenir enamorats e usar carnalment ab aquells per que aquell
s'es emprenyada." ARV G 2314: 444r.

Margalida contended that in providing clothing for Michalet, Johan Ros was "displaying love" for his son. Indeed, there was even a strong physical resemblance between the two. Margalida insisted that simply by looking at the faces of her master and her child, "one can tell that they are father and son."[79] Skillfully manipulating the paternalistic rhetoric that, in other circumstances, legitimated (and perpetuated) their subjugation, several of these slave women successfully sued for their freedom. Out of a total of seventeen *demandes de libertat* brought before the court of the governor between 1425 and 1520 by slave women claiming to have given birth to their master's child, six (including Margalida's) were successful and a seventh was resolved by means of an arbitrated settlement. Although six of the remaining ten cases are incomplete, making an evaluation of the overall success rate difficult, only three claims, definitively, were rejected.

Given the prevailing customs of the time, of course, masters could hardly deny that they had sexual relations with their slave women. Instead, they attempted to cast doubt on claims that they had fathered their children by portraying slave women as sexually promiscuous. In an effort to displace (if not entirely disown) responsibility, masters, mistresses, and their heirs emphasized their slave women's lack of discretion and attributed to them prodigious sexual appetites. Thus, when the aforementioned slave woman named Ysabel demanded recognition of her freed status for having given birth to two of her master's children,[80] her master's heirs retorted that it was impossible for Ysabel to affirm that her master undeniably was the father of her two children. For, she was nothing short of a "public whore," "laying carnally with slaves as well as free persons." They contended that before, during, and after each of her two pregnancies she had "lived very dishonestly, committing adultery and fornicating with all men." Ysabel allegedly had sex "with anyone who came to her, not saying no to anyone."[81]

Similarly, when Ursola, the daughter of Russian slave woman named Maria, filed a demand for her liberty, claiming that her master (Jofré d'Anyo) was her biological father, Jofré's sister retorted that Maria was notorious "for having carnal relations with slaves both white and black."[82] Indeed, Jofré's widow, Francesqua, maintained that Maria was

79. "Ex facie del dit mossen Johan e del dit Miqualet poreu conexer aquells esser pare e fill axi com realment ho son." ARV G 2314: 440v.

80. I noted earlier (in chapter 4) Ysabel's argument that Alfonso's participation in Ysabel's daughter's baptism constituted irrefutable "proof" that he was the child's biological father. See pp. 130 and 132.

81. "Vivia molt desonestament jaent se carnalment axi ab catius com ab altres persones franques... era publica bagassa fent so de tots los qui venien davant no dient de no a nengu.... Axi ans que paris com stant prenyada com apres que hague parit continuament ha vixcut desonestament adulterant e fornicant ab tot hom.... Que puix moltes gents han comunicat e praticat carnalment ab la dita Ysabel nos pot inferir que aquella parint ni emprenyant se se sia emprenyada del dit N'Alfonso de la Barreda amo seu in tal cosa seria provat ni fundat de justicia." ARV G 2395: M. 11: 39v–41r.

82. "Se jahia carnalment ab catius axi blanchs com negres e ab molts homens als quals liurava la sua persona en tant que la dita Maria axi vivia liurant se ab huns e ab altres carnalment." ARV G 2305: M. 11:

so sexually promiscuous that her husband, in exasperation, had offered her freedom in exchange for a promise to abstain from having carnal intercourse during a seven-year term of service. Maria, reportedly, had refused, declaring that she would rather be a perpetual slave than swear off sex. This widow insinuated that Maria had been so outraged by even the suggestion that she curtail her sexual activities that, henceforth, in defiance, "she would not say no to anyone who asked for it."[83]

In their testimony before the court of the governor, then, masters and mistresses frequently linked a slave woman's sexual promiscuity with rebellion. A witness appearing on behalf of Jofré d'Anyo's sister adduced as "proof" that the Russian slave woman named Maria was a "bad woman" the fact that she had had sexual relations with black men. This barber testified that he "never considered the slave of Jofré d'Anyo to be a good woman and had heard many people say that she was a bad woman." Not only had he seen the slave drunk on several occasions but he also knew she had given birth to a "black" baby girl.[84]

Similarly, when a friend expressed interest in purchasing the aforementioned slave woman named Margalida, Johan Ros reportedly urged him to reconsider, warning him that Margalida was "very insolent and immoral."[85] Johan also testified that Margalida frequently complained to him that he was committing "a grave sin by making her live without a man."[86] Unsuccessful in his efforts to rein in his slave's libido, Johan lamented that a male servant named Anthonet (Anthoni) had fled his household due to Margalida's incessant sexual advances. Anthoni testified that he left Johan Ros's service because Margalida "did nothing but grab him by the ass, demanding that he lay carnally with her." Reproaching this slave woman for her faithlessness and lack of restraint, Anthoni maintained that he, in contrast, never lost control. While Margalida was an "impudent and dissolute woman," Anthoni, in contrast, "protected the honor of the household" by steadfastly resisting all her demands.[87]

11r. I discussed the role the nobleman Jofré d'Anyo played in Ursola/Yolant's baptism in chapter 4, see pp. 131–32.

83. Francesqua testified that "lo dit en Jofré d'Anyo la volia fer franqua a la dita Maria a set anys ab esta condicio que dins los VII anys nos acostas ab nengun home carnalment e la dita Maria dix que no li venia be que mes amava esser sclava per esta raho li portava mala voluntat lo dit son amo e ella dita testimoni e tant era mala la dita Maria que creu ella testimoni que no vedava a nengu que liu demanas." ARV G 2305: M. 11: 16r.

84. The barber testified that "may he tenguda la dita sclava del dit en Jofré d'Anyo per bona dona ans hoy dir a molts que era mala dona ... veu ell dit testimoni que la dita Maria pari una filla negra. ... Ha hoyt dir en la dita cassa del dit en Jofré d'Anyo ... que la dita Maria se seria jaguda ab hun negre." ARV G 2305: M. 11: 18r–v.

85. "Era molt fort viciosa e havia comes en casa tal acte lo'n volgue avisar." ARV G 2314: 441r.

86. "Aquella no podia star sense home e que son amo havia gran peccat de fer la star sense home." ARV G 2314: M. 1: 36v; M. 9: 441v.

87. "La dita sclava es molt viciosa disoluta enamoradica que hun jove que lo dit mossen Ros tenia en casa apellat Anthonet per causa de la dita sclava se hisque de casa que no fahia sino gafar lo per lo cull

Thus, in opposition to this depiction of slave women (regardless of ethnicity) as natu-rally libidinous creatures, unable to control their passions,[88] masters projected an image of discipline and restraint. Masters generally denied having feelings of lust or desire for their slave women. Such an admission, after all, would imply a lack of "mastery." Johan Ros, for one, declared that "he was not accustomed to perform such acts with the slave women of his household."[89] Although other masters admitted that, on occasion, they had sex with their slave women, they invariably insisted that they did so only out of necessity—because their wives were unavailable or because of health reasons. The notary Bernat Johan, for instance, contended that he slept with his wife's slave woman, Johana "the Bearded," "more as a remedy for his kidney stones" than out of lust. At the time, his wife had been away in Murviedro, helping to bring in the wine harvest.[90] In a similar vein, a widow dismissed charges that her husband was the father of the aforementioned slave woman named Rosa's child by proclaiming that, at the time when the slave had been impregnated, her master had been a happily married man.[91]

Left to her own devices, in contrast, a slave woman's sexual appetite inevitably provoked disorder. To take just one notable example, the romantic entanglements of the Russian slave woman named Rosa allegedly wreaked so much havoc in her master's household that one of her lovers, a black male slave named Diego, had to be resold in order to avoid bloodshed. Having carnal relations with Diego at the same time that she was having an affair with a white squire of the household named Angelo, when Rosa gave birth to a black child (her daughter, Margalida, the plaintiff in this *demanda de libertat*), Angelo re-putedly became so enraged with jealousy that Rosa's owner (the notary Arnau Castello) had to sell Diego "to prevent the scandals that would have erupted between them."[92]

---

requirent lo se jagues ab ella carnalment." The squire, not surprisingly, concurred, testifying "que la dita Margalida es fort dona e viciosa e stant ell testimoni en la casa de mossen Johan Ros aquella se enamora d'ell testimoni empero ell testimoni no hague amistat carnalment ab ella. Es ver que no resta per aquella sino ell testimoni guardava la honor de casa." ARV G 2314: 441v and 445r.

88. For the image of the black woman in the American South as a person "governed almost entirely by her libido, a Jezebel character," see Deborah Gray White, *Arn't I a Woman? Female Slaves in the Plantation South* (New York: W. W. Norton, 1985), esp. 27–46.

89. "No ha fet ni acostumat fer tals actes a les sclaves de la casa sua." Thus Johan Ros insisted that "ella non poria dir que fos de mossen Ros com ab veritat aquell no acostuma tractar axi sua companya." ARV G 2314: 441r.

90. Bernat Johan explained that "esta en veritat que ell dit responent s'es jagut carnalment ab la dita sclava Johana cativa mes per vici que per exercir luxuria e per remeys de sos mals de pedra." ARV G 2311: 55r.

91. This widow insisted that Rosa's claim "no es prova suficient per a demostrar aquell dit Jolia esser son fill... considerat majorment que en lo dit temps fonch prenyada e pari la dita Rosa ja lo dit en Arnau Castello era casat." ARV G 2384: M. 24: 31r.

92. "Lo dit Angelo vehent que la dita Rosa havia parit de aquell lo dit fill appellat Jolia e apres havia parit del dit Diego negre l'altra filla appellada Margarida pres gran hoy e mala voluntat contra lo dit Diego

Similarly, the notary Bernat Johan protested that at the time she became pregnant, his wife's dark-skinned (llora) slave woman, Johana Abarba (Johana "the Bearded"),[93] reputedly had at least three "notorious friends or lovers with whom she habitually had carnal relations": a chaplain (whom her master declined to name "[out of respect] for the holy orders"[94]); Johanet, a slave living in the household of the nobleman Guillem Masco; and Antoni, a squire living in the Centelles household. Not content with just having sex with the men who approached and propositioned her, Johana is depicted as a sexual predator who actively "goes out looking for men." The residents of a neighboring household kept their side entrance locked since "they did not dare keep it open because of a dark-skinned (llora) slave woman with painted lips who does nothing but come and go," bringing her lover (the aforementioned Johanet) "at times, rose water, at times, sweets, and many other things."[95] Publicly reputed to be "a sex-crazed woman" who had carnal relations "incessantly, sometimes with certain men, other times with other men," Johana was depicted by her male "victims" as a strange and formidable force that could not be denied. "Those who are unwilling to lie with her," her master contended, "would be tricked into doing so." Johana reportedly "played so many games with them" that it could be argued that she compelled them to sleep with her "by force."[96]

A cobbler living in a room off Bernat Johan's entryway related how "on the day of Saint Nicholas," he had fallen prey to Johana's charms. Having been lured upstairs by the slave woman, he soon found himself having sexual intercourse with her on a daybed located in her master's chamber. Not assuming any culpability for his actions, the cobbler insisted that Johana had seduced him, "making many alluring gestures in such a manner that he could not keep himself from sleeping with her." When he subsequently had sex with

---

e lo dit Diego contra lo dit Angelo e per evitar scandels que entre aquells se hagueren seguits lo dit en Castello vene lo dit Diego sclau." ARV G 2383: 505r.

93. I first discussed Johana "the Bearded" in chapter 2, pp. xx–xx.

94. The laborer Alfonso Garcia testified that whenever he came to Bernat Johan's household, his slave, Johana, was nowhere to be found. He always had to look for her, invariably finding her "in the home of a chaplain." Convinced that she and the chaplain were lovers, when Alfonso confronted this slave woman with his suspicions, Johana allegedly replied, "Mind your own business! I don't have to give an explanation to you about what I do." ARV G 2311: M. 12: 11v.

95. "No gosam teniren la dita porta uberta per una sclava lora qui te los morros pintats que may fa sino anar e venir a veure Juhanet qui sta malalt e totstemps li porta ades ayguarros ades çucres e moltes altres coses e per ço que no volen que y entre no la gosam tenir uberta." ARV G 2311: M. 12: 8r.

96. Bernat Johan maintained that Johana was "una gran bagasa la qual va cerquant los homens que la y fareu convidants los a mengar formatges frescs e donant los a beure montonech e com alguns de aquells nos volguessen jaure ab la dita sclava aquella los feya tants jochs que per força s'avien a jaure carnalment ab ella carnalment [sic] ... en tant que per los dits testimonis se mostra que la dita sclava no solament se jau carnalment ab moltes persones mas encara va cerquant los homens per que ab aquella carnalment se jaguen." ARV G 2311: M. 12: 17r–v.

her "on the day of the Virgin Mary of the Conception" (this time, in the master bedroom), she allegedly had plied him with "fresh cheese and young white wine."⁹⁷ A laborer named Domingo Granada told a similar tale of being victimized by this dark-skinned slave woman. Subjecting Domingo to a constant barrage of amorous overtures, Johana reputedly "assaulted him so many times and so often" that he "could not avoid doing what the slave woman wanted him to do." Johana "teased" him so forcefully, "doing so many shameful things to him," that he had to have intercourse with her.⁹⁸

In stark contrast to their sexually voracious slave women, masters were occasionally depicted in these paternity suits as sexually impotent. The heirs of Ysabel's master, the baker Alfonso de la Barreda, for instance, argued that Alfonso could not possibly have fathered his slave woman's (second) child. At the time when she had been impregnated, Alfonso had been "so sick and indisposed that he did not have the disposition to practice carnal intercourse with any woman." He was "unable to work or even walk, except with great difficulty."⁹⁹ Similarly, in opposition to his indomitable llora slave woman, Bernat Johan described himself as old and feeble, someone who had sex only to relieve the pain caused by his kidney stones. His advocate argued that "although the said en Bernat Johan had lain with the said slave woman," one must bear in mind that "he is old." While Johana had "many lovers with whom she had carnal relations and invited to have fresh cheese and white wine,"¹⁰⁰ Bernat was "ill and infirm [i.e., unable to have an erection]."¹⁰¹

97. "Fent li moltes gests enamorant en lo manera que ell dit testimoni no poch tenir es jague carnalment ab aquella en un llit de repos que esta en la cambra del dit en Bernat Johan. E encara se jague carnalment ab aquella lo dia de la verge Maria de la conceptio propasada en lo lit major de la casa del dit en Bernat Johan el convida almorzar a formages frechs e vin blanch." ARV G 2311: M. 12: 8v. On the significance of food as the medium through which women (particularly ethnically, culturally, and socially marginalized women) "ensorcelled," bewitched, and corrupted men, see Ruth Behar, "Sexual Witchcraft, Colonialism, and Women's Powers: Views from the Mexican Inquisition," in Sexuality and Marriage in Colonial Latin America, ed. Asunción Lavin (Lincoln: University of Nebraska Press, 1989), 178–206.

98. Domingo Granada testified that "moltes e diverses vegades la dita Johana...stomeja a ell dit testimoni de amas tantes vegades e tant sovint que ell dit testimoni no y poch de fugir de fer ço que la dita sclava volia. E hun dia entre los altres ell dit testimoni es acordant que la dita sclava prega a ell testimoni que no s'en anas que volia parlar ab ell dit testimoni e de fet ans que ell dit testimoni s'en anas parla ab aquella dita Johana en axi que aquella dita sclava se pres tant forcivent a burlar fent li tantes tanquanyeries que ell dit testimoni se jague carnalment ab aquella." ARV G 2311: M. 12: 12v.

99. "Li porta tanta indisposicio que lo dit Alfonso de la Barreda no tenia disposicio per a treballar ni anar sino ab molta dificultat.... Que del principi de la dita malaltia fins que mori...aquell dit n'Alfonso de la Barreda stigue tant mal e tant indispost e de tal malaltia que aquell no tingue disposicio per aquell praticar carnalment ab dona alguna." ARV G 2395: M. 11: 39v.

100. "Jatsia lo dit en Bernat Johan se fos jagut ab la dita sclava enpero ates que aquell es vell e la dita sclava tenia enamorats ab los quals se jahia e la convidava a formatges freches e a vins blanchs." ARV G 2311: M. 12: 17v.

101. "Esser ell dit responent malalt o invalt." ARV G 2311: M. 12: 2r.

Although claiming impotency in order to rebut a paternity suit likely enjoyed only a limited currency in a society in which honor was so closely related to sexual performance, it is striking, nevertheless, how slave women were represented here as dominating free men sexually. Paradoxically, a master's continued domination over his slave woman was occasionally predicated on a declaration of his own weakness and impotence.

Slave women themselves, however, presented their relationships with their masters in radically different terms. A black slave woman named Leonor (aka Elionor), for example, hardly characterized sexual intercourse with her master as willing or consensual. Rather, she claimed that her master forced himself on her, "seeing himself lord of the said Leonor, seeing that she could not contradict him or his wishes."[102] Similarly, although the heirs of the baker Alfonso de la Barreda disparaged her as nothing less than a prostitute or a whore, Ysabel stressed how her master had taken her virginity (la haguda fadrina) when she was only eleven years old.[103] Rather than hold their masters' sexual exploitation of them up for censure, however, most slave women appearing before the courts cited it as an indication of their privileged status, entitling them to preferential treatment.

Witnesses, for example, recounted how during Ysabel's pregnancy, her master had taken notably better care of her, "keeping and treating her like a woman who was bearing his child."[104] A former male slave in the household named Pere Andreu testified that, during Ysabel's pregnancy, Alfonso treated her very well and "held her in great affection. He gave her treats from the bakery and she almost always slept with the said en Alfonso de la Barreda [in his chamber]."[105] A former slave woman of the household named Sperança reported that she overheard Alfonso instruct Ysabel not to work so hard. "Be careful!" Alfonso cautioned. "Don't overburden yourself!" Thus "displaying great affection for her," Sperança concluded that Alfonso "was doing all this because he knew it was his child."[106]

102. "Vent se senyor de la dita Leonor e vent que aquella no li podia contradir a sa voluntat pres amor ab aquella e coneguda aquella carnalment per una e moltes vegades per lo qual acostament enprenya aquella." ARV G 2405: 399r. I discussed Leonor's experiences earlier, in chapters 4 and 5, pp. 88 and 131–32.

103. "Lo dit en Alfonso de la Barreda . . . compra a la dita Ysabel . . . era en aquell temps de edat de XI anys poch mes o menys. . . . Que stant en poder e servitut de aquell lo dit en Alfonso de la Barreda s'es jagut carnalment ab la dita Ysabel e la haguda fadrina." ARV G 2395: 38r.

104. "Essent prenyada la dita Ysabel la tenia e tractava com a prenyada de aquell e lo prenyat de aquella lo tenia per seu." ARV G 2395: 38r–v.

105. "Tractava molt be a la dita Ysabel e li tenia molta amor e que donava recapte al forn e dormia quasi continuament ab lo dit Nalfonso de la Barreda." ARV G 2395: 46v.

106. Sperança testified that "lo dit en Alfonso de la Barreda tractava molt be a la dita Ysabel essent prenyada creu ella testimoni quen feya sabent que lo prenyat era de aquell dient a la dita Ysabel guarda no't carregues e semblants paraules mostrant tenir molta amor a aquella." ARV G 2395: 41v.

Although this, their first child, died in infancy (with Alfonso reportedly attending the baby's burial wearing the pointed hood or capiro, "indicating that she was his daughter"), Ysabel was pregnant a second

"To the Testimony and/or Oath Sworn by a Slave No Faith Ought to Be Given"

Not confident that a declaration of sexual impotence would suffice to rebut his slave's charges, the notary Bernat Johan attempted to further discredit the claims of Johana "the Bearded" by smearing her reputation as a good Christian. Bernat contended that this dark-skinned slave woman was a serial renegade who had previously abjured the Catholic faith and had imminent plans to do so once again. Bernat purchased this Muslim female from a Neapolitan merchant in 1452. Almost immediately upon her arrival in his household, Bernat recounted that his wife, along with other women, took it upon themselves to "encourage the slave to become a Christian." After an unspecified period of instruction in the Catholic faith, his slave woman, who had originally been called Fatima, was baptized "Johana" in a ceremony that likely took place in the local parish church. Twelve years later, however, Bernat charged that he had since discovered that, before her arrival in Valencia, Johana/Fatima had already been baptized "Bonaventura" in Palermo, Sicily (at the time of her initial capture and enslavement). When she was subsequently resold to a new master in Barcelona, Bernat continued, Fatima/Bonaventura had renounced her Christian faith and returned to Islam. What was even more contemptible, however, Bernat argued, was that several years later, upon her arrival in Valencia, Fatima (aka Bonaventura) had deceived his wife into believing that she was an unbaptized Muslim and fraudulently accepted a second baptism.

Johana attempted to defend herself against these charges by claiming ignorance of her first baptism. "If they baptized her or not in Palermo, Sicily, she cannot recall since she had been very young and childish."[107] It is important to note here how while the double baptisms of Canary Islander captives (related in the previous chapter) passed by without remark in contemporary sources,[108] in this dark-skinned Muslim woman's case, having accepted a second baptism was held up as proof of her perfidious character.

While Fatima/Johana attempted to assure the court that she was a devout and practicing Christian, her master and mistress fomented suspicion that she was a faithless apostate and pathological liar. Bernat related a rumor that Johana (along with several other Muslim slaves) had secretly contracted the services of a *morisca* poultry seller to lead them

---

time within the year. Though Alfonso died before Ysabel's son was born, Ysabel insisted that this child, too, was her master's.

107. "Si ella dita responent bategaren en Caragoça en Çiçilia o no que no s'en recorda per tant com ella dita responent era molt petita e minyona." ARV G 2311: M. 12: 3v.

108. For a revealing analysis of the relative understanding of Catholic doctrine among newly baptized Canary Islander, Muslim, and black African slaves in the Canary Islands, see Luis Alberto Anaya Hernández, *Judeoconversos e Inquisición en las Islas Canarias (1402–1605)* (Las Palmas de Gran Canaria: Ediciones del Cabildo Insular de Gran Canaria, 1996), esp. 114–28.

to the Nasrid Sultanate of Granada so that, upon reaching Islamic territories, they could revert to Islam. Thus, Bernat protested, for these and many other reasons, "no faith ought to be given to her oath or anything she says."[109] Bernat's tactics here were hardly unique. Masters, mistresses, and their heirs frequently contended that a slave woman's claims regarding her child's paternity were outright lies. In addition to decrying their sexual promiscuity, masters and mistresses affirmed a marked tendency among slave women toward lying and deceit.[110]

After disparaging her Russian slave woman named Maria's practice of "delivering her person to many, indeed to everyone as far as she could tell," Francesqua, the widow of the nobleman Jofré d'Anyo, emphasized how, on several different occasions, Maria had lied about her children's paternity.[111] Before coming to Valencia, Jofré had been a bachelor, living with his slave woman Maria on the island of Sardinia. On the first occasion that she found herself pregnant, Maria had initially claimed that the local market inspector (*mustaçaff*) was the child's father. When this market inspector managed to prove, in the court of the local governor, that the timing of the infant's birth made it impossible for him to be the child's father, Maria then convinced Jofré that a silversmith of Alghero was the culprit. Though this silversmith accepted responsibility for the child, rumors continued to circulate in the community, particularly given the strong physical resemblance between the child and another one of Maria's reported lovers, a local mason.[112] Several years later, Maria became pregnant once again and this time she claimed that the child's biological father was Jofré. In this incident (which took place four or five years before the birth of the plaintiff in this case, Ursola, aka Yolant), Maria reportedly had sworn a false oath on the four books of the Evangelists that she was carrying her master's child. When Maria

109. "A jurament ne dit de la dita cativa fe alguna no pot esser donada." ARV G 2311: M. 12: 2v. For her part, Johana protested that this incident had been blown out of proportion and her intentions had been completely misunderstood. Angered by an excessive beating from her mistress, Johana explained that she had let her master and mistress think that she had plans to run away in the hopes that it might prompt them to reconsider how they had been treating her and, perhaps, even repent their violent actions. Insisting that she never would have even considered renouncing Christianity, she averred that even having such a thought would be a great offense to God.

110. Kenneth S. Greenberg similarly has noted a widespread "contempt" for the words of slaves in the Old South. Noting how masters "controlled truth," Greenberg observes that by "whipping slaves from truth to lie and from lie to truth, the master was telling both the slave and himself that truth was a matter of assertion and force—and the master had it in his control." Greenberg, *Honor and Slavery*, 39–41.

111. Earlier, I discussed the role Jofré d'Anyo had played in his slave woman's child's baptism. See chapter 4, pp. 131–32.

112. Although this mason reportedly had also sued for custody of this slave woman's child, ultimately the court ruled in the silversmith's favor. See the testimony of Jofré's widow, Francesqua Vinader. ARV G 2305: M. 11: 17r.

gave birth to a black baby girl, however, the slave's duplicity was made plain. Francesqua concluded that the child's father must have been one of the two black male slaves that she and her husband owned, both of whom lived on their rural property (alqueria), located near Picanya.[113]

To a certain extent, then, contemporaries felt confident that the "truth" of the matter would be revealed at the time of the infant's birth. When Castellona, the wife of the nobleman Arnau Castello, expressed doubts about the claim of her Russian slave woman named Rosa that she was carrying her master's child, her neighbor attempted to soothe her anxieties by assuring her that soon they would know for certain. For, she reasoned, if the father was, as they suspected, a dark-skinned (llor) freedman, the child, "if a girl, would have 'black' features, and if a boy ['black'] testicles."[114] The squire of the household, Angelo de Capoa, similarly reasoned that if, Rosa, as she claimed, had been impregnated by her master, the child, also, should have been white, for she and her master were both white. When Rosa gave birth to a daughter who was "dark" in skin tone and "had the mouth of a black person," it thus "became known that she had spoken falsely." The child's paternity was, in fact, so glaringly obvious that the midwife who delivered the child immediately rebuked Rosa, stating, "You could never say that you had been impregnated by your lord, Arnau Castelló."[115]

Although sexual dalliances with slave women in and of themselves would not necessarily taint a master's reputation (the double standard with respect to male versus female sexual activity is well documented), the impregnation of his slave woman had more serious implications. The pregnancy could not only compromise his rights of ownership but also, if he were married, it could jeopardize his marriage; his wife and extended family might very well regard this as an act of betrayal. Exploiting the preexisting tensions between masters and mistresses regarding their relations with their slave women, slave women were accused of deliberately fomenting marital discord by making false claims concerning their child's paternity. The aforementioned Francesqua, for example, testified that when (four or five years before Ursola/Yolant's birth) Maria made allegations that she was carrying her master's child, they were the source of considerable conflict

113. "E aquella stant prenys dix e fonch hoyda dir prestament jurament sobre los quatres sants evangelis que era prenyada del dit en Jofré Danyo e segui del dit part pari una fillata negra com se fos emprenyada de cert sclau negre." ARV G 2305: M. 11: 9r.

114. This rope maker's wife told Castellona not to worry because Rosa had told her "que lo dit prenyat era del dit llor e no de son amo." When Castellona asked her how she could know this for sure, she responded, "si es dona tendra la natura negra e si es home los botons." ARV G 2384: M. 24: 32v.

115. "Quant vench al parir vent la madrina que la dita criatura era llora dix e fonch oyda dir... aquesta criatura detena deya yames be podies dir tu Rosa eres prenyada del senyor n'Arnau Castello increpant la de la falsia que havia dit." ARV G 2383: M. 20: 3v.

between her and her husband. She recalled how, "because of that which the slave woman had said, she became very upset with her husband."[116] When the child Maria gave birth to turned out to be a dark-skinned baby girl, her mistress, clearly relieved, sternly rebuked the slave woman, reportedly crying out, "Evil woman! Don't you realize how upset you made me and your master all because of your child?"[117]

The widow of the nobleman Arnau Castelló also accused her slave woman of deliberately causing friction in her marriage. Even though Rosa allegedly knew that the child she was carrying was not her master's, she had declared publicly that Arnau was the father. Witnesses testified that during the slave's pregnancy, they overheard the couple fighting, with "na Castellona saying that the child Rosa was carrying was her husband's, and [Arnau] saying that this was not true." One witness noted "thus it remained for a long time that they [Arnau and his wife] were not speaking with one another."[118] Only after Rosa gave birth to a dark-skinned baby was harmony restored in the Castelló household. After seven months of "not sleeping together in one bed," Arnau and na Castellona "made peace."

In some instances, rather than being "exposed" at the birthing bed, slave women, professedly of their own accord, withdrew their claims and admitted that they "had spoken falsely" (ha dita falsia). Indeed, in cases in which the slave mother was black and/or the child she gave birth to was white, it was much more difficult to rule the master out as the child's biological father. Disputes thus could become prolonged indefinitely—unless the slave woman backed down. In 1458, a Bulgar slave woman named Johana withdrew her complaint, admitting that "certain individuals" had advised her to say that her master was her child's father, even though she knew that this was not the case. She confessed that her daughter's "true" father was one of his household squires. Though Johana herself now had no claim to freedom, by insisting that her child's father was a freeborn Christian, Johana perhaps was attempting to salvage (at the very least) her daughter's claim to freedom.[119] According to the kingdom of Valencia's legal code, a child born of a free father was considered freeborn.[120]

---

116. "E ella testimoni congoxant s'en molt ab so marit de ço que la sclava deya que era sua." ARV G 2305: M. 11: 16r.

117. "Mala fembra no t'as conegut que has fet viure ab congoxa a mi e a ton amo per sa criatura." ARV G 2305: M. 11: 16r.

118. "Quant la dita Rosa era prenyada de la dita Margalida per que entre la dita na Castellona e lo dit son marit havia gran questio sobre lo dit prenyat dient la dita na Castellona que lo prenyat de la dita Rosa era del dit son marit e aquell deya que no era veritat que desque havia haut fil no la havia coneguda. E axi stigueren gran temps que nos parlaren." ARV G 2384: M. 24: 32v

119. Johana acknowledged that "aconsellada d'algunes gents dix e fon hoyda dir que la dita filla sua havia hauda del dit noble mossen Pero Roiz amo e senyor seu empero la veritat del feyt era e es que la dita sua filla ella la hague de hun scuder de la casa del dit noble amo seu appellat... [blank] Binguet." ARV G 2291: M. 1: 43v.

120. Furs de València, Colon and Garcia, eds. (Barcelona, 1990), V: 110.

Indeed, one of the more compelling passages to be encountered in the *demanda de libertat* filed by Ursola (aka Yolant, the daughter of the slave woman named Maria) is the widow Francesqua's recollection of a discussion she had had with Maria following the birth of her second child, the aforementioned dark-skinned baby girl. After admitting that, even during her pregnancy, she had known full well that Jofré d'Anyo was not the girl's father, Maria explained that a neighbor had convinced her to make the false claim as a means to achieve her liberation. Struck by a crisis of conscience, however, Maria, just before the infant's birth, had decided to alter her claim. Knowing that Jofré could not possibly be her child's father, she remained genuinely uncertain with respect to the child's true paternity. She had been sleeping with two different men at that time: a slave and a free man. Maria opted to name the free man (a squire in the household of a neighboring widow) as the child's father in the hopes of securing her child a better future. When her baby was born with dark skin, of course, Maria was forced to recognize that the black male slave was the child's father, but, Maria reportedly had protested that, in all fairness, she had been sleeping with both of them at the same time.[121]

Francesqua presented Maria as equally pushy and manipulative in her quest to secure freedom for her third (white) child, Ursola (aka Yolant). Thus, Francesqua testified that, about three years ago, Maria had come to her house, "begging her to give testimony saying that Yolant (aka Ursola) was the daughter of Jofré d'Anyo." Unwilling to accept "No" as an answer, Maria told her that she would return shortly with two men to serve as witnesses for this testimony. Two days later, all three of them showed up on Francesqua's doorstep. When one of the men asked her to confirm that Ursola was the daughter of Jofré d'Anyo and Francesqua replied that "she did not know this and had never heard anyone say such a thing," the two men became angry and said to Maria, "Why did you make us come?"[122] Francesqua's second husband, the notary Jacme Vinader, similarly recounted how Maria had come to their household "many different times... beseeching his wife to testify and say that Ursola was the daughter of Jofré d'Anyo, her first husband." Indeed, he continued, he had seen Maria "work with great diligence in the courts

121. "Be sabia ella que no era de son amo mas havia lo y consellat la muller d'en Jacme Marti per que fos franqua per la senyora reyna que lavors era aci en Valencia dient que era de son amo la faria franqua." ARV G 2305: M. 11: 16r.

122. "La dit Maria mare de la dita Ursola vingue a la cassa d'ella testimoni pregant la que li fes testimoni que la dita Yolant alter Ursola era filla d'en Jofré d'Anyo e que ella portaria dos homens per testimonis e que li fers tanta de gracia que'n digues davant los testimoni. E a cap de dos jorns vench la dita Maria ab los dos homens... los quals li diguren a ella testimoni que la dita Maria los havia dit que ella testimoni sabia que la dita Ursola filla de la dita Maria era fila del dit en Jofré d'Anyo e lladonchs ella testimoni dix e respos que ella no sabia tal cossa ni havia hoyt dir e los dits homens reptaren la dita Maria dihent per que'lls havia fet venir." ARV G 2305: M. 20: 20v–21r.

in order to attain freedom for her daughter."[123] To the modern reader, of course, Maria's efforts seem heroic. In presenting such testimony, however, Jofré's heirs were attempting to discredit Ursola's claims by presenting Maria as someone who would do anything (including suborning perjury) to secure her daughter's freedom.

Contemporaries hardly assumed, however, that the slave women advancing these claims were never telling the truth. Indeed, despite the vehement denials that they voiced in public, masters, according to the testimony of witnesses, occasionally acknowledged their paternity in private. One laborer (admittedly, a former slave who was rumored to be Maria's lover) related how Jofré d'Anyo confessed to him that he was the father of Maria's (his white slave woman's) daughter. When this witness had protested "then Maria is free and her daughter as well," Jofré responded that although this "certainly" was the case, he could not afford to make such an admission publicly. For, it would cause his wife "to harbor ill will" both toward him and this slave woman. This was something that had to be avoided because Maria also was the wet nurse to his and his wife's children. Jofré reportedly explained that "she is my daughter but, so as not to displease my wife, I would not dare say so."[124]

To a certain extent, then, masters felt torn. On the one hand, to please their wives and preserve harmony in the household, masters felt pressure to renounce their slave women and their children. On the other, contemporary norms dictated that they had an obligation to take responsibility for both the slave mother and child. Should it be discovered that he had denied his own child and repudiated the mother of his children, a master would be dishonored in the eyes of his community as a man who did not fulfill his obligations. The notary Berthomeu Queralt, for example, testified that many members of the community

123. "Moltes e diverses vegades ha vist ell dit testimoni que la dita Maria venia a la casa dell testimoni e pregava a la muller del ell dit testimoni que volgues testifficar e dir que la dita Ursola era filla del dit en Jofré d'Anyo marit qui primer fon de la muller del testimoni. E axi mateix . . . ha vist treballar a la dita Maria ab gran diligencia per les corts per atenyer libertat a la dita Ursola filla sua." ARV G 2305: M. 20: 20r.

124. The laborer Antoni Ferrer (aka Fevoli) recounted how Jofré had admitted, "ma filla es empero per no fer desplaer a ma muller no gosse dir que es ma filla per que la dita Maria crie les criatures e ma muller no haia enuig ab ella. Mas ella es certament ma filla dihent ho de la dita Ursola filla de la dita Maria. Lavors dix e respos ell dit testimoni donchs Maria francha es e sa filla tambe. Diu que respos lo dit en Jofré d'Anyo que francha era ella e sa mare empero per que crie les criatures mies e ma muller no haia enuig non gosse dir." ARV G 2305: M. 20: 16r–v.

Protesting that it was highly suspicious that Maria only made the claim that Jofré was Ursola's father *after* her master's death, Jofré's heir, Orfresina also pointed out that Anthoni Ferrer (Ursola's star witness) was Maria's longtime lover. Witnesses testified that Maria and Anthoni had been having an affair even while Jofré was still alive. After catching them in *flagrante delicto*, Jofré chased Anthoni out of his house with a knife. Onlookers reportedly had to intervene to prevent Jofré from killing him. Anthoni allegedly had bribed people to testify in support of Ursola's *demanda de libertat* and reportedly was so in love with Maria that he would do anything—even die—for her.

disapproved of Jofré's behavior toward his slave woman. After Maria gave birth to his child, many reportedly speculated, "What sort of conscience must Jofré d'Anyo have that he has impregnated his slave woman and gives her such a hard time, beating her grievously?" Similarly, when Jofré's sister and heir, Orfresina Sanyes, sold Ursola (Maria's daughter by Jofré) as a slave, this same notary commented that "he viewed this as a great offense. A person of conscience who fears God would not have done such a thing!"[125] Francesqua herself was overheard saying that her sister-in-law, Orfresina Sanyes, was a despicable woman. Francesqua allegedly had fumed, "How could she sell that little girl [Ursola/Yolant] as a slave? She is the sister to my daughters and the daughter of my husband, Jofré d'Anyo. It is not fitting that the sister of my daughters be forced to spend her life in servitude!"[126]

When a slave woman filed a paternity suit against her master, then, she was resented not only for the tension she created within the household (provoking feelings of jealousy between the slave woman and her mistress) but also for the social stigma her accusations of neglect generated as they were repeated throughout the community. As anthropologist David Gilmore has observed, in an honor-conscious society, male status is founded not only on "a minatory phallic dominance" but on possession of a whole range of virtues, "chief among them being the fulfillment of one's obligations and living up to the expectations of one's peers." Dishonor stems not just from sexual shame "but also from neglect of duty."[127] Thus, Francesqua testified that although her husband had always been secure in the knowledge that he was not the father of his slave woman's child, he felt so profoundly threatened by Maria's allegations that he "was anxious to kill her."[128] Such claims, even when voiced by slaves, were an indictment against a master's honor-integrity, damaging his reputation among his peers.

125. The notary Berthomeu Queralt reported that many in the community had wondered, "quina consciencia te en Jofré Danyo que ha emprenyat la sua sclava e li dona mala vida com la bates legament." In addition, Berthomeu stated that he considered Orfresina's sale of Ursola into slavery a "gran offensa... tals coses no les faria persona de consciencia qui temes deu. Tal venda de lege divina disponente no s'es poguda fer." ARV G 2305: M. 11: 13r.

126. Francesqua reportedly protested, "malvada fembra com havia pogut vendra la dita fadrina per sclava car germana es de mos filles e filla de mon marit en Jofré d'Anyo. Mas no li cal que no passara tal fahena que germana es de mies filles." ARV G 2305: M. 20: 17v.

127. David D. Gilmore, "Honor, Honesty, Shame: Male Status in Contemporary Andalusia," in Honor and Shame and the Unity of the Mediterranean, ed. David D. Gilmore (Washington, D.C.: American Anthropological Association, 1987), 90–103.

128. Francesqua, the widow of Jofré d'Anyo (now remarried to the notary Jacme Vinader), testified that her former husband "la cuyda matar com sabes que no era sua la dita criatura." ARV G 2305: M. 11: 16r. This case, unfortunately, lacks a conclusion. Ultimately we do not know what happened to Ursola. Perhaps the governor found her mother Maria's version of events the most convincing. But, perhaps Orfresina's efforts to discredit Maria and, by extension, her daughter Ursola's claims were successful.

Masters contended that their slave women filed false paternity suits not only in an attempt to win their (and their children's) freedom but also to discredit their masters' reputation in the community. When the dark-skinned slave woman Johana "the Bearded" filed a demand for liberty before the court of the governor, her master chastised her for not trusting him to do the right thing, opting instead to air the household's dirty laundry in public. Outraged to have his slave woman publicly questioning his integrity, Bernat allegedly cried out, "Come here, evil woman! You have defamed me and are defaming me in many places throughout the city, going around and saying to everyone that you are carrying my child. Don't you think that I have a soul and that I fear God so that if you are pregnant with my child I will make you free?"[129]

Slave women like Johana, however, knew that they could not always rely on their master's good conscience. Instead, they sought recognition of their freed status in a court of law. Explicitly invoking the paternalistic ideals that had justified her subjugation, the aforementioned slave woman named Ysabel likewise challenged her master's "honor-integrity" by filing a *demanda de libertat* subsequent to his death. Assuming a morally superior position to her master, Ysabel maintained that not only had her master been the one who had "deflowered her" at the age of eleven, but that she had also given birth to no fewer than two of his children. Successfully deflecting all the attacks leveled against her character by her master's heirs, Ysabel steadfastly asserted that she was entitled to freedom as the mother of her master's children. When her master's heirs contended that Alfonso de la Barreda had been "such a good man and such a good Christian that if he had had relations with the said Ysabel, or if she had given birth to his child he would have freed her of all servitude,"[130] Ysabel retorted that her master's failure to acknowledge her status properly in his last will and testament revealed that he had been neither a good

---

129. The wife of a silversmith recounted how she overheard Bernat say to Johana, "vine açi mala fembra tu'm difames he'm vas difamant per molts lochs de la ciutat e vas dient a tot hom que est prenyada de mi. Non faces pensa que yo tinch anima e tem deu que si tu es prenyada de mi que yo't fare francha." Bernat reportedly concluded this outburst by promising, in the presence of all the aforesaid witnesses, to free Johana if she was carrying his child. When Johana swore "by my faith, lord, I am pregnant with your child and no one else's and you know very well that I speak the truth," Bernat reportedly replied, "Don't worry. If this is true and you are carrying my child, I will free you and buy another slave woman to serve my wife." ARV G 2311: M. 12: 7v. Johana, of course, had very good reason to worry and thus ended up filing a claim before the governor. After hearing the testimony of witnesses produced by her master, the governor dismissed Johana's *demanda de libertat;* for the short run, at least, Johana would remain in servitude. With respect to the fate of Johana's son, the extant records remain frustratingly silent. It is possible he died in infancy or, perhaps, was resold to another household.

130. "Lo dit en Alfonso era tant bon home e tan bon xristia que si aquell hagues praticat ab la dita Ysabel ni aquella hagues parit de aquell aquell la haguera jaquida franqua de tota servitut." ARV G 2395: M. 11: 38r.

man nor a good Christian. Indeed, she rather boldly proclaimed, because of this, she believed that his soul should end up "in the infernal flames."[131]

Beyond shaming individual masters (or securing freedom for individual slaves), such allegations, taken to the extreme, had the potential to call into question the paternalistic ideology undergirding slavery's legitimacy. These slave women's charges drew attention to the disjuncture between the dictates of paternalism (what a "good" Christian master owed his slaves) and the rights of ownership (the absolute authority, including sex right, that masters enjoyed over their slaves). Judging from contemporary legislation, their claims provoked a great deal of anxiety. At the meeting of the Corts held in Orihuela in 1488, King Fernando issued the following decree:

> Since it often occurs that slave women living in the kingdom of Valencia, lying carnally with squires, male servants, and other members of their masters' households, as well as with men residing outside [their masters'] households, become pregnant and afterward, when they give birth, claim that the child was their master's and, for this reason, [both mother and child] are free, we provide and ordain that these slaves shall not and cannot obtain freedom for this reason. If their masters swear an oath that the child is not his she will have to remain [in his service] and shall not otherwise obtain her liberty.[132]

Thus, partially in response to the complaints of masters confronting what seemed to them to be a continuous stream of paternity suits, an amendment was added to the statute awarding freed status to slave women who gave birth to their master's child. From now on, these slave women would not be granted their freedom if their masters denied their claims under oath. Certainly this statute reasserted the moral authority of masters over their slave women by privileging the master's testimony and assuming a more marked tendency among slave women to lie. Nevertheless, it maintained intact the notion that masters were obliged to award freedom to slave women who had given birth to their children. Inasmuch as, with or without said oath, a child's paternity (in the eyes of his contemporaries) remained uncertain, masters remained vulnerable to charges that they were

---

131. "No era bon xristia puix no la jaquia franqua e la anima sua ne vull en mig dels inferns." ARV G 2395: M. 11: 39r.

132. "Com sovint s'esdevinga que les catives dels habitants en lo regne de València se jaen carnalment ab los scuders, moços e altres de la casa de lur senyor, e encara ab altres fora de la dita casa, e se emprenyen e aprés quan pareixen dien que lo part és de lur senyor e que per açò són franques, provehim e ordenam que les dites sclaves, per la dita rahó, no obtinguen o puixen obtenir franquea, si lur senyor jurarà que la criatura no és sua ab jurament, al qual se jaha a star e altrament no obtinga libertat." Furs de València, Colon and Garcia, eds. (Barcelona, 1990), V: 111.

neglecting their paternal responsibilities. Slave women would continue to file paternity suits against their masters well into the sixteenth century.

Masters regarded their slave women's sexuality with considerable trepidation, then, because their pregnancies put them in an exceptionally vulnerable position. By making claims that she was bearing her master's child, a slave woman might not only win her (and/or her child's) freedom, but also, at the very least, disrupt the harmony of her master's household. What was even more troubling, masters complained, was the fact that a slave woman's protests could tarnish their reputation in the community. By making claims that they were denying their own progeny and abandoning the mothers of their children, slave women exposed their owners to public censure for being disreputable men who did not honor their responsibilities. The threatening portrayal of slave women's sexuality, thus, becomes more intelligible upon consideration of the fact that those who gave birth to their master's child could take him to court.

Throughout this chapter, I have highlighted evidence for what historians of slavery have termed "slave agency" and we have seen the myriad ways in which slave owners as well as royal and municipal officials presented the enslaved as historical actors. Accepting contemporary descriptions of a slave's actions as "voluntary" or "by choice" is, of course, highly problematic and one could legitimately question the authenticity of many of the instances of "slave agency" depicted in court records. With respect to the discussion of enslaved women who purportedly exploited their sexuality as a tool to secure their freedom, for example, although it is certainly true that some enslaved women might have tried to turn their master's sexual desire to their own advantage, the power inequities at play here meant—as Edward Baptist has observed with respect to the Antebellum South— that these women "chose, at best, between, a negotiated surrender on the one hand and severe punishment, and possible death, on the other." Since it was not unusual for enslaved women to be beaten brutally for refusing to comply with their owners' demands, "force and threat made these relationships, to a large extent, inevitable."[133]

Whether bearing their masters' swords or bearing their masters' children, enslaved men and women participated in the Valencian culture of honor even though, as slaves, theoretically, they personally had none.[134] Although this chapter has highlighted how

---

133. I am paraphrasing here an argument made by Edward Baptist that, though it concerns the position of domestic slaves in the antebellum South, seems equally pertinent in the late medieval Iberian context. Edward E. Baptist, " 'Cuffy,' 'Fancy Maids,' and 'One-Eyed Men': Rape, Commodification, and the Domestic Slave Trade in the United States," *American Historical Review* 106, no. 5 (December 2001): 1644 n. 68.

134. I draw here on the essays by Boyer et al. in *The Faces of Honor*. One of the central contention of this book is that "plebeians . . . especially covet[ed] a reputation for honor because the economic and political vulnerability of their lives put them in perilously close proximity to squalor, forced labor, prostitution, and illegitimacy," 10.

masters and mistresses were obsessed with making sure that their slaves' behavior enhanced rather than compromised their reputation in the community, what seems most noteworthy about the court testimony discussed above is the recognition that enslaved men and women were making their own judgments concerning their master's "honorability."

After all, when Johan, the "arrogant" and "despicable" black male slave whom we discussed at the beginning of this chapter, burst into his master's bedchamber, he did so in order to chastise his master for abusing his mistress "without cause." Admittedly, those witnessing the confrontation hardly expressed admiration for the slave's gallantry, nor did they seem to view it as the legitimate response of a loyal dependant. Rather, the female servant recounting the incident portrayed it as an act of gross insubordination. Ignoring the injunctions that she and other members of the household had given him to "mind his place," Johan bounded up the stairs to his master's chamber and demanded "What are you doing? Why are you fighting with my mistress without cause?" Indeed, it was viewed as an especially egregious affront to his master's honor since the slave had said these words, "with his hand on the sword that he possessed."

Order was quickly restored, however, as soon as the "impudent" black male slave was humiliated. Present also at this dramatic confrontation were the nobleman's squires and ladies who, as faithful household dependants, immediately came to their master's aid. "Seeing these things," they "did not let the black male slave approach any closer to their master." Rather, the squires "seized the black man and shoved him toward the stairs." They did so, the female servant informs us, "so that he would go back down."

The black male slave, however, was "not willing to go down." Instead, "he cried out, 'Let me be since I can die but once!' "[135] Johan's purported plea brings to mind Orlando Patterson's depiction of slavery as "social death"; that is, that Johan's request could be read as an admission that, as a slave, he was already "dead" in the eyes of the community and thus had no part to play in disputes over honor.[136] Considered, however, alongside the testimony offered by the dozens of enslaved men and women discussed in this chapter, Johan's plea takes on added poignancy: though slaves may have been treated juridically as men without honor, they hardly conceded their debased condition without a struggle.

135. This former female servant recounted how "lo dit negre sentint les dites noves que la senyora e senyor tenien munten damunt... dix al dit magnifich en Johan Roic de Corella amo seu... que haveu per que us barallau ab la senyora sense causa revis lo dit negre la ma a una papagorga... e los scuders del magnifich en Johan Roic de Corella vehent les dites coses e les dones no dexaren acostar al dit magnifich en Johan de Corella... los dits scuders prengueren al dit negre e empenyien lo per la scala per que s'en devallas. E aquell no s'en volia devallar dient los tals o semblants paraules dexa'l virir (sic-viure) que no puch morir sino una vegada." ARV JCiv 923: M. 13: 44r–48v; M. 14: 11r–12v.

136. See Orlando Patterson, *Slavery and Social Death*.

Shortly after Christmas, 1461, the merchant Joan Rossell lay on his death-bed surrounded by his wife Ysabel, his brother Dionis, and his slave woman Maria. Fearful of what lay ahead of her after her master's de-mise, Maria seized this opportunity to make one final plea for her liberation. Climbing into her master's bed to help put him in a more comfortable position, Maria reportedly burst into tears, begging her master to "make me free so that I do not fall into the hands of another!" Although other witnesses' descriptions of this scene feature a more asser-tive Maria pointedly questioning her master, "Lord, am I to stay like this forever?" by all accounts, Joan promised his slave woman a speedy liberation. Joan allegedly had replied, "Don't worry, Maria. I have instructed my brother to see to it that you are well taken care of. I have told everyone that I am leaving you free to live in liberty and act according to your will."[1] Grateful for this act of lordly munificence, Maria kissed her master's hands and, according to one observer, exclaimed, "God grant you salvation" (salut).[2]

This death scene conforms neatly to the conventional view of slavery in the late medi-eval Mediterranean world. Slavery, for most, was but a temporary condition. Manumis-sion was frequent, if not customary upon a master's and/or mistress's death.[3] Recent

1. One witness recounted that Maria said, "senyor no'm dius res? E lo dit en Johan Rossell respos que vols que't digua? E ella dix plorant senyor que'm dexes franqua que no vaga a mans de negu. E ell dit Johan Rossell respos ja't dexe franqua a totes tes voluntats e a ta libertat e axiu ha fet scriure açi Benet Salavador e encara ho dit a mon frare e a tots los de casa que no vull que vages a mans de negu. E llavors la dita Maria dix e respos senyor deu te do salut." ARV G 2304: M. 2: 26v; M. 7: 47r–48r; M. 8: 1r–v and ARV G 2305: M. 12: 43r–44v and ARV G 2306: M. 25: 7r.

2. Since Maria's liberation would become effective only upon her master's death, one can assume Maria was praying for the salvation of her master's soul rather than for his physical recovery.

3. Jacques Heers, for example, suggests that the practice of granting slaves their freedom effective upon their masters' or mistresses' deaths is a defining characteristic of domestic slavery. It "perfectly cor-responds to the idea of 'personal' domestic service. The slave is attached to his master, whom he serves; when the master dies, the bond is broken . . . we are dealing, in effect, with a personal tie that is not easily transferable to another." Heers, Esclavos, 234–35.

research, particularly by scholars studying the more ethnically and religiously diverse slave populations of the Iberian Peninsula, has revealed, however, that the practice of outright manumission in this period was not as widespread as had previously been believed. In her study of slavery in sixteenth-century Granada, for example, Aurelia Martín Casares found that only about 12 percent of the overall slave population received charters of freedom; these lucky few, in turn, were often required to pay exorbitant redemption fees.[4] Close inspection of the archival evidence from fifteenth-century Valencia similarly reveals that slaves faced significant challenges in recovering their liberty.

Despite all her master's assurances to the contrary, Maria's path to freedom was not without obstacles. Indeed, we only learn of this eleventh-hour manumission because it was later contested (albeit unsuccessfully) by Joan's brother and heir, Dionis. Denying that he ever heard his brother make such a promise, Dionis argued that, even if he had, it was not legally binding. Not only had the requisite three witnesses been lacking,[5] but inasmuch as the alleged promise was made only orally, it was of doubtful sincerity. Masters habitually promised their slaves freedom as an incentive for providing better service. Hence, Dionis contended, if Joan did, in fact, tell Maria she would be freed upon his death, he would have said so "only in order to persuade her to serve him well during his illness, giving her the [false] hope that he would make her free." For, Dionis insisted, had Joan truly intended to make Maria free, he would have done more than just "say" this (de paraula); he would have put his professed desire into execution, "issuing her a [notarized] charter of freedom" (carta de libertat). Although Joan may have told Maria that the notary Benet Salvador would record his promise to her in writing, there evidently was no record of her alleged manumission.[6]

<hr />

4. Alfonso Franco Silva, for example, had claimed that "in Andalusian society during the end of the Middle Ages the concession of liberty to slaves was fairly common. Liberation was the prize that the slave whose behavior toward his master had been faithful, caring, and respectful received." Alfonso Franco Silva, Esclavitud en Andalucía 1450–1550 (Granada: Universidad de Granada, 1992). In contrast, Aurelia Martín Casares found that "in general, neither Christian nor Morisco owners of slave labor showed any intentions of freeing their dependents 'gratis.' To the contrary, the number of liberations was relatively small, and they often demanded exorbitant ransoms." Aurelia Martín Casares, La esclavitud en la Granada del siglo XVI (Granada: Universidad de Granada, 2000), 438–40. Martín also cites several other studies that found similarly reduced rates of manumission among the slave populations of Jaén and Cordoba. See Juan Arandel Doncel, "Los esclavos de Jaén durante el último tercio del siglo," Homenaje a Antonio Domínguez Ortiz (Madrid: Ministerio de Educación General de Enseñazas Medias, 1981), and Albert Ndamba Kabongo, Les esclaves a Cordue au debut du XVIIème siècle (1600–1621), doctoral thesis, 1975.

5. Furs de València, ed. Colon and Garcia (Barcelona, 1990), V: 148.

6. After denying that he had ever heard his brother say he wished to grant Maria her liberty, Dionis Rossell insisted that, even if he had, these words "no serien suficients a prestar a la dita Maria com sien confessio extrajudicial la qual no es de efecte algu sino es provada per dos testimonis dignes de fe n'es pot dir que les dites paraules haien força de legat com no haia fet testament ne codicil e serien hi necessaris al menys tres testimonis." Moreover, he continued, "Si lo dit en Johan Rossell hagues volgut fer francha

Though in Dionis's perspective, manumission was a unilateral act of largesse, a gift masters and mistresses bestowed upon their slaves for which they should be eternally grateful, in daily practice emancipation was far more contentious. Maria was hardly unique among slaves living in fifteenth-century Valencia in her conviction that she was "entitled" to freedom. Slaves of all backgrounds were preoccupied with regaining their freedom. Their prospects for actually doing so, however, varied significantly according to their gender, religion, and ethnic identity. Although many slaves attempted to secure their freedom in cooperation with their owners, others laid claim to it in open defiance of their wishes. In addition to the fugitive slaves who took flight and sought refuge in both Muslim and Christian communities, a significant proportion of slaves filed *demandes de libertat*, taking their masters and mistresses to court.

Pious Bequests and "*Cartes de Libertat*"

According to the kingdom of Valencia's legal code, slave owners could free their slaves in one of three ways: by making an oral statement before witnesses, by inserting a clause in their last wills and testaments, or by issuing a document produced specifically for the occasion: a charter of freedom (referred to, alternatively, as a *carta de libertat, carta de franquea*, or *instrumentum franquitatis*). All three modes of enfranchisement were equally effective; all three were to be considered legally binding.[7]

Judging from the language owners used to record their slave's enfranchisement, manumission was an act of charity. In the charter of liberty issued to Elena, a black slave woman owned by Johan de Monblanc, Johan stated that he was freeing her "spontaneously and out of sheer liberality."[8] When the attorney Pere Valcanell amended his last will and testament, he affirmed that he was enfranchising his black male slaves Johan and Miqualet not because they deserved it (indeed, they were rebellious and ungrateful), but "because giving freedom to slaves is an act of piety and mercy."[9] A donation made "for

---

a la dita Maria ell la haguera dexada francha fahent li carta de franquea axi com fer se deu." Thus, he concluded, "Se mostra que lo dit en Johan Rossell no deya les dites paraules a la dita Maria sino perzuaduyir la que'l servis be en la dita malaltia metent la en sperança que la faria francha. Car si hagues tengut voluntat de fer la francha no ho haguera dit de paraula ans realment ho haguera posat en execucio fahent li carta de franquea." ARV G 2304: M. 2: 26v; M. 7: 47r–48r; M. 8: 1r–v and ARV G 2305: M. 12: 43r–44v and ARV G 2306: M. 25: 7r.

7. *Furs de València*, ed. Colon and Garcia (Barcelona, 1990), V: 147.

8. "Ex mea mera liberalitate et spontanea voluntate." ARV P 816 (nonpaginated): 31 July 1470.

9. Pere Valcanell explained that he was postponing the enfranchisement of his black male slave Miqualet for ten more years "considerant la perversitat de aquell com nos vulla corregir ni esmenar per la qual raho la libertat entregament li degues esser levada empero per esser acte de misercordia e pietat ab lo present codicil vull e orden que axi com lo dit Miqualet havia de servir a la dita muller mia per temps de cinch anys vull que aquell la servixqua per temps de quinze anys los quals passats lo dit Miqualet

the benefit of one's soul as well as those of all the faithful," the manumission of one's slaves (like the redemption of Christians held in Muslim captivity)[10] was thought to be an act pleasing to God. Thus, it would bring spiritual rewards to the giver. Voicing concerns about her ultimate salvation, Yolans, the widow of the nobleman Johan Gasco, instructed her executors that "out of reverence for our lord God" they should see to it that "Beatriu, my slave, be freed from all servitude immediately after my death."[11] Similarly, in a *carta de libertat* issued by the nobleman Gisbert Valleriola to his black male slave Pere, Gisbert stated that he was doing this "out of piety, for the redemption of my soul, and for the remission of my sins."[12]

Although the overwhelming majority of slaves receiving such grants of freedom were baptized Christians of Muslim, pagan, or Eastern Orthodox Christian origin, unbaptized Moors were also to be found among slaves receiving "pious" bequests of liberty. In 1470, the innkeeper Manuel Pardo granted his Muslim slave Ali his freedom in his last will and testament.[13] Thus, although conversion to Latin Christianity certainly helped pave the way for a slave's manumission, it was by no means required. In 1475, a Christian couple from Manises instructed the executors of their last wills and testaments to free their jointly held slave, a black male who was also named Ali, immediately upon the surviving spouse's death. Although there is some suggestion here that they hoped Ali would

---

vull sia e reste franch e libert de tot jou de servitut." With respect to the manumission of his black slave Johan, Pere explained that he had initially believed that Johan would be grateful and improve his behavior ("aquell me hauria grat e se esmenaria"), but that "apres per aquell esser estat rebelle e ingrat…li havia revocat axi lo dit legat de libertat com les altres dexes." Be that as it may, Pere, in this, his latest last will and testament, stated that he now, "out of reverence for God," wished to reinstate Johan's manumission, "considerat que donar libertat als catius es acte de pietat e misercordia." ARV P 10251 (nonpaginated): 11 November 1501.

10. In his study of the redemptionist order of the Mercedarians, James Brodman notes how, from the twelfth century onward, "Catalans had come to consider captives, alongside the poor, to be fit objects of their charity." Brodman argues that testators donated money toward the ransoming of Christian captives both out of a sense of obligation and because they "believed that this was personally redemptive." Brodman, *Ransoming Captives*, ix, 12, 117–21. For two examples of testamentary bequests directed toward the redemption of Christians in Muslim captivity, see ARV P 1109 (nonpaginated): 9 September 1469 and ARV P 2398 (nonpaginated): 3 August 1472.

11. Yolans specified that "per reverencia de nostre senyor deu vull e man que de continent apres obit meu sia francha de tota servitut Beatriu sclava mia la qual ara per lavors e lavors per ara fac francha." APPV 26182 (nonpaginated): 18 July 1442.

12. Gisbert stated that "intuitu pietatis et ob remedium anime mei et ob remissionem peccatorum meorum manumitto [fra]nchum quitium liberum et alforrum facio et voco te Petrum servum et captivum meum de genere nigrorum." ARV P 10443 (nonpaginated): 29 March 1476.

13. Although in the *carta de libertat* Manuel had issued him, Ali's liberation was contingent upon either payment of an eighty lliure redemption fee or twelve more years of service, in his last will and testament Manuel specified that Ali could secure his freedom by paying him a redemption fee of only sixty lliures. ARV P 1911 (nonpaginated): 31 August 1470.

convert to Christianity (they note that the black male slave from Guinea "at present" is called Ali), there is no indication that baptism was a requirement for his manumission.[14] The language used by masters and mistresses to explain their motives for freeing their Muslim slaves, moreover, does not differ all that markedly from that employed for Christianized slaves. When the merchant Pasqual Verdego stated that he was freeing his slave Caçim, he stated that he did so "induced by piety and the love he had for his slave, on account of the good service he provided me and my household."[15]

In the best case scenario, slaves were freed "purely, freely, absolutely, and without any further obligation or condition."[16] Indeed, as was noted in chapter 4, many slave owners even threw in some parting gifts. Some masters and mistresses bequeathed to their former slaves furniture, bed linens, clothing, usufruct of certain properties, and/or sums of money. Maria, "the Galician," for example, instructed the executors of her last will and testament to give Luisa, her (dark-skinned) slave woman, in addition to a charter of freedom, "the bed where she was accustomed to sleep, together with all its linens."[17] A pharmacist's wife directed that the executors of her last will and testament see to it that her former slave woman Lucia was give a wooden bed frame, a straw mattress, a pair of burlap sheets, a blanket, and a bedspread, albeit "the thinnest one that I possess." On the second anniversary of her mistress's death, moreover, Lucia was to be given twenty-five lliurcs, presumably to go toward her dowry.[18]

There were, of course, some inherent dangers involved in masters and mistresses making their slave's liberation contingent upon their own deaths.[19] In 1452, Aldonca Pardo, the widow of a money changer, revoked her promise to grant Johanota, her black slave woman, her freedom immediately following her death on the grounds that Johanota, ostensibly in an effort to hasten said manumission, had surreptitiously been poisoning her. Lying on her deathbed and in the presence of several witnesses, Aldonca confirmed that she had decided to resell the slave woman and stated that she also did not wish the testamentary bequest of forty lliures she had made to Johanota to come into effect. Being "in

14. ARV P 1914 (nonpaginated): 17 April 1475.

15. "Intuhitu pietatis et amoris quod ergo te Caçim servum meum gero propter bonam servitutem pro te michi ac domui mee in pensam." ARV P 1109 (nonpaginated): 3 January 1469. In actuality, however, Caçim's manumission was contingent upon a five-and-a-half-year term of service.

16. Didacus de Torres, the bailiff general of the kingdom of Valencia, for example, freed Johannes de Castilla, his eighteen-year-old black male slave, "pure libere et absolute et absque aliqua retencio ne sine condicione." In addition, Didacus promised to give Johannes a gift of twenty lliures at the time of his marriage. ARV P 10440 (nonpaginated): 22 March 1491.

17. ARV P 2240 (nonpaginated): 21 March 1477.

18. APPV 22731 (nonpaginated): 7 November 1471.

19. Steven Epstein informs us that for this very reason (lest a slave hasten his or her owner's death) a law was enacted in Genoa and its colonies that made it illegal for a master to free a slave by will. Epstein, Speaking of Slavery, 96.

full possession of her senses and speaking clearly and intelligently," Aldonca reportedly exclaimed, "This is my intention because she killed me with poisons."[20]

However much masters and mistresses may have liked to congratulate themselves on their piety and generosity, a close reading of these documents reveals that these "gifts" of freedom frequently came at a considerable cost. When Garcia d'Agramunt awarded his three slaves—Francesc, Pere, and Jordi—freedom in his last will and testament, he specified that this bequest was contingent upon them working in his tannery for a period of at least two years following his death. If any one of them should fail to live up to the terms of this agreement—either by fleeing his wife's custody or refusing to perform the stipulated labor (i.e., cleaning animal hides)—his widow was empowered to sell them back into slavery.[21]

The conditions specified in this tanner's last will and testament were not unusual. Out of the thirty-nine testamentary manumissions encountered in notarial records dating from 1442 to 1504, fewer than half (eighteen) were freed without any further obligation or condition. More than half (thirty-five) of the sixty-two *cartas de libertat* encountered for this same period specified that the slave's liberation was contingent upon him or her providing several additional years of unpaid service and/or paying a substantial redemption fee. Even clerics imposed conditions on their slaves. A priest named Francesch Olzina stipulated that the manumission he was "giving" his Bulgar slave woman named Maria was contingent upon Maria reimbursing him for her initial purchase price. Granting freedom both "out of love for God" and in exchange for payment of a redemption fee, slave owners did not perceive these motives to be mutually exclusive. Five years later, when Maria completed a term of service that earned her a salary equivalent to her sales price, the executors of Francesch's last will and testament declared that they now conceded to Maria "freedom without exception...as much out of reverence for God and his life-giving soul, in contemplation of holy Christianity, as in compensation for your payments."[22]

---

20. A broker who was present at this widow's deathbed testified that he heard Aldonca revoke the legacy she had promised her slave woman Johanota, saying "yo'l revoque e vull que no vaia per fet com tal sia ma entencio per com com aquella m'a mort ab metzines." She said these words, moreover, "diverses voltes perserverant en allo mateix." And, he added, "quant la dita n'Aldonca dix les dites paraules aquella stava en tot son seny e entrega paraula." ARV JCiv 916: M. 12: 9r–10v.

21. "Leix a Francesc a Pere e Jordi catius meus franchs ab condicio que aquells serveixsch e que sien tenguts de servir a la dita muller mia dos anys comptadors del dia an avant del obit meu per que aquells exaguen e sien tenguts exaguar a la dita muller mia los cuires. E si aquells dins los dits dos anys s'en fugien e o no volien servir en tal cars aquell o aquells qui contrafara sia e resta catiu com no vull en lo dit cars que sien franchs sino catius e sien venuts per la dita muller mia o altra de aquells qui contrafara sia venut." ARV P 442 (nonpaginated): 23 July 1476. I noted earlier, in chapter 3, this condition imposed on their manumission, see p. 114.

22. In a notarized document, the executors of Francesch Olzina's last will and testament noted how Maria had been put in a contract of service "a soldada a tant temps tro que la soldada munte tant com lo

Redemption Agreements

While the aforementioned Bulgar slave woman raised her redemption fee by work-ing as a domestic servant in the household of a merchant's widow, many Muslim slaves raised the requisite sum by securing loans and/or charitable donations from their core-ligionists. In such instances, slaves first negotiated a redemption price (*se atallar*) and then solicited friends, relatives, and coreligionists to cosign the debt agreement with their owners. As soon as the slave had paid in full the stipulated ransom (*rescat*), she or he would be issued a charter of freedom.

Indeed, given the sizable free Muslim population in the kingdom of Valencia, Muslim slaves were well positioned with respect to raising funds to "buy" their freedom. In 1480, for example, a penally enslaved Mudejar from Vilamarchant entered into an agreement with his master, the carpenter Bernat Ferrer, whereby he promised to pay a redemption fee of seventy lliures. The debt agreement, promising full payment within the follow-ing year, was cosigned by his wife Xuxa, his mother Axa, as well as three other residents of Vilamarchant, all Muslims.[23] In 1475, Faat Bonet made a similar arrangement with his owner, the carpenter Jacme Lombart, and Faat's wife, son, daughter-in-law, and grandson as well as some Mudejars from Bellido and Petrés guaranteed the payment of his eighty lliure redemption fee.[24]

Although it was never institutionalized in the form of Christian redemptionist reli-gious orders such as the Mercedarians and the Trinitarians, the ransoming of Muslim captives was a recognized form of charity among members of the kingdom's Mudejar community.[25] As a Muslim tailor from Manises explained:

Among the Moors of the present kingdom such is the practice and custom that, en-countering captives, they give [alms] to them for the love of God, especially to those who are in irons. And, it can be seen manifestly and has been shown that in recent years in the present kingdom diverse captives have been redeemed by the Moors of the present kingdom, in accordance with the said obligation of giving [alms] to them for the love of God.[26]

---

preu que costas." Now that Maria had completed this contract of service, they were awarding her freedom "sine aliqua retencione" both "ob dei reverenciam et eius alme genitricis ac contemplacione sancte cristi-anitatis" and "in premiorum tuorum compensacione." APPV 20972 (nonpaginated): 16 March 1470.

23. ARV P 1113 (nonpaginated): 7 May 1480.

24. It bears noting, however, that these Mudejar vassals needed the permission of their lord, Francesc Aguilo, to cosign this debt agreement. ARV P 442 (nonpaginated): 22 June 1475.

25. See Meyerson, "Slavery and Solidarity," 286–343. For a recent study comparing Muslim, Chris-tian, and Jewish attitudes toward redeeming captives, see Yvonne Friedman, *Encounters between Enemies: Captivity and Ransom in the Latin Kingdom of Jerusalem* (Leiden: Brill, 2002). See also Rodriguez, *Captives and Their Saviors.*

26. Testifying on behalf of a dark-skinned freedman and *faqīh* named Abdalla Alfaqui (charged with aiding and abetting a Muslim slave's flight), this Muslim tailor from Manises noted that "entre moros del

Contemporary documentation bears witness to the collective efforts of Valencian Mudejars to redeem children, spouses, and neighbors from captivity. In 1475, when Ali Thagari, a Mudejar vassal of Beniopa, and his wife Mudia, redeemed their son, Macot, from captivity, they did so with the intercession of the local *faqīh* (Muslim jurist).[27] Similarly, in 1478, Fotayma, the wife of Galib Galbon, a penally enslaved Mudejar, redeemed her husband from captivity with the help of two other Mudejar women. Promising jointly to pay the lord of Chiva the eighty lliure redemption fee, the three women acknowledged that if the sum was not paid within the next year that all three of them would join Fotayma's husband in captivity.[28]

Although, as noted earlier, the kingdom's legal code dictated that "foreign" Muslim captives could not be ransomed with local monies (*rescatarse con dinero de la terra*), members of the local Mudejar community still seem to have contributed toward the redemption of their North African and Granadan coreligionists. In 1478, Abdalla Benferich, a Mudejar from the Vall de Sego (whose nickname, according to this record, was Compare, or "godfather"), acknowledged that he owed a baker's widow 30.5 lliures "by reason of the manumission" of Mahomat Benzahit, "a Saracen, of the nation of Haha."[29] Similarly, in 1475 a Valencian merchant told Caat, the son of Mahomat, a native of Morocco, that he had received forty-five lliures, "the price you had agreed to pay to me as your redemption price (*ab ipse atallavit*) . . . from the hands of Mahomat Zichnell, a Saracen and a resident of the Vall de Alfandech."[30]

Penally enslaved Mudejars and Moorish victims of corsair activity, however, were not the only slaves who redeemed themselves from captivity. A black male slave named Nicholau negotiated a similar type of agreement with his master, the hosier Pere del Mas. In this black African's case, however, the contract of debt, rather than being consigned by a wife and/or relatives, was consigned by the local butcher, a fishmonger, two knife makers, and a man whose trade was not specified. Each of these men individually assumed liability for ten lliures of the fifty lliure ransom.[31] Although the support network available to black African slaves certainly paled in comparison with that available to their Muslim counterparts, there is, nevertheless, evidence of cooperative activity among the slave and free members of the city's burgeoning black African community. In particular, there was

---

present regne es tal practica e consuetut que trobant los catius los donen per amor de deu e molt millor als qui estan ferrats e manifestament se pot mostrar es mostra que en estos anys passats en lo present regne se son rescatats diversos moros per los moros del present regne seguint lo dit orde de dar lo per amor de deu." ARV B 1431: M. 2: 344r–368v; M. 3: 369r–375r. This passage has been quoted in Meyerson, "Slavery and Solidarity," 313.

27. ARV P 442 (nonpaginated): 15 September 1475.
28. APPV 21819 (nonpaginated): 11 October 1478.
29. APPV 25003 (nonpaginated): 1 May 1478.
30. ARV P 442 (nonpaginated): 17 October 1475.
31. ARV G 2315: M. 15: 40r and ARV G 2316: 273r–275r.

the confraternity of black freedmen, founded in Valencia in 1472.[32] In addition to being dedicated to lending charitable assistance (i.e., food, shelter, and medical assistance) to those in their community "who otherwise would not be able to survive or sustain their lives," members of this confraternity were actively engaged in negotiating redemption contracts and collecting alms to help ransom black African slaves.[33] Although their activities were hardly on the same scale as Muslim redemptionist activities, the following two court cases reveal that they achieved, nonetheless, a certain measure of success.

After being subjected to an especially brutal beating by her master, the stonemason Francesch Martinez (aka Francesch "the Hothead"), a black slave woman named Ursola suffered a major head injury. Her master later recounted how, after a failed attempt to try and unload the gravely injured slave woman on some unsuspecting buyer, he opted (on the advice of some unnamed individuals) to let her go to "the house of the blacks" (la casa dels negres), a house leased by the confraternity of freed blacks. There, under the supervision of its "housemother" (madrastra), he had hoped that Ursola would be "cured" (se guarria) as well as "cheered" (se allegraria—read pacified).[34] Shortly after Ursola had been sent there, however, a woman (most likely the madrastra) appeared on Francesch's doorstep, beseeching him to grant Ursola her liberty in exchange for payment of a ransom.

Although Francesch testified that he only grudgingly accepted the terms of this redemption agreement—doing so only "so that he would not be forced to beat her again due to the disturbances she [otherwise] would have continued to cause him"[35]—he had achieved, at least on paper, the best of all possible solutions. Not only would he recoup the slave's initial purchase price, but, he would also retain Ursola's services. Until she paid off the forty lliure redemption fee, Ursola was obliged to continue making bread for his household. Most significantly, however, Francesch had achieved all of this without having to accept the unruly slave back into his household or pay the expenses of her upkeep. Throughout this entire period, Ursola would remain in the casa dels negres.

32. I discuss the foundation and growth of this "confraternity of freed blacks" in greater detail in my article, "La casa dels negres: Black African Solidarity in Late Medieval Valencia," in Black Africans in Renaissance Europe, ed. K. Lowe and T. F. Earle (Cambridge: Cambridge University Press, 2005), 225–46.

33. Miguel Gual Camarena transcribed, edited, and published this confraternity's foundation charter in his article, "Una confradia de negros libertos en el siglo XV," Estudios de Edad Media de la Corona de Aragón 5 (1952): 457–66.

34. Francesch testified that "hague de consell per aquells no sent rischs o moris de la naffra que la leixas anar a la casa dels negres hon tenia madastra e que alli se allegraria e guarria. E axi ho feu ell dit responent." ARV G 2348: M. 7: 2r. I discussed Ursola's distaste for making bread in chapter 3, see pp. 94–95.

35. "E ell dit responent per que no hagues a tornar a batre la per los desordes de aquella poria venir en algun inconvenient dix que era content." ARV G 2348: M. 7: 2r.

At least initially, Ursola seems to have honored this arrangement, "coming to his household two or three times to make bread." Very soon thereafter, however, Ursola simply stopped showing up. Francesch's wife, thus, had been obliged to go over to the *casa dels negres* to fetch her, demanding that, in accordance with their agreement, Ursola come to his household to make bread. Emboldened, perhaps, by the fact that she no longer lived under her master's roof, Ursola reportedly had refused, responding that she was no longer willing to serve him inasmuch as "this did not seem satisfactory to her. She was unwilling to give him both money and service."[36] Hardly inclined to allow his black slave woman to dictate the terms for her redemption, Francesch sent his apprentices over to the *casa dels negres*, instructing them to seize Ursola and have her incarcerated in the municipal prison.

The members of the black African community, however, quickly mobilized and interceded, once again, on Ursola's behalf. Francesch noted how the group of "black men and others" came and begged him to give Ursola another chance to buy back her freedom. This time, they offered, in compromise, to pay the forty lliure redemption fee in slightly larger installments of twenty-five sous per month, which, if they made their payments every month, would be paid off in a little over two and a half years, or thirty-two months.[37]

More than a decade later, we encounter a similar campaign being mobilized by the confraternity of freed blacks. This time, it was being made on behalf of a black slave woman named Johana. In 1495 members of "the confraternity of the blacks" propositioned the nobleman Bernat Sorrell, requesting that he let them redeem Johana, his black slave woman. Bernat, similar to Francesch "the Hothead," had been dissatisfied with his slave woman's services. Contending that his generosity toward Johana was "being poorly repaid," Bernat decided "to deliver himself" of his black slave woman. Despite his broker's best efforts, however, Bernat was unable to find a buyer. For, "wherever they went, the slave represented herself so poorly that no one wanted to buy her." Frustrated with Johana's misbehavior, Bernat placed Johana in the municipal prison where he intended to keep her until he could ship her off to Ibiza and be rid of her once and for all. Before he

36. "E seguis de la dita Ursola en virtud de la dita concordia vench a pastar a la casa de ell dit responent dos o tres veguades. E com haguessen en casa dell dit responent pastar trametiha la muller del dit responent per aquella demanant la que vingues a pastar. E aquella respos que no li venia be car no li volia donar dines e fahena." ARV G 2348: M. 7: 2r.

37. "E ell dit responent vehent que no era volguda venir segons promes havia trames dels seus jovens e feu la portar a la preso ab cor de sperar li comprador e vendre la puix aquella no li atenyia lo que promes li havia. E tenint la presa fonch preguat per negres e alguns altres que la dona a capleuta ab fermances. E que si volia que ella li daria les quaranta lliures empero que no hagues a pastar e que les dites quaranta lliures li paguaria ves cascun mes vint e cinch solidos e que ja tenia quaranta solidos que'ls hi donaria." ARV G 2348: M. 7: 2r.

could do so, however, Bernat's broker was approached by "the black men who beg alms in the city in order to redeem black slaves. They told him that if he [Bernat] wished to come to an agreement with them, that they would ransom her."[38] This broker testified that Johana also had badgered him to let her negotiate her redemption, telling him "not to look for a buyer or a new owner for her because she could not and would not serve anyone." Rather, this black slave woman boasted that "she would seek out and secure the assistance of some black friends and relatives of hers in the city who would redeem her."[39]

Four black men are mentioned in the court transcript as the principal participants in Johana's redemption. Interestingly enough, they were not all freedmen. Two of them were slaves. In addition to the mattress maker named Joan Monpalau, the former slave of the nobleman Joffre de Monpalau, and a free black porter named Joan Moliner, were Pere, the slave of a nobleman named en Pallars, and Antoni, the slave of the nobleman Antoni Johan.[40] This slave named Pere, moreover, seems to have not only been a member of the confraternity but also held a key post in its administration. Pere reportedly was the treasurer or manager of the confraternity's coffers (its baci or alms box).[41]

When first approached by this group of black Africans, Bernat testified that he had been skeptical, telling them "that the slave was worth a lot of money to him and that he did not think that they could pay him what she was worth to him." After several meetings, however, over the course of some twenty days, Bernat's concerns had been satisfied, and they set Johana's redemption fee (rescat) at thirty-six lliures.[42] Nevertheless, reflective of the significant economic constraints under which the black freedmen's confraternity operated, when it came time to pay Johana's ransom they found themselves a significant number of lliures short. Although some witnesses insisted that they were only ten lliures short of the thirty-six lliure redemption fee, others claimed that they had only managed to

---

38. Johana's former master, Bernat Sorrell, testified that "dix lo dit corredor a ell dit testimoni que huns negres qui acaptaven per Valencia per a rescatar catius negres li havien parlats dihent que si ell dit testimoni si posava en la raho ells la rescataren." ARV G 2411: 54r.

39. The broker hired to resell Johana, Miquel Ramon, testified that "essent la dita Johana negra en poder de ell dit testimoni aquella dix a ell dit testimoni que no li cerquas comprador ni amo per que ella no poria servir ni serviria a nenguna persona pero que ella treballaria e procuraria ab alguns negres amichs e parents de aquella de la present ciutat que la rescatarien." ARV G 2411: 55r–v.

40. The broker Miquel Ramon testified that "los negres qui menejaven lo dit rescat se nomenen la hu Johan lo traginer e l'alter Johan lo matalafer de mossen Monpalau e l'altre Anthoni catiu del dit mossen Anthoni Johan." ARV G 2411: 55v.

41. The notary Miquel Gari, who acted as Bernat Sorell's procurator, recounted how "hun negre del noble mossen Pallars e altre negre de mossen Anthoni Johan treballaven que lo magnifich mossen Sorell vene als dits negres la dita Johana per obs de enfranquir aquella de les caritats del baci que aquells tenien. Lo qual baci regia lo dit negre del dit noble mossen Pallars." ARV G 2411: 58v.

42. Bernat reportedly replied, "Que la dita sclava li stava en gran preu e que no creya la y pagassen segons lo que valia per que sola y pagaven be que ell dit testimoni lals vendria e lliuraria." ARV G 2411: 54r.

raise five or six lliures.[43] The agent contracted to broker the transaction recounted how, shortly after making the agreement, "some differences arose [between the members of the black freedmen's confraternity] such that they could not move forward nor could those with whom he had negotiated the slave's redemption bring anything into effect." After assuring Bernat that they could get him the money, telling him that they would give him the thirty-six lliures "very soon," the members of the confraternity of the blacks turned to a local nobleman for assistance.[44]

Instrumental to securing Johana's redemption were the efforts made by the black male slave named Anthoni Johan, the namesake of his noble master. All accounts describe this black male slave as being linked romantically to Johana—some describing Anthoni as Johana's "husband,"[45] others saying that Johana had given birth to Anthoni's daughter. Desperate to secure Johana's redemption, Anthoni pleaded with and ultimately convinced his master to provide the remainder of the sum needed to pay Johana's ransom. Thus the confraternity of the blacks was, once again, successful in securing a black African slave's redemption.

Despite this striking evidence of the organization and cohesion of the black African community, the actual extent of their powers must be kept in perspective. After all, relative to the free Muslim population (to which Muslim slaves had access), the black African community was much smaller in terms of its size, wealth, and degree of political influence. In consequence, black Africans were much more dependent on the financial support and cooperation of others to secure their freedom. Returning to the first case, it bears noting, for example, that while Ursola and her black African benefactors had argued that Francesch, since he had accepted payment of the first installment of her ransom, was obliged to honor the redemption agreement, and, upon payment in full, grant Ursola her freedom, Francesch insisted that he had no obligation to free her and, in fact, could still change his mind.[46] Thus, in glaring contravention of what the members of the

43. According to a document submitted on Johana's behalf, the nobleman Anthoni Johan had donated ten lliures toward her ransom. According to the testimony of the broker hired by Bernat to coordinate Johana's sale/redemption (Miquel Ramon), however, Anthoni paid thirty lliures. See ARV G 2410: 219v, G 2411: 50v, and G 2410: 225v.

44. "Que'l possaven per noves e no portaven res a effecte a los quals li avia concordat ell dit testimoni que per lo rescat de la dita Johana negra donassen al dit mossen Bernat Sorell xxxv (sic) lliures aquells digueren a ell dit testimoni que nos envias que de ora e ora staren per haver diners e que molt pres li donaris les dites xxxv [sic] lliures." ARV G 2411: 55v.

45. According to Johana's advocate, the "negre appellat Anthoni Johan sclau qui es del dit mossen Anthoni Johan... era marit o enamorat de la dita Johana per lo qual causa tenia gran passio que la dita Johana fos enfranquida." ARV G 2410: 219r.

46. Francesch maintained that he received the sum *en comanda* (in deposit) rather than in payment of Ursola's ransom. Thus, he was under no obligation to grant Ursola her freedom. Denying that he had ever agreed to the terms of this new arrangement, Francesch insisted that accepting this money in no way

black African community considered a legally binding contract, Francesch sold Ursola back into slavery.[47]

Similarly, turning to the second case, we see how five years *after* the confraternity of freed blacks redeemed Johana from captivity, her noble benefactor, Anthoni Johan, suddenly resurfaced and claimed her as his slave. Although witnesses testifying on Johana's behalf affirmed that this nobleman had donated only a small sum of money toward Johana's ransom "out of charity" (or, alternatively, "out of love for his black male slave and to keep him out of trouble"),[48] Anthoni Johan insisted that he had *purchased* Johana, presenting the document recording the payment he had made to Johana's master as proof of sale. Despite the fact that Johana had, ever since then, been living as a freedwoman, "maintain[ing] her own household, work[ing] for her own benefit... [and] doing all those things that persons freed from servitude are accustomed to perform," this nobleman threatened to thrust Johana back into a life of servitude.[49]

Ursola and Johana were both fortunate in that they managed to win access to the court of the governor and, ultimately, secured official recognition of their freed status by filing successful *demandes de libertat*.[50] Their struggles, nonetheless, demonstrate that liberty did not come cheaply in fifteenth-century Valencia, particular for members of the local black African community who had fewer resources at their disposal.

---

precluded him from being able to sell her. Indeed, Francesch argued, Ursola herself had recognized this. When he resold her, no fewer than two subsequent times, he did so "with her cooperation and complicity." By allowing herself to be sold, first to a notary and then to the bailiff of Puçol, Ursola, in Francesch's view, had both acknowledged and affirmed her slave status. ARV G 2348: M. 7: 2v, 36r.

47. Ursola's advocate protested that Francesch, "no curant e oblidant se de la dita concordia contra tota raho e justicia secretament una nit pres aquella dita Ursola e mes aquella en poder de hun qui dien Segarra al qual se diu la havia venuda." Even worse, Ursola's advocate continued, her new master intended to ship her off for resale on the island of Ibiza, "en manera que may s'en sabes res in francam libertatis ja per ell atorgada a la dita Ursola." ARV G 2348: M. 7: 1r.

48. Johana's advocate maintained that "quant lo mossen Anthoni Johan dona per rescat les dites x lliures dix que aquelles donava per caritat per sguart de seu negre." Elsewhere, it was affirmed that, at the time of payment, the nobleman "dix e fonch hoit dir tals paraules aquestes deu lliures done pero per amor de meu negre per traure'l de mal." ARV G 2410: 219v and ARV G 2411: 50v.

49. In the *demanda de libertat* filed on her behalf, Johana protested that for the past five years she had been "en sa pacifica possessio de libertat," that "continuament ha tengut la casa e feta fahena per sustenacio sua stant en possessio de persona liberta e exercint tots aquells actes que persones libertes de servitut acostumen exercir e per tal es tenguda e reputada en la present ciutat entre los conexents aquella." ARV G 2410: 200r.

50. In a sentence issued on 25 May 1478, the governor ordered Francesch to accept payment of the redemption fee negotiated on Ursola's behalf by the members of the *casa dels negres*. ARV G 2348: M. 7: 36v. Similarly, on 5 March 1501, the governor affirmed Johana's freed status and ordered the nobleman Anthoni Johan, "under great penalties," not to "disturb" or "molest" her in any way. ARV G 2411: 62r–v.

Earning Freedom through Service:
"Contracts" of Manumission

Though, as we have just seen, some Muslim and black African slaves "bought" their freedom by paying a redemption fee, the "price" paid by most Valencian slaves for their freedom was several additional years of unpaid service. Grants of freedom were often made contingent on completion of a fixed term of service, ranging from two to fifteen years. In her last will and testament, for example, Maria, the widow of the carpenter Francesch Selva, specified that she was freeing her slave Johan "under the condition that he serve and be obliged to provided good service to her heir—or anyone substituted [for her] by me—for a period of nine years... subsequent to my death."[51] In some instances, however, the exact term of service required was left open-ended—for example, for the duration of a surviving spouse's or child's lifetime.[52] In the last will and testament of Elvira de Ribelles, she specified that her black slave named Anthoni would win his freedom only after her husband's death. For however long her husband lived, Anthoni was "to serve him and follow all of his orders."[53] Other masters and mistresses stipulated that the manumission would take effect only after a suitable marriage partner for the slave had been found or she or he had provided "enough" service to compensate their owners for their initial purchase price. Slaves often protested that such indefinite clauses enabled their masters and mistresses to postpone their manumissions unjustly—for example, by rejecting all potential suitors or undervaluing the service a slave had already provided. Another circumstance that potentially could compromise a conditionally freed slave's manumission was if their owners sold and/or transferred their services over to a third party. For example, although the innkeeper Manuel Pardo promised Johan, his black male slave, freedom contingent on serving his wife and children for ten more years, he inserted a clause stipulating that "if his wife thought it preferable, she could sell him for said period... to whomever she saw fit."[54] Although Johan technically was to be freed upon completing ten years of service, his new master might not have been inclined to respect

51. "Ab tal condicio que aquell servescha e sia tengut de ben servir a la herena mia... e successivament als substituhits per mia aquella per temps de nou anys contadors comptats apres obte meu." APPV 25214 (nonpaginated): 24 April 1470.

52. For one example among many, see ARV P 588 (nonpaginated): 27 February 1475. Miquel Fort and his wife Francina specified that the manumission of Gostancia, their thirty-five-year-old black slave woman from "Guinea," would take effect upon Francina's death.

53. Elvira "do e leix al dit noble senyor marit meu Anthoni negre catiu meu lo qual haia de servir aquell e fer tots sos manaments durant la vida tant solament del dit marit meu. E apres mort de aquell vull e orden que lo dit Anthoni negre sia franch e delliure de tota servitut e puixa anar e contractar a sa voluntat axi com qualsevol persona franqua e libera pot fer." APPV 18557 (nonpaginated): 15 December 1477.

54. "Volent que la dita muller mia si a ella benvist li sera lo puxa vendre als dits deu anys a aquell o aquella que benvist sia." ARV P 1911 (nonpaginated): 31 August 1470.

this prior arrangement. Indeed, in 1478, a conditionally freed black slave woman named Lucia requested the governor's assistance in protecting her from just such a fate. Lucia's master, a Sardinian merchant, had granted her freedom contingent upon her serving his heir for ten years following his death. Rather than retain Lucia in his service, however, the curator of her master's estate had hired a merchant to take Lucia to Valencia where he intended to sell her services to a third party. Fearful that this merchant "would sell her for a period of time greater than that she was obliged to serve," Lucia asked the governor to issue an order that she be sent back to Sardinia. There she felt more confident that the terms of her manumission would be respected.[55]

Though masters and mistresses often presented manumission as an act of charity, in practice, it was treated as a business arrangement. Manumissions were typically drawn up as contractual agreements. For example, in the carta de libertat Pere de Palomar issued to his slave, Galceran Jacobi, Galceran was depicted as an active participant (if not an equal partner) in this transaction. Noting how the slave was present at the time of the document's composition, Pere specified that Galceran's manumission was contingent upon him providing four more years of "loyal and faithful service."[56] Although the notary emphasized how Galceran accepted the gift of freedom "with many acts of gratitude, kissing humbly his hands and feet," he also carefully registered this slave's acceptance and approval of Pere's offer of freedom, "under the terms and conditions expressed above." Thus, Galceran promised to serve Pere and his household (or whomever else Pere specified) "well, lawfully, and faithfully, for the entire aforementioned period of four years as specified above." Affirming, finally, that the terms of this agreement had been read aloud to him so that "he understood them very well," Galceran "knowingly" and "freely" pledged his person and any property that he owned in surety for his promise: "to perform and uphold completely and firmly each and every one of the aforementioned obligations."[57]

55. Lucia, "de linatge de negres . . . tement que aquella no fos venuda a mes temps del que deuia servir reclama e recorregut al illustrissimo senyor infant." ARV G 2348: M. 3. 42r. The governor acceded to Lucia's request, ordering that she be returned to Sardinia, into the custody of the curator of her master's estate.

56. Pere granted Galceran his freedom "sub condicione . . . quod tu tenearis michi et meis et domui mei aut cui seu quibus ego volvero loco mei bene fideliter et legaliter per tempus quatuor annorum a presenti die continue computandorum servire prout decet quod si non feceris tali casu volo quod revertaris penitus in servitute et captivitate ac si numquam esset tibi cognita libertas aut per me concessa et data." APPV 11436 (nonpaginated): 22 February 1469.

57. "Ad hec autem ego predictus Galcerandus Jacobi acceptans a vobis prefato magnifico domino Petro de Palomar domino meo libertatem manumissionem et franquesiam predictam per vos de presenti mei concessam cum multiplici gratis accione manus et pedes vestras humiliter osculando sub modis formis et condicionibus superius expressatis mei presencialiter dictis lectis et per me bene intellectis. Promitto vobis predicto domino Petro de Palomar domino meo . . . servire bene legaliter et fideliter per

The balance of power in these so-called contractual agreements, however, clearly favored the master. They set the terms and they claimed the exclusive prerogative of determining whether or not the terms had been met. Promises of freedom, therefore, were hardly ironclad. If not renounced by masters and mistresses while they were still living, conditional grants of liberty were often ignored, challenged, or rejected by heirs. A quick perusal of contemporary court records reveals that masters and mistresses frequently appeared before local authorities, requesting—on allegations of breach of contract—that *cartas de libertat* be declared null and void.

On an early autumn day in 1472, the Valencian merchant Bernat Gilabert had ordered his two slaves—one white, the other black—to assist him in bottling his latest vintage of *vi muntonech* (*montonec*: a white wine or sherry). When Bernat directed his white slave, a twenty-five-year-old man named Nadal, to begin bottling the wine, Nadal allegedly had responded by abusing his master verbally, grabbing him and then throwing him to the ground, pummeling him with some "powerful blows." Not content with this outrageous act of rebellion against his master, Nadal thereupon attempted to hurl his master into a vat of wine. According to Bernat's complaint and the testimony of several witnesses, had not Bernat's other slave, a black man named Joan, as well as several bystanders immediately come to his assistance, Nadal would have succeeded in his "deliberate plot" against his master, drowning him in a tub of wine.[58]

The alleged incident took place just a few months after Bernat, in response to the pleas of "friends and well-wishers," had agreed to grant Nadal his freedom. In his complaint, Bernat emphasized how the notarial charter (*carta de libertat*) promising Nadal his freedom had been contractual in nature, with Bernat granting and Nadal "accepting and receiving" his liberty in accordance with certain mutually agreed upon terms. Nadal's liberation was contingent upon him serving Bernat "well and faithfully" for five more years, "without committing any fraudulent, evil, or treasonous act against said Bernat Gilabert (or whomever he wishes him to be with)."[59] Hardly serving his master "well and

---

totum predictum tempus quatuor annorum ut superius iam dictum est. Et pro predictis omnibus et eorum singulis sich attendendis firmiter et complendis obligo scienter et gratis vobis et vestris personam meam et omnia bona mea mobilia et inmobilia." APPV 11436 (nonpaginated): 22 February 1469.

58. "Et aquell dit catiu tenint ja la pença delliberada de rebellar se contre son senyor...entrant lo dit en Bernat Gilabert en altres paraules ab lo dit catiu lo dit catiu desmenti lo dit en Bernat Gilabert per tres vegades. E lo dit en Bernat Gilabert abrassars ab lo dit catiu com sia home de xxv en xxviii anys llança en terra lo dit en Bernat Gilabert donant li de grans punyades e volent llançar al dit en Bernat Gilabert en hun llach de vi com fos plena en aquell cars de vin...sino per hun altre catiu negre del dit en Bernat Gilabert e altres vehins que sentint la rancor e tempesta...acorregueren e ajudaren al dit en Gilabert lo dit catiu haguere llançat dins lo dit lloch de vi ple al dit en Bernat Gilabert en lo qual se fora offegat." ARV JCiv 924: M. 12 (bis): 44v–46v.

59. The contract of manumission stipulated that during this term of service, Nadal was obliged to "servis be e diligentment e sens fer frau malvestat e trahicio al dit en Bernat Gilabert ho lla hon ell volgues

faithfully," Bernat contended that Nadal's act of rebellion invalidated his claim to free-dom. In Bernat's estimate, Nadal's attempt on his life rendered the contract of manumis-sion null and void.[60]

What is remarkable about this episode, beyond the fact that a slave allegedly attempted to drown his master in a vat of wine, is that we only learn of this incident because Bernat felt it necessary to get official recognition of his right to maintain Nadal in slavery. Bernat was not pressing criminal charges against his slave. He was not asking the authorities to condemn his slave to death. Rather, Bernat was appearing before the civil court of the city of Valencia to ask the Justícia to confirm his right to sell Nadal to another, no doubt, unwitting, master. He wished the Justícia to lend its authority and back up his claim that Nadal's act of rebellion invalidated any right he may previously have had to freedom. Whether or not we can accept Bernat's account of this episode as true and accurate, whether or not Nadal, in fact, attempted to drown his master in a vat of wine, Bernat's avowed scrupulous attention to the legal process is revealing of how the dominance of a master over his slave was established, justified, and understood by his contemporaries. Whereas in the previous chapter I discussed similar court cases in the context of an ex-amination of how masters and mistresses responded to assaults against their "honor," here I explore what these cases tell us about contemporary attitudes concerning a slave's claims to freedom.

"Against Their Masters' Will": *Demandes de Libertat*

Considered in isolation, Bernat's efforts to block his slave's enfranchisement might not seem all that noteworthy. That the Valencian legal system would affirm a master's right to keep a "rebellious" slave in captivity is not terribly startling. Yet, when Bernat's request is considered in conjunction with dozens of demands for liberty filed before royal and municipal courts between 1425 and 1520, Bernat's allegations take on added signifi-cance. It becomes evident that Bernat's actions were likely motivated by more than legal

---

en axi que aquell durant lo dit temps no furtars no jugars fugirs ne fahes malesa nenguna contra son senyor. E aço ha fet lo dit Bernat Gilabert per amor de deu e per prechs de alguns amichs e ben volents de aquell." ARV JCiv 924: M. 12 (bis): 44v–46v.

60. Bernat argued that "per les quals coses e altres lo dit catiu de justicia ha perdut qualsevol grat que aquell en la dita carta haia promesa al dit catiu puix aquell dit catiu no ha servat la promesa ne les condicions contengudes en la dita carta de libertat. E per ço que a vos molt magniffich justicia sia cert de les dites coses vos requer que per vos dit magniffich justicia sia reebuda sumaria informacio de les dites coses e si a vos constara axi en veritat passar la dita rebellio feta per lo dit catiu al dit en Bernat Gilabert declarets la dita gracia feta al dit catiu de libertat a cinch anys no procehir com ab les dites condicions li haia donada la dita libertat e no sens aquella no obstant lo dit Bernat Gilabert poder vendre com a catiu la persona de aquell." ARV JCiv 924: M. 12 (bis): 44v–46v.

scrupulousness. His actions appear more defensive in nature, reflective of a concern that his slave might contest his right to keep him in servitude by citing the legally binding terms of his manumission. Bernat's actions are demonstrative of an awareness among slave owners that (to a limited degree) slaves, too, had access to the courts. In addition to appealing to their masters' munificence, begging for alms, or taking flight, slaves living in late medieval Valencia could regain their liberty by taking their owners to court.

We noted in the first chapter how, upon their arrival in the kingdom of Valencia, captives were closely questioned concerning their faith, parentage, and place of residence. Before they could legitimately be sold into slavery, captive men, women, and children were granted a public hearing at which they, theoretically, could contest the legitimacy of their seizure. Given the timing and setting of this hearing, it is hardly surprising that few captives spoke out openly or disputed the legality of their seizure. With the passage of time, however, slaves living and working in the city of Valencia not only adopted the dress, religious practices, and language of their new community, they also became conversant with its laws and legal procedures. In addition, they formed support networks, securing friends and advocates both within and outside their master's households who could be enlisted to help slaves navigate the kingdom's legal system in an effort to sue for their freedom.

A close reading of Valencia's legal records reveals that slaves could demand their liberty by advancing a number of different claims. *Demandes de libertat* filed before Valencian courts in the latter half of the fifteenth century can be grouped roughly into two broad categories: slaves claiming unlawful enslavement and slaves claiming to have earned freed status. Slaves claiming unlawful enslavement argued that they should not have been enslaved in the first place. Children of slave mothers, for example, appeared before the governor's court insisting that since their fathers had been freeborn Christians, they too were entitled to freeborn status. Other slaves protested that their capture and enslavement had been illegal. Hardly "captives of good war," these slave plaintiffs claimed that they had been kidnapped and sold illicitly into slavery. In 1493, for example, Nicholau Marquo, a fifteen-year-old neophyte Christian, recently redeemed from Muslim captivity, successfully demanded his freedom before the court of the governor. Fleeing his Muslim master's custody in Tunis, Nicholau contended that he had been divinely inspired to convert to Christianity. Surreptitiously boarding a Christian vessel bound for Sicily, upon his arrival in Palermo, Nicholau (along with several other enslaved *moros*) was baptized and proclaimed "free" by the viceroy of Sicily.[61] Almost immediately subsequent to his conversion/liberation, however, Nicholau claimed he had been tricked into boarding a

---

61. Nicholau explained that he had secured these privileges through the intercession of another Moorish convert, who was a member of the viceroy's court. We first met Nicholau Marquo in chapter 2, see p. 73.

vessel bound for Valencia where, "without being presented before the bailiff general," he was secretly and fraudulently sold back into slavery.[62] Insisting that his sale into slavery had been a case of mistaken identity, Nicholau and other plaintiffs protesting unlawful enslavement presented themselves as the innocent victims of unscrupulous merchants.

Slaves claiming freed status, by way of contrast, argued that, though their initial enslavement had been legitimate, for a variety of different reasons their masters and mistresses were legally obliged now to grant them their freedom. I noted in the previous chapter, for example, how, according to the kingdom of Valencia's legal code, slave women who gave birth to their masters' children were entitled to an automatic manumission. Thus, we saw how when their owners failed to recognize their *de jure* freed status, the aforementioned Johana, Rosa, and Ysabel sought justice at the court of the governor.

The *Furs de València* also dictated that slaves who converted to Christianity while in "infidel" custody in Valencia were entitled to an automatic manumission.[63] Thus, in 1487, despite the protests of his Mudejar master,[64] the Justícia Civil declared "free from all captivity and the yoke of servitude" a black male slave, formerly named Halof, now a baptized Christian named Luis Villes.[65] Citing the "dispositions of both canon and civil law, as well as the *Furs de València*," the Justícia affirmed that "if any Jew, pagan, or heretic should be master of and possess a Moorish or pagan captive and that black captive, trusting in God, should be baptized or request holy baptism and learn the holy Catholic faith, he immediately shall acquire the better condition, attaining full liberty and liberation from the

62. Nicholau Marquo claimed that "quatre o cinch anys ha poch mes o menys... hixque fugitivament de la ciutat de Tunis per fer se xristia lo qual s'en fugi ensemps ab altres moros de la dita ciutat e s'en anaren a la ciutat de Palerm per fer se xristians.... Essent aquell ensemps ab los altres moros companyons de aquell en la dita ciutat de Palermo tots se feren xristians e per lo semblant ell dit propossant e lo virrey de Sicilia los feu xristians e franchs." Shortly thereafter, however, an unscrupulous merchant "vene a ell dit propossant amagadament sens manifestar lo al batle per que manifestant lo se fora descubert se com aquell era e es franch." ARV G 2397: M. 13: 21r–24v. Though Nicholau's *demanda de libertat* was successful and the governor declared him "free," what later became of this Moorish convert—whether Nicholau returned to Palermo or remained in Valencia—is not indicated in the extant records.

63. *Furs de València*, ed. Colon and Garcia (Barcelona, 1990), V: 106–7.

64. Luis/Halof's owner, Azmet Mengat, a Mudejar of Picasent, attempted to refute Luis's claims by arguing that he had sold this black Muslim to a Christian prior to his conversion. Moreover, he insisted, that since Halof/Luis had converted "against his master's will," he was not entitled to an automatic manumission. In Azmet's view, the *Furs de València* stipulated Luis/Halof was obliged to remain in his master's custody until he had fully reimbursed him for his purchase price. ARV JCiv 932: M. 8: 44r–45r.

65. The Justícia Civil rejected both of Azmet's arguments, noting that the clause barring manumission to slaves who converted against their master's will was applicable only in the case of Christian masters and that the clause ordering slave converts to Christianity to pay a redemption fee was "a special dispensation applicable only to Jewish slave owners." The Justícia, nevertheless, did order Halof/Luis to pay Azmet the token sum of six *morabatins*. ARV JCiv 932: M. 8: 44r–45r.

captivity or servitude in which the said convert had been held."[66] To prevent the outrage of seeing a Christian made subject to infidels, local authorities dictated that slaves belonging to "infidels" would be freed immediately upon receipt of baptism.

Most commonly, however, slaves filed *demandes de libertat* when grants of freedom (both oral and testamentary) were not being honored by masters, mistresses, or their heirs. In 1480, Joan Fernandiz, the black male slave held by Elvira de Ladro, the widow of the viscount of Vilanova, complained to the governor that, about a month after his master's death, Elvira had him arrested on trumped-up charges of theft in an effort to forestall his manumission. Joan protested that by imprisoning him in a *serra* (a device akin to the aforementioned *ballesta*, a wooden or metal contraption that was used to confine and discipline unruly slaves), Elvira effectively was preventing him from fulfilling the requirements outlined in his contract of manumission: providing his master's heirs with five more years of service.[67] Similarly, in July 1465, Nicholau, the aforementioned black male slave owned by the hosier Pere del Mas, appeared before the governor, accusing his master of contravening their agreement. Ever since his master granted him his freedom, contingent upon payment in full of a redemption fee of fifty lliures, Nicholau insisted that he had been making an "honest" living as a porter, hauling merchandise (with the aid of the horse his master gave him) between the city's center and its port. Indeed, Nicholau had already paid off between ten and twelve lliures of the 50 lliure debt. Observing how well his former slave was managing his own affairs, however, Pere reputedly had come to regret his act of "charity." Thus, Nicholau protested, in violation of his conditionally freed status, Pere had ambushed him while he was working down by the port. In an effort to drag him, literally, back into his service, Pere had grabbed him by the hair, tearing out a large clump of it. Stunned and confused by his master's attack, Nicholau ran off and sought shelter in a friend's house (one of the five cosigners of his contract of debt) and then appealed to the governor for assistance.[68]

Presented with a relatively broad array of legal arguments with which they could demand their liberty, some enslaved men and women took their masters to court. To do so, they typically sought out the assistance of a little-studied municipal official known as the

66. "Attenent que ali per disposicions de drets canonich e civil e de furs del present regne...es statuhit e ordenat que si algun juheu paga o heretge sera senyor tenia e possehiria algun catiu moro o paga e aquell catiu negre senyor deu espresant se batejara o petita lo sant babtissme e deuers e connehira a la santa fe cristiana e ali a millor condicio e o ipso consegue e a ateny plens libertat e libertacio de captivitat e o de cativeri de aquell e de servitut en la qual era lo dit bategat e devengut a la santa fe xristiana ne algun juheu paga o heretge no pot haver ne tenir en maners alguns en son servey com a catiu o servent xristia algu." ARV JCiv 932: M. 8: 44r–45r.

67. ARV G 2354: M. 1: 27r and ARV G 2357: M. 38: 23r–24r. Unfortunately, we do not know the governor's ultimate ruling on this case.

68. ARV G 2315: M. 15: 40r and ARV G 2316: 273r–275r.

procurator of the miserable (Procurador dels Miserables). The procurator of the miserable was an annually elected municipal official entrusted with overseeing the conditions in the city prison (*preso comuna*)—making sure that inmates were properly fed, clothed, and provided with suitable bedding. More important, however, he was responsible for seeing to it that they were not detained there indefinitely at the municipality's expense.[69] In connection with this latter responsibility, the procurator of the miserable came to play a role somewhat akin to that of a court-appointed attorney. In return for a nominal salary, paid by the municipality, the procurator saw to it that the poor and indigent of Valencia received a fair and timely hearing in city courts. Hence, on behalf of the so-called miserable, the procurator collected testimony, filed motions, and appeared at court hearings on his clients' behalf, free of charge.

Hence, in 1454, when a twenty-five-year-old slave named Johan decided to demand his liberty, he sought out the assistance of the procurator of the miserable. Claiming he was a Hungarian Christian who had been mistaken for a Muslim Turk and sold into slavery, Johan asked the procurator to assist him in filing his claim. On Johan's behalf, the procurator collected testimony from a number of witnesses, including three German merchants and a German cobbler. All four men testified that after interrogating Johan (aka Almancor) thoroughly in both German and Hungarian, they were convinced, "based on his language," that "Johan was from the kingdom of Hungary and a natural-born Christian, not a Moor."[70] Leaving no stone unturned, the procurator also had Johan examined by a physician, who, in a sworn written statement, assured the court that Johan had never been circumcised, proof positive that he was not a Moor. Thanks to the procurator of the miserable's prodigious efforts, the court affirmed Johan's natural-born Christian status, ruling that Johan was a free man with faculty "to come, go, and make contracts as he pleased."[71]

69. For a brief overview of the role and functions traditionally assigned to the Procurador dels Miserables (as well as a list of officeholders from 1344 to 1708), see F. Carrerres i de Calatayud, "El Procurador dels Miserables: Notes per a la seua històrica," *Anales del Centro de Cultura Valenciana* (Valencia, 1931), 41–53.

70. A cobbler named Albert who had been born in Cologne, for example, testified "que'l ha interrogat ab lenguatge ongres e alamany... e aquell li havia respost en lo dit lenguatge verdader que era del regne de Ongria qui es del imperi d'Alamanya e era xristia de natura de xristia de part de pare e mare. E ell testimoni reinterroga aquell ab la dita lengua com era stat cativat e menat en la present ciutat e aquell recita en lo dit lenguatge per menut lo cas segons desus es contengut de que ell testimoni segons la sua lengua creu que aquell es del dit realme d'Ongria e xristia de natura e no moro." ARV G 4581: M. 5: 36r–37v; M. 6: 2r.

71. Before issuing his ruling, the governor noted, among the many pieces of evidence that had been presented before him, "lo acte ab lo qual fe se mostre lo dit Johan Serec no esser circumcis." Finding Johan "to be a natural-born Christian, the son of a Christian father and a Christian mother, a native of the kingdom of Hungary," the governor affirmed that he saw no legitimate cause for someone to say he was

Slaves claiming they had a legitimate claim to freedom not only had the ability to solicit the procurator of the miserable's counsel to help them file a suit, but their continued access to him throughout the duration of the trial was also protected by the courts. Upon filing a demand for liberty, slaves turned themselves over into the protective custody of the governor. Then, they would be placed either in the city's prison or in a designated safe house. Nevertheless, in many instances, at a master's or mistress's urging, the court would release the slave back into their owner's custody. The court would only do so, however, upon receipt of a sworn promise from the master (or mistress) that they would neither physically harm the slave nor take him or her outside the city limits. In this way, the court worked to ensure the slaves could not be intimidated or bullied into withdrawing their claims. Most notably, some masters and mistresses were required to swear an oath promising that they would permit their slaves continued access to the procurator of the miserable. For example, when a slave woman named Juliana filed an (ultimately successful) demand for liberty in 1456 (citing a clause in her master's last will and testament granting her freedom after six years of service), in order to regain custody of her slave woman, Juliana's owner, Agostança, the widow of the innkeeper, Ferrando "lo Portogues," was obliged not only to promise the court that she would not beat Juliana "like a slave" for the duration of the trial but also that she would allow Juliana to meet with the procurator of the miserable at least two days a week. The bail-bond agreement specified that "every Tuesday and Friday, after supper," Juliana would be permitted "to go ... and consult with the procurator or advocate" for one hour.[72]

The degree to which these promises were actually honored, however, clearly varied. Sworn promises were not always effective in assuring a slave's physical safety, much less his or her continued access to the procurator of the miserable. Consider, for example, the experiences of the aforementioned Russian slave woman named Anna. In 1457, Anna filed a demand for liberty against her master, demanding freed status as a consequence of giving birth to her master's child. As was typical, upon filing the suit Anna placed herself in the protective custody of the governor. At her master's request, however, Anna was released back into his custody for the duration of the trial. When the

---

a slave. Emphasizing how Johan was neither "de nacio de moros ni de turchs," the governor "pronuncia e declara lo dit Johan Serec ... esser ingenu e franch e no esser moro ni sclau e per consequent aquell no poder esser venut com a moro sclau declarant aquell haver libera facultat com a franch anar star e contractar com a persona franqua e libera." ARV G 4581: M. 5: 36r–37v; M. 6: 2r.

72. The bail-bond agreement specified that Agostança "promes es obliga de no maltractar aquella axi com si no fos sclava e aço sub pena de docents florins aplicadors als cofrens del dit molt alt senyor rey encara promes es obliga en poder del dit honorable tinent loch de governador que lexava aquella ho permetra que dos dies de la setmana ço es lo dimarts e lo divendres en lo apres dinar una hora en cascu dels dits dies que aquella puxa venir a parlar e comunicar ab lo procurador e advocat per la present causa." ARV G 2287: M. 16: 19r–21v.

governor's agent escorted Anna back to her master's household, the agent admonished her master that he could neither take Anna outside the city limits nor mistreat Anna in any way. Nevertheless, as soon as she was back in his custody, Anna complained, her master beat her savagely—whipping her naked body with a hempen rope. Anna testified that the beating was so vicious that she remained bedridden for days. Not confident, moreover, that he had fully cowed her into submission, several days later, under cover of darkness, Anna's master allegedly took her outside of the city, packing her off to the town of Benafer, about twenty-six miles north of Valencia. His only motive for doing so, Anna insisted, was to prevent her from pursuing her legitimate claim to freedom. Once she had been taken out of Valencia, he had believed it would be almost impossible for Anna to get justice—for, in Benafer, no one knew her and, therefore, no one would likely take an interest in helping her.[73]

In addition to countering their slaves' demands for liberty with brute force, however, masters and mistresses also appealed to their self interest. They tried to discourage their slaves from litigating by making grants of liberty contingent on promises that they would not take their masters and mistresses to court. In 1485, a slave named Pedro appeared before the court of the governor in order to distance himself from the demanda de libertat that had been filed on his behalf. According to the terms of his contract of manumission, Pedro was forbidden to pursue his liberty in a court of law. Hence, in an effort to prevent the nullification of this contract, Pedro now appeared before the court of the governor to insist that the suit had been filed against his will by "certain Castilians from Valladolid." Affirming his legitimately enslaved status and admitting that he had no legal grounds on which he could demand his immediate liberation, Pedro concluded his sworn statement by affirming that he was quite content to serve the twelve years stipulated in his contract of manumission. Thus, Pedro stated,

> He wills and it is pleasing to him to remain in his service for said time and to serve his master well and loyally as he promised in the said agreement. He said that he renounced any right to freedom [he may have] until the completion of said period of twelve years; he was certain, however, that he did not have any. And thus, in order that said mestre Pere Crespo, his master, could not be dragged into any argument

---

73. Anna's advocate explained that she had been unable to pursue her claim to freedom until now because "no solament lo dit en Marti de Vaquena fonch e es stat inobedient al dit noble governador e manament de aquell per batre la dita sclava mas encara per ço com una nit lo dit en Marti de Vaquena ... amagadament hora de miga nit trague de la ciutat de Valencia la dita Anna ... a fi que la dita Anna essent fora de Valencia no proclamara la dita libertat ni negun per aquella no s'en curaria axi com fins açi nengu no s'en curat e axi tendria aquella per força axi com de fet ha fet tengut maltractant e batent aquella." ARV G 2314: M. 1: 10r and ARV G 2317: M. 35: 32r–33v. We discussed Anna's relationship with her master, Martí de Vaquena, in chapter 5, see pp. 173–74.

concerning those things that have been alleged and attempted, he says to your majesty that he wishes to stay and persevere in the agreement.[74]

Manumission: A Master's Prerogative?

A slave's fulfillment of the terms imposed in a contract of manumission, of course, was almost always open to dispute. In 1457, a black male slave named Johan Viscaya appeared before the governor, protesting that he had "earned" his freedom. According to the terms of his master's last will and testament, Johan Viscaya, and his mother, Johana the Black, were to be freed as soon as "they earned [an amount equivalent to] what they cost him."[75] Citing his prodigious skills as a farmer, Johan estimated that in the seventeen years since his master's death, he had provided services which were worth more than two hundred lliures. Since his initial purchase price at the age of six could not have been more than thirty lliures, Johan insisted that not only had he earned his freedom but also that his master's widow, Damiata Ferrer, owed him close to 150 lliures in back salary. In addition to their differences of opinion concerning Johan's initial purchase price (thirty versus sixty lliures) and the monetary value of his labor, Johan and his master's widow also disagreed about who ultimately had the right to determine whether Johan had fulfilled the terms of his manumission. Was it a public or a private matter?

In his efforts to demonstrate that he had provided more than enough service to pay back his master, Johan Viscaya produced two brokers who supported his claim that he had cost his master no more than thirty lliures. Both affirmed that, at the time when Johan had been purchased, "twenty-five lliures would have been a very good price for a six-year-old 'untrained' (boçal) slave."[76] Damiata, the widow of the merchant Johan Ferrer, however, contended that her husband "paid" nearly twice as much for this slave, at

---

74. Affirming that "ell no ha sabut res en la dita proclamacio de libertat feta per los dits castellans de Valladolit," Pedro stated that, "ell no vol proclamar nenguna libertat com no la puxa proclamar e que verdaderament aquell es catiu e estat venut be e legittimament per catiu e que la libertat per ell dit proposant fonch proposada...per vexar de despeses e conguoxes al dit mestre Pere Crespo amo de aquell e no per que ell pogues tenir libertat com no la tingues," and concluded that, "vol e li plau de estar en lo dit servey per lo dit temps e servir lo dit son amo be e lealment segons ha promes en la dita concordia. E diu que renuncia a qualsevol dret de libertat jatsia ell dit proposant sia cert non tinga alguna durant lo temps dels dits dotze anys. E per que lo dit mestre Pere Crespo amo de aquell no li puxa traure en argument alguna de les coses fetes e attemptades fer diu a la senyoria vestra que ell vol estar e perseverar en concordia." ARV G 2374: M. 4: 39r and ARV G 2376: M. 21: 10r–v.

75. "Que servexquen tractant que hagen guanyat lo que costaren a coneguda de la dita muller mia e del dit en Frances Julia." ARV G 2290: M. 22: 27r–29v; M. 25: 1r–9v; M. 27: 32r–33v. I discussed this black slave named Johan Viscaya's training and experiences as an agricultural laborer in chapter 3, see pp. 96–97.

76. ARV G 2290: M. 22: 27r–29v; M. 25: 1r–9v; M. 27: 32r–33v.

least twelve hundred sous or sixty lliures.[77] Emphasizing his extreme youth at the time of "purchase," Damiata complained that they were unable to extract any meaningful service from Johan until he was nine or ten years in age. Even then, she insisted, neither she nor anyone else in their household had much use for him. She already had many slaves who could serve her and she was unable to find anyone interested in hiring his services until several years later. Thus, Damiata concluded, Johan had given her only about six or seven years of service—a period that, in her estimate, fell far short of that requisite to "pay off" the aforementioned sixty lliure debt. Pointing, moreover, to the many expenses she had incurred in supporting Johan and his mother for all of these years, Damiata protested that the costs of feeding and clothing the two slaves far outweighed any service they provided.[78]

Most strident of all, however, were Damiata's protests against the governor for agreeing to hear Johan's case. She questioned his very authority to intervene in disputes between masters and their slaves. How they disposed of their private property, how, when, and, indeed, whether or not they freed their slaves, she argued, was hardly the court's concern. In his last will and testament, Damiata's husband had left the timing and execution of Johan's manumission at the determination of his widow and his executor ("*a coneguda de la muller mia e del dit en Frances Julia*"). Thus, in Damiata's perspective, the court had no business hearing Johan Viscaya's *demanda de libertat*. Arguing that, "in accordance with justice, the determination concerning said servitude cannot be made by you ... most noble, lieutenant governor," this widow insisted that neither the governor nor any other public official could dictate when or whether or not her slave had "earned" his freedom.[79]

77. Rather than purchase the slaves because he needed their services, Damiata explained that her husband had been given the three slaves in payment of a debt. Since this man had owed her husband more than thirty-six hundred sous, Damiata reasoned, Johan's "price" or "ço que costa al dit en Johan Ferrer" was at least a third of this amount. ARV G 2290: M. 22: 27r–29v; M. 25: 1r–9v; M. 27: 32r–33v.

78. ARV G 2290: M. 22: 27r–29v; M. 25: 1r–9v; M. 27: 32r–33v.

79. Damiata argued that "per la clausula del derrer testament del dit quondam honorable en Johan Ferrer ... aquell no puxa esser dit franch sino finida la servitut de ço que aura guanyat a coneguda de la dita na Damiata Ferrer e d'en Francesch Julia com la dita conexenca sia donada en virtud del dit testament a la dita Damiata e al dit en Francesch Julia en e sobre la dita servitut seguex se que de aquella dita conexenca de justicia no pot esser fet per vos ne deu esser feta comission alguna per vos dit molt noble tenint loch de governador al dit Dionis Dolit pare dels orfens de la present ciutat que tache la dita servitut segons es request per lo dit Johan de Vischaya." Thus, Damiata requested that "la dita demanda o requesta feta per lo dit Johan de Viscaya no sia per vos dit molt noble tenint loch de governador admesa ... remetent a la dita na Damiata la dita conexenca segons la voluntat e disposicio del dit testador e tenor de la dita clausula aposada en lo dit testament." ARV G 2290: M. 22: 27r–29v; M. 25: 1r–9v; M. 27: 32r–33v. The case, unfortunately, ends here. We do not know what ultimately happened to Johan de Viscaya, his mother, or, for that matter, his baby brother (see the discussion of Johan Ferrer's last will and testament

Be that as it may, the governor, at least initially, issued a ruling that was supportive of this black male slave's petition. Citing Damiata's unwillingness to consider fairly Johan's claim, the governor ordered the *pare dels òrfens*[80] to look into the matter and make an assessment regarding the financial value of Johan's services. Before the *pare del orfens* could make his assessment, however, a letter from King Juan II arrived, forbidding the governor to intervene any further in the matter.[81]

Although in this instance the absolute authority of a mistress over her slave was upheld by the Crown, similar protests, when voiced by a Genoese merchant, were completely ignored. In 1488, a Genoese merchant objected to the governor's order that he accept payment of the ransom being offered for his slave woman's redemption. Raffel Gentil argued that even if he had promised to allow his slave woman Magdalena to buy her liberty in exchange for her agreeing to have sex with him, "Justice simply did not allow Magdalena that could win her freedom against her master's will."[82] In spite of her master's protests, however, in this case, the governor affirmed Magdalena's claim to liberty. He ordered Raffel Gentil to accept the fifty-seven lliures, ten *sous* Magdalena had collected in pious offerings from friends and supporters and give her her freedom.[83]

The frustration expressed by the aforementioned mason, Francesch "the Hothead," in 1478 was perhaps reflective of the feelings of many Valencian slave owners upon being taken to court by their slaves. This mason complained that "it sets a very poor example if slave women, in a state of servitude, by [merely] claiming that they had made an agreement with their masters that they could redeem themselves in exchange for [paying] a certain quantity, have the capacity to go wherever they like and demand their liberty."[84] It bears emphasis that Francesch directed his complaint regarding frivolous lawsuits toward enslaved women in particular. Indeed, his slave woman named Ursola's *demanda de libertat* was filed in the very same year that King Fernando issued the edict restricting

in chapter 3, note 61). Although his baby brother may very well have become a notary or a barber, there is no further record of any of them.

80. The *pare dels òrfens* (or "father of the orphans") was a municipally appointed official entrusted with the responsibility of looking after minors who lacked legal guardians, often placing them in contracts of service. See Agustín Rubio Vela, "Infancia y marginación. En torno a las instituciones trecentistas valencianas para el socorro de los huérfanos," *Revista d'Història Medieval* 1, 1990, 111–53.

81. ARV G 2290: M. 27: 32r–33v.

82. Raffel Gentil protested that Magdalena's claim "no procohex ni te fonament algu de justicia per quant la dita Magdalena volrria haver libertat ultra voluntat de son senyor lo que justicia no comporta." ARV G 2385: M. 4: 10r and ARV G 2386: M. 12: 40r–43r.

83. ARV G 2386: M. 12: 42r–43r.

84. "Es cosa de mal exemple que les sclaves constituhides en stat de servitut per dir que tenen concordia ab lurs senyor de quitar se per certa quantitat stant tingue...[smudge—la facultat?] de anar s'en e proclamar en libertat." ARV G 2348: M. 7: 1r–2v; 36r–v.

the ability of slave women to file *demandes de libertat* on the grounds that they had given birth to their master's child.[85]

A slave owner had raised similar objections in 1459, arguing that it was absurd to accept a slave's claims at face value. Imploring the court to err on the side of conservatism, he insisted that slaves should be treated in accordance with the condition (legal status) in which they were found. Unless preventative measures were taken, he warned, *all* slaves would file false claims, if only for the benefit of temporarily (for the duration of the trial) being treated as free persons.[86]

In contrast with this slave owner's dire predictions, however, research in the records of the court of the governor between 1425 and 1520 uncovers, on average, only about two *demandes de libertat* a year (see appendix). In some years, however, such as in 1457, there were as many as seven. Although perhaps few in number, the *demandes* nevertheless had a fairly respectable success rate. Given the aforementioned Dionis Rossell's contention that masters habitually made insincere promises to free their slaves to inspire them to provide better service, it is not surprising to discover that many of these slave plaintiffs were claiming that their masters and mistresses had made oral promises to grant them freedom without condition. Though a good portion of these disputes quickly degenerated into "he-said, she-said" squabbles, five out of the eleven *demandes* of this type were successful. Slave plaintiffs citing the legally binding terms of a contract of manumission, in turn, had more than a 50–50 chance of success. The governor affirmed the legitimacy of ten of the eighteen *demandes de libertat* based on written promises made in last wills and testaments or *cartes de libertat* that were contingent upon payment of a redemption fee or completion of a term of service.

Enslaved persons protesting that they should not have been sold into slavery in the first place encountered a relatively sympathetic ear in the court of the governor. Nine out of the eighteen slaves who alleged they were long-lost Christians languishing in Muslim captivity or victims of unscrupulous merchants were pronounced "free." Although allegations of "free" paternity were extremely hard to prove and could, fairly easily, be repudiated by the purported father, five out of the fourteen slave children claiming to have freeborn fathers were declared "free."

The outcome for slave women demanding freedom on the grounds of having given birth to her master's child or for being forcibly prostituted, however, was considerably

---

85. *Furs de València*, Colon and Garcia, eds. (Barcelona, 1990), V:111.

86. The owner of a Tartar slave woman named Marta warned that "se seguiria que cascun catiu o cativa diria que son franchs sabents que durant la questio de la llibertat deguessen esser tractats com a franchs car al menys obtendrieu libertat per aquells temps en lo qual se examinaria la causa de la libertat." Thus, "per evitar les absorditats sobre dites," he argued that "determenat es per justicia que segons lo stat e possesio en lo qual algu es trobat deu esser tractat." ARV G 2294: M. 1: 47r; M. 24: 37r–39v.

more mixed. Both of the *demandes de libertat* filed by slave women claiming that their owners exploited their bodies for illicit gain are incomplete. And, out of the seventeen *demandes de libertat* filed by slave women claiming to have borne their master's child, only
six were definitively successful.

With thirty-nine out of ninety-four demands for liberty having favorable outcomes—
an overall success rate of at least 40 percent—it is clear that in a period when adjudicat-
ing status had become exceedingly complex, savvy slaves learned how to navigate the
kingdom's courts. Here, slaves could contest the legitimacy of their enslavement by affirming new faiths, asserting different ethnic origins, or adopting other paternities. By
making these claims, some legitimate, others perhaps less so, a significant proportion
of these slaves managed to recover their freedom.

Yet what at the outset might appear to have been an extremely effective instrument
slaves could use to regain their liberty was, more often, turned against them. Consider,
for example, the case of Maria, the Greek Orthodox Christian slave woman from Nicosia,
Cyprus. In 1470, Maria filed a *demanda de libertat* against her current mistress, a nun living in the Dominican convent of St. Mary Magdalene. Claiming she had been kidnapped
from her parents at the age of eight by some Genoese merchants and had been sold illicitly into slavery, Maria, now, some twenty years later, appeared before the court of the
governor to reclaim her liberty. In their attempt to refute Maria's claims, Maria's owners,
both past and present, not only insisted that Maria was of Russian rather than Greek ancestry[87] but also, more curiously, pointed to her many years of "willing" service. This, they
argued, was evidence of her legitimately enslaved status. For, if Maria had solid legal
grounds on which to challenge the legitimacy of her enslavement, why had she not contested her slave status earlier? If Maria truly was, as she now alleged, a freeborn Christian
who had been captured and enslaved illegally by other Christians (as opposed to Muslim
Turks), she would not repeatedly have permitted herself to be sold.[88]

---

87. Rejecting her claim that she had been kidnapped by a group of Genoese merchants and wrong-
fully enslaved, Maria's owners argued that not only was she of Russian (not Greek) descent but that her
captors had been Muslim Turks. Thus, while Maria very well may have been an (Orthodox) Christian, she
could not benefit from Urban V's reported pronouncement. Only Greeks who had been captured and
enslaved by other Christians were entitled to an automatic liberation. Thus, they argued that "cessa esser
ver...que la dita Maria sia grega ni de nacio de grechs." The "truth" of the matter was that "la dita na
Maria sclava es de nacio de Rosos e aquella es stada presa per turchs" and "essent en poder de turchs fonch
comprada per hun genoves per sexanta ducats." ARV G 2331: M. 16: 3r–8v and ARV G 2332: M. 26: 1r–4v.
We discussed Maria's suit in greater detail in chapter 1, see pp. 36–40.

88. Thus, Maria's owners also argued that "cessa esser ver...que la dita Maria fos portada contra
sa voluntat a la present ciutat de Valencia." Rather, "the truth is that the said Maria was transported to
the present city of her own free will (de sa propria voluntat)." Indeed, Maria had been living in the city
of Valencia for more than a year and a half, in the service of Raffael and Pau Mercader, "without her ever
having resisted, protested, or said that she was free (sens que james no ha contradit ne reclamat ne dit que

The dogged persistence with which masters and mistresses advanced such arguments to justify their continued dominance over their slaves is revealing of the strength of their conviction that slavery was an institution based on the rule of law, not brute force and domination.[89] In refuting their slaves' *demandes de libertat*, masters and mistresses continually emphasized how slaves were given ample opportunity to contest the legitimacy of their subjugation. Slaves could proclaim their free status, they noted, in a variety of different venues: immediately following their capture, at the time of their presentation before the bailiff general, in the marketplace prior to the contraction of their sale, and, ultimately, with the assistance of the procurator of the miserable, before a court of law. As a broker in 1477 rather disingenuously instructed Jacobo, the slave he had been hired to sell, "Mind you, if you are free, say so, because here in Valencia they will not cheat you!"[90] Ironically, in providing slaves with the means to contest the legality of their subjugated status, masters could more confidently assert slavery's legitimacy.

The vast majority of slaves did not file suits demanding their liberty. Despite their owner's contentions, however, we cannot conclude from this that they simply did not want to or that they did not think that they had legitimate grounds. The testimony of slaves concerning the violence they had to overcome in order to win a hearing before the governor suggests otherwise. Be it through physical violence, verbal intimidation, or the offer of incentives, masters and mistresses had many mechanisms at their disposal to prevent slaves from filing claims. The Greek slave woman named Maria, for example, successfully countered her previous master's allegation of "consent" by explaining that the reason why it had taken her twenty years to voice these claims was because, previously, she had been physically prevented from doing so. Every time she made mention of her legitimate claim to freedom, her previous master allegedly had beaten and dragged her around the house. Indeed, she maintained that he was so anxious about keeping her from filing a *demanda de libertat* that he would not allow her to do work near any doors or windows, much less let her out of the house.[91]

---

fos libertat)." When, subsequently, these two brothers decided to resell her, they insisted that they sold her "de voluntat e expres consentiment de la dita Maria sclava ... sens que la dita Maria no y feu ne y ha fet contradiccio alguna." ARV G 2331: M. 16: 3r–8v and ARV G 2332: M. 26: 1r–4v.

89. This is not to say, however, that the law and brute force were mutually exclusive mechanisms for establishing a master's authority over his slaves. The law both limited and affirmed a master's power to discipline his slaves.

90. The broker Bonanat Pujol testified that he had advised Jacobo, a slave he had been hired to sell, "si era catiu que'n digues que en ciutat era que no li farien sobres algunes." ARV G 4854: M. 21: 34r–38v.

91. Maria's advocate maintained that "no gosa demanar libertat car com la demanava e li dehia que ella volia exir en totes maneres de sa casa puix no la volia libertar e aquell hoyint les dites coses la batia e rocegava per casa e no la dexava fer [sic—fahena?] a la finestra ni a la porta tant la tenia desstreta e per aquesta raho no li gosava demanar libertat." ARV G 2331: M. 16: 3r–8v and ARV G 2332: M. 26: 1r–4v.

That the burden of proof weighed most heavily on slaves themselves in the determination of their status is reflected most starkly in the case of the aforementioned slave named Jacobo. A freeborn Christian who insisted that he had been sold into slavery illicitly, Jacobo filed his first *demanda de libertat* in the Catalan port of Tarragona. His master at that time, however, easily had refuted Jacobo's claims by noting how, at the time of sale, Jacobo affirmed publicly (in the presence of both notary and witnesses) that he was a slave. Frustrated in this "legitimate" attempt to reclaim his liberty, Jacobo subsequently decided to take flight, running away to Barcelona at the time of the Catalan Revolt of 1462–72. A fugitive slave, Jacobo joined a band of Catalan rebels there, only to be captured by Crown forces and resold into slavery. Jacobo was purchased by a cobbler who happened to live in Valencia. In 1475, Jacobo filed his second *demanda de libertat* before the court of the Justícia Civil and this time he was successful. And yet, while Jacobo recovered his liberty, the efforts made by this cobbler to recoup his losses are revealing, and merit further comment. In his attempt to counter Jacobo's *demanda de libertat*, this cobbler had argued that even if Jacobo's initial capture and enslavement had been illegal, by failing to speak out immediately Jacobo effectively had forfeited his right to freedom. The cobbler argued, "It can be concluded, and the justice of this is clear, that even if Jacobo had possession of liberty, for having permitted himself to be sold so many times, each time Jacobo confessing that he was a slave, Jacobo cannot (now) demand his liberty."[92]

This cobbler, in fact, would appeal the Justícia Civil's ruling, insisting that Jacobo's failure to proclaim his free status actively and continually not only discredited his claim to liberty but had, in fact, invalidated them. Indeed, this cobbler was so firm in his conviction that Jacobo not only had the faculty but a legal responsibility to demand his freedom that he also sued Jacobo for fraud. Seeking compensation for the expenses he had sustained as a result of being party to an illegal sale, the cobbler subsequently sued his former slave for fraudulently allowing himself to be sold. The complaint stated that he was seeking compensatory damages since "said Jacobo...at the time of sale, knew very well that he was free and permitted himself to be sold."[93]

---

92. "Ex quibus et alter se conclou e resulta en clar de justicia que en cars hon lo dit Jacobo tingues franquea alguna per aquell haver permes tantes voltes esser stat venut e aquell cascuna volta haver confessat esser catiu aquell dit Jacobo no pot demanar libertat." ARV G 2346: M. 2: 19v and ARV G 2347: M. 15: 26r–29r.

93. "Que puis lo dit en Jacobo de Seguer en lo temps de la dita venda sabia be que era franch e permete que fos venut e axi mateix expressament dix que era catiu de justicia seria e es tengut de dol e frau al dit mestre Jaume qui ha feta la dita fermansa e es compellit restituhir lo preu de aquell per que lo dit Jacobo deu esser condemnat en tot so e quant lo dit mestre Jaume haura pagat per aquell e li convendra pagar e en tots los dayns e damnages que haura sostenguts e li haura convengut sostenir per la dita raho com axi de justicia fer se deja." ARV G 4854: M. 21: 34r–38v.

Unfortunately, we do not know the governor's ultimate verdict in this case. Neverthe-less, considered in their totality, these *demandes de libertat* reveal how slaves such as Jacobo effectively exploited the judicial channels made available to them and sued for their free-dom. Those slaves fortunate enough to secure themselves a court hearing were able to profit from what was presented as a uniquely "Valencian" concern with upholding the rule of law. Yet what at first glance seems a powerful tool with which slaves could win their liberty was, by the same token, wielded by their masters to maintain the vast major-ity of slaves in servitude under an aura of fairness and legality. Granting access to a select handful of Muslim, eastern, and black African slaves to challenge the legality of their continued enslavement in the kingdom's courts served only to enhance the legitimacy of the slave owner's dominion. That being said, the achievement of these thirty-nine slaves in regaining their freedom becomes all the more impressive.

"Theft of One's Person": Flight to Freedom

Early one morning before Christmas in 1470 a compost seller was pushing a cartful of manure through the streets of Valencia. Tripping over a long piece of rope lying in the middle of the road, he reportedly called out, "Whose rope is this that is on the ground? Could you remove it?" This compost-seller's complaint provoked an immediate uproar. For, when the members of the cotton merchant Johan Ferrandiz's household woke up and discovered that, sometime during the previous evening, the slave named Pedro de Mena had used this length of rope to lower himself down from the upper-story terrace and escape, the slave's owner "began to shout and got very upset." Although Johan im-mediately alerted the guards posted at the city gates and sent out a search party, the slave seemingly had vanished without a trace.[94]

Since it offered the distinct advantage of liberty without payment, additional service, or delay, flight was, for some slaves, the most appealing path to freedom. Flight, of course, was not without its dangers. Most of what we know about fugitives and the paths they took toward freedom, in fact, comes from reports concerning their arrest and recovery. The records of the bailiff general contain numerous reports of fugitive slaves apprehended on land and at sea. In 1434, a band of fugitive slaves was discovered hiding in a cave in the Foya de Buñol.[95] Similarly, in 1407, the bailiff general was informed that a group of Mus-

94. ARV JCiv: 923: M. 16: 31r–33v. I discussed Pedro de Mena's reputation as a loyal slave and pious Christian in chapter 4, p. 139.

95. ARV B Lletres y Privilegis, IV, 103v. Cited in Piles Ros, *Estudio Documental sobre el Bayle General de Valencia, Su Autoridad y Jurisdicción* (Valencia: Instituto Valenciano de Estudios Históricos, Institución Al-fonso el Magnànimo, Diputación Provincial de Valencia, Consejo Superior de Investigaciones Científicas, 1970), 150 (#121).

lim slaves had been captured off the coast of Cullera. They had tried, unsuccessfully, to escape by boat (en un laut), perhaps with the intention of returning to Islamic-controlled territories.[96] Such reports illuminate how fugitive slaves set off in multiple directions. Although many Muslim slaves sought shelter in nearby Mudejar communities, others traveled beyond the borders of Valencia into Castile. The aforementioned fugitive Pedro de Mena (a baptized "Saracen"), for example, was found one year later living in the Castilian town of Lorca and calling himself "Ali of Castile."[97] Antonio, a baptized Muslim slave belonging to a nobleman from Játiva, was recaptured in Cartagena;[98] and Faraig, a forty-five- to sixty-year-old black Muslim slave owned by the carpenter Jacme Lombart, was recovered in Xirixella.[99] Traffic moved in the opposite direction as well. In 1477, a priest from Córdoba traveled to Valencia to recover Ali, his twenty-six-year-old slave who had gone "missing" about a year and a half ago.[100] Other slaves ventured even further abroad, to the Nasrid Sultanate of Granada and to the kingdoms of Navarre and France.

No matter which direction they took, however, fugitive slaves ran the risk of being recaptured and punished for the crime of "theft of one's person" (furt a si matexa).[101] In 1445, for example, Johan Saranya, a notary, requested that the Justícia Criminal punish his black slave named Johan corporally "as a penalty . . . since he had taken flight." Rather than leave the exact form of corporal punishment up to the determination of the Justícia Criminal, this slave owner specified that he wished to see Johan tied to a stake in front of the courthouse and whipped at least fifty times.[102] Similarly, in 1445 the Justícia Criminal approved a request made by a local baker to place his slave woman, a former fugitive, in chains. After the baker recovered her from the home of a local silk weaver, the Justícia

---

96. ARV B Lletres y Privilegis, II, 208r. Cited in Piles Ros, *Estudio Documental*, 131 (#43).

97. ARV JCiv: 923: M. 16: 31r–33v.

98. ARV Bailía Lletres y Privilegis, IV, 202v. Cited in Piles Ros, *Estudio Documental*, 168 (#198).

99. ARV P 438 (nonpaginated): 27 September 1465.

100. Ali, for his part, claimed that he had come to Valencia as a freedman, not as a fugitive slave. Kidnapped from this Cordoban priest four or five years ago, Ali claimed that the thieves subsequently had sold him to a man named Diego Fajardo who, in turn, accepted payment of the redemption fee offered for him by a group of his coreligionists from Guadalajara. Recalling how he had been ambushed by three men while taking this priest's mule to get a new set of horseshoes, the bandits had dragged Ali off his mule and took him away with them. Covering up his mouth so that he could not cry out and masking his face so that he could not see where they were taking him, they held Ali captive in an abandoned well for eight to ten days. Later, they took him to Castile where they sold him to the nobleman Diego Fajardo. Ali testified that after the group of Muslims from Guadalajara had redeemed him, he stayed in Guadalajara for a while and then moved to Valencia, where he had been living as a free man for almost a year and a half. ARV G 2346: M. 2: 33r; M. 8: 23r–26r.

101. Thus, Luis Collar charged that his fugitive slave, Mahomat Jach, "haga comes e fet furt a si matex." ARV G 2342: M. 14: 6r–v.

102. ARV JCrim 22: Clams: M. 2: (nonpaginated) 31 March 1445.

Criminal empowered him to put a leg iron on his slave woman in order to prevent her from running away again.[103]

Even years later fugitives remained in danger of being recognized and arrested. After vanishing "without a trace" from her master's custody on the island of Majorca, for example, a black slave woman named Caterina was spotted in Valencia more than a decade later. A former acquaintance of the reported fugitive's, a freed slave woman named Lucia, described Caterina as an argumentative, "full-figured, and well-built woman with a round and pretty face." After witnesses such as Lucia positively identified her as the missing fugitive, Caterina found herself aboard the next ship bound for Majorca, where her former master, presumably, would reassume custody of her.[104]

In contrast with the situation in the principality of Catalonia, where an official known as the *guarda d'esclaus* pursued and recaptured fugitives, in fifteenth-century Valencia slave owners seem to have been left largely to their own devices. Although slave owners in Catalonia had been required to register their slaves and to pay an annual premium to cover both the *guarda*'s expenses and the compensatory payments made to owners whose fugitive slaves could not be recovered,[105] in the kingdom of Valencia slave owners relied on tips from the local populace and reports made to the bailiff general and the Justícia Criminal.[106] Desirous of securing the monetary reward customarily given in exchange for information leading to a fugitive's recovery, residents alerted local authorities when they encountered suspicious-looking characters. In 1452, for example, two men from Mosquerola sent an agent to Valencia to report to the Justícia Criminal their discovery of a twenty-three-year-old dark-skinned male, presumably a fugitive, in the precincts of Morvedre (Sagunto). Upon receipt of this report, the Justícia Criminal ordered the town crier (*trompeta*) to announce "throughout the entire city and accustomed places" that a fugitive slave had been found and that "any man who lost a dark-skinned male slave, twenty-three years, more or less, in age" had five days to notify the Justícia Criminal of this and claim him.[107] The

---

103. ARV JCrim 22: Clams: M. 2: (nonpaginated) 8 February 1445.

104. Given the fact that the last time Lucia had seen Caterina was more than a dozen years ago, she speculated that Caterina likely had put on even more weight in the interim. ARV B 1430: M. 1: 53r–v; M. 2: 25r–31v; 46r–v.

105. See Roser Salicrú i Lluch, *Esclaus i propietaris d'esclaus a la Catalunya del segle XV: L'assegurança contra fugues* (Barcelona: Consell Superior de Investigacions Científiques, 1998).

106. In 1449, for example, a slave owner reported that his thirteen- to fourteen-year-old slave girl had gone missing. After giving a physical description of the missing slave girl (even noting how she had been "dressed in blue" on the day of her disappearance) the Justícia Criminal declared that anyone with information about the fugitive slave girl's whereabouts had three days to either report this or return the slave girl to her owner; otherwise, they would incur the penalties for theft. ARV JCrim 23: Clams: M. 3: (nonpaginated) 15 July 1449.

107. For the report filed before the Justícia Criminal, see ARV JCrim 102: M. 3 (nonpaginated): 16 June 1452. Two weeks later, the town herald reported that he had announced publicly that "tot hom qui hagues

two men who found the fugitive, Joan Daus and Domingo Nicholas, likely expected to be rewarded for their efforts. Indeed, in 1456, the seamen Roderic de Santarem and Christofor de Vallcarcre (from the kingdoms of Portugal and Castile, respectively) appointed an agent to travel to Majorca to collect the finders' fees (trobadores) that had been offered for aid in the recovery of a slave owned by a Majorcan merchant. Although no details were given concerning how these two seamen captured the fugitive, the slave, Francesc Ungre, had been recovered and was now being held in the municipal prison of Valencia.[108]

If tips from local residents or officials were not forthcoming, slave owners might contract the services of a professional broker or a merchant to help track down their fugitives, men who worked essentially as bounty hunters. The druggist Marti Despinal, for example, hired the merchant Bernat Gil to aid in the recovery of a fugitive Muslim slave of his named Muça. Bernat had promised Marti that if he was unable to recover his slave within the next six months, he would pay him sixty lliures and, thereupon, assume "ownership" of the fugitive. Since this merchant-cum-bounty hunter ultimately failed to deliver, Bernat, in accordance with this agreement, paid Marti sixty lliures and, Marti, in turn, transferred his rights over the fugitive slave to Bernat. When Muça, eventually, resurfaced, Bernat signed an agreement with Muça (likely in exchange for some sort of ransom payment), granting Muça safe conduct to return to Valencia.[109] Similarly, in 1503, the boot maker Marti Lopes hired two merchants and a broker to help him pursue and recover his black male slave. While Marti himself took responsibility for publicly announcing the slave's flight and offering a reward for information leading to the fugitive's recovery, these three men were charged with the task of tracking down his twenty-four-year-old slave. Though these three men promised Marti that they would pay him, collectively, forty-five lliures if they failed to produce the slave within the next six months, they insisted that if the slave fled overseas (i.e., to the parts of the Crown of Aragon "deça mar"), they would be under no obligation to pay said forty-five lliures and, thereby, assume "ownership" of the fugitive slave. Rather, they only were obliged to inform Marti that the slave was overseas. If Marti still wished to recover him, he himself would travel there to recover him at his own expense. This contract, in addition, stipulated that if, within a year of paying Marti the forty-five lliure penalty, the bounty hunters were able to produce the fugitive, Marti would be obliged to accept delivery of the slave and refund their money.[110]

Judging from the information given in these reports of runaway slaves, certain points in time seemed particularly propitious ones for taking flight: when a slave was sent on

perdut hun sclau lor de edat de xxiii anys poch mes o menys ... que dins cinch jorns ho haguessen notificar al dit honorable justicia e demanat aquell." ARV JCrim 102: M. 4 (nonpaginated): 3 July 1452.

108. ARV P 436 (nonpaginated): 9 January 1456.
109. ARV P 2005: 166v–167r.
110. ARV P 2020: 771r–v.

an errand taking him or her a fair distance away from his master's household, in the confusion immediately following a master's death,[111] and when a slave was being transferred into the custody of a new owner.[112] Slaves, of course, had to weigh the costs and benefits of seizing this opportunity to regain their freedom. A failed attempt at flight could seriously jeopardize any progress they had made toward securing a legal enfranchisement. Slave owners not infrequently appeared before the Justícia Civil, requesting the nullification of contracts of manumission based, among other things, on allegations of a slave's attempted flight.[113] When the aforementioned black male slave named Nicholau appeared before the court of the governor, protesting that his master was violating the terms of his contract of manumission by detaining him in prison, his owner, Pere del Mas, insisted that the truth of the matter was that he had every right to have his slave arrested. Painting a lurid picture of a black male slave run amok, Pere complained that not only had his conditionally freed slave refused to hand over his earnings, as required, each day, but he had frequently "run off" to get drunk, gamble, and commit many other "shameful acts" (tacanyeria). Notorious for his drunk and disorderly behavior, Nicholau was in the habit of picking fights in taverns and going to the stables to perform "those acts that drunks do, taking out his member."[114] Nicholau, moreover, had "gone missing" for three, ten, and even fifteen days at a time. Thus, as a consequence of his repeated attempts at "flight,"[115] Pere insisted that Nicholau no longer had any legitimate claim to freedom. Indeed, Pere complained, Nicholau ought to be forced to reimburse him for the more than one hundred reals he had spent publicizing his slave's flight and sending a search party out as far as Requena (approximately 67 kilometers

---

111. For example, see APPV 15927 (nonpaginated): 4 February 1478, in which a widow and her son reported that, following the death of a Valencian attorney, his forty-five-year-old black male slave had gone missing.

112. See, for example, APPV 499 (nonpaginated): 16 December 1476, in which a Turkish slave named Johanet was reported missing following his sale to the nobleman Berenguer Marti Turribus. See also ARV P 1996 (nonpaginated), in which a black male slave named Joan took flight following his sale to the nobleman Anthoni Johan.

113. For one notable example, see ARV JCiv 923: M. 13: 44r–48v; M. 14: 11r–12v. See also ARV JCiv 926: M. 13: 30r–31v.

114. "Nicholau s'en es anat e fogit una e moltes vegades de la casa del dit en Pere del Mas no sabent hon era fahent cercar e cridar aquell.... apres feta la dita carta lo dit Nicholau s'es embriagat moltes vegades e axi ambriach anava al corral dels bous fent actes de embriach trahent lo membre e fent altres coses qu'es acostumen d'embriachs.... axi mateix lo dit Nicholau fogint de la casa del dit en Pere del Mas e anant com a vagabunt." ARV G 2315: M. 15: 40r and ARV G 2316: 273r–275r.

115. Admittedly, drunkeness and repeated attempts at flight were just two in a long list of charges Pere leveled against Nicholau to justify the nullification of his contract of manumission. More damning, perhaps, was Pere's charge that Nicholau repeatedly had threatened him, "telling him that if God should permit him to grasp him by the feet" that, dangling him upside down, "he would make him eat dirt." ARV G 2315: M. 15: 40r and ARV G 2316: 273r–275r.

from Valencia). Finally, Pere suggested that public safety concerns demanded Nicholau's continued detention. Depicting his black male slave as a dangerous and unruly figure with superhuman strength, Pere claimed that though his slave had been bound in chains and locked securely inside a chamber, he still managed to unchain himself, break down the chamber's doors, and make his escape by leaping across the terraces of neighboring buildings.[116]

Although Pere depicted Nicholau's alleged repeated attempts at flight as the actions of a wild and irrational animal, practical considerations likely determined when or whether or not a slave attempted flight: (1) their current material conditions (i.e., how desperate they were, whether they had any other option for securing their freedom); (2) opportunity (i.e., whether they had a realistic chance of escaping safely); and (3) their prospects for success (i.e., whether they had access to shelter and support and believed they could survive and elude recapture). Inasmuch as slave women primarily were employed as household domestics and, consequently, were under the closer supervision of masters, mistresses, and free servants, they likely had fewer opportunities to take flight. Few of the reports of fugitive slaves encountered in Crown and notarial records involved women.[117] Muslim men, in contrast, seem to have been the slaves most likely to take flight. Sixty percent of reported runaways were of Muslim origin.[118]

An Underground Railroad? Muslim *"Ladres de Catius"*

We noted earlier how enslaved Muslims could count on the financial support of the local Mudejar population in helping them pay off their redemption fees (*rescats*). More problematic for Valencian Christian officials, however, was the role their Muslim coreligionists allegedly played in aiding and abetting their flight. Free Mudejars were suspected not only of sheltering Muslim fugitives but also of "stealing" Muslim slaves, actively encouraging them to take flight. In 1451, for example, the *jurats* of Valencia sent a pointed

116. "Lo dit Nicholau fon ferrat e tancat dins una cambra e aquell se desliga e rompe les portes de la cambra e anassen per los terrats e lo dit en Pere del Mas lo feu cerquar fins a Requena entrevenint hi diverses persones qui li costaren pus de cent reals e feta crida per la ciutat de Valencia." ARV G 2315: M. 15: 40r and ARV G 2316: 273r–275r.

117. Though most of the references I encountered did not provide details about their ethnic and/or religious identities, almost all of these fugitive slave women (six of eleven) had "Christian" names: Beatriu, Caterina, Elena, Juliana, Magdalena, and Margalida. The remaining five female fugitives included an unnamed "crazy" woman in the custody of the queen and a conditionally freed Mudejar woman named Axa who, along with her father and brother, skipped town without paying her redemption fee. For the former, see Piles Ros, *Estudio Documental*, 192 (#293); for the latter, see ARV G 2338: 63r–64r.

118. Out of a total of fifty-five reports of fugitive slaves encountered in notarial and Crown records, thirty-three concerned slaves of Muslim origin: nineteen were explicitly described as baptized "Saracens" or "moros," and fourteen had "Muslim" names.

letter to the nobleman Alfonso Fajardo, "*adelantado*" (Castilian term for the political and military ruler of a frontier province) of Murcia, expressing their alarm concerning "the flight, in recent days, of many slaves from this city" and requesting his assistance in their recovery. The city councilmen feared that these fugitives would soon be joined by many others since some unnamed "bad persons" (likely Muslims) were "taking them away" and secreting them in places where their masters would never be able to find them. The *jurats* also recounted how they had heard rumors that some seventeen fugitive slaves, both whites and blacks, had already made it to Murcia and that some twenty-five more were meeting in Lorca with the intention of securing passage into the Nasrid Sultanate of Granada.[119]

In 1493 charges were filed jointly against three Mudejars who happened to be passing through the city of Valencia the same weekend that the "Moorish" slave owned by a traveling Castilian official went missing. Alasdrach (an *alfaqui* [jurist] of Buñol), Ali (his son-in-law), and Abdalla Simbe (another *moro* from Buñol) were charged with inciting Mahomat—a "Moorish" slave who was a guest at the same inn where they were staying—to take flight. Witnesses testified that after speaking with these three Mudejars (whom he met, seemingly by chance, at the fountain located in the inn's courtyard), Mahomat mysteriously disappeared. His owner, the Castilian nobleman Johan de Talavera, felt that there was only one possible explanation for his slave's flight: these three Muslims must have put him up to it. Even though all three of these Mudejars denied exchanging even one word with the fugitive, since the four men had been seen speaking privately together "in Arabic," the bailiff general pronounced Alasdrach, Ali, and Abdalla guilty and demanded that they financially compensate the slave's owner, paying the Castilian nobleman the "price and estimated value of the said slave."[120]

Christian suspicions about Mudejar support of Muslim fugitives, of course, do not seem to have been entirely unfounded. Çahat Alvaquil, a penally enslaved Mudejar who, in 1470, fled his master's service in Alcasser, was found subsequently living in the predominantly Mudejar region known as the Vall d'Alfàndec (Valldigna).[121] Similarly, after fleeing his master's custody in Valencia, a penally enslaved Mudejar named Mahomat Jach was spotted, years later, living in "Benizano." His master complained that for the past four

119. See document #147, in Agustín Rubio Vela, ed., *Epistolari de la València Medieval II* (València/Barcelona: Institut Interuniversitari de Filologia Valenciana, 1998), 358–59.

120. ARV B 1431: 278r–286r.

121. On 28 November 1470, a merchant acting on behalf of the nobleman Johan Vilanova, the lord of Alcasser, sought the governor's assistance in recovering Vilanova's fugitive slave, Çahat Alvaquil, who reportedly was living in the Vall d'Alfàndec. ARV G 2331: M. 17: 33r–v. For a fascinating study of this community, see Ferran Garcia-Oliver, *La vall de les sis mesquites: El treball i la vida a la Valldigna medieval* (Valencia: Universitat de València, 2003).

years he had been unable to find any trace of his slave because Mahomat, originally from Ribaroja, had been concealed in "many places and *morerías* of the present kingdom."[122]

The harboring of Muslim fugitives, it bears noting, was achieved often with the complicity of these Mudejars' Christian overlords. Seigneurial lords, after all, were always anxious to recruit new vassals to work their lands. In 1479 the nobleman Galceran de Soler complained that the lord of Navarres was sheltering his fugitive slave, a penally enslaved Mudejar named Yaye Ambroni.[123] Similarly, in 1477 the nobleman Joan de Cardona complained that Diego Fajardo was sheltering his fugitive slave on some properties Diego controlled in the Vall de Xalop. Protesting that "the slave belonging to one person ought not to be received or held by another," Joan demanded that the governor send a porter to the Vall de Xalop to retrieve the fugitive and see to it that Diego Fajardo receive "the punishments specified in the *furs* and *privilegis*."[124] Implying that Christian lords and Valencian Mudejars were jointly implicated when it came to the concealment of Muslim runaways, Joan requested that, in the event that the local officials should refuse to hand over the slave, the porter be empowered to arrest the "*alami* [al amīn, or chief financial officer of the Muslim community], *jurats*, and notable members" of the Mudejar community of Vall de Xalop and hold them hostage until the fugitive slave was returned.[125] Finally, in 1475 the lord of Gilet accused the lord of Alcudia de Veo (a town located in the predominantly Mudejar Vall d'Uxó) of harboring a fugitive slave of his named Obaydal Gadi. When the slave's "owner," Manuel Lancol, demanded Obaydal's return, the lord of Alcudia de Veo cited the terms of a thirteenth-century surrender treaty whereby Mudejars found living within the boundaries of the Vall d'Uxó were to be considered "free." Thus, according to the terms of this treaty, a Mudejar slave who managed to return to the Vall d'Uxó would automatically regain his or her liberty. Henceforth, their masters would be unable to reclaim them. Noting how Obaydal Gadi presently was living in the "safe haven" of the Vall de Uxó, Joan Torrelles, the lord of Alcudia de Veo, argued that his owner no longer had any claim to him. Joan affirmed that while he was more than willing "to obey the orders of the lord king," his vassal, a *moro de la Vall*, "enjoyed the privilege

122. The slave's owner complained that for the past four years his fugitive slave—a "catiu serahi" named Mahomat Jach from Ribaroga—"es stat receptat de molts lochs e moreries del present regne de Valencia en manera que fins ahuy lo dit en Luis Collar no ha pogut saber res del dit catiu." ARV G 2342: M. 14: 6r–7v.

123. ARV G 2351: M. 13: 6r–7r.

124. "Los catius de alguna persona nos poden receptat e tenit en loch algu ans les persones qui'ls recepten son encorregudes en penes statuhides en los dits furs e privilegis." ARV G 2346: M. 9: 30r–v.

125. "Si la citat o amagat seria en la dita vall prenga los alami e jurats e altres prohomens moros de la dita vall e aquells porte en poder vestre e de vestra cort e sien detenguts per vestra spectabilitat fins que lo dit catiu sia lliurat e restituhit al dit Egregi don Johan de Cardona." ARV G 2346: M. 9: 30r–v.

whereby a *moro de la Vall*, immediately upon placing his foot within the boundaries [of the Vall de Uxó], cannot be a captive."[126]

Although Muslim fugitives had found shelter in Mudejar communities throughout the fifteenth century, anxiety regarding what Mark Meyerson has termed a Muslim underground railroad reached its peak in the 1490s. Noting the "dramatic influx of [foreign] Muslim captives in the final decades of the fifteenth century" (captured in the final conquest of the Nasrid Sultanate of Granada), Meyerson has argued that an obvious "corollary" to the presence of more Muslim slaves in the kingdom was a "more worrisome runaway problem."[127] Between 1492 and 1494, three cases concerning alleged "slave stealers" (*ladres de catius*) were heard before the court of the bailiff general. While we discussed the charges that were filed against Alasdrach, the *alfaqui* of Buñol, above, in the remaining two cases, the purported "slave stealers," rather than locals, were "foreign" Muslims, from the "kingdoms" of Tunis and Tripoli, respectively.

When Luys (formerly Mahomat), the "Moorish" captive he had purchased and then converted to Christianity, went missing the night after the feast day of Santa Caterina, the Valencian baker Luys Cabanes immediately suspected the "Moor" who had been visiting his slave. Indeed, this baker claimed, Azmet Çahat, a conditionally freed *moro* from Tunis, was "a great thief of captives, who many and diverse times has stolen slaves from the present city, taking them out of the present city and kingdom." Thus, Luys charged that Azmet had conducted his slave Luys, aka Mahomat, to some secret location in the Vall de Castro.[128]

Four slaves were brought before the court of the bailiff general to confirm this slave owner's story: that Azmet was notorious for promising Muslim slaves a quick ticket to freedom. Ali, a slave owned by the carpenter Vincent Calamocha, claimed that about a week after Luys/Mahomat's disappearance, Azmet had tried to convince him to run away while he was working in the household of a neighboring carpenter. Noting how this carpenter's workshop was located just in front of the *taverna de la morería*, Ali recounted how, at about seven in the evening, Azmet sidled up to him, offering, in exchange for four

---

126. In response to Manuel Lancol's charge that he was sheltering a fugitive slave, Joan Torrelles, the lord of Alcudia de Veo, retorted, "Los moros de la Vall tenien priviletgi que lo moro de la Vall de continent que metra lo peu en lo terme que no podia esser catiu." Doubting Obaydal's claim that he was a native of the Vall de Uxó, however, Manuel, in turn, protested that the court should not accept a fugitive slave's claims at face value—"seria fort cosa que sols per tal assertcio de la part altra lo dit catiu pogues esser detengut." ARV G 2339: M. 9: 48r–v and ARV G 2340: M. 13: 7r–8r.

127. Meyerson, "Slavery and Solidarity," 336. Meyerson discusses all three of these cases in this article, 340–42.

128. Luys Cabanes contended that Azmet Çahat was a "gran ladre de catius e aquell moltes e diverses vegades ha furtats molts catius de la present ciutat portant s'en aquells de la present ciutat e regne. E per tal l'es haut tengut e reputat lo dit delat comuniter per omnes." ARV B 1431: 324r–343r.

ducats, to take him where he took "the slaves [formerly] belonging to Luys Cabanes, Johan Insa, and Jacme Lombart" (three, apparently, infamous fugitives). Ali Amar, a slave owned by the baker Johan Soler, similarly charged that about eight days before Azmet's detention, Azmet had propositioned him while he was selling bread in the marketplace. First attempting to lure Ali Amar with flattery—saying that "since he knew the sea so well," fleeing his master's custody would be a piece of cake—Azmet allegedly boasted that, if he wanted him to, he could get him a boat. Hardly seduced by Azmet's advances, both slaves insisted that they sent the seditious Moor packing. While Ali (the slave owned by Vincent Calamocha) testified that he brusquely replied, "Go away! I have no intention of fleeing my master," Ali Amar more patiently explained that he had a good master and that, inasmuch as he expected to be able to redeem himself, he did not think it prudent for him to run away.

Although Luys Cabanes, not surprisingly, argued that the evidence marshaled against Azmet was overwhelming and demanded (in addition to 140 lliures in recompense for his financial loss) that the bailiff general sentence this "slave stealer" to death, the bailiff general was unwilling to convict him. Not only had Azmet denied his involvement, but, most problematically, he steadfastly maintained his innocence through repeated torture sessions. Azmet, moreover, was not an entirely unsympathetic figure. The former slave of a Valencian dyer, Azmet presented himself as a loyal subject who was in the process of paying off his redemption fee. Since he possessed no trade with which he could support himself, Azmet, with the requisite license from the bailiff general, begged for alms in the Mudejar communities of the Vall de Uxó and Xativa. Ultimately, however, "considering the frequency of this crime and considering the many cases of flight that have recently occurred in the present city and kingdom," the bailiff general was equally unwilling to absolve Azmet of all charges. Thus, he released Azmet on bail, forbidding him to leave the kingdom and instructing his guarantors, two moros of the Vall de Uxó, to see to it, under penalty of two hundred gold florins, that Azmet would be returned, whenever requested, into the bailiff general's custody.[129]

Less than four months later, the bailiff general heard charges leveled against another alleged "slave stealer." This time, the accused, Abdalla Alfaqui, was a respected jurist (alfaqui), described as a "dark-skinned" man (llor) originally from Tripoli. Although Ab-

---

129. Acknowledging that Azmet's stubborn persistence in maintaining his innocence under torture "attenuated and diminished" the weight of the evidence marshaled against him, the bailiff general ruled that "we cannot, at present, proceed with and condemn the accused to the death penalty, nor to any other corporal penalties, with justice." Nevertheless, the bailiff general continued, he was not absolving him completely, "especially considering the frequency of such crimes and the many flights that have taken place recently in the present city and kingdom within a brief period of time." In addition, he felt it prudent to keep tabs on Azmet, "considering the condicio of the accused, who is a stranger in the present kingdom, not having his own residence here." ARV B 1431: 342v–343r.

dalla insisted that he had spent a quiet weekend in Valencia, sharing a meal with the *alfaqui* of Manises and then visiting the *alfaqui* of Paterna to exchange some books, the carpenter Johan Insa was absolutely certain that Abdalla "stole" his twenty-five-year old slave named Azmet. Captured in the conquest of the Nasrid Sultanate of Granada, Azmet, in Johan Insa's estimate, would have fetched at least two hundred lliures in ransom. Producing several witnesses who said that they had seen Azmet chatting with Abdalla in Arabic "in a very low voice," Johan Insa insisted that the two men were in conspiracy.[130] Perot Coll, a slave who worked for a neighboring carpenter, said that he saw this dark-skinned man in a grayish-black tunic with a ribbed charcoal-gray linen cape visit the slave so many times that he found it rather remarkable that Johan Insa did not tell him to go away. Once again, however, the bailiff general found the case presented against the purported "slave stealer" less than conclusive. Abdalla insisted that he had only had a brief verbal exchange with Azmet. The slave apparently had signaled to him while he was passing in the street. The only reason he came up to him, Abdalla claimed, was to offer him a *diner* "out of love for God." When Azmet, however, asked him, unprompted, if he had any tips on how to make a safe getaway, Abdalla, conscious that this was a compromising situation, made a hasty exit. Abdalla, moreover, was able to produce ten witnesses who confirmed his account of the weekend's events and no fewer than five of these witnesses attested to Abdalla's unimpeachable character. Himself a former captive, Abdalla had been redeemed two years previously with the help of the *alfaqui* of Ondara, who reputedly had admired Abdalla for his piety and learning. Ever since then, Abdalla had lived in Ondara, supporting himself by, alternatively, giving classes to young Muslim boys in the winter and, in the summer, traveling and collecting alms from various Mudejar communities. Axir, the *alcadi* of the *morería* of Xativa, testified that Abdalla was so well respected in his community that when their *alfaqui* died, the *aljama* or Muslim community of Xativa wanted to appoint Abdalla as his successor.[131] For these and other reasons, the bailiff general felt that the evidence presented was not sufficient to sentence Abdalla to death. Nevertheless, "considering that the crime with which the said Moor is accused is occurring with heightened frequency in the present city and kingdom," the bailiff general, once again, was unwilling to absolve the defendant of all charges. Indeed, he noted, "in just the past few months, many slaves have escaped from the custody of their masters, despite the fact that they were kept in irons and well guarded." Since it was obvious that "[the slave] could not have executed the flight without the help of other Muslims," and since the accused had been seen talking with the fugitive immediately before his

130. Johan's apprentice, Miquel Pinyava, testified, for example, that Abdalla spoke with Azmet "very affectionately" and that whenever Abdalla visited, Azmet kissed Abdalla's hands. ARV B 1431: 344r–368v; 369r–375r.

131. ARV B 1431: 344r–368v; 369r–375r.

disappearance, the bailiff general concluded that Abdalla could not be ruled out as the most likely culprit and, for this reason, should be kept under watch.[132]

Although the bailiff general expressed alarm concerning the flight of slaves toward Muslim-dominated regions, in the opinion of a certain group of fugitives, the most secure path to freedom was to flee to the kingdoms of Navarre or France. Residence in either one of these territories, it was rumored, made slaves "free" and released them permanently from all yoke of servitude.[133] A penally enslaved Mudejar convert named Perot de Benimaclet attempted this northern path to liberty at least two separate times. Fleeing first to the kingdom of Navarre and then to France, Perot returned to Valencia in the hope of being reunited with the "wife" he had left behind: a servant girl who worked in his former master's household.[134] Quickly learning, however, that his master did not subscribe to the view that a slave's residence in the kingdoms of Navarre or France effected his or her immediate and irreversible manumission, Perot was reenslaved and placed in chains. Indeed, to reinforce his subjugated position, when Perot's owner became cognizant of the slave's relationship with his servant girl, he resold Perot's services to another baker to avoid a scandal. Two months later, Perot took flight again. This time he was recovered in his purported birthplace, Benimaclet (a rural community located just outside the city walls).[135] Similarly, in 1495 a black male fugitive named Geronim testified that, two years before, "some other slaves" had convinced him to take flight by telling him that if they made it into French territory, "four days later, they would all be free." In an effort to alleviate Geronim's fears of leaving everything that was familiar behind, these slaves reportedly had assured him that later on he could return to Valencia. They led him to believe that residence in French territory was such a universally respected pathway to

132. "Et actenent que lo crim del qual lo dit moro delat es acusat e denunciat es molt fraquentat en la present ciutat e regne e de poch temps ença hagen fallit e s'en sien anats molts catius de poder de llurs amos estant aquells ferrats e molt guardats la qual fuga nos farris pot fer sens auxili de altres moros e consta d'orde que en lo temps proxime e pro tunch a la fuga del dit catiu del dit en Johan Inça es estat atrobat lo dit Abdalla Alfaqui moro delat parlant ab lo dit catiu... resulte alguna presumpcions e suspicions les quals encars no basten ni sien sufficients e condemnarien del dit delat ni a procehir pronunch contra aquel empero aquelles basten e son sufficients per a poder e deure detenir la persona del dit delat e encautararse e assegurarse de la persona de aquell. Per tal e als pronuncia e declara lo dit delat deure esser sots ydoneus e sufficients capllevadors ab sagrament en la dita sua cort dins deu dies comptadors." ARV B 1431: 374r–375r.

133. For a discussion of France's reputation as "land of the free," see Sue Peabody, "There are no slaves in France": The Political Culture of Race and Slavery in the Ancien Regime (New York: Oxford University Press, 2002).

134. The nobleman Luis Masco testified that, shortly following his recovery, Perot told him "que no era tornat de França e de Navarra sino que tenia amor a la dita fadrina la qual era sa muller la qual havia sposada." ARV G 2394: M. 4: 7v; M. 10: 15r–18r.

135. ARV G 2394: M. 4: 7v; M. 10: 15r–18r.

freedom that "afterward they could come back here to Valencia and they would no longer be slaves."[136]

Although Valencian officials seemed most preoccupied with "Muslim" runaways, black African fugitives were hardly uncommon. Since they did not have an extensive, ready-made support system they could turn to for shelter and protection, black Africans seem to have been more likely to take flight in groups. In 1462, two noblemen named agents to help them recover two black male fugitives who, aged twenty-one and thirty-two years old, respectively, were reportedly headed in the direction of the kingdom of Aragon.[137] Also in 1462, a Valencian attorney appointed an agent to assist in the recovery of his two black male slaves whom he suspected had fled toward the kingdom of Castile. While one of the missing slaves was described as a thirty-five-year-old named Joan de Flores who had a brand on his left hand and whose right hand was missing the thumb, his companion-in-flight, Orlando, was "smaller in person" and about twenty-five years in age.[138] Geronim's master, Johan Rufach, in fact, contended that his black male slave was the ringleader of a band of fugitives who encouraged and abetted other slaves in taking flight. Since their attempted flight to France had failed (Geronim returned one month later), Geronim's master claimed his slave was now plotting an escape by sea. Geronim reportedly was assembling a group of prospective fugitives at the Portal of the Jews, the entrance to the former Jewish quarter and reputedly the unofficial meeting place for slaves interested in fleeing the kingdom by boat. Having gotten wind of Geronim's latest conspiracy, Johan testified that he and several of his neighbors had gone down to the Portal of the Jews to arrest the attempted fugitives. Rather than surrender peaceably to his master, Geronim reportedly offered violent resistance. "Defending himself with two swords, one in his left hand and another in his right," Geronim only relented when two of Johan's companions "put the points of their lances to his chest" and forced Geronim to lower his swords. Even then, however, the fight had not ended. Geronim "turned the corner and took flight," forcing Johan and his companions to chase him. After Geronim once more had threatened his master's life, Johan himself finally erupted and stabbed Geronim in the thigh. Although Geronim "fell immediately to the ground," Johan was loath to leave his slave any further avenues of escape. Thus he and his companions tied Geronim up, triumphantly returning the slave "bound and injured" to his master's household.[139]

136. Geronim testified that "dos meses ans que ell dit responent s'en fugis ell dit responent fonch pregat per aquels dits altres sclaus ab les quals s'en fugi que s'en fugis ab ells donant li a entendre que de continent que fosen en França quatre dies apres tots serien franchs. E que puix fosen franchs apres porien venir açi en Valencia e pus no serien catius e que per la dita raho ell dit responent s'en era fugit ab aquels." ARV G 2398: M. 3: 1v and ARV G 2399: M. 20: 28r–31r.

137. ARV P 4406 (nonpaginated): 7 October 1462.

138. ARV P 4406 (nonpaginated): 18 February 1462.

139. One of Johan Rufach's companions described how "quant foren entre los portals de la mar e dels juheus trobaren lo dit Geronim negre e trobat aquel volgueren lo pendre aquel dit Geronim negre se

Though Geronim's repeated attempts at escape exposed the tenuous hold masters had over their slaves, in his testimony Johan reworked the incident to celebrate his own mastery and control. Thus, he emphasized how this dangerous and disorderly black man was subdued, humbled, and returned, "bound and injured," back into his master's custody. Such a spectacular display of slave agency, of course, was profoundly unsettling to masters. Since, as we have seen, slavery's legitimacy as an institution depended, to a surprising extent, on the illusion that slaves "accepted" and "acquiesced in" their subjugation, the fugitive slave's rejection of his or her subordinate position posed a significant problem. Consequently, rather than blame the slave for "theft of their person," slave owners seemed more comfortable pawning responsibility for the flight off on someone else—the corrupting influence, say, of a subversive *moro* or slave stealer ("*ladre de catius*").

Indeed, rather than corporally punish their fugitives, in most instances it seems that owners tried to protect their investment by quietly attempting to unload the unruly fugitive onto someone else. At the time of sale, naturally, they downplayed the flight risk. Thus, in 1472, when a disgruntled buyer protested that he had been tricked into buying a habitual fugitive, the slave's sellers insisted that, while in their custody, the black male slave named Andria had always been "very passive and subdued." In fact, "even though he had had many opportunities to run away from them," the slave never had. Laborers testifying on the sellers' behalf painted an equally bucolic scene. They had seen Andria go off on multiple occasions "to mow grass, pick carob beans (*garrofes*), and gather wood in the mountains." In addition, this slave often had been sent a distance of more than a league and a half away in order to work his master's fields. Although Andria thus had many opportunities to take flight (*avinenties de fugir*)—"if he had wanted to" (*si hagues volgut*)— the slave never did.[140] Similarly, in 1456 a slave seller dismissed his black male slave's reported flight as a brief moment of panic. The nobleman Dalmau Ferrer explained that, on the vespers of San Joan, his eighteen-year-old slave named Jordi had been too afraid to come home since one of the mules he was taking care of ran off when he took it for a drink of water. Offering the court a remarkably reassuring portrait of master-slave relations, this nobleman maintained that Jordi had hid out on the stairs of the portal of Valldigna, "out of fear that he [his master] would beat him." Insisting that Jordi was missing for only about two hours, this nobleman urged the governor to reject the plain-

---

deffensava ab dues spases que aquel tenia arranquades la una en la ma squerra e l'altra en la ma dreta." It was only after "Geronim negre tira ab la spasa una gran coltellada al dit son amo" that his master "li dona una lancada en la cuxa." Geronim, thereupon, "caygue en terra e llavors tots lo prengueren ell ligaren e axi ligat e naffrat lo aportaren a la casa del dit en Johan Rufach amo de aquel." ARV G 2398: M. 3: IV and ARV G 2399: M. 20: 28r–31r.

140. According to the sellers "lo dit Andriu catiu james stant en poder dels dits Marti e Johan Castralbo fugi ne fonch vist fugir ne reputat per persona fugitiva ans stigue continuament molt reposat he asosegat jatsia que aquell tingues moltes avinenteses de poder s'en fogir si volgues." ARV G 2336: M. 10: 9r–12v. For more on this black male slave named Andria, see chapter 2, pp. 64–65.

tiff's characterization of his slave as a hardened fugitive. Rather, he urged the governor to treat this episode "for what it was," a childish attempt to avoid punishment, not a serious or concerted attempt at flight.[141] Based on the records we have, it is impossible to know what Jordi was thinking as he sat on the steps of the Portal of Valldigna that night. Although the working assumption for this chapter has been that slaves universally yearned to be "freed"—risking their physical well being, if not their lives, to reclaim it, masters and mistresses, for obvious and self-serving reasons, insisted that this was not necessarily the case.

Equally self-serving, of course, were the statements made by masters and mistresses promising their slaves freedom. Was the promise "sincere"? Or, was it a calculated ploy to mollify a slave? By juxtaposing statements made in a slave owner's last will and testament with the fine print in a slave's *carta de libertat*, I have also exposed the marked disjuncture between rhetoric and reality with respect to a master's so-called gift of freedom. Considering, however, slave owners' petitions that the Justícia Civil declare contracts of manumission null and void alongside the *demandes de libertat* that were filed by dozens of slaves, this chapter has also complicated the issue of the master's "agency" in freeing his slaves. Even though there were multiple paths to freedom in fifteenth-century Valencia, these paths were not equally accessible to all and (as we'll highlight in the concluding chapter) they were hardly unidirectional.

141. Dalmau insisted that "may li fogi sino la vespra de sent Johan de juny propassat per que lo dit negre portava dos mules a beurar e fugi l'en una e per por que no'l bates amaguas en les scales de Valdigna no stech dues hores." Thus, he urged the court, "veus la dita fuyta del dit negre com es stat." ARV G 2288: 101r–v; 147r–148r.

CHAPTER 7 LIVING *"COM A FRANCH"*— "LIKE A FREE PERSON"

In 1470, a Tartar freedman named Anthoni Peralda sat languishing in Valencia's municipal jail. Describing himself as a "foreigner" with no local ties, Anthoni threw himself on the mercy of the court, beseeching the governor to collect testimony from abroad that would confirm his freed status since there was no one in Valencia who could vouch for him.[1] A blanket weaver whose liberty was being challenged more than a decade following his manumission, Anthoni's plea illustrates the precarious position of freed persons in late medieval Iberian society.

Almost immediately following his liberation, Anthoni departed from his master's house, moving from Barcelona to Genoa where he exercised his new prerogatives as a freed person by getting married and setting up his own household. Shortly thereafter, however, Anthoni was taken captive once again, this time in Muslim territory.[2] Although Anthoni would be redeemed two years later, Anthoni's grasp on freedom remained less than firm. After a brief stop in Barcelona (ironically, to secure documentary proof of his freed status, a *carta de franquea*, from his former owner),[3] Anthoni moved to Valencia where he contracted his services out to a local blanket weaver. Though he had been "earning his salary and making a living as other [free] persons are accustomed to do," royal officials had appeared one day and abruptly arrested him.[4] Since the master who liberated him

---

1. Anthoni described himself as a "foraster e no tingua fermanca ne troba fermança en la present ciutat." ARV G 2332: M. 30: 30r–v.

2. ARV G 2332: M. 30: 30r–v.

3. In light of his recent experience of reenslavement, Anthoni appears to have felt it prudent to secure documentary proof of his freed status. Thus, he related, "since he did not have a *carta de franquea*," he returned to Barcelona and asked his former master, Berthomeu Peralada, to issue him a charter of freedom. The charter reportedly was drawn up by the notary Anthoni Vilanova on 15 September 1468. ARV G 2332: M. 30: 30r–v.

4. Anthoni insisted that he "residens e residexca en la present ciutat com a franch e en possesio de franch e stigue affermat al offici de flaçader ab en Pere Barcelo guanyant sa soldada axi com altres acostumen de vivir e guanyar." ARV G 2332: M. 30: 30r–v.

happened to have been Catalan, the *procurador fiscal* (public prosecutor) now claimed that his manumission, granted ten years ago, in the midst of the Catalan Revolt, was invalid. The *procurador* charged that Anthoni had been freed unlawfully by a "rebel" against the Crown: a Barcelonan blanket maker named Berthomeu Peralda.[5]

Anthoni's vulnerability to reenslavement was hardly unique. Manumissions could be reversed on a variety of different grounds. In some instances, manumissions were declared null and void on the basis of legal technicalities, that is, the liberator was not the slave's true owner or lacked the authority to unilaterally free her. In other instances, owners pointed to their former slaves' alleged "ingratitude." In 1452, for example, Aldonça Pardo, the aforementioned widow of a money changer, revoked her promise to free Johanota, her black slave woman, immediately upon her death on the grounds that Johanota, ostensibly in an effort to hasten said manumission, was poisoning her. Lying on her deathbed and in the presence of several witnesses, Aldonça confirmed that she had decided to resell the slave woman and stated that she did not wish the testamentary bequest of forty lliures she had made to Johanota to come into effect.[6]

Although Johanota's promised manumission never came to fruition, Anthoni's experiences beg the question of whether, even if it had, the stain of servitude would entirely have been blotted out. For, in the decade following his manumission, Anthoni, perhaps as a consequence of his poverty, perhaps as a consequence of his Tartar ethnicity, continued to occupy a position in society that seemed fixed at its margins. What did it mean, then, for a slave to be freed? Were freed persons, as some have suggested, integrated economically and socially into late medieval Iberian society? What was the status of freed persons in fifteenth-century Valencia?

The fates of freed persons and their offspring are extremely difficult to trace in the extant documentation. Although in many instances an individual was explicitly described as either a freed person (*libert* or *libertina*) or a former slave (*olim sclau* or *olim serva*), freed persons were not consistently identified as such in contemporary records. A freed person's prior identity was most likely to be acknowledged when their status was in dispute

5. The *procurador fiscal* justified his seizure and detention of Anthoni by claiming that Anthoni's master, Berthomeu Peralada, "qui seria cathala...no'l hauria pogut fer franch per esser rebelle a la magestat del senyor rey." ARV G 2332: M. 30: 30r–v. For another example of someone questioning the validity of a manumission granted by a "Catalan rebel," see the successful *demanda de libertat* filed (also in 1470) by Catherina, "de nacio de alarbs," the former slave woman of Blanquina, the widow of the lawyer Jacme Jorda, of Lleida. ARV G 2331: M. 19: 28r–30v; 35v; 41v; 45r–v and ARV G 2332: M. 25: 17r–v.

6. A broker who was present at this widow's deathbed testified that he heard Aldonça revoke the legacy she had promised her slave woman Johanota, saying "yo'l revoque e vull que no vaia per fet com tal sia ma entencio per ço com aquella m'a mort ab metzines." She said these words, moreover, "diverses voltes perserverant en allo mateix." And, he added, "quant la dita n'Aldonça dix les dites paraules aquella stava en tot son seny e entrega paraula." ARV JCiv 916: M. 12: 9r–10v. I discussed this case earlier, in chapter 6, see pp. 198–99.

or when they laid claim to something promised them by their former owners. In other circumstances, their former condition was perhaps deemed irrelevant or, for a variety of different reasons, it might not have been deemed prudent to make reference to it. In cases where individuals were referred to as *"moros,"* *"negres,"* or *"xarxes,"* it is not always clear whether this meant that they were slaves. For example, was Margalida, a woman "of Russian lineage" (*de linatge de Rossos*) accused by a lawyer's widow of stealing fifty gold florins from her household, a former slave?[7] Was Johan Diez, the black herald (*"negre trompeta"*) purchasing a house in the parish of San Juan del Mercado, a former slave?[8] It remains uncertain. In one case, it was due only to an incidental reference to her possession of a *carta de libertat* that a woman's servile past was discernible in the historical record.[9] In the pages that follow, I will distinguish between individuals described explicitly as former slaves and individuals identified simply as "black" (*negre*) or "Moorish," Tartar," "Russian," or "Greek."

Given the diversity of Valencia's slave population, it seems more than likely that the experiences of freed persons would have varied (as they had while still in slavery) according to their gender and their religious and ethnic identities. Indeed, Teresa Vinyoles i Vidal has suggested that, in late medieval Barcelona, the future prospects for an enslaved woman were better than those for her male counterparts. Vinyoles reasons that since affective bonds were much more likely to develop within the confines of a household, masters and mistresses were more likely to free their slave women, who worked predominantly as household domestics.[10] Although freed women did confront certain prejudices—namely, the belief that they were sexually licentious—Vinyoles concluded that most could nevertheless secure a respectable position for themselves in free Barcelonan society by finding work as a domestic servant and/or by getting married.[11]

In stark contrast, Fabiana Plazolles Guillèn has painted a fairly grim picture of the position of "Moorish" and black African freed persons (both men and women) in late medieval Barcelona. She cautions against taking notarial charters of freedom at their word, as conferring "pure and perfect liberty, releasing the freed person from any and every yoke and restoring to him his original birth rights" (*pura y perfecta libertat eximiendo al liberto de cualquier*

7. ARV JCrim 50: M. 8: 24r–33v; M. 9: 45r.

8. ARV P 439 (nonpaginated): 28 January 1471.

9. See the inventory postmortem of the property belonging to Magdalena Cabata, deceased. ARV P 3162 (nonpaginated): 28 April 1480.

10. Vinyoles i Vidal does admit, however, that this was often only after they provided many additional years of service or otherwise compensated their masters and mistresses for the "favor."

11. Teresa Vinyoles i Vidal, "Integració de les llibertes a la societat Barcelonina baixmedieval," in *De l'esclavitud a la llibertat: Esclaus i lliberts a l'edat mitjana*, ed. Maria Teresa Ferrer i Mallol and Josefina Mutgé i Vives (Barcelona: Consell Superior d'Investigacions Científiques, Institució Milà i Fontanals, 2000), 593–614.

yugo restaurándole sus antiguos derechos de ingenuidad). In Plazolles Guillèn's estimate, it would be extremely naïve to believe that Muslim converts and black Africans were admitted into Barcelonan society without a second glance. The evidence she presents to the contrary is highly convincing. Muslim and black African freed persons were hardly treated like everybody else. Their aspirations for social and economic advancement were, for the most part, frustrated. Barred by guild ordinances from practicing the most skilled professions (some of which, ironically, they had practiced while enslaved), their employment options were generally limited to occasional work as manual, unskilled laborers in exchange for low wages. Though it is certainly true that some enjoyed economic success—owning substantial pieces of property and purchasing their own slaves—Plazolles argues that most freed blacks and Muslim converts lived lives that were segregated from the prosperous and respected members of society. Living and socializing predominantly among themselves, their choice of marriage partners was restricted to other freed persons—usually freed persons from their own ethnic community. In those instances when they did marry outside their community, they married other social outsiders: foreigners and immigrant workers coming from other parts of the Crown of Aragon, Castile, or even further afield.[12]

Vinyoles's and Plazolles's contrasting portraits of the lives of freed persons in late medieval Barcelona expose some significant differences in experiences, not only between freed men and women in late medieval Iberian societies but also between freed blacks and whites. But ought we to ascribe these differences to an incipient "racism" that was developing in late medieval Iberia? In this final chapter I will consider, first, what we know about the experiences of Muslim, "eastern," and black African freed persons and, second, those of their children. Then, in the conclusion, I will tackle the question of what the Valencian case tells us about the so-called medieval "roots" of modern racism.

"Usant de la Dita Libertat": Exercising One's Freedom

Upon receipt of manumission, freed persons demonstrated (and, to a certain extent, legally established) their newly "free" status by performing certain acts: leaving their owner's household, contracting out their labor, and getting married. In order to substantiate his claim that, for the past ten years, he had been "living like a free person," Anthoni sought testimony from witnesses who could confirm that he had left his master's household in Barcelona, that he had been "earning his own salary and making a living," successively, in Genoa, Islamic territories, and Valencia, and finally, that he had married

---

12. Fabiana Plazolles Guillen, "Trayectories sociales de los libertos musulmanes y negroafricanos en la Barcelona tardomedieval," in *De l'esclavitud a la llibertat: Esclaus i lliberts a l'edat mitjana*, ed. Maria Teresa Ferrer i Mallol and Josefina Mutgé i Vives (Barcelona: Consell Superior d'Investigacions Científiques, Institució Milà i Fontanals, 2000), 615–42.

and set up his own household in Genoa.[13] Similarly, in 1474, when the daughter of their former master had them arrested as fugitives, two freedmen, a Muslim named Mahomat and a Muslim convert to Christianity named Perico, adduced as proof of their "freed" status the fact that they had left their master's estate, the castle of Ricote, without protest. While Perico had gone to Valencia to learn a trade, Mahomat went to Orihuela where he found employment as a blacksmith. Mahomat, moreover, had gotten married and was raising children in Fanavella, a town near Orihuela.[14] Although opinions may have varied with respect to what it took for a slave to "earn" his or her freedom, there was little debate among contemporaries regarding what it meant to be free. In fifteenth-century Valencia, freedom meant the ability to live where one pleased, exercise control over one's own labor, own and dispose property, marry, and have a family.

Living Where One Pleased

One of the clearest expressions of a former slave's new status was their ability to "stay, go . . . whenever and wherever you should choose and like."[15] For some freed persons, this meant returning to their place of origin. Penally enslaved Mudejars, for example, frequently were ransomed with the assistance of family members and other residents of their former communities. Postredemption, they returned to these predominantly Muslim communities scattered across the kingdom of Valencia. Similarly, once redeemed, many "foreign" Muslim slaves emigrated back to the Nasrid Sultanate of Granada or to North Africa. Vicenta Cortes documented some 330 freed *moros* who emigrated back into Islamic territories between 1470 and 1516.[16] To do so legally, they needed to secure a license from the bailiff general as well as pay certain passage duties. In much the same way that alms had been collected to help redeem Muslims from Christian captivity, the funds used to pay these passage duties had likely also been contributed by coreligionists out of piety. On 8 and 13 November 1477, for example, the bailiff general granted licenses, respectively, to Azmet Alaziz, a native of Arzilla, the former slave of the silk weaver Joan Despuig, and to Mahomat, the former slave of the notary Bernat de Bellmont.[17] Similarly, on 13 January 1483 Abdallah Achayre, his wife Axa, and their daughter Mariem, "*moros*"

13. Thus, "apres de la qual franquea," Anthoni, "s'en ana en la ciutat de Genova e alli a contractat de matremoni e te son domicili e cap major." Similarly, in Valencia, "aquell dit n'Anthoni residens e residexca . . . com a franch e en possesio de franch e stigue affermat al offici de flaçader ab en Pere Barcelo guanyat sa soldada axi com altres acostumen de vivir e guanyar." ARV G 2332: M. 30: 30r–v.

14. ARV G 2340: M. 11: 7r–8v.

15. Most *cartas de libertat* granted freed slaves (among other things) the right "morari ire . . . quocumque et ubique volveris et elegeris." For an example, see ARV P 442 (nonpaginated): 19 July 1476.

16. Emigrants paid a passage duty (the *diezmos* or *delme*) that typically amounted to 136 sous. Vicenta Cortes, *La esclavitud en Valencia durante el reinado de los Reyes Católicos (1479–1516)* (Valencia: Ayuntamiento de Valencia, 1964), 141.

17. ARV MR 87: M. 6: 112v–113v.

from Tangiers, the former "*catius*" of the Valencian merchants Enrique Bosch and Jaime Navarro, were issued licenses to emigrate to "*terra de moros.*"[18]

Although Muslim freed persons could count on the support of relatives and coreligionists to find their way "home," it would have been considerably more challenging for "eastern" and black African freed persons to return to Cyprus or Guinea. Some freed persons, nevertheless, seem to have opted to put some distance between themselves and their former owners. The aforementioned Tartar freedman named Anthoni, for example, left his master's household in Barcelona to go live in Genoa, subsequently moving to Islamic territories, and then, finally, settling in Valencia.[19] Likewise, one of the first things a former slave named Pere Garcia did as a freed person was to depart Valencia and move to Naples.[20]

The majority of freed persons, however, likely did not possess the economic means to move overseas. Freed persons who had lived in rural areas occasionally opted to move to the city, drawn, perhaps, by the promise of greater economic opportunities. A black freedman named Joan Muntanya, for example, left his master's estate in rural Meliana to seek his fortune in Valencia. There he found work as a servant in the Crown-managed *fonduk* (*alfondech*—an inn/warehouse, occasionally also functioning as a tavern).[21] A fair number of freed persons (especially women), however, opted to (post-manumission) remain in their masters' or mistresses' households. Although they might testify that they did so out of a sense of obligation and affection for their former owners, other no less significant considerations were the comfort of living in a known environment and the promise of continued support and lodging. Indeed, we noted in an earlier chapter how in their last wills and testaments, masters and mistresses frequently granted their former slaves lifetime usufruct of a room in their households. In 1474, Johana Barcelo, the widow of a surgeon, granted her freedwoman named Margalida (along with her son Johanot) lifetime usufruct of a building that her husband formerly had used as a stable.[22]

---

18. Cortes, *Esclavitud*, 224 and 483.

19. Though, in 1470, the *procurador fiscal* had him arrested and detained as an "unlawfully freed" slave, by 1474 it appears that Anthoni was well along the way to buying back his freedom. Having purchased Anthoni in 1470 as "property belonging to a Barcelonan rebel against the Crown" (*de bonis Barchinonensium tunch rebellotis dicte regie magestati*), the noblewoman Toda de Centilles acknowledged on 16 September 1474 that Anthoni was making payments toward his thirty lliure redemption price. He now owed her only 117 more sous. ARV P 511 (nonpaginated): 16 September 1474.

20. ARV G 2348: M. 16: 33r–44v and M. 19: 45r–46v.

21. ARV B: Letra P: 46 (1470). For a thorough discussion of the historical evolution of the *funduq*, see Olivia Remie Constable, *Housing the Stranger*.

22. See the last will and testament of Johana, the widow of the surgeon Guillem Barcelo. Johana bequeathed to "Margalida quativa qui era del dit Guillem Barcelo," among other things, lifetime usufruct of "un alberch meu en que tenien lo stable com lo dit marit meu era viu." Upon Margalida's death, Margalida's son Johanot would inherit said *alberch* (along with the other household furnishings Margalida

Similarly, in a last will and testament drawn up in 1477, the merchant Manuel Muncada bequeathed to Damiata, a slave woman whom he had freed "orally" (*de paraula*) four years previously, lifetime usufruct of a room (*statge o habitacio*) in his household.[23]

Collecting a Salary

At the same time that it afforded them a certain degree of security, continuing to live under a former master's or mistress's roof posed certain risks for a freed person. Their new status would not necessarily be respected and it seems to have been more difficult for them to assert and protect their property rights. Freed women who remained in their former masters' or mistresses' households typically would continue performing much the same tasks that they had performed while in servitude: cooking, cleaning, doing the laundry, and spinning raw fiber into thread. The difference was that now they were entitled to receive some form of financial compensation for their efforts. And yet, judging from the complaints filed by freed women in the courts of the governor and the Justícia Civil, their former owners were not always willing to pay for services they had previously enjoyed "for free." The aforementioned merchant Manuel Muncada, for example, acknowledged in his last will and testament that he had not given his former slave woman, Damiata, any of the money he had collected over the past four years from the sale of the thread she had spun while living in his household as a freed woman.[24]

Freed persons often charged that not only were their former masters failing to remunerate them for their labors but they were also pocketing the wages that they earned working in other households. In 1465, for example, a freedwoman named Crestina filed a complaint against the widow of her former master, Ursola Venturelli, alleging that Ursola had not only failed to pay her for the five months of service she had provided her—at a rate of ten sous a month, Crestina demanded a back salary of fifty sous— but had also unlawfully retained the more than thirty lliures she had earned working in the households, respectively, of a doctor, a notary, and a merchant. Ursola, the widow of the merchant Berthomeu Venturelli, categorically denied receiving these sums on Crestina's behalf. She retorted that any sums she withheld from Ursola were taken either in payment for a pink tunic or skirt (*gonella*) she had had made on Crestina's behalf or were rightfully "hers" by virtue of former ownership. Of the thirty lliures she reportedly kept hidden underneath a wooden beam in her room, Crestina allegedly had amassed at least twenty of them while she was still a slave in her husband's household. Thus, Ursola

---

was given), though only if he took her husband's surname—only if "se nomene Johan Barcelo." ARV P 1914 (nonpaginated): 3 September 1474.

23. See the last will and testament of Manuel Muncada. APPV 22551 (nonpaginated): 29 March 1477.

24. Manuel acknowledged in his last will and testament that he had not given Damiata the money he had collected on her behalf for "la filaça que aquella ha feta e fara fins al dia de la mia mort." APPV 22551 (nonpaginated): 29 March 1477.

insisted, this money was "hers" since at the time when Crestina came into possession of it, she had been a slave living under her "dominion and lordship."[25]

Similarly, in 1477 a freedwoman named Johana filed a (successful) complaint against Luis Amalrich, the son of her former master, charging him with stealing eighteen lliures from a locked coffer in her bedroom. After serving Luis Amalrich's parents, Johan and Caterina Amalrich, for many years, Johana had been freed, jointly, by two of their sons, Luis and his brother Francesch (now deceased). Johana acknowledged that, when she entered Luis's service, Luis had not promised to pay her any salary. He had assured her, however, that her efforts ultimately would be rewarded and that, while living in his service, she would not want for anything. To earn extra pocket money, Johana took in additional laundry and spun raw fibers into thread.[26] Johana testified that she kept all of her money as well as a variety of other items that belonged to her in a locked coffer in her bedroom. She complained that while she was lying ill in the household of Luis's other brother (the priest Johan Amalrich), Luis deliberately had broken into this coffer, taking the eighteen lliures that were inside. She insisted that Luis knew very well that this coffer was hers and that, for this reason, he had had to cut the lock off.

Luis retorted that if anyone was guilty of committing theft in this household, it was Johana. He stressed how since Johana effectively managed his household, she had in her possession the key for every door, coffer, and box. Thus, she had custody of all of Luis's most precious possessions: silver, gold, and jewels, as well as currency in the amount of more than three hundred lliures. He explained how whenever any money came into his possession, i.e., the rents he collected regularly as well as revenues from his assorted *censals* and *violaris* (long-term loans liquidated by the debtor through the payment of annual pensions, with interest, to the creditor), it was immediately transferred over into Johana's custody for safekeeping. Luis disputed Johana's contention that this coffer was "hers" and that he had deliberately broken into it to defraud her of her property. He maintained that all sorts of boxes and coffers were kept in Johana's bedroom. The day he broke into the coffer in question, he was desperately searching for something that he needed. When

25. Ursola claimed that "en lo temps que la dita Crestina sclava fonch del dit micer Berthomeu Venturelli e lo temps que la dita Crestina fonch de la dita Ursola aquella dita Crestina fonch vista tenir e se sabia que aquella tenia xxx o xxxi timbre poch mes o menys amagats. E axiu es hoyda stada dir la dita Crestina." Thus, she insisted, "la dita quantitat es de la dita Ursola per la domini e senyoria que ella havia de la dita Crestina en lo qual temps aquella fonch vista e se sabe tenir aquelles." ARV G 2316: 341v.

26. A female witness who testified on behalf of this freedwoman noted how Johana had shown her some tufts of flax, exclaiming excitedly, "Look *madona* Maria, Domingo has brought this to me in order that I spin it for making shirts!" This witness likewise testified that she had also overheard Domingo, Johana's alleged lover, tell Johana, "Speaking of this flax, don't worry, Johana! Spin it and I will pay you for it." ARV G 2346: M. 6: 25r–39v and ARV G 2347: M. 14: 1r–2v; 6r–v. I discussed how this freedwoman named Johana earned extra income by spinning raw fibers into thread in chapter 3. See p. 115.

he came across this particular coffer and discovered that he could not open it with any of his keys, he cut the lock off—an act that he insisted was perfectly within his rights. Although it was true that Johana kept some of her things in locked coffers, he insisted that all the coffers were technically his. Moreover, Luis insisted, rather than being strictly segregated, Johana's things were intermixed with his own things, and vice versa. Thus Luis denied Johana's claim that the coffer contained only "her" things and insisted that the eighteen lliures that were in there were his.[27] Indeed, Luis argued that since Johana had not been able to accurately describe this money, it was clearly his.[28]

Instead, painting himself as the victim, Luis, in turn, claimed that, subsequent to Johana's departure from his household, more than fifty lliures worth of property had been discovered missing. Luis charged that Johana's accomplice in these crimes had been a former (and disgraced) servant of his named Domingo Ysert, whom Johana intended to marry. In anticipation of this marriage, Johana allegedly had stolen many of his household furnishing so that she and Domingo could more easily set up a household of their own. Luis contended that Johana, in fact, had been defrauding him for years, secretly providing food, drink, and clothing to her lover Domingo, who, most definitely, was no longer welcome in Luis's household. To add insult to injury, Johana was not only laundering Domingo's clothes for him, at Luis's expense, but she was perfuming them with his musk. Thus, Luis insisted that even if these eighteen lliures did belong to Johana, he had every right to claim them in compensation for the more than fifty lliures Johana owed him. In the end, however, despite all of Luis's protests and countercharges, the governor issued a ruling in Johana's favor. Since everyone, including Luis, had acknowledged that this coffer was used to store Johana's things and that Johana had the key, the governor concluded that "one ought to presume" that the eighteen lliures that were discovered inside this locked coffer belonged to Johana.[29]

Though Johana's property rights were upheld (ultimately) by the governor, this dispute (over what was not a particularly substantial sum of money[30]) amply demonstrates the difficulties freed women faced in protecting what was theirs[31]—particularly while living

27. ARV G 2346: M. 1: 10r; M. 6: 25r–39v and ARV G 2347: M. 14: 1r–2v; 6r–v.

28. Although Johana testified that the eighteen lliures worth of currency she kept in her coffer were in small denominations, Luis insisted that the money he recovered in the coffer was in large denominations. ARV G 2346: M. 1: 10r; M. 6: 25r–39v and ARV G 2347: M. 14: 1r–2v; 6r–v.

29. ARV G 2346: M. 1: 10r; M. 6: 25r–39v and ARV G 2347: M. 14: 1r–2v; 6r–v.

30. Indeed, the dispute initially was not deemed worth the expense of recording it in writing. To save the costs of scribes, paper, and so forth, "petty" disputes—that is, those concerning sums less than three hundred sous or fifteen lliures—were typically pled and/or adjudicated orally.

31. Reflective of the difficulties freed women seem to have faced in defending their property rights, in 1449 a freedwoman named Caterina was charged with stealing a black tunic valued at eight *reals* from the wife of a neighbor. In response to these charges, Caterina protested that she was innocent, that her

under their former owner's roof. Johana's success here owed much to the support and influence of Luis's brother, the priest Johan Amalrich. His testimony—that Luis had admitted to him that he took the money from Johana's coffer—was pivotal in establishing Johana's claim and likely was instrumental in securing a favorable outcome for Johana.

According to the letter of the law, in fact, there was little a freed person could do if their former master or mistress decided to defraud them. The Furs de València decreed that a freed slave could not file "defamatory or criminal" charges against his or her padron or padrona—the master or mistress who freed them. Courts technically were not to admit complaints made by freed persons accusing their padrons or padrones with "theft, violent seizure (rapina), or other similar things."[32] In 1470, when a freedwoman named Magdalena (aka Elena), along with her husband, the tailor Pere Saboya, charged Dionis Verdu, her former master, of unlawfully retaining the salaries she had earned in the households, respectively, of a shopkeeper and a farmer's wife, Dionis's procurator argued that Magdalena's complaint was inadmissible not only on the grounds that this former slave woman possessed no official proof that she had been awarded her freedom but "especially" because it was directed "against her master."[33] Though Magdalena did secure a hearing before the court of the governor, she had been struggling to win recognition of her rights as a freed person for more than thirteen years—ever since the birth of her daughter Barbereta, whom she claimed was Dionis's child. Magdalena's husband contended that although his wife's employers explicitly had directed that the money they were giving him should be given to Magdalena (or, if she got married, to her husband), Dionis reportedly had retorted, "Give me the money and it will be as God wills."[34] Indeed, given the fact that there is no record of the governor ever issuing a ruling, it seems more than likely that Magdalena's struggle continued.[35]

---

neighbor, actually, had given her the tunic in pledge for some money that she had loaned her. ARV JCrim 23: Clams: M. 4 (nonpaginated) 7 August 1449.

32. Furs de València, ed. Colon and Garcia (Barcelona, 1974), II: 130.

33. "La present demanda posar volguda per part de la dita Magdalena contra lo dit honorable en Dionis Verdo no pot ne deu esser admesa en manera alguna com a aquella puis se diu sclava del dit en Dionis Verdu no es persona legitima per entrevenir en juhi maxime contra dominum suum car es dispost de fur e raho natural scrita quod servus in iudicio interesse non posa sino en certs casos de libertat." ARV G 2331: M. 17: 16v; M. 19: 32r–33v and ARV G 2332: M. 25: 33r.

34. "Als quals paraules respos lo dit en Verdu da me los diners e tals paraules en effecte et sera lo que deus volra." ARV G 2331: M. 17: 16v; M. 19: 32r–33v and ARV G 2332: M. 25: 33r.

35. In his first hearing before the governor, Dionis dismissed every one of the charges that had been laid against him by proclaiming that he never had a slave woman named Magdalena. One week later, Magdalena's husband Pere appeared before the governor to explain that Magdalena was also known commonly as Elena. When Pere requested that Dionis once again be brought in to respond to these charges, Dionis's procurator replied that unless Magdalena could (within a certain period of time) produce concrete evidence that she had been manumitted, the case should be thrown out. ARV G 2331: M. 17: 16v; M. 19: 32r–33v and ARV G 2332: M. 25: 33r.

Not all freed persons, however, lived and worked as salaried domestic servants in other people's households. Some of the freed men who appear in the surviving documentation practiced skilled trades, describing themselves, variously, as bakers and bread makers (*flaquers, pistors,* or *pastadors*), blacksmiths (*ferrers*), gold-leaf makers (*batifullas*), blanket weavers (*flaçaders*), and dyers (*tintorers*).[36] Nevertheless, they remained, for the most part, in positions of dependence, working as apprentices or salaried workers in someone else's workshop. After his master freed him in 1470, for example, a black freedman (*niger libertinus*) named Joan left Lérida (about 155 kilometers west of Barcelona) for Valencia where, in 1472, he put himself in a three-year contract of apprenticeship with the cloth preparer Johan Fandos.[37] When the freedman Jordi (aka Georgius) Daries, the former slave of the espadrille maker Johan Daries, pooled his resources with the freedwoman Magdalena (also the former slave of Johan Daries) in contemplation of marriage, he also described himself as an espadrille maker (*tapiner*). Indeed, in a document drawn up on the very same date, Jordi recognized that his manumission was contingent upon his completion of a term of service. Thus, for the five years remaining in his contract of service, Jordi was obliged to continue to provide Johan's wife with fifteen pairs of espadrilles a week.[38]

Inasmuch as the freed persons most likely to be documented in the surviving notarial and court records were those who secured apprenticeships, earned salaries, and owned property, freed men such as Johan Marroma—"a black man and former slave"—may have been the exception rather than the rule. The former slave of a deacon at the cathedral of Valencia, Johan Marroma had learned a trade and supported himself as a cloth preparer. In April 1478, we encounter him purchasing a piece of unfinished cloth he hoped to work on and resell at a profit. It bears noting, however, that, rather than acting independently, Joan Marroma had to have this purchase agreement cosigned by a fellow cloth preparer, Joan Sorolla, and the baker Joan Torrent. Suggestive, moreover, that this freedman was not necessarily thriving financially is the fact that, although according to

36. The freedman Joan Verdecho, for example, was described variously as a *pistor,* a *pastador,* and a *flaquer.* See APPV 21593 (nonpaginated): 24 January 1476 and APPV 21593 (nonpaginated): 17 April 1476. For an example of a blacksmith, see ARV G 2340: M. 11: 7r–8v, in which the freedman Mahomat, the former slave of Garcia de Eredia, deceased, described himself as a *"ferrer."* For an example of a gold-leaf maker, see APPV 23000 (nonpaginated): 3 August 1477, in which the freedman Johan Rocha was described as a *"batifulla"* in the document recording his redemption. For an example of a blanket weaver, see the case concerning the aforementioned Tartar freedman Anthoni, ARV G 2332: M. 30: 30r–v. For an example of a dyer, see the testimony of Jordi Sanc, described as a *"tintorer libert olim catiu,"* in a dispute concerning the ownership of several dozen wooden bins (*portadores*). ARV G 2422: 355r–36or.

37. In 1472, Joan, "niger libertinus pro nunch Valencie comorans," put himself in a contract of apprenticeship with the cloth preparer Johan Fandos "ad tempus vero trium annorum . . . ad adepiscendum officium vestrum lanifici seu panniparatorie." ARV P 822 (nonpaginated): 16 January 1472.

38. ARV P 436 (nonpaginated): 3 July 1459. We discussed the freedman Jordi Daries' marriage to a freedwoman named Magdalena in chapter 4, see p. 145.

the terms of this agreement, Joan was supposed to pay the sales price of eleven lliures by the following June, the debt was not canceled until almost three years later.[39]

Reflective of the difficulties freed persons faced daily finding employment in an environment where freeborn artisans often seem to have resented them as unwelcome competition, when, in the 1440s, a black freedman named Luch Ametler came to Valencia, though a miller by trade, he seems to have had no choice but to reinvent himself as a poultry seller. Even so, one Sunday evening, he was the victim of an assault by one of his competitors. While en route to buy some more chickens, he was attacked by a hired laborer in the butcher shop located in the Muslim quarter.[40] In 1441 a freedman named Vicent Junquera was seized and detained by the Justícia del Grau on suspicion that he was violating a municipal statute that prohibited slaves from working as porters on the city's wharf. Vicent (referred to in later documentation as "lo negre") was able to secure his release only after producing documents proving that he had been freed by his master's widow. Even then, the municipal councilmen (jurats) demanded, as an added security measure, that this widow be questioned. Only after this widow had confirmed, under oath, that she really and truly had freed Vicent would the city councilmen issue the order declaring that Vicent "be allowed to work as a porter and practice his trade without any impediment." Even then, the extent to which this order was honored by Vicent's competitors is open to debate.[41]

Black African freedmen seem to have been particularly vulnerable to this sort of harassment. As early as 1425 we find a Valencian artisan petitioning for the release of a former black male slave of his named Silvester. More than twelve years earlier (when Silvester was eight years old), this artisan had issued Silvester a carta de libertat. Making his living as a sailor on the island of Sicily, Silvester was subsequently captured by a band of Genoese corsairs. His captors, looking no further than his skin color, presumed he was a slave. Though all his fellow seamen had affirmed, repeatedly, Silvester's freed status, the Genoese corsair reportedly refused to release him "because, since he is black, he assumes he is a slave."[42] Likewise, in 1470, a black freedman named Joan Muntanya

---

39. ARV P 1998 (nonpaginated): 3 April 1478.

40. ARV JCrim 22: M. 6 (Clams): (nonpaginated): 13 November 1445.

41. Indeed, suggestive that his problems continued, some four years later Vicent's wife would be charged before the court of the Justícia Criminal with assault. A physical altercation between Vicent's wife and another woman living in the port district reportedly occurred when this presumably "white" woman discovered the slave owned by her "black" neighbor (Vicent, described as "lo negre" and "barquerador [sic] del Grau") washing clothes in the public fountain and tried to discipline him. For the document reporting Vicent's arrest by the Justícia del Grau in 1441, see document #146 in Agustín Rubio Vela, ed., Epistolari de la València Medieval II (València/Barcelona: Institut Interuniversitari de Filologia Valenciana, 1998), 358. For the altercation involving Vicent's wife, see ARV JCrim 22: M. 5 (Clams): (nonpaginated) 2 September 1445.

42. The Genoese corsair Phelip de Vinaldaz reportedly had refused to release Silvestre "com sia negre pensa esser catiu jatsia li fos dit per los de la dita nau que aquell era franch." ARV G 2235: M. 13: 9r–10v.

protested that he was the victim of prejudice, citing his black skin color as a factor in his relative powerlessness. Soon after he had been granted his freedom, Joan departed from his master's rural estate in Meliana and found work as a servant in the royal inn (*al-fondech*) in Valencia. Like many freed persons in Valencia, Joan complained that he was having difficulty collecting his wages. Joan maintained that his repeated demands for payment of his salary so antagonized his boss (Simó Mascardell, the *alfondech's* administrator) that Simó had him arrested on trumped-up charges of theft. Joan protested that Simó was using him as a scapegoat, transferring onto him the responsibility for thefts that, in fact, had been perpetrated by Simó, his wife, their domestic servant, "as well as his many other accomplices in said hostel." Acutely conscious of his vulnerability as a freedman, an accused thief, and a black person, Joan charged that Simó "had resolved to denounce him so that, if, by chance, the [other] thefts ever were discovered," the local authorities would not believe Joan if he disclosed Simó's role in these crimes. Acknowledging how his own testimony would carry little weight since it came "from the mouth of a black man," Joan reasoned that Simó had denounced him for theft as an added insurance measure. For, if Joan ever attempted to reveal this innkeeper's guilt, the bailiff would discount his testimony, since now it could be argued that he, "a black man, had [implicated Simó Mascardell] not because it was true, but out of malice, or out of revenge for Mascardell having denounced him." In this way, Joan explained, his boss had tried to ensure that any testimony that he could make against him would not be believed and thus he, and not Simó, would be punished for his master's crimes.[43]

Contracting Marriage

In the eyes of many contemporaries, marriage was possible only between free persons.[44] According to the kingdom's legal code, although slaves technically could marry, a slave's marriage could in no way compromise a slave owner's property rights. Marriage (like the sacrament of baptism) would not, in and of itself, bring a slave freedom. Rather, it had to be accompanied by an explicit act performed by the slave's master or mistress granting the slave freedom: that is, the issuance of a *carta de franquea*. The statute read, "if a male or female slave or captive marries another, this by no means means that he [or she]

43. Joan contended that his boss "delibera denunciar aquell a fin que si res descobria e dehia dels dits furts vos dit molt magnifich batle e altres que de aquell havrien noticia per la boca del dit negre haguessen a veure que lo dit negre ho dehia per malicia per ço com lo dit en Mascardell lo avià denunciat e no per que fos veritat e que ab aquesta color lo dit negre no feria cregut de res que digues contra lo dit Mascardell e axi aquel restara inpunit dels dits furts." ARV B (Procesos) Letra P: 46.

44. See Michael Sheehan, "Theory and Practice: Marriage of the Unfree and the Poor in Medieval Society," *Mediaeval Studies* 50 (1988): 457–87.

will no longer be in his power or under his lordship, [rather, he or she would remain] just as he [or she] had been prior to contracting the marriage."[45]

Several slave couples, in fact, appear to have contemplated, if not formally contracted, marriage prior to their manumissions. In the contract of manumission for Caterina, the black slave woman owned by Damiata, the widow of Guillerm Paella, Caterina already described herself as the wife (uxor) of a black slave named Johan. Johan formerly had also been the slave of Guillerm Paella. Now, however, Johan was owned by the count of Oliva. Despite the fact that Johan himself was still in servitude, he cosigned his wife's debt agreement, promising to help pay Caterina's redemption fee of twenty-five lliures.[46] Similarly, in 1476, Anna, a forty-six-year-old partially manumitted Russian slave woman, the former slave of the merchant Galceran Martí, contracted marriage with Joan Verdecho, the baker and the former slave of the baker Pasqual Verdecho. Though Anna immediately gave Joan twenty lliures in dowry, Anna and Joan stated that (under penalty of fifteen lliures) they would solemnize their union in a church (literally, in facie sancte matris ecclesiae) within the next four years. The ceremony was likely timed to coincide with Anna's completion of a four-year term of service. Her contract of manumission required that she provide this service to her master's heir, the merchant Ludovic Martí.[47] Finally, in 1491, two former slaves, Joana Haha and Jacobo Plasent, affirmed that they would solemnize their marriage as soon as Jacobo, a partially manumitted freedman of Tunisian descent, completed a term of service with his master's widow. In the meantime, Jacobo would help pay off his fiancée's twenty-five lliures redemption fee. In this same document, Joana's master recognized that Jacobo, as Joana's future husband (futur vir) had paid him the first installment of said redemption fee (three lliures and three sous).[48]

45. "Si servu o serva o catiu o cativa d'alcun farà matrimoni ab altre, gens per açò no roman que sia sots poder e sots senyoria de son senyor, axí com era de primer ans que hagués feyt lo matrimoni." Furs de València, ed. Colón and Garcia (Barcelona, 1990), V: 109.

46. Damiata, the widow of the merchant Guillerm Paella, freed Caterina, "uxor Johannis etiopis captivi spectabilis comiti Olive et olim dicti honorabilis Guillermi Paella quondam viri mei...sub hoc condicione...quod in continenti mei dare teneatis decem llibris monete regalium Valencie." Similarly, in a document issued on the same date, Johan, "olim captivus honorabili Guillermi Paella quondam mercatoris et nunch multum spectabilis comitis de Oliva," jointly with Caterina, "eius uxor olim captiva honorabilis dompne Damiate uxore dicti honorabile quondam Guillermi Paella et in presenciarum liberta et a jugo servitutis penitus liberata," promised to pay Damiata the remaining fifteen lliures they owed her "ex illis xxv llibris monete predicte pro quibus odierna die paulo...dictam Caterinam a jugo servitutis liberastis et liberam francham et alforiam." APPV 24956 (nonpaginated): 28 December 1477.

47. APPV 21593 (nonpaginated): 17 April 1476. I discussed Joan Verdecho's marriage to Anna in chapter 4, see pp. 143–44.

48. Jacobo and Joana were to be married when "ille (Jacobo) perfecerit servitutem quam facere et prestare tenetur honorabile Catherine Plasent eius dicte uxorique et heredi dicti Jacobi Plasent iuxta disposicione ille testamenti." APPV 26597 (nonpaginated): 7 September 1491.

With respect to these "marriages" between slaves, it is not always clear what the living arrangements would be. Although Ludovic Martí explicitly specified that Anna was required to complete her four-year term of service "while living in my household" (*in domo mea cohabitando*),[49] it was not indicated whether Caterina and Johan would continue to live apart or whether Joana would move into the household where Jacobo was completing his term of service.

The ability to contract marriage and set up their own household, nevertheless, was frequently adduced by freed persons as the very essence of freedom. In 1451, for instance, the laborer Domingo Garcia contested the merchant Matheu Corones's assertion that he could sell Domingo's wife Marta as a slave by citing how "Marta, with the consent and approval of said Corones and his wife, contracted marriage with the said Domingo." Thus, Domingo insisted, "for this reason she should be considered and truly is free."[50] Many slave couples seem to have formalized their unions immediately upon enfranchisement. The priest Marti Dalfambra, for example, recounted how he had officiated at the wedding of the freed persons Marti and Lucia Bossa that took place soon after the death of their former master.[51] In 1448–49, when the nobleman Johan Olzina freed all the slaves living in his household in celebration of his marriage, three of the five slaves also turned around and almost immediately got married. While two of his former slaves, Margalida and Domingo "the black," married each other, Elena, "exercising the said liberty" (*usant de la dita libertat*), married the silversmith Marti Mendes.[52]

As Teresa Vinyoles has suggested, for some freedwomen marriage was a mechanism for social integration, a means for securing themselves a respectable position in society. Indeed, masters and mistresses explicitly stated that they gave dowries to their former slave women to ensure that they could secure a "good" husband. In 1448, a freedwoman named Ursola, the former slave of the tanner Vicent Boix (deceased), collected the fifty lliures promised her in her master's last will and testament. The sum had been earmarked for her dowry and was payable only after her marriage had been solemnized in a church ("*quant fos collocada en matrimoni en fac de santa mare ecclesia*"). Thus, the tanner Thomas Albarrazi, having contracted marriage with Ursola (ostensibly in a ceremony that took place in front of a church), now appeared before the court of the Justícia Civil to collect this sum.[53] A white freed woman named Ysabel, the former slave of the merchant Daniel

---

49. APPV 21593 (nonpaginated): 17 April 1476.

50. Marta's husband, Domingo Garcia, protested that Corones could not sell his wife's services "com sia e es en stament de franquea juro verius francha com ella dita Marta de voluntat e beniplacit del dit en Corones e muller d'aquell contracta e ha contractat matrimoni ab lo dit Domingo per consequent seria e verdaderament es franqua." ARV G 4580: M. 9: 46v and ARV G 2280: M. 13: 44r–48r.

51. ARV G 2290: M. 21: 34r. I discussed Marti and Luisa Bossa's marriage in chapter 4, pp. 145–46.

52. ARV G 2348: M. 5: 20v and ARV G 2349: M. 6: 33r–44v; M. 19: 45r–46v.

53. ARV JCiv 913: M. 5: 34r and ARV JCiv 914: M. 12: 41r.

Pardo (deceased), was similarly promised twenty-five lliures for her dowry in her master's last will and testament. Though Ysabel died before she had a chance to collect this sum, Ysabel's husband and universal heir, Alamay de Cervello, appeared before the Justícia Civil to collect this bequest.[54] As these selected examples demonstrate, freed women not only married other slaves or freedmen, they also married men with no apparent slave ancestry, artisans such as tanners, carpenters, tailors, cobblers, tanners, masons, locksmiths,[55] and even merchants.[56]

To secure their "respectable" husbands, freedwomen offered dowries that typically ranged between twenty and thirty lliures, though some offered as much as fifty to sixty lliures.[57] More exceptional was a freedwoman named Magdalena who offered her fiancé, a cobbler named Anthoni Rey, twenty-four hundred sous (roughly 120 lliures) as dowry— a sum provided by her former master, Angelino de Prato, a Lombard merchant.[58] Anthoni, in turn, promised Magdalena some eight hundred sous (roughly forty lliures) in creix (escreix)—the sum customarily offered by the husband to supplement her dowry, a gift traditionally offered in recognition of the wife's virginity.[59] In 1486, when the freedwoman Elionor Donas, a domestic (criata) in the service of the abbess of the local Dominican

54. ARV JCiv 921: M. 10: 26r–v.

55. For example, Magdalena, the former slave woman of Dionis Verdu, married the tailor (sastre) Pere Saboya. ARV G 2331: M. 17: 16v; Magdalena, the former slave woman of the Lombard merchant Angelino de Prato, married a cobbler (cabater) named Anthoni Rey. ARV JCiv 931: M. 2: 15r; Johana, the former slave of the broker Pau Vives, married a mason (operaris ville) named Joan Martí. ARV P 1823 (nonpaginated): 18 February 1460; Magdalena, the former slave woman of Jacme Aguilo, married a locksmith (manya) in Morvedre (Sagunto) named Berthomeu Cabata. Later on, however, this couple seems to have run into some problems. In the inventory postmortem of Magdalena's possessions, reference was made to the lawsuit she filed against her husband in 1454 demanding restitution of her dowry. ARV P 3162 (nonpaginated): 28 April 1480.

56. In her last will and testament, a freedwoman named Maria described herself as the wife of the merchant Berenguer Marti. APPV 15927 (nonpaginated): 31 August 1477.

57. For one example among many, see ARV P 1823 (nonpaginated): 18 February 1460, in which Johana, the former slave of a broker, offered the mason Johan Marti thirty lliures in dowry. See also APPV 21819 (nonpaginated): 16 May 1476, in which the libertina Lucia de Sent Marti offered Pere Salvador, a porter, thirty lliures in dowry. Less than two months later, however, Lucia supplemented the thirty lliures she gave Pere in dowry with fifteen additional lliures, transferring over to him the title to a house that she owned. APPV 21819 (nonpaginated): 5 July 1476. For another example of a freedwoman offering her fiancé a dowry worth roughly fifty lliures, see ARV P 19071 (nonpaginated): 26 June 1477, in which Caterina, the former slave of a cathedral canon, offered the mason Johan Martinez five hundred sous (roughly twenty-five lliures) worth of clothing and jewelry and then transferred over into his custody the annual allowance of five hundred sous (twenty-five lliures) she was promised in her former master's last will and testament.

58. ARV JCiv 931: M. 2: 15r; M. 9: 31r–32v.

59. The combined sum of thirty-two hundred sous (roughly 160 lliures) was later invested in a house (alberch) located in the parish of San Bartolomé. ARV JCiv 931: M. 2: 15r; M. 9: 31r–32v.

convent of St. Mary Magdalen, contracted marriage with the carpenter Dominic Vines, Elionor offered Dominic some fifty lliures in dowry, while Dominic, in turn, promised to give Elionor twenty-five lliures "since, by disposition of the *Furs de Valencia*, a supplementary payment (*augmentum*) or donation for marriage (*donacionem propter nupcias*), commonly referred to as the *creix*, ought to be made in recognition of virginity."[60]

Most freed women, however, do not seem to have been promised a *creix* by their prospective husbands. Perhaps this was because most spouses of former slave women (freedmen and laborers) simply did not possess the financial means necessary to do so. An equally important consideration, however, was that in the estimate of their contemporaries, they perhaps did not merit this supplementary payment "made in recognition of virginity." Many fifteenth-century Valencians, after all, claimed that slave women were naturally licentious. Thus, perhaps they could not be presumed virgins. It seems, then, that it was only in exceptional cases that a fiancé offered a *creix* if his future wife was a former slave woman. In 1478, the black freedman Mathias Cardona (the former slave of an attorney) promised to give to his intended, Honesta, the former (white?) slave woman of Pere Vilarasa, a deacon and canon at the cathedral of Valencia, thirty lliures "on account of her virginity" (*propter earum virginitatem*), in supplement to the sixty lliures she had given him as dowry.[61]

It remains debatable, therefore, that freed women were successfully integrated into "respectable" Valencian society through marriage. Contemporary testimony suggests, in fact, that for some free men, marrying a freedwoman significantly compromised their social standing. Thus, the free-born laborer Domingo Garcia emphasized how marrying a freedwoman led to the degradation of his social status and complained that he now was subjected to a constant stream of insults from his wife's master and mistress. Stressing how he endured this "out of love for his wife," despite the fact that he himself was of free birth and had no slave ancestry whatsoever, Domingo's procurator noted,

> It ought to be recognized that he, the said Domingo, in order to redeem the said Marta from captivity, obligated himself to serve four years with said Corones. While other men were accustomed to get a dowry from their wives, he has not received anything

60. "Et quia virginibus per disposicionem fori huius regni Valencie fieri debeat augmentum sine donacionem propter nubcias dictam vulgo creix premio sue virginitatis eas obres vobis dicte Elionori future sponse mee facio vobis augmentum sine donacionem propter nupcias dictam vulgo creix de viginti quinque libris dicte monete." ARV P 10270 (nonpaginated): 4 February 1486. For a thorough discussion concerning the *creix*, its purpose, and composition, see Dolores Guillot Aliaga, *El regimen económico del matrimonial en la Valencia foral* (Valencia: Biblioteca Valenciana, 2002), 179–93.

61. Honesta's skin color was not indicated. "Et cum secundum forum Valencie virginibus dos cum augmento fieri mereatur. Ideo facio vobis dicte Honeste domicelle ut virgini et propter earum virginitatem augmentum sive donacionem propter nupcias de triginta libris dicte monete." ARV P 2067 (nonpaginated): 30 August 1478.

and instead was obliged to offer four years of his service and labor, subjecting himself to such extreme subjugation that there is not a slave in the world who suffers so many hardships, is exposed to so much abuse, and is so poorly provided for.

Domingo was appearing before the court of the governor, moreover, because his wife's former master, the merchant Matheu Corones, was now threatening—as a consequence for their alleged ingratitude—to sell him, a free-born laborer (along with Marta) into slavery.[62]

Exercising Their Parental Rights: Freed Persons as Mothers and Fathers

Though a slave's rights as a parent were not officially acknowledged, much less respected in fifteenth-century Valencia, contemporaries, nonetheless, recognized the strong bonds linking enslaved parents and their children. Shortly following the flight of the black slaves Johan and Caterina, the widow Damiata Paella (curator of her husband's estate) alarmingly reported that the fugitive slave couple was now plotting the escape of their two children. In 1473, Damiata Paella appeared before the Justícia Civil requesting permission to sell the "sclavets" ("little slaves," a diminutive form of sclau) Baltasar and Damiata (aged between ten and twelve years old) before their parents, the fugitive slaves Johan and Caterina, engineered some way to "steal" them. Though, according to the terms of her husband's last will and testament, Baltasar and Damiata could not be sold or otherwise alienated, his widow protested that since it was more than likely that she would lose these slave children—either to seizure by her many creditors or to "theft"— the most expedient thing for her to do, as curator of her husband's estate, was to sell the two sclavets to help pay off the estate's many debts.[63] Damiata's logic apparently proved convincing to the Justícia Civil; he issued a ruling authorizing Damiata Paella to resell the two black children. Though there is no further record concerning what eventually

---

62. "E deu se molt attendre com lo dit Domingo per traure la dita Marta de captivitat s'es obligat de servir quatre anyades al dit en Corones e los altres homens acostumen de pendre dot ab les mullers e aquest no ha pres res ans fa tornes que li dona la servitut e sos treballs de quatre anys es subuga en tanta manera que no es sclau en lo mon pus mala vida pogues passar e axi esser vituperat e molt mal provehit de mala provisio." ARV G 4580: M. 9: 46v and ARV G 2280: M. 13: 44r–48r.

63. Witnesses appearing on Damiata Paella's behalf testified that they believed that the two sclavets posed a significant flight risk "since they have as their father and mother slaves who have run away from the custody of the female curator [of this estate]. Moreover, the said father and mother will pursue them with great energy and also will have others search for them in order that they could see and be reunited with them and they will work hard to recover them." Other witnesses testified, respectively, that Baltasar and Damiata's parents were most certainly the type of people "who would not hesitate to order the said Baltasar and Damiata, their children, to run away, or even steal them." Indeed, "they had little doubt that they would steal them or make them run away." ARV JCiv 926: M. 13: 30r–31v.

happened to these two children, their resale to a new owner would hardly have facilitated a reunion with their biological parents. Indeed, four years later, in a document recording the terms of Caterina's manumission, while reference was made to Caterina's husband, Johan (who would help pay the twenty-five lliure redemption fee), no mention was made of either one of their two children.[64]

Freedom brought the authority to raise and make decisions concerning the livelihood of one's children. A former slave woman, thus, argued in her *demanda de libertat* that the fact that her master had allowed her to retain custody of her child was an implicit recognition of her freed status. Thus, in 1462, the procurator representing the interests of Ursola (aka Yolant), the daughter of a freedwoman named Maria and Jofré d'Anyo, Maria's former owner, cited as "proof" of both Ursola's and Maria's freed status the fact that mother and daughter had remained together: Maria "raising and nourishing" Ursola (aka Yolant), throughout her entire infancy, and Ursola (aka Yolant) "following her mother every place that she went" (*seguia la mare d'aquella en tot loch hon aquella stava*).[65]

Reflective of their new status, freed persons appear in contemporary records assuming responsibility for the support and well-being of their children. Most notably, we see them providing for their sons and daughters in their last will and testaments. The black freedman Johan Puig, for instance, named his "legitimate and biological son" (*fill seu legittim e natural*), Luiset Puig, his universal heir.[66] Similarly, in 1478, a gravely ill Marti Pardo, *negre* and *habitant* of Tavernes Blanques, named his son, Francesch Pardo, *negre*, his universal heir in his last will and testament.[67]

Freed persons also acted as their children's advocates: filing suits to secure recognition of their freeborn status. The slave woman named Rosa, for example, filed two *demandes de libertat* on behalf of her daughter Margalida. Rosa filed the first one in 1476, in conjunction with her own *demanda de libertat*, when Margalida was about a year and a half old. In 1487, after she had secured her own freedom, Rosa filed a second *demanda*—when Margalida was about twelve or thirteen years old. Although in the first *demanda* Rosa had insisted that Margalida had been born free since "the fetus inherits the status of the mother" (*partus sequitur ventrem*—literally, "that which is brought forth follows the womb"),[68] in the

---

64. APPV 24956 (nonpaginated): 28 December 1477. Unfortunately, there is no information given here concerning *how* the fugitive slaves Caterina and Johan came back into Damiata Paella's custody.

65. "Item diu que...aquella [Ursola] era en poder de la dita Maria mare de aquella la qual la nodria e criava ja essent mort lo dit en Anyo sens que no stava ni era ab la dita na Sanyes ans seguia la mare d'aquella en tot loch hon aquella stava." ARV G 2304: M.3: 45r, and ARV G 2305: M. 11: 8r–23v; M. 20: 13r–21v; and ARV G 2306: M. 25: 16r–v; 17r–v; M. 26: 36r–37v; 42r–43v; M. 29: 19r–v.

66. ARV JCiv 921: M. 9: 43r–44r.

67. APPV 21200 (nonpaginated): 9 July 1478.

68. ARV G 2343: M. 4: 37v; ARV G 2344: M. 12: 9r–10r. I discussed Rosa's relationship with her master, Arnau Castello, in chapter 5, see pp. 173, 179, 185–6.

second *demanda* (which was successful), rather than stress her own free status at the time of her daughter's birth, Rosa argued that Margalida was entitled to freedom because she was the daughter of a free man.[69]

The aforementioned Russian freedwoman named Maria also lobbied for recognition of the freed status of her daughter Ursola (aka Yolant). Noting how her daughter was born free since her father was her (Maria's) former master, Maria protested that her former master's sister and heir, Orfresina de Sanyes, had tricked her, convincing her to release Ursola/Yolant into her custody on the pretense that she would find her daughter employment as a servant in a respectable household.[70] Orfresina had convinced Maria that she had her daughter's best interests at heart—that she would see to it that her daughter earned a decent salary and could amass a dowry sizable enough to attract a good husband. Maria insisted that she did not become aware of Orfresina's duplicitousness until more than fifteen years later. Having learned that her daughter, now around twenty years in age, had, in reality, been sold as a slave rather than hired as a salaried domestic servant, Maria noted how she had immediately appealed to the procurator of the miserable for assistance in filing a *demanda de libertat* on her daughter's behalf.[71]

Although the freedman Pere Garcia (in 1478) filed a successful *demanda de libertat* on behalf of his daughter, Johana, we ought not to exaggerate the power of freed persons as advocates for their children. The noblewoman whom Pere charged with detaining his child unlawfully had, afterall, been unwilling to recognize Pere's claims as father for an

---

69. ARV G 2382: M. 3: 43r; ARV G 2383: 501r–510r; ARV G 2384: 180r–185r. Although no mention was made of Margalida's biological father in the first *demanda de libertat* filed on her behalf, in the second one Rosa affirmed that Margalida's father was a dark-skinned freedman named Pere, a hosier. The governor ultimately issued a ruling in Margalida's favor, proclaiming her free and ordering that she be released from servitude. The passage of time, thus, seems to have in no way prejudiced her legitimate claim to freedom, particularly given their advocate's protest that both she and her daughter were "foreigners" who were unfamiliar with the kingdom's customs.

70. Maria insisted that her four-year-old daughter Ursola/Yolant had entered Orfresina's household as a free person. She acknowledged, however, that there would have been very little discernible difference between how a four- or six-year-old girl would be treated, be she a slave or a free-born child. Rosa, moreover, also protested that her former mistress, Ursola Castello, had made false promises that she would respect her daughter Margalida's freeborn status. Thus, she claimed that she had been fooled for more than a decade, until she learned, to her amazement, that Ursola was plotting to sell Margalida as a slave.

71. Orfresina Sanyes allegedly "cortesament dix e dona a entendre a la dita Maria mare d'aquella que seria bona cosa la dita Ursoleta fos mesa a criar e que la affermassen ab alguna bona dona que servis o guanyas soldada ab que's pogues collocar en matrimoni quant fos gran e tingues per a exovar." Thus, "donant fe la dita Maria al que la dita na Sanyes li havia dit del affermar de la dita Ursoleta e esser de edat de vint anys vel quasi ha sabut que aquella es stada venuda o d'aco es stada feyta clamor als procurador dels miserables lo qual ha mogut aquell a posar la dita demanda de libertat." The case, unfortunately, lacks a conclusion. Ultimately, we do not know what happened to Ursola. ARV G 2304: M.3: 45r; ARV G 2305: M. 11: 8r–23v; M. 20: 13r–21v; ARV G 2306: M. 25: 16r–v; 17r–v; M. 26: 36r–37v; 42r–43v; M. 29: 19r–v.

unspecified time period. His former mistress allegedly kept Pere's daughter so closely confined that she was unable "to communicate or speak with her father or any other persons." When a court official was sent to the household to investigate, the young woman, upon being interrogated, immediately burst into tears and related how her mistress kept her locked up (*tancada*) and would not let her speak with either her father or her mother. Contrasting the power (*potencia*) of his former mistress to his own weakness and impotence as a freedman, Pere pleaded for the governor's assistance, protesting that this noblewoman had secret plans to sell his daughter overseas.[72]

Given the tireless energy with which freed persons such as Rosa, Maria, and Pere fought for their children's freedom, it is somewhat perplexing to find that most of the slave women who filed suits demanding freedom as a consequence of giving birth to their master's child did *not* demand their child's enfranchisement in conjunction with their own. Judging from these trial transcripts, the fates of their children generally did not seem to have been a cause of great concern for these women. What ought we to make of this? Did this indicate a lack of affection on their part for offspring conceived in circumstances of extreme physical duress and psychological coercion?

At least some of these children had died by the time their mothers appeared before the court of the governor. Barbera, the daughter of a Russian slave woman named Anna, for instance, had already died by the time her mother filed her *demanda de libertat*.[73] Luisset, the son of Nicholana, a twenty-five-year-old Russian slave woman, however, was living and reportedly seven months of age when his mother sued for her freedom.[74] Similarly, both of the two children a Canary Islander slave woman named Catherina allegedly conceived by her master (the silversmith Jacme Puig) were referred to as "living" in the *demanda de libertat* she filed before the court of the governor.[75] Though most of these children were mentioned by name in these records, once the circumstances of their births were recounted, they received no further mention. One possible explanation for this apparent lack of concern was that their mothers were fairly confident that their children would be acknowledged (and perhaps even embraced) as free persons by their masters and/or biological fathers. In 1477, for example, the merchant Gracia Pelegri acknowledged that Johana, the child of a dark-skinned slave woman named Domenega, was his daughter.

---

72. Pere's former mistress allegedly "te la dita Johana tant stretament que per demanar la sua justicia que no te facultat ni liberalitat de poder comunicar ni parlar ab lo dit son pare ni ab altres persones." Similarly, when an official from the governor's court came to question Johana, "la qual dita Johana prenent se a plorar dix e respos que ... quant la dita senyora exia de casa la lexava tanquada en casa e que no la lexava anar a parlar ab son pare ne sa mare." ARV G 2348: M. 5: 20v and ARV G 2349: M. 6: 33r–44v.

73. ARV G 2314: 15r and ARV G 2317: 234r–235v. I discussed Anna's relationship with her master and her *demanda de libertat* in chapters 5 and 6, see pp. 173–4 and 215–16.

74. ARV G 2266: M. 14: 10r.

75. ARV G 2410: 388r–v.

In addition to formally admitting his paternity, Gracia paid Domenega's master, the merchant Marti Sanchiz, twelve lliures ten sous in child support. Five lliures were given to cover the expenses Marti sustained in connection with his slave woman's pregnancy and childbirth, and the remaining seven lliures ten sous were in payment for the milk and other necessities Domenega provided Gracia's daughter.[76] Likewise, the Genoese merchant Albert de Pont not only recognized Ysabel, the daughter of a slave woman named Caterina, as his freeborn daughter, but he also had her sent (against her mother's will) from Valencia to Genoa to live with him. In a letter Albert allegedly wrote to his former slave concubine, pleading with her to send Ysabel to live with him, Albert told her that "if you wish to think of your profit, my honor, and the honor of your daughter, I beg you to send our daughter as quickly as you can." Time, in Albert's view, was of the essence: the younger Ysabel was when she arrived in Genoa, the easier it would be to pass her off as his wife's daughter and integrate her into the community.[77] In such circumstances, slave mothers might have "assumed" that their child's freeborn status would be recognized and hence felt there was no need to lobby for their enfranchisement.

Birth and Status in the Later Middle Ages

In a recent article, Sally McKee has argued that, sometime around the beginning of the fourteenth century, there was a major shift in how jurists and legal practitioners in Italy and Venetian Crete defined the inheritance of status. Status was no longer determined by the maternal line but was inherited patrilineally.[78] In her research in the notarial archives of Venetian Crete, for example, McKee found that after 1270 it was no longer necessary for masters explicitly to free the children they had by slave mothers in their last wills and

76. APPV 20425 (nonpaginated): 8 July 1477.

77. Albert, moreover, assured Caterina that she need not fear his wife since "I am determined that she [Ysabel] will come here, God willing." With respect to his wife, he informed Caterina that "I have advised her that I want her [Ysabel, Caterina's daughter] to come here very much. I have told her that she [Ysabel] is very pretty and that there should be no further delay . . . that the younger she is when she arrives here, the more it will seem like she is my wife's daughter and so that, with the aid of a good upbringing, she will not be considered a bastard (borda)." Thus, he urged Caterina "to send Ysabel [to him] with the first [i.e. the next] passage." ARV G 2317: 91r.

78. It bears emphasis, however, that this was not the rule in every Mediterranean society. The law varied even within the territories of the Crown of Aragon. While status was inherited patrilineally in the kingdom of Valencia, it was inherited matrilineally in the kingdom of Majorca. Status was also inherited matrilineally in the neighboring Castilian kingdom of Murcia. In 1400, for instance, a master rejected the procurador of the miserable's claim that his infant client had been born free by pointing out that the boy technically had been born in Castilian rather than Valencian territory. Thus, since he was born in Villena (located 121 kilometers from Valencia) he was not entitled to the "benefit" offered by Valencian law to children born of slave mothers and freeborn fathers. See document #112 in Agustín Rubio Vela, ed., Epistolari de la València Medieval (Valencia: Institut de Filologia Valenciana, 1985), 287.

testaments.[79] McKee contends that this was a response, essentially, to popular pressure. She argues that Venetian, Genoese, and Florentine patricians who fathered children by their slave women were loath to have their progeny "bear their mothers' burden" and wished to make them their heirs. Insisting that contemporaries did not necessarily view their slaves and their offspring "as profoundly and innately different from their masters," McKee observes:

> As the picture becomes clearer, a family portrait with the father at the center takes shape. The father is extending his hand to motion into the picture's frame his children by his slave women, standing visibly but subserviently in the background. It is a crowded and uncomfortable space, but there the children are, standing a little to the side, unsure of their placement and in uneasy proximity to their father's legitimate kin.[80]

The protest of a Valencian money changer named Gabriel Torregrossa in response to a *demanda de libertat* filed on behalf of Jacme, the eleven-year-old son of Marta, Gabriel's former slave woman, on its surface provides eloquent testimony in support of McKee's contention. Though Gabriel vehemently denied that he was Jacme's biological father, he nonetheless insisted that if this truly had been the case, he—a well-to-do money changer with no children of his own—would have had no problem accepting this white Russian slave woman's son as his own. Indeed, Gabriel's procurator argued, "Considering the fact that he is a rich man with no sons, it is not at all plausible, nor believable, nor could it be presumed, nor does it follow, nor could it follow by employing any type of reasoning, that the said Torregrossa, if he knew or believed that the slave woman was pregnant with his child, that he would have sold the said slave woman."[81]

Though the Furs de València did automatically ascribe "free" status to any child born of a free father (regardless of the mother's status), it seems that in practice, masters and mistresses still assumed the authority to confer free status on the children borne by their slave women. In 1477, for example, Johana Verdecho, the widow of the baker Pasquasius

---

79. Sally McKee, "Inherited Status and Slavery in Late Medieval Italy and Venetian Crete," *Past & Present* 182 (2004): 41.

80. Thus, McKee argues that "a simplistic notion of slave-owning that allows little room for the unpredictable agency of human emotions will hinder us from exploring the possibility" that high-ranked Venetian, Genoese, and Florentine patricians, "whether out of affection or fear of extinction" wanted to "keep" their illegitimate children. Sally McKee, "Inherited Status and Slavery," 43.

81. "No es versemblant ne de creure ne presomidor ne cau ne pot caure en cap de algun rectament iutjant que lo dit en Torregrossa si sabes o cregue que la dita sclava fos prenyada de aquell considerant que es home rich e no te fills hagues venut la dita sclava." Thus, although Gabriel Torregrossa admitted that he had sex with Marta "a few times," he insisted that the child's "true" father was a white slave who worked in a nearby oven. ARV G 2351: M. 15: 1r–4v.

Verdecho, issued a *carta de libertat* to Lucas Cubells, the son of her former slave woman, the aforementioned Anna, and the cuirass maker Bartholomeu Cubells.[82] Although it could be argued that Johana was merely confirming the child's *de jure* "freeborn" status as a safety measure, it is clear that masters and mistresses wielded a considerable amount of influence with respect to determining the status of their slave women's children.

Status, after all, was a hotly contested issue in the kingdom of Valencia's courts. Children of slave mothers and free fathers often had to fight for recognition of their freeborn status. Hardly being beckoned into the frame of the family portrait, between 1450 and 1582, sixteen slaves protesting that they had been born free filed *demandes de libertat* before the court of the governor. In eight of these sixteen cases, admittedly, the alleged father was someone other than the slave mother's master, usually a man of modest social status (a farmer, cobbler, harness maker, hosier, or cook) or a household servant or squire (*moço* or *scuder*). Rather than turning the child over to his biological father's custody (or abandoning it in a local hospital), in all eight of these instances the slave's owner had been unwilling to relinquish his or her claim to the slave woman's child. When it was discovered that Marti Dutrea, a servant (*moço*) in the household of the merchant Jaume Francesquo (of Alicante) had impregnated Caterina, Jaume's Canary Islander slave woman, his master responded by expelling Marti from his household. Though Marti formally had acknowledged that he was the father of Caterina's child and clearly was willing to take custody of him, Marti was, nevertheless, powerless to prevent his child (Johanot) from being shipped off to the island of Majorca where Johanot and his mother were resold to a new owner. In spite of the great distance between them, however, Marti still managed to keep tabs on his son. And thus, more than twenty years later, when a grown-up Johanot gained access to the court of the governor and filed his successful *demanda de libertat*, Marti was instrumental in gathering witnesses in Alicante (Johanot's birthplace) who could affirm his son's freeborn status.[83]

The vast majority of these paternity suits, indeed, were pursued decades after the child's birth. Many of these "children" of slave mothers and free fathers were adults when they demanded their freedom. Such a pattern suggests that although their mothers might have assumed their child's freeborn status would be respected, their future was hardly assured. Though contemporary legislation stipulated that they were juridically to be treated as individuals of freeborn status, their actual position in society was considerably less secure.

This more complicated reality can be seen in the varying fates of the children of slave mothers whose siblings had a different biological father. A freedwoman named

---

82. APPV 21593 (nonpaginated): 22 December 1476. I noted earlier how Anna had married another freedperson, Joan Verdecho. See chapter 4, pp. 143–44.

83. ARV G 2410: 155r–161v.

Margalida, for example, reportedly had given birth to two children: a son, Berthomeu, and a daughter, Lucia. Berthomeu was the son of Margalida's former master, Asensi de Morales, the lord of Finestrat (a territory located about one hundred miles south of Valencia, near Alicante). The freeborn status of Margalida's son, known popularly as Berthomeu de Morales, seems to have been recognized without dispute. Berthomeu, in fact, would eventually marry the daughter of a local bailiff. Berthomeu's stepsister, Lucia, however, experienced a much different fate. The daughter of Johan Taracol, a squire in Asensi de Morales's service, Lucia was raised in the Morales's household in the company of her mother and step-siblings. Though she had assumed that everyone in the household recognized and would respect her freeborn status, Lucia had a brutal awakening when, in her twenties, one of Asensi's legitimate daughters, Beatriu de Morales, claimed Lucia as her slave and sold her to the broker Gaspar Riudaura. Though Lucia ultimately secured official confirmation of her freeborn status, the fact that she had been obliged to appeal to the governor for assistance in the first place suggests that she would remain vulnerable to being "mistaken" for a slave in the future.[84]

A similarly revealing comparison could be made between the respective fates of the three children of the aforementioned Russian slave woman named Rosa. Rosa's first two children, Lucrecia and Julia, were, reputedly, the daughter and son of her master, the notary and royal scribe Arnau Castello. Based on the testimony of contemporary witnesses, while Lucrecia died in infancy, Julia publicly had been embraced by his father—if not by his father's heirs. Julia allegedly had been raised and treated as a free person in the Castello household. Rosa's third child, Margalida, in contrast, was the daughter of a dark-skinned freedman named Pere. It took tremendous persistence on her mother's part to get Margalida's freeborn status recognized. The process took more than ten years and, as noted above, necessitated the filing of two separate *demandes de libertat*.[85]

Although both Margalida's and Lucia's suits ultimately were successful, their struggles illustrate well the fact that the children of slave mothers (be they black or white) were not automatically welcomed into the bosom of Valencian society—particularly if their father was someone other than their mother's master or a wealthy merchant or nobleman. Indeed, if we are to accept the contentions made on behalf of eleven-year-old Jacme, even if they were the sons of well-to-do Valencians, they could be put into chains and leg irons by their own father (the aforementioned money changer Gabriel Torregrossa) and sold into slavery.[86] The position of the children of slave mothers and free fathers, thus, defies easy

---

84. ARV G 2398: 25v and ARV G 2399: 529r–537v.

85. For the first *demanda de libertat* (1476), see ARV G 2343: M. 4: 37v; ARV G 2344: M. 12: 9r–10r. For the second *demanda* (1487), see ARV G 2382: M. 3: 43r; ARV G 2383: 50rr–51or; ARV G 2384: 18or–185r.

86. Jacme's advocate protested that "lo dit en Gabriel Torregrossa . . . sabent lo dit Jacme esser franch lo haia ferrat e li haia posada una anella en la una cama significant e designant aquell esser catiu e encara

categorization. Their fates were dependent on a variety of different factors: their father's willingness to recognize them, his social as well as marital status, and whether or not he had any other legitimate children.

Whether their biological fathers recognized them or not, however, dark-skinned children appear to have been in the most vulnerable position. In 1479, Francesquet Carlos, the son of a white (freeborn) bridle maker and a dark-skinned (llora) woman, protested that he had been mistaken for a slave. Raised as a free person on the island of Sardinia, when Francesquet's parents died he was entrusted to the care of his uncle. Doubly vulnerable as both an orphan and a person of color (the son of a llora), when his uncle (a sailor) set off on a sea voyage Francesquet fell into the hands of some "diabolical persons" who sold him, "against all reason and justice," into slavery. Thus, reportedly due to the dark color of his skin, Francesquet (not unlike the aforementioned freed black sailor named Silvester) had been mistaken for a slave and now suddenly found himself traveling the streets of Valencia with an iron ring around his ankle.[87]

Although it is clear that, subsequent to their manumission, liberts and libertès were granted the ability to act "like free persons"—going where they pleased, collecting salaries, getting married, raising children—the freedom they enjoyed could, depending on the terms of their manumission, be, in actuality, rather limited and was often tenuous. Accused, alternatively, of being fugitives, having violated the terms of their contracts of manumission, or (if their manumission was contested by a disgruntled heir) having been "unlawfully freed," freed persons could, seemingly without warning, find themselves arrested and sold back into slavery, sometimes even more than a decade later. Moreover, some, while possessing the legal title to freedom, never truly managed to break free from their masters, remaining in a perpetual position of socioeconomic dependence. A black freedman named Johan, for example, struggled post-manumission and ultimately decided that he was unable to provide food and clothing for his five-month-old son. Thus, he reentered his former mistress's service.[88] Perhaps the clearest evidence of the continued vulnerability of freed persons were the preventative measures that many felt it necessary

---

haia temptat de vendre de aquel per les quals coses ha encorregut grans crims e delictes per los quals mereix punicio." ARV G 2351: M. 15: 1r–4v.

87. Francesquet's advocate protested that the boy "es stat a giny e tracte de diaboliques persones venut com a sclau et tandem de huns en altres es stat venut al dit en Johan Navarro lo qual lo te contra tota raho e justicia axi com a sclau e ab una anella al peu." ARV G 2350: M. 3: 33r; ARV G 2351: M. 15: 24r–30v; M. 16: 47r–48r.

88. In this notarized document, Johan's former mistress noted that "atendens quod tu Johannes niger olim servus et captivus meus tenes unum filium etatis quinque mensium parum plus vel minus et non teneas de quo possis illum facere nutrire fuit inter me et te conventum et in pactum deductum quod ego teneat nutrire et criare dictum filium tuum usque sit desmamatum et tu tenearis servire me per tempus unius anni et novem mensium." ARV P 2005: 192r–v.

to take to protect their status. In 1509, Pasqual Exea, a freedman and blacksmith from Chilches (thirty kilometers north of Valencia), decided to resettle in Valencia. To protect himself from any possible "tricks" or deceptions, Pasqual—likely a former Mudejar who had been penally enslaved and then, subsequently, had converted to Christianity and been redeemed—filed a request before the governor, asking him to confirm his free Christian status and to forbid anyone, under penalty of five hundred florins, to harass or disturb him in any way. Pasqual Exea, thus, like many liberts, did not feel secure in his freedom. He needed protection—a special court order—affirming his right to do the things that other free men took for granted: be they "to sell and cultivate his own properties" or merely "to come or go, stay or return."[89]

89. Pasqual Exea's request read as follows, "Iatsia per esser xristia e per esser persona liberta no fos tengut de fer e fermar de dret en poder de la senyoria vestra per a maior cautela e per fugir de rigor del senyor del dit loch com tinga de libertat e deia vehinarse desavehinarse del dit loch e fer se vehi de la present ciutat de Valencia e . . . e dubte que volent se desavehinat del dit loch no sien fetes sobres algunes per la dita raho diu que ferma de dret en poder del senyoria vestra e promet fer dret e star a dret. . . . Requirent la senyoria vestra li plasia fer comissio ab lo qual sia manat axi al senyoria del dit loch com als officials de aquell sots pena de cinchcents florins que no'l enugen ni molestar axi en dexar li vendre com coltivar ses heretats anant e venint stant e tornant com axi de justicia proceheixca e ferse dega." ARV G 2427: 475r–476r.

CONCLUSION

A bustling Mediterranean port located near Islamic territories, the city of Valencia boasted a slave population of pronounced religious and ethnic diversity. Although a significant proportion of them were Muslims who had been seized in land raids or sea battles, over the course of the fifteenth century the slaves directly captured in warfare progressively were outnumbered by shiploads of sub-Saharan Africans and Canary Islanders sent by Portuguese and Italian traders based in clearinghouses along the Atlantic coast. Nevertheless, enslaved men and women would continue to be referred to as "captives of good war" (*catius de bona guerra*) well into the sixteenth century. The rhetoric of warfare helped perpetuate an image of slavery as the legitimate consequence of belligerent actions.

Once introduced into the Valencian marketplace, enslaved men, women, and children became commodities to be exchanged: resold, inherited, and/or mortgaged for debts. The conventional wisdom about their fate—that they were set to work in predominantly, if not exclusively, domestic occupations and, for this reason, experienced a less brutal and exploitative form of slavery does not stand up to closer scrutiny.[1] Slaves in fifteenth-century Valencia participated in a broad range of economic activities, with their contributions not limited to domestic service but encompassing agricultural and industrial production as well. Most slaves (both male and female) at one time or another during the year did field work and some slaves seem to have been acquired principally for work on agricultural estates. The enslaved workers employed by artisans, in turn, were engaged, by and large, to perform menial labor—sawing wood or shoveling loaves of bread in and out of hot ovens. For the most part, they did not work as skilled laborers. Whether in the field, workshop, or household, however, enslaved laborers worked alongside free laborers. What distinguished the slave experience was not really the type of work they performed but the circumstances under which they labored. Although all female domestic

---

1. As David Brion Davis has pointed out, "the 'benign' and 'paternalistic' image was also long applied to slavery in Latin America and the American South."

servants (whether free or slave) were vulnerable to sexual violence and exploitation, enslaved women did not possess the same social and legal protections. Nor did enslaved and free male laborers share the same opportunities for advancement.

Similarly, though baptism, naming, and testamentary practices gave substance to the claim that masters and mistresses treated slaves as members of their extended family, we ought to take care not to romanticize their paternalism. Such practices, after all, were no less self-serving than the pronouncements issued by the bailiff general branding them "enemies of the Catholic faith and Crown." They helped to naturalize as well as legitimate their authority. Nevertheless, masters were not all-powerful tyrants with power over every aspect of domestic relations. Consideration of contemporary civil and criminal court records reveals a much more complicated picture, in which courts took seriously the claims of enslaved persons that masters, as heads of households, had certain obligations. In other words, we should not assume a static patriarchy with little room for legal contestation. Slaves could manipulate this paternalistic rhetoric to achieve their own ends. Thus we saw in chapter 4 how the Christian Tartar slave named Miquel attempted to defend himself against charges of brutally murdering his mistress and assaulting his master by suggesting to the Justícia Criminal that his actions were perhaps, to a certain extent, justifiable since his master and mistress had betrayed him when they decided to sell him after his many years of faithful service. Although, in this case, Miquel's protests fell on deaf ears, such arguments were not all that uncommon. Others experienced better results and even managed to win their freedom.

Indeed, the court records analyzed in this book demonstrate conclusively that enslaved persons were keenly aware of the power of law in their lives. Consequently, those seeking to improve their position sought a hearing in Valencia's courts. Acts of resistance, then, not infrequently took place in the courtroom. And, when enslaved men and women hauled their owners into court, this resistance had a very clear "public" and "political" dimension. They challenged their "mastery" as well as their honor. Ultimately, of course, even though enslaved persons had access to the courts, the courts more often than not worked to maintain and reinforce their servile status. Nevertheless, as Ariela Gross has pointed out, the point of calling attention to this form of slave agency is "not so much to paint a picture of glorious resistance and triumphant agency, but to show that even hegemony takes work."[2]

As their *demandes de libertat* demonstrate, enslaved persons of all backgrounds in fifteenth-century Valencia were preoccupied with regaining their freedom. Their prospects for doing so, however, varied according to their gender and their ethnic and religious identities. Though there were multiple paths to freedom, these paths were not

2. Ariela Gross, "Beyond Black and White: Cultural Approaches to Race and Slavery," *Columbia Law Review* 101, no. 3 (April 2001): 655.

equally accessible to all. Not only did they face significant economic challenges with respect to securing a place for themselves and their families in this city but their status and claim to possess the rights of free persons remained open to dispute. Thus we saw in chapters 4 and 7 how Marti Bossa—a freedman who, following the death of his wife (a freedwoman named Lucia), was tossed out of his former mistress's household since he "was old and no longer of any use"—struggled financially, scrounging for work and sustenance in the neighboring towns of Denia and Ruzafa, only to, several years later, be confronted with a mistress who, "suddenly," was denying that he had ever been freed.

Slavery and the Construction of Race

Although I am convinced by Orlando Patterson that much about slavery was and remains universal, I have also been at pains to point out the differential meanings of slavery for the diverse population of men and women who lived as slaves in fifteenth-century Valencian society. Given the significant differences in resources at their disposal, Muslim, "eastern," and black African slaves (and their free coreligionists) dealt with the problem of slavery, both individually and collectively, in divergent ways and with divergent outcomes.

Freed persons of all origins confronted significant challenges when it came to reintegrating themselves socially into "free" society. But, for several different reasons, black slaves seem to have had a harder time than most. Do we see an incipient "racism" developing in late medieval Iberia by the fifteenth century? George Frederickson, David Brion Davis, and James Sweet have all speculated that the roots of modern-day racism may be found in late medieval Iberia.[3] Looking at Italy and Italian colonies, Sally McKee and Steven A. Epstein have also stressed, respectively, the force of "ancestry" and skin color as boundary markers. Their work has significantly complicated the prevailing vision of premodern Mediterranean slavery as a less stigmatizing brand of servitude.[4] Did inherited stereotypes of "blackness" combine with inherited stereotypes about slaves to create a race-based slave system or racialized slavery in fifteenth-century Iberia?

3. See George Frederickson, Race: A Short History (Princeton: Princeton University Press, 2002); James H. Sweet, "The Iberian Roots of American Racist Thought," special issue, "Constructing Race: Differentiating Peoples in the Early Modern World," William and Mary Quarterly 54 (January 1997): 143–66; and David Brion Davis, Challenging the Boundaries of Slavery (Cambridge: Harvard University Press, 2003).

4. Steven A. Epstein, Purity Lost: Transgressing Boundaries in the Eastern Mediterranean, 1000–1400 (Baltimore: Johns Hopkins University Press, 2006), 204; Epstein, Speaking of Slavery: Color, Ethnicity, and Human Bondage in Italy; Sally McKee, "Inherited Status and Slavery in Late Medieval Italy and Venetian Crete," Past & Present 182 (2004): 31–53; and McKee, Uncommon Dominion: Venetian Crete and the Myth of Ethnic Purity (Philadelphia: University of Pennsylvania Press, 2000).

McKee's and Epstein's assertions of a hardening of ethnic distinctions and categories over the course of the thirteenth and fourteenth centuries—particularly in borderlands where "mixing" was more likely to occur—echo the observations of scholars examining Muslim, Christian, and Jewish interaction in Iberia in the wake of the mass baptisms of Muslims and Jews in the fourteenth and fifteenth centuries. Though their focus has been on the status of *conversos* and *moriscos* (as opposed to black African or Greek freedmen), many have likewise emphasized "the increasingly widespread use of ideas about the biological reproduction of some somatic and behavioral traits in order to create legitimate hierarchies and discriminations"—what David Nirenberg has termed "the genealogical turn" in medieval discussions of difference.[5] Such assertions of the utility of "race" as a category of analysis for premodernists merit more serious consideration among historians of slavery in late medieval Iberia.

Although assimilation in fifteenth-century Valencia was first and foremost a question of religion, it bears emphasis that the rate of baptism was not uniform for all slaves. Though enslaved men and women of "pagan" or Eastern Orthodox origins were almost unilaterally baptized and initiated into the Latin rite—be they Greek Orthodox Christians or "pagan" Circassians—we have seen that enslaved Muslims, in contrast, often did not convert to Christianity. This was most likely due to the presence of a sizable free Muslim population that was actively engaged in redeeming their coreligionists. If the Christians purchasing Muslim captives ultimately intended to ransom them to their coreligionists, it simply was not practical for them to convert them to Christianity since, once baptized, their redemption by their former coreligionists became a much thornier proposition. Nonetheless, although the fewer number of baptized Muslim slaves is perhaps more attributable to economic pragmatism than Christian prejudice against *moros*, the subsequent history of Muslims who did convert suggests that, by the end of the fifteenth century, the barriers hindering their social acceptance were more than simply "religious." In late medieval Iberia, at least, identities were no longer so easily shed by embracing new faiths, learning new languages, or accepting new laws.[6]

The introduction into the slave population of an increasing number of black Africans in the latter half of the fifteenth century unquestionably altered the dynamics of slavery

5. David Nirenberg, "Was There Race before Modernity? The Example of 'Jewish' Blood in Late Medieval Spain," in *Origins of Racism in the West*, ed. Ben Issac, Yossi Ziegler, and Miriam Eliav-Feldon (Cambridge University Press, forthcoming).

6. See, for example, Mary Elizabeth Perry, *The Handless Maiden: Moriscos and the Politics of Religion in Early Modern Spain* (Princeton: Princeton University Press, 2005), and Vincent Barletta's recent translation of the Granadan *morisco* Francisco Nuñez Muley's impassioned protest against the Spanish Crown's assimilationist policies: Francisco Nuñez Muley, *A Memorandum for the President of the Audiencia and Chancery Court of the City and Kingdom of Granada*, ed. and trans. Vicent Barletta (Chicago: University of Chicago Press, 2007).

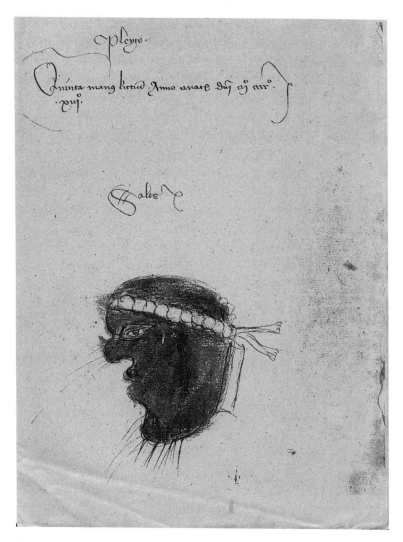

Sketch of the head of a black African man on the frontispiece of a quire (*manus*) in a volume of the records of the Gobernación dating from the fifteenth century (ARV Gobernación 2341: M. 5: fol. 1r).

in the kingdom of Valencia. Although Valencian Christians and Muslims had shared a long history of conflict and interaction, black Africans were relative newcomers. The novelty presented by these sub-Saharan black Africans is evident in even a cursory reading of documents recording their presentation before the bailiff general. While Muslim captives were closely questioned concerning the circumstances of their capture and their testimony carefully transcribed by Crown notaries, the sub-Saharan black African "*moros*," in contrast, were adjudged legitimately enslaveable largely on the basis of their "obvious" infidel-like appearance. Herded like cattle into the courtroom of the bailiff general, they were labeled "barbarous" (*bozal*) explicitly because they spoke languages that their inter-preters did not understand. While Muslim captives arriving in the port of Valencia were presented as feared but respected enemies, these black African *moros* seem to have been regarded as beneath fear and beneath contempt. What impact did such shifts in the com-position of the slave population have on contemporary understandings of slavery as well as perceptions of ethnic differences?

Color Consciousness in Fifteenth-Century Valencian Society

There is ample evidence that fifteenth-century observers increasingly were associating black or dark skin color with slave status. This linkage is evident not only in the rulings issued by the bailiff general adjudging black Africans *catius de bona guerra* on the basis of their obvious "infidel" appearance, but also in complaints filed by black and dark-skinned free persons—like the aforementioned Silvester and Francesquet Carlos, both discussed in chapter 7—that, due to the color of their skin, they were being "mistaken" for slaves and sold into slavery.

Not only were some Valencians automatically attributing slave status to persons of dark skin color, but others attributed to them certain mental deficiencies. In chapter 2, for ex-ample, we discussed how the sellers of a twenty-three-year-old black African slave named Andria argued that a buyer's protests that the slave's "foolishness" rendered him "defec-tive" ought to be rejected out of hand since *all* blacks "are irredeemably vain." Similarly, we observed in Chapter 5 how the fact that some Valencians considered black Africans the most "vile" and "despicable" persons in their society made them ideal candidates for individuals on the lookout for hit men to degrade their enemies. We heard, moreover, in chapter 7, the frustration expressed by the black freedman named Joan Muntanya, who protested that his boss was not only refusing to pay his wages but had also had him ar-rested on trumped-up charges of theft. He noted how he was the ideal scapegoat for this white Christian wishing to deflect responsibility for his crimes.

Silvester's, Francesquet's, Andria's, and Joan's stories, admittedly, are hardly conclu-sive evidence for the existence of "protoracism" in late medieval Iberian society—whereby certain people, purely on the basis of physiological characteristics deemed fixed and im-mutable, were regarded as inferior and hence barred systematically from full participa-tion in the political, religious, and social life of the community. Was skin color, in fact, the most significant factor here? And, more important, how representative were their experiences of contemporary attitudes toward black and dark-skinned people?

Though we noted in chapter 6 how the founding of a black freedman's confra-ternity was prompted by a concern that black Africans "would not be able to survive or sustain their lives" without charitable assistance, judging from extant property transactions people of color do not appear to have been ghettoized in fifteenth-century Valencia. Indeed, we find them buying and selling real estate in parishes and neighborhoods scattered throughout the city and its surrounding countryside. The black free man named Johan Diez, for example—who was employed as a herald (*trompeta*) by the municipality—purchased (in conjunction with his wife) a house near the church of San Juan del Hospital, which was located in the city's center.[7] A black free woman named Anthonia, the widow of Jacme Adria, owned at least two houses located in the parish of San Lorenzo—which José Hinojosa numbers as one of the wealthiest parishes during the Middle Ages. We only learn of this because after she bequeathed the houses to two other free blacks, a dispute arose between them over who had the stronger claim to ownership.[8] Black free men also owned property in the surrounding countryside, property that bordered on land owned by "white" farmers in rural communities such as Almassera, Ruzafa, Tavernes Blanques, and Torrent.[9] There is no indication that the property they owned was "marginal" or any less valuable. Indeed, in several cases the property had previously belonged to the black freedman's former master.

We also encounter black and dark-skinned persons alongside "white" artisans and merchants making purchases in public auctions. Although in some instances, the items they acquired were basic necessities (i.e., a pair of boots for two sous),[10] in other instances they are buying what might be termed luxury items, like the black freedman who spent sixty-three sous for what appears to have been an altar cloth or a coverlet made for a throne.[11]

Though we noted in chapter 3 how certain guild statutes barred "blacks" (as well as freed slaves and *moros*) from admission into their ranks, we also occasionally find in contemporary notarial records references to black freedmen practicing skilled trades. One black freedman (*niger olim servus*) for instance, was described as a wool clothier (*perayre* or *parator pannorum*);[12] Vicent, the son of at least one "black" parent (Beatriu, "*negra*," and her husband, Anthoni Nom de Deu) was described as a jerkin or doublet maker

---

7. It bears noting, however, that Johan needed his fellow (white) *trompeta*, Pere Boynach, to cosign the purchase agreement. ARV P 439 (nonpaginated): 28 January 1471.

8. ARV G 2291: M. 4: 7v; ARV G 2292: M. 14: 31r–33v; 48r–49r. José Hinojosa Montalvo, *Diccionario de historia medieval del Reino de Valencia*, tomo III (Valencia: Biblioteca Valencia, 2002), 345.

9. In 1475, Jaume Batea, *negre* and a *comorant* (resident) of Ruzafa, filed a complaint against Caterina, his former master's widow, demanding payment of the fifteen lliures and one *cafficada* (unit of land measure, equivalent to the amount of land that can be sown with a "calís"—or forty-eight bushels—of grain) of *terra campa* that had been promised him in his master's last will and testament. ARV G 2342: M. 14: 22r. The property bordered land owned by Michel Alba, *negre*. ARV P 1115 (nonpaginated): 11 January 1503. A slave woman named Magdalena filed a *demanda de libertat*, claiming that she was daughter of a free black farmer named Anthoni Martinez, who lived in Torrent. ARV G 2412: 199r; ARV G 2413: 151 r–172r.

10. ARV P 1996: 199r and 207r.

11. ARV P 10252: 21 December 1502.

12. ARV P 1998: 4 April 1478.

(*giponer*).[13] Such references to black free persons in contemporary notarial records, admittedly, are few and far between. Nevertheless, they call into question any easy or "neat" equation between skin color and status in fifteenth-century Valencian society. What we can definitively conclude from these fragmentary bits of evidence is that the position of "black" and "dark-skinned" men and women could vary in fifteenth-century Valencian society. Although many freed blacks encountered considerable difficulties (as evidenced by the charitable activities of the black freedmen's confraternity), some appear to have made the transition from servitude to freedom as successfully as any other freed person. They, too, found work, as well as a spouse, and set up their own household. The last will and testament drawn up by the black freedwoman Johana Gralla in 1475, for example, does not stack up unfavorably with that drawn up in 1477 by a white freedwoman named Rosa. While Rosa appears to have never been married, Johana Gralla married twice. First, she married a black free man named Johan Coll, a cook (*cuyner*), and then she married Johan Fexinet, whose trade and ethnic identity were not specified. Postmanumission, she directed her three executors—a priest, a mason, and a butcher—to set aside "as much money as was necessary" to pay not only for her funeral, anniversary masses, and burial in the cemetery near the Hospitaler convent but also to pay for masses (with candles and customary offerings) at both the local Trinitarian convent and the parish church of San Lorenç, where, presumably, she lived. In addition, Johana left ten lliures to her current husband (plus money to buy him a set of mourning clothes); one hundred sous to a woman named Margalida; two florins and a coffer to Sicilia, a black woman who was in the service of a nun named sister Ballestera; one florin to a choirboy at the parish church of San Lorenç; and, finally, "the tunic and skirt that I wore every day" to a woman named Margalida Canelera. Johana concluded her will by directing that all her remaining property was to be donated to charity—not surprisingly, perhaps, she indicated a preference for redeeming Christians from the captivity of infidels.[14]

Rosa, by contrast, post-manumission, was working as a household domestic for the widow of a local laborer. At the time when she drew up her last will and testament, Rosa did not possess much more than the fifteen lliures in salary that she had earned while in this widow's service. Outside of this salary, Rosa disposed of no more than a bed frame, a mattress, pillows, a comforter, and two coffers, which she bequeathed to the woman who had cared for her during her illness.[15]

13. ARV P 1997: 7 October 1477.

14. ARV P 442 (nonpaginated): 14 April 1475.

15. Thus, the bulk of her estate (ten lliures) went toward covering the costs of her funeral and anniversary masses at the Augustinian convent. Suggestive of a high level of piety, Rosa donated the remaining third of her salary (five lliures) to help pay for an altarpiece depicting the Visitation of the Virgin that her executor commissioned for the same Augustinian convent where she was to be buried. ARV P 1997: 6 December 1477.

Testaments and property transactions, of course, illuminate only part of the picture. The black freed persons who turn up in notarial records are generally the success stories: the fortunate ones who were able to find employment and had the financial wherewithal to buy property and/or draw up a will. We do not typically encounter here the homeless or the unemployed. Social and economic barriers impeding a freed person's full integration are revealed much more starkly in contemporary litigation: the black freedwoman accused of stealing an ankle-length tunic from a priest, the black female prostitute who requested the Justícia Criminal's protection from a squire whom she feared might come after her person or her property, the black freedman who reportedly suffered from pneumonia and died shortly following an attack in which a group of slaves owned by a local espadrille maker threw stones at him.[16] The frequency with which black freed persons appear here are certainly suggestive that people of color confronted distinct challenges in fifteenth-century Valencian society and, if we dig a little deeper, we encounter more telling evidence that some Valencians regarded "blacks" as profoundly different and were uneasy about embracing them as part of their community.

Plaintiffs, defendants, and witnesses in contemporary paternity suits frequently expressed disapproval of sexual relations between "whites" and "blacks." In most of the marriages involving "black" or "dark-skinned" persons I encountered in notarial records, free blacks and mixed-race men and women married other persons of color.[17] Though in several instances the ethnic identity of one spouse was not explicitly indicated, leaving the door open for one or several of these couples to be a "mixed" or "interracial" marriage,[18] discussions in contemporary court records of what modern observers would call "miscegenation" reveal that fifteenth-century Valencians were not only concerned about sexual intercourse between Christians and Muslims and Christians and Jews[19] but also expressed disapproval for (white) women who "had relationships with black slaves, dark-skinned slaves (llors), as well as other slaves."[20]

16. See, respectively, ARV JCrim 22: M. 6 (Clams): (nonpaginated) 2 December 1445; ARV JCrim 23: M. 1 (Clams): (nonpaginated) 27 January 1449; and ARV JCrim 23: M. 2 (Clams): (nonpaginated) 25 April 1449.

17. Caterina, *etiopam de nacione de Guinea* (literally, an Ethiopian from Guinea, or a black woman from Guinea) and the former slave of Damiata, the widow of Guillermus Paella, married Johan, *etiopum*, the *captivum* of the count of Oliva and also formerly the slave of Guillermus Paella. APPV 24956 (nonpaginated): 28 December 1477. Similarly, Ysabel, "llora natural de Areguli," married Pedro, "negre del senyor batle general." ARV P 44 (nonpaginated): 27 September 1501.

18. The aforementioned Johana Gralla, *negra*, described her first husband, Johan Coll, as *negre*, but in the very next sentence her second husband, Johan Fexinet, was conspicuously not so described. ARV P 442 (nonpaginated): 14 April 1475.

19. See David Nirenberg, *Communities of Violence: Persecution of Minorities in the Middle Ages* (Princeton: Princeton University Press, 1996).

20. Here I am quoting from the court case in which Joanot Corrals's paternity was challenged because Joana, Joanot's mother, "tenia amistat ab catius negres lors e altres catius." ARV G 2465: 458r.

A fairly common (though not always successful) tactic used to repudiate slave children claiming "free" paternity was to claim that their mothers were notorious for having sexual relationships with both white and black lovers. In 1462, when Ursola, the daughter of Maria, the aforementioned white Russian slave woman, filed a *demanda de libertat* claiming that her master, Jofré d'Anyo (now deceased), was her biological father, the heirs of Jofré D'Anyo's estate responded by attempting to smear Maria's reputation, charging that Maria had been notorious for having "carnal relations with slaves both white and black."[21] A barber testifying in support of Jofré's heirs cited as "proof" of Maria's depraved character—that she was a "*mala dona*," not a "*bona dona*"—that she was rumored to have "had a sexual relationship with a black man" and had "given birth to a black daughter."[22]

Linking sexual intercourse with black men with sexual promiscuity, the implication here was that color-crossing unions were disreputable, if not unnatural, acts. Indeed, Jofré's heirs insisted that as soon as Jofré discovered that his Russian slave woman had been impregnated by a black man, he became so disgusted with Maria that he wanted to have nothing more to do with her.[23] Charges of such "indiscriminate" sexual coupling, however, not only discredited the women involved, they also (seemingly in contrast with the union of slave women and free men when the parties involved were both "white") had the potential to damage the man's reputation. When the Russian woman named Rosa gave birth to a dark-skinned daughter named Margalida, the rumored daughter of a black slave named Diego,[24] her other lover, a white squire named Angelo de Capoa (the rumored father of Rosa's "white" son Julia),[25] reportedly became so enraged at this black male slave's offense to his honor that Rosa's master was obliged to resell Diego in order to avoid bloodshed in his household.[26] Although it is likely that Angelo would have felt dishonored no matter what color his rival's skin was, color-crossing seems to have been an exacerbating factor.

Intercourse between slaves and free persons had always been a potential source of dishonor. We noted in chapter 5 how even when they were only informally acknowledging these children as their own in the presence of friends and confidantes, masters felt compelled to provide some sort of explanation. Nevertheless, though there had always been a slight stigma attached to having sex with slaves of any ethnic origin (falling prey to a slave

21. Maria allegedly "se jahia carnalment ab catius axi blanchs com negres." ARV G 2304.

22. ARV G 2304: M. 3: 45r.

23. ARV G 2304: M. 3: 45r.

24. According to Rosa's testimony, however, she was the daughter of a free dark-skinned hosier named Pere.

25. Though Rosa, of course, insisted that Julia's biological father was her master, Arnau Castello.

26. ARV G 2305: M. 11: 8r–23v; M. 20: 13r–21v; ARV G 2306: M. 25: 16r–17v; M. 26: 36r–37v; 42r–43v; M. 29: 19r–v.

woman's charms, after all, did suggest a certain lack of mastery), the evidence presented above seems to suggest that, as the complexion of Valencia's slave population changed, the taboo against sex between slaves and free persons was expressed progressively in more "black and white" terms.

Although the above discussion has offered some suggestive evidence for the development of racialized ideas in connection with slavery, it still seems misleading to label what we see here in fifteenth-century Valencia as "racism" or even "protoracism." As George Frederickson has argued, racism involves "more than theorizing about human differences or thinking badly of a group." It is an ideology that "either directly sustains or proposes to establish a racial order, a permanent group hierarchy that is believed to reflect the laws of nature or the decrees of God," even though this ideology does not necessarily have to have "the full and explicit support of the state and the law."[27] Although we certainly see racially inspired stereotyping taking place in fifteenth-century Valencia, "racist practices"—that is, habits of thought that treat as inalterable and hence hereditary certain characteristics of particular types of slaves—do not seem to have been implemented here in a consistent or comprehensive fashion. To be sure, Valencia was hardly a tolerant paradise for religious and ethnic minorities. Nevertheless, though the boundaries between slave and free in the premodern Mediterranean world were clearly not as fluid as previous generations of scholars wished to believe, this was not the racialized slavery that subsequently developed in the Spanish colonies in the Americas and in the Atlantic World.

27. Frederickson, *Race*, 43.

Appendix Demandes de Libertat Filed before the Court of the Gobernación in the City of Valencia between 1425 and 1520

Total Sample Size: 94

35 filed by male plaintiffs

59 filed by female plaintiffs: 1 filed jointly with daughter; 2 filed jointly with son; 1 filed jointly with sister

Outcome

Successful: 39 (though 8 of which had a pending appeal)

Arbitrated Agreement: 3

Withdrawn: 3

Dismissed: 2

Unsuccessful: 7

Incomplete: 40

Grounds: Wrongful Enslavement (38 total)

I. Unlawful seizure: 18 total (9 successful, 1 unsuccessful, 7 incomplete, 1 withdrawn)
   - 11 male (4 successful, 6 incomplete, 1 withdrawn)
   - 7 female (5 successful, 1 unsuccessful, 1 incomplete)

II. Born free: 16 total (9 successful, 1 unsuccessful, 6 incomplete)
   - Free father: 5 male (4 successful, 1 incomplete); 9 female (3 successful, 1 unsuccessful, 5 incomplete)
   - Free mother: 1 male (successful); 1 female (successful)

III. Already freed: 4 total (2 successful, 2 incomplete)
   - 3 male (2 successful, 1 incomplete)
   - 1 female (incomplete)

Grounds: Entitled to Freed Status (48 total)

I. Fulfilled terms of contract of manumission: 18 total (8 successful, 2 arbitrated, 1 unsuccessful, 1 dismissed, 6 incomplete)

- 8 male (2 successful, 1 arbitrated, 1 unsuccessful, 1 dismissed, 3 incomplete)
- 10 female (6 successful, 1 arbitrated, 3 incomplete)

II. Verbal promise: 11 total (5 successful, 1 unsuccessful, 5 incomplete)
- 5 male (2 successful, 1 unsuccessful, 2 incomplete)
- 6 female (3 successful, 3 incomplete)

III. Bore master's child: 17 total (all female)
- 6 successful
- 1 arbitrated
- 1 withdrawn
- 3 unsuccessful
- 6 incomplete

IV. Forcibly prostituted: 2 total (both female, both incomplete)

Grounds: Unspecified—8 Total (1 Withdrawn, 1 Dismissed, 6 Incomplete)

- 2 male
- 6 female

Bibliography

Primary Sources

Archival Sources

Arxiu del Regne de València (ARV):

Bailía

Presentaciones e Confessiones de Cautivos: 193 (1419–34), 194 (1494–97), 195 (1502–3)
Contratos: 217–18 (1479–84, 1484–86)
Letra P: 43 (1466), 46 (1470), 72 (1482), 85 (1481)
Lletres y Privilegis: II (1407), IV (1434)
Pleitos: 1430–31 (1416–17, 1491–94)

Gobernación

Criminum: 4261, 4384, 4287, 4288 (1472–73, 1479–80)
Litium (149 volumes, dating 1425–1520): 2235, 2266, 2267, 2268, 2272, 2278–81, 4580–3,
  2283–2297, 4846–50, 2299–2300, 2302, 2304–6, 2308–11, 2314–2327, 2330–44,
  2346–52, 4854–5, 2354–8, 2362, 2371–2, 2374, 2376, 2378–80, 2382–7, 2390, 2392–
  2401, 2403, 2405–6, 2409–13, 2416–7, 2419–24, 2426–36, 2439–41, 2445, 2455, 2458,
  2460, 2464, 2467–9.

Justícia Criminal

Clams, Cedules, y Lletres: 20 (1435), 21 (1440), 22 (1445), 23 (1449), 102 (1452), 24 (1456),
  36 (1464), 103 (1478–9), 25 (1487)
Denunciaciones: 44 (1378), 50 (1400), 97 (1440), 104 (1441), 52 (1454), 53 (1456), 54
  (1459), 55 (1476), 103 (1479), 25 (1487)
Processos: 97 (1440)
Registres: 86 (1440), 87 (1442), 88 (1442), 89 (1442).

Justícia Civil

Requests (31 volumes, dating 1440–1500): 895–97 (1440), 903–4 (1443), 907 (1445), 912–936 (1447–48, 1450, 1452–53, 1456, 1459, 1461, 1469–74, 1477–78, 1482, 1487–88, 1491, 1500–1501).

Justícia De 300 Sueldos

1091–93 (1473, 1478, 1480)

Mestre Racional

87 (1477)

Protocolos (136 volumes from 55 different notaries)

Garcia de Artes 4406, 9950, 9952
Andreu Artigues 9954
Pedro Avella 9956
Pau Agustin Beses 9986
Juan de Campos Sr. 437
Juan de Campos Jr. 436, 438, 2529, 439, 2785, 440, 442, 443, 444, 445, 446, 447
Berenguer Cardona 502
Jaume Carnicer 10035
Galceran de Castellar 511
Domingo Català 519
Onofre Cobrena 588
Juan Comes 593
Martin Doto 795
Bertomeu Escriva 814, 816, 817, 818
Luis Espinal 3096
Nicolau Esteban 4302
Jaime Estevan 2847
Nicolau Esteve 822, 2863, 823
Juan Fenollar 3205, 3105, 3110
Joan Forner 949
Domingo Garcia 1086, 1087, 1088
Joan Garcia 1099
Mateo Gil 1116, 1123, 1124
Bernat Julia 1253
Andres Julian 1271
Bartholome de la Mata 1392
Joan Mora 1565

Juan Nadal 4305

Nicolas Oller 3021

Miquel Ortigues 3162, 10440, 10251, 2752, 10252

Francisco Perez 2663

Miquel Perez 10266

Guillem Peris 1795

Pere Perpinya 3126, 10270

Jaume Piles 1823, 2667, 2668, 2895, 1825, 2669, 2670, 2966

Jaime Pinosa 1838

Francisco Pintor 1844, 1845, 1846

Jaime Prats 1854, 1855

Joan Gil de Puigmicha 1108, 1109, 1110, 1111, 1112, 4267, 1113, 1115

Miquel Puigmicha Jr. 1911, 1912, 1913, 1914, 1915, 1916, 1918

Benito Salvador 10310

Jaume Salvador 1994, 1995, 1996, 1997, 1998, 1999, 2005, 2006, 2007, 2008, 2020, 2022

Ausias Sans 2063, 2067, 2068, 2078, 2079

Bernat Sans 2092

Francisco Soler 2163, 2164, 2165, 2770, 2771

Pere Sorell 2182

Jaume Tolosa 3183, 3184, 2240, 2241

Joan Tortosa 2463, 2464

Guillem Tovia 4301, 10443

Miquel Villafarta 2379, 2380

Ramon Vives (Vines) 2396, 2398, 2399

Pedro Juan Zabrugada 4140

Vicente Zaera 4391

Miquel Zavila 2440, 3187

Desconocido 11260, 11274

Archivo de Protocolos de Patriarca de Valencia (APPV): (100 volumes from 83 different notaries)

Jaume Albert 10205, 11245, 11248, 11249, 11253

Joan Aldabert 11440

Miquel Aliaga 022580

Jeroni Amalrich 25534

Vicent Ambros Artes 20066

Joan de Aragó (Joan d'Aragó) 18424

Joan Argent 25214, 25217, 25218, 25219, 25226

Gabriel Lluis Arinyo 816

Alfons de Ayerve (d'Ayerve) 20515, 20496

Pere Badia 13660

Genis Barrot 10795

Joan de Bas 752, 10927, 10928

Bertomeu Batalla 11436

Jaume Bataller 19195

Joan Beneyto (Jr.) 26957

Joan Beneyto (Sr.) 26958

Jaume Blasco 24981, 24983

Bertomeu Bodi 14399, 14400

Pere Bonanat 16894

Onofre Buera 25367

Martí Cabanes 20972

Bertomeu Cabater 26579

Joan Calaforra 13415

Pere de Campos 20903, 20919

Joan de Carci (Calci) 21593, 21594

Francesc Cardona 6486

Joan Carnicer 27255

Bertomeu de Carries 20425

Joan Casanova 6161

Galceran Castellar 23289

Andreu Cirera 20619

Joan Comaleres 24025

Joan Comes 22731

Bernat Dassio 26815

Francesc Dezpi 2162

Luis Erau 28885

Miquel Eroles 09653, 9636

Miquel de Esparca 11380

Guillem Exernit 23000

Jaume Ferrando 18557

Bernat Ferrer 21819

Esteve Font 12500

Pere Fortuny 22391

Luis Gacet 23042

Galceran Gamiça 24558

Joan Gamiça 21514

Luis Gil 25777

Jaume Gisquerol 19042
Pere Gisquerol 19071
Joan Jorba 26850
Antoni Julia 15927
Bernat Julia 15939
Bertomeu de Losques 21200
Joan Marroma 26182
Antoni Martí 2399
Gaspar Martí 19281
Guillem Matali 24076
Francesc Menor 26629
Joan de Molina 22059
Pere Monsoriu 9614
Joan Navarro 21498
Luis Orti 18792
Pere Palomar 26674
Vicent Pedro 25225
Francesc Perez 25101
Joan Perez 23406
Miquel Perez 499
Jaume Piles 24316
Francesc Pintor 22546, 22551
Joan Pla 15546
Pere Ros 26926
Jordi del Royo 26288
Joan Sabater 23228
Benet Sant 24369
Antoni Sendra 24956
Jeroni Tovia 25003
Lluis Tovia 20161
Garcia Uguart 20123
Jaume Valero 28485
Joan Verdancha 24143
Pere Vilaspinosa 1670
Joan Vives 22772
Mateu Yviça 23837

Archivo Municipal de Valencia (AMV):
Manuals de Consell: A–17, A–18, A–38, A–41

Published Sources

Aureum Opus Regalium Privilegiorum Civitatis et Regni Valentie. Valencia, 1515. Luis Alanya, ed. In Textos Medievales, 33. Valencia, 1972.

Eiximenis, Francesc. Regiment de la cosa pública. Barcelona: Editorial Barcino, 1927.

Furs de València. Edited by Germà Colon and Arcadi Garcia. 9 vols. Barcelona: Editorial Barcino, 1970–2000.

Lopez, Robert S., Irving Raymond, and O. R. Constable. Medieval Trade in the Mediterranean World: Illustrative Documents. New York: Columbia University Press, 2001.

Miralles, Melchior. Dietari del Capella d'Alfons el Magnanim. Edited by Vicent-Josep Escarti. Valencia: Editions Alfons el Magnanim, 1988.

Münzer, Jerónimo. Viaje por España y Portugal (1494–1495). Edited by Christoph Weiditz. Madrid: Polifemo, 2002.

Nuñez Muley, Francisco. A Memorandum for the President of the Audiencia and Chancery Court of the City and Kingdom of Granada. Edited and translated by Vincent Barletta. Chicago: University of Chicago Press, 2007.

Rubio Vela, Augustín. Epistolari de la València Medieval. Valencia: Institut de Filologia Valenciana, 1985.

———. Epistolari de la València Medieval II. Valencia/Barcelona: Institut Interuniversitari de Filologia Valenciana, 1985.

Zurara, Gomes Eanes de. In The Chronicle of the Discovery and Conquest of Guinea (Works of the Hakluyt Society), edited by Charles Raymond and Edgar Prestige Beazley. New York: Burt Franklin, 1963.

Secondary Sources

Anaya Hernández, Luis Alberto. Judeoconversos e Inquisición en las Islas Canarias (1402–1605). Las Palmas de Gran Canaria: Ediciones del Cabildo Insular de Gran Canaria, 1996.

Arandel Doncel, Juan. "Los esclavos de Jaén durante el último tercio del siglo." Homenaje a Antonio Domínguez Ortiz. Madrid: Ministerio de Educación general de enseñazas medias, 1981.

Austen, Ralph A. "The Mediterranean Islamic Slave Trade out of Africa: A Tentative Survey." Slavery and Abolition 13, no. 1 (1992): 214–18.

Balard, Michel. "Remarques sur les esclaves à Gênes dans la seconde moitié du XIIIe siècle." Mélanges d'archéologie et d'histoire publiés par l'École française de Rome (1986): 627–80.

Baptist, Edward E. " 'Cuffy,' 'Fancy Maids,' and One-Eyed Men': Rape, Commodification, and the Domestic Slave Trade in the United States." American Historical Review 106, no. 5 (December 2001): 1619–50.

Bartlett, Robert. The Making of Europe: Conquest, Colonization, and Cultural Change, 950–1350. Princeton: Princeton University Press, 1993.

———. "Medieval and Modern Concepts of Race and Ethnicity." *Journal of Medieval and Early Modern Studies* 31, no. 1 (Winter 2001): 39–56.

Behar, Ruth. "Sexual Witchcraft, Colonialism, and Women's Powers: Views from the Mexican Inquisition." In *Sexuality and Marriage in Colonial Latin America*, edited by Asunción Lavin, 178–206. Lincoln: University of Nebraska Press, 1989.

Belenguer Cebrià, Ernest. *València en la crisi del segle XV*. Barcelona: Edicions 62, 1976.

Bénesse, D. "Les esclaves dans la société ibérique aux XIVe et XVe siècles." University of Paris X, 1970.

Benítez Bolorinos, Manuel. *Las cofradías medievales en el reino de Valencia (1329–1458)*. Alicante: Universidad de Alicante, 1998.

Bensch, Stephen. "From Prizes of War to Domestic Merchandise: The Changing Face of Slavery in Catalonia and Aragon, 1000–1300." *Viator* 25 (1994): 63–93.

Bisson, T. N. *The Medieval Crown of Aragon: A Short History*. Oxford: Oxford University Press, 1986.

Bloch, Marc. "How and Why Ancient Slavery Came to an End." In *Slavery and Serfdom in the Middle Ages: Selected Essays*, 1–31. Berkeley: University of California Press, 1975.

Blumenthal, Debra. "La casa dels negres: Black African Solidarity in Late Medieval Valencia." In *Black Africans in Renaissance Europe*, edited by K. Lowe and T. F. Earle, 225–46. Cambridge: Cambridge University Press, 2005.

Bonnassie, Pierre. *From Slavery to Feudalism in South-Western Europe*. Translated by Jean Birrell. Cambridge: Cambridge University Press, 1991.

———. *La organización del trabajo en Barcelona a fines de siglo XV*. Barcelona: Consejo Superior de Investigacions Científicas, 1975.

Braude, Benjamin. "Ham and Noah: Sexuality, Servitudinism, and Ethnicity." In *Proceedings of the Fifth Annual Gilder Lehrman Center International Conference*. Yale University, 2003.

———. "The Sons of Noah and the Construction of Ethnic and Geographical Identities in the Medieval and Early Modern Periods." *William and Mary Quarterly* 54 (1997): 103–42.

Braudel, Fernand. *The Mediterranean and the Mediterranean World in the Age of Philip II*. New York: Harper and Row, 1973.

Bresc, Henri. *Un monde méditerranéen: Économie et société en Sicile, 1300–1450*. 2 vols. Palermo-Roma: Bibliothèque des Écoles Françaises d'Athènes et de Rome, 1986.

Brodman, James William. *Ransoming Captives in Crusader Spain: The Order of Merced on the Christian-Islamic Frontier*. Philadelphia: University of Pennsylvania Press, 1986.

Bugner, Ladislas, ed. *The Image of the Black in Western Art*. 4 vols. Cambridge: Harvard University Press, 1983–89.

Burns, Robert I. "Piracy as Islamic-Christian Interface in the Thirteenth Century." *Viator* 11 (1980): 165–78.

Cabrera, E. "Cautivos Cristianos en el reino de Granada durante la segunda mitad del siglo XV." In *Relaciones exteriores del reino de Granada*, edited by C. Segura Graino. Almería: Instituto de Estudios Almerienses, 1988.

Cariñera i Balaguer, Rafael, and Andrés Díaz i Borrás. "Corsaris valencians i esclaus barbarescs a les darreries dels segle XIV: Una subhasta d'esclaus a València en 1385." *Estudis Castellonencs* 2 (1984–85): 439–56.

Carrerres i de Calatayud, F. "El Procurador dels Miserables: Notes per a la seua històrica." *Anales del Centro de Cultura Valenciana* (1931): 41–53.

Cohen, Jeffrey Jerome. "On Saracen Enjoyment: Some Fantasies of Race in Late Medieval France and England." *Journal of Medieval and Early Modern Studies* 31, no. 1 (2001): 113–46.

Constable, Olivia Remie. "Muslim Slavery and Mediterranean Slavery: The Medieval Slave Trade as an Aspect of Muslim-Christian Relations." In *Christendom and Its Discontents*, edited by S. L. Waugh and P. Diehl, 264–84. Cambridge: Cambridge University Press, 1996.

——. *Housing the Stranger in the Mediterranean World: Lodging, Trade, and Travel in Late Antiquity and the Middle Ages*. Cambridge: Cambridge University Press, 2003.

Cortés Alonso, Vicenta. "La conquista de las Islas Canarias a traves de las ventas de esclavos en Valencia." *Anuario de Estudios Atlanticos* 1 (1955): 479–547.

——. *La esclavitud en Valencia durante el reinado de los reyes Católicos (1479–1516)*. Valencia: Ayuntamiento de Valencia, 1964.

——. "La trata de esclavos durante los primeros descubrimientos (1489–1516)." *Anuario de Estudios Atlanticos* 9 (1963): 23–46.

——. "Los pasajes de esclavos en Valencia en tiempo de Alfonso V." *Anuario de Estudios Medievales* 10 (1980): 791–819.

Cortés López, J. L. *La esclavitud negra en la España peninsular del siglo XVI*. Salamanca: Ediciones Universidad de Salamanca, 1989.

Davis, David Brion. *Challenging the Boundaries of Slavery*. Cambridge: Harvard University Press, 2003.

——. *In the Image of God: Religion, Moral Values, and Our Heritage of Slavery*. New Haven: Yale University Press, 2001.

——. *The Problem of Slavery in Western Culture*. Ithaca: Cornell University Press, 1966.

Davis, John. *People of the Mediterranean*. London: Routledge, 1977.

Davis, Robert C. *Christian Slaves, Muslim Masters: White Slavery in the Mediterranean, the Barbary Coast and Italy, 1500–1800*. London: Palgrave Macmillan, 2003.

Díaz Borrás, Andrés. *Los orígenes de la piratería islámica en Valencia: La ofensiva musulmana trecentista y la reacción cristiana*. Barcelona: Consejo Superior de Investigacions Científicas, Institucion Milà y Fontanals, 1993.

——. *El miedo al Mediterraneo: La caridad popular Valenciana y la redención de cautivos bajo poder musulmán, 1323–1539*. Barcelona: Consejo Superior de Investigacions Científicas, 2001.

Diccionari català-valencià-balear, inventari lexicogràfic i etimològic de la llengua catalana. Edited by Antoni M. Alcover, Francesc de B. Moll, Manuel de Sanchis Guarner, and Anna Moll Marquès. Palma de Mallorca: Editorial Moll, 1964.

Dockès, Pierre. *Medieval Slavery and Liberation.* Translated by Arthur Goldhammer. Chicago: University of Chicago Press, 1982.

Douglas, Mary. *Natural Symbols: Explorations in Cosmology.* New York: Pantheon Books, 1970.

———. *Purity and Danger: An Analysis of the Concepts of Pollution and Taboo.* London: Routledge and Kegan Paul, 1966.

Dufourcq, Charles-Emmanuel. *L'Espagne Catalane et le Maghrib au XIIe et XIV siècles.* Paris: Presses Universitaires de France, 1944.

Epstein, Steven A. *Purity Lost: Transgressing Boundaries in the Eastern Mediterranean, 1000–1400.* Baltimore: Johns Hopkins University Press, 2006.

———. *Speaking of Slavery: Color, Ethnicity, and Human Bondage in Italy.* Ithaca: Cornell University Press, 2001.

Evans, Daniel. "Slave Coast of Europe." *Slavery and Abolition* 6, no. 1 (1985): 41–58.

Evans, William McKee. "From the Land of Canaan to the Land of Guinea." *American Historical Review* 85 (1980): 15–43.

Ferrer i Mallol, Maria Teresa. *La frontera amb l'Islam en el segle XIV: Cristians i sarraïns al País Valencia.* Barcelona: Consell Superior d'Investigacions Científiques, 1988.

———. "Els redemptors de captius: Mostolafs, eixees, o alfaquecs (segles XII–XIII)." *Medievalia* 9 (1990): 85–106.

———. *Els sarraïns de la Corona catalano-aragonesa en el segle XIV: Segregació i discriminació.* Barcelona: Consell Superior d'Investigacions Científiques, 1988.

Ferrer i Mallol, Maria Teresa, and Josefina Mutgé i Vives, eds. *De l'esclavitud a la llibertat: Esclaus i lliberts a l'edat mitjana (Actes del Colloqui Internacional celebrats a Barcelona del 27 al 29 de maig de 1999).* Barcelona: Consell Superior d'Investigacions Científiques, Institució Milà i Fontanals, 2000.

Fildes, Valerie. *Breasts, Bottles, and Babies: A History of Infant Feeding.* Edinburgh: Edinburgh University Press, 1986.

———. *Wet Nursing from Antiquity to the Present.* Oxford: Basil Blackwell, 1988.

Fox-Genovese, Elizabeth. *Within the Plantation Household: Black and White Women of the Old South.* Chapel Hill: University of North Carolina Press, 1988.

Franco Silva, Alfonso. *Esclavitud en Andalucía 1450–1550.* Granada: Universidad de Granada, 1992.

Frederickson, George. *Race: A Short History.* Princeton: Princeton University Press, 2002.

Freedman, Paul. *Images of the Medieval Peasant.* Stanford: Stanford University Press, 1999.

———. *The Origins of Peasant Servitude in Medieval Catalonia.* Cambridge: Cambridge University Press, 1991.

Freedman, Paul, and Monique Bourin, eds. *Forms of Servitude in Northern and Central Europe: Decline, Resistance and Expansion*. Turnhout, Belgium: Brepols, 2006.

Friedman, Ellen G. *Spanish Captives in North Africa in the Early Modern Age*. Madison: University of Wisconsin Press, 1983.

Friedman, Yvonne. *Encounters between Enemies: Captivity and Ransom in the Latin Kingdom of Jerusalem*. Leiden: Brill, 2002.

García Herrero, María del Carmen. *Las mujeres en Zaragoza en el siglo XV*. 2 vols. Zaragoza: Ayuntamiento de Zaragoza, 1990.

García Marsilla, Juan Vicente. *La jerarquía de la mesa: Los sistemas alimentarios en la Valencia bajomedieval*. Valencia: Historía Local/13 Diputació de Valencia, 1993.

Garcia-Oliver, Ferran. *La vall de les sis mesquites: El treball i la vida a la Valldigna medieval*. Valencia: Universitat de València, 2003.

Gaspar, David Barry, and Darlene Clark Hine, eds. *More Than Chattel: Black Women and Slavery in the Americas*. Bloomington: Indiana University Press, 1996.

Gilmore, David D. "Honor, Honesty, Shame: Male Status in Contemporary Andalusia." In *Honor and Shame and the Unity of the Mediterranean*, edited by D. Gilmore, 90–103. Washington, D.C.: American Anthropological Association, 1987.

——. "The Shame of Dishonor." In *Honor and Shame and the Unity of the Mediterranean*, edited by D. Gilmore, 1–11. Washington D.C.: American Anthropological Association, 1987.

Gioffré, Domenico. *Il mercato degli schiavi a Genova nel secolo XV*. Genoa: Fratelli Bozzi, 1971.

Giordano, Christian. "Mediterranean Honour Reconsidered: Anthropological Fiction or Actual Action Strategy?" *Anthropological Journal on European Cultures* 10, no. 1 (2001): 39–58.

——. "Mediterranean Honor and Beyond: The Social Management of Reputation in the Public Sphere." *Sociologija: Mintis ir veikmas* 1 (2005): 44–45.

Goldenberg, David M. *The Curse of Ham: Race and Slavery in Early Judaism, Christianity, and Islam*. Princeton: Princeton University Press, 2003.

Graullera Sanz, Vicente. *La esclavitud en Valencia en los siglos XVI y XVII*. Valencia: Instituto Valenciano de Estudios Históricos, Institución Alfonso el Magnànimo, Diputación Provincial de Valencia, Consejo Superior de Investigaciones Científicas, 1978.

Greenberg, Kenneth S. *Honor and Slavery: Lies, Duels, Noses, Masks, Dressing as a Woman, Gifts, Strangers, Death, Humanitarianism, Slave Rebellions, the Pro-Slavery Argument, Baseball, Hunting, and Gambling in the Old South*. Princeton: Princeton University Press, 1996.

Gross, Ariela. *Double Character: Slavery and Mastery in the Antebellum Southern Courtroom*. Princeton: Princeton University Press, 2000.

——. "Beyond Black and White: Cultural Approaches to Race and Slavery." *Columbia Law Review* 101, no. 3 (April 2001): 640–90.

——. "Pandora's Box: Slave Character on Trial in the Antebellum Deep South." *Yale Journal of Law & the Humanities* 7, no. 2 (1995): 267–316.

Gual Camarena, Miguel. "Un seguro contra crimenes de esclavos en el siglo XV." *Anuario de Historia del Derecho Español* 23 (1953).

———. "Una confradia de negros libertos en el siglo XV." *Estudios de Edad Media de la Corona de Aragon* 5 (1952): 457–66.

Guarducci, Piero, and Valeria Ottanelli. *I servitori domestici della casa borghese toscana nel basso Medioevo.* Florence: Libreria editrice Salimbeni, 1982.

Guillot Aliaga, Dolores. *El regimen económico del matrimonial en la Valencia foral.* Valencia: Biblioteca Valenciana, 2002.

Guiral-Hadziiossif, Jacqueline. "Course et piraterie à Valence de 1410 à 1430." *Anuario de Estudios Medievales* 10 (1980): 759–65.

———. *Valencia, puerto mediterráneo en el siglo xv (1410–1525).* Valencia: Edicions Alfons el Magnànim, 1989.

Hahn, Thomas. "The Difference the Middle Ages Makes: Color and Race before the Modern World." *Journal of Medieval and Early Modern Studies* 31, no. 1 (2001): 1–37.

Hair, P. E. H. "Black African Slaves at Valencia, 1482–1516: An Onomastic Inquiry." *History in Africa: A Journal of Method* 7 (1980): 119–31.

Hamilton, Earl J. *Money, Prices, and Wages in Valencia, Aragon, and Navarre, 1351–1500.* Cambridge: Harvard University Press, 1936.

Hammer, Carl I. *A Large-Scale Slave Society of the Early Middle Ages: Slaves and Their Families in Early Medieval Bavaria.* Burlington, Vt.: Ashgate, 2002.

Heers, Jacques. *Esclaves et domestiques au Moyen Age dans le monde méditerranéen.* Paris: Librairie Arthème Fayard, 1981.

———. *Esclavos y sirvientes en las sociedades mediterráneas durante la Edad Media.* Valencia: Edicions Alfons el Magnànim Institució Valenciana d'Estudis i Investigació, 1989.

———. *Family Clans in the Middle Ages: A Study of Political and Social Structures in Urban Areas.* Amsterdam: North-Holland Publishing, 1977.

———. *Les négriers en terres d'islam: La première traite des Noirs VIIe–XVIe siècle.* Paris: Editions Perrin, 2003.

Herlihy, David. *Medieval Households.* Cambridge: Harvard University Press, 1985.

Hernando, Josep. *Els esclaus islàmics a Barcelona: Blancs, negres, llors i turcs: De l'esclavitut a la llibertat (s. xiv).* Barcelona: Consell Superior D'Investigacions Científiques, 2003.

Herzfeld, Michael. "The Horns of the Mediterraneanist Dilemma." *American Ethnologist* 11, no. 3 (1984): 439–54.

Hillgarth, J. N. "A Greek Slave in Majorca, 1419–26: New Documents." *Mediaeval Studies* 50 (1988): 546–58.

———. *The Spanish Kingdoms, 1215–1516.* 2 vols. Oxford: Clarendon Press, 1976–78.

Hinojosa Montalvo, José. "La esclavitud en Alicante a fines de la Edad Media." In *Les sociétés urbaines en France meridionale et en péninsule ibérique au Moyen Age: Actes du colloque de Pau, 21–23 septembre 1988.* Paris: Éditions du CNRS, 1991.

——. "Piratas y corsarios en la Valencia de principos del siglo XV (1400–1499)." *Cuadernos de Historia* 5 (1975): 100–114.

——. "Tácticas de apresamientos de cautivos y su distribución en el mercado valenciano (1410–1434)." *Qüestions Valencianes* 1 (1979): 5–45.

Hunwick, John. "Arab Views of Black Africans and Slavery." In *Proceedings of the Fifth Annual Gilder Lehrman Center International Conference.* Yale University, 2003.

——. "Black Slaves in the Mediterranean World: Introduction to a Neglected Aspect of the African Diaspora." *Slavery and Abolition* 13, no. 1 (1992): 5–38.

Iradiel Murugarren, Francisco Paulino. "Familia y función de la mujer en actividades económicas no agraria." In *La condición de la mujer en la edad media: Actas del coloquio celebrado en la Casa de Velázquez del 5 al 7 de noviembre de 1984,* edited by Yves-Ree Fonquerne and Alfonso Esteban. Madrid: Casa de Velázquez, Universidad Complutense, 1986.

Jiménez González, M. "Esclavos andaluces en el reino de Granada." In *Actas del III Colloquio de Historia Medieval Andaluza: La sociedad medieval andaluza: Grupos no privilegiados.* Jaén: Diputación Provincial de Jaén, 1984.

Johnson, Lyman L., and Sonya Lipsett-Rivera, eds. *The Faces of Honor: Sex, Shame, and Violence in Colonial Latin America.* Albuquerque: University of New Mexico Press, 1998.

Johnson, Walter. "On Agency." *Journal of Social History* (Fall 2003): 113–24.

——. *Soul by Soul: Life Inside the Antebellum Slave Market.* Cambridge: Harvard University Press, 1999.

Jordan, William Chester. "Why Race." *Journal of Medieval and Early Modern Studies* 31, no. 1 (2001): 165–73.

Jordan, Winthrop. *White over Black: American Attitudes toward the Negro, 1550–1812.* Chapel Hill: University of North Carolina Press, 1968.

Juan, Rafael. "Confradía de libertos en Mallorca." *Boletin de la Sociedad Arqueológica Lulliana* 34 (1973): 568–84.

Karras, Ruth. *Slavery and Society in Medieval Scandinavia.* New Haven: Yale University Press, 1988.

——. *Common Women: Prostitution and Sexuality in Medieval England.* Oxford: Oxford University Press, 1998.

Kedar, Benjamin. *Crusade and Mission: European Approaches to Muslims.* Princeton: Princeton University Press, 1984.

Klapisch-Zuber, Christiane. "Women Servants in Florence during the Fourteenth and Fifteenth Centuries." In *Women and Work in Preindustrial Europe,* edited by Barbara A. Hanawalt, 61–68. Bloomington: Indiana University Press, 1986.

Ladero Quesada, M. A. "La esclavitud por guerra a fines del siglo XV: El caso de Málaga." *Hispania* 27 (1967): 63–88.

Lewis, Bernard. *Race and Slavery in the Middle East.* New York: Oxford University Press, 1990.

Livi, Ridolfo. *La schiavitù domestica nei temps di mezzo e nei moderni: Richerche storiche di un antropologo*. Padova: CEDAM, 1928.

Lobo Cabrera, Manuel. *La esclavitud en las Canarias orientales en el siglo XVI: Negros, moros y moriscos*. Las Palmas: Cabildo Insular de Gran Canaria, 1982.

Lop, Miguel. *Un aspecto económico de la Valencia del siglo XVI: Los salarios*. Valencia: Ayuntamiento de Valencia, 1972.

López Beltrán, María Teresa. "La accesibilidad de la mujer al mundo laboral: El servicio domestico en Málaga a finales de la edad media." In *Estudios historicos y literarios sobre la mujer medieval*. Málaga: Diputación Provincial de Málaga, 1990.

López Elum, Pedro. "Apresamiento y venda de moros cautivos en 1441 por 'acaptar' sin licencia." *Al-Andalus* (1969): 329–56.

López Pérez, María Dolores. *La Corona d'Aragón y el Magreb en el siglo XIV (1331–1410)*. Barcelona: Consejo Superior de Investigacions Científicas, Institución Milà y Fontanals, 1995.

Lourie, Elena. "Anatomy of Ambivalence: Muslims under the Crown of Aragon in the Late Thirteenth Century." In *Crusade and Colonization: Muslims, Christians, and Jews in Medieval Aragon*. Aldershot: Variorum, 1990.

Marmon, Shaun. "Islamic Concubinage." In *Dictionary of the Middle Ages*, 527–29. New York: Charles Scribner's Sons, 1982.

Martín Casares, Aurelia. *La esclavitud en Granada del siglo XVI: Género, raza, y religión*. Granada: Universidad de Granada y Diputación Provincial de Granada, 2000.

Marzal Palacios, Francisco Javier. "Una presencia constante: Los esclavos sarracenos en el Occidente Mediterráneo bajomedieval." *Sharq al-Andalus* 16–17 (1999–2002): 73–93.

McKee, Sally. "Greek Women in Latin Households of Fourteenth-Century Venetian Crete." *Journal of Medieval History* 19 (1993): 229–49.

——. "Households in Fourteenth-Century Venetian Crete." *Speculum* 70 (1995): 27–67.

——. "Inherited Status and Slavery in Late Medieval Italy and Venetian Crete." *Past & Present* 182 (2004): 31–53.

——. *Uncommon Dominion: Venetian Crete and the Myth of Ethnic Purity*. Philadelphia: University of Pennsylvania Press, 2000.

Meyerson, Mark D. *The Muslims of Valencia in the Age of Fernando and Isabel: Between Coexistence and Crusade*. Berkeley: University of California Press, 1991.

——. "Prostitution of Muslim Women in the Kingdom of Valencia." In *The Medieval Mediterranean: Cross-cultural Contacts*, edited by M. Chiat and K. Reyerson, 87–96. St. Cloud, Minn.: North Star Press, 1988.

——. "Slavery and Solidarity: Mudejars and Foreign Muslim Captives in the Kingdom of Valencia." *Medieval Encounters* 2, no. 3 (1996): 286–343.

——. "Slavery and the Social Order: Mudejars and Christians in the Kingdom of Valencia." *Medieval Encounters* 1, no. 1 (1995): 144–73.

Morgan, Jennifer L. *Laboring Women: Reproduction and Gender in New World Slavery.* Philadelphia: University of Pennsylvania Press, 2004.

Narbona Vizcaíno, Rafael. *Pueblo, Poder y Sexo: Valencia Medieval (1306–1420).* Valencia: Història Local 10/ Diputació de València, 1991.

——. *Malhechores, violencia y justicia ciudadana en la Valencia bajomedieval.* Valencia: Ayuntamiento de Valencia, 1990.

Navarro Espinach, Germán. *El despegue de la industria sedera en la Valencia del siglo XV.* Valencia: Consell Valencià de Cultura, 1992.

Nirenberg, David. *Communities of Violence: Persecution of Minorities in the Middle Ages.* Princeton: Princeton University Press, 1996.

——. "Was There Race before Modernity? The Example of 'Jewish' Blood in Late Medieval Spain." In *Origins of Racism in the West,* edited by Ben Issac, Yossi Ziegler, and Miriam Eliav-Feldon. Cambridge University Press, forthcoming.

Orellana, D. Marcos Antonio de. *Valencia antigua y moderna.* Valencia: Librerías París-Valencia, 1924.

Origo, Iris. "The Domestic Enemy: The Eastern Slaves in Tuscany in the Fourteenth and Fifteenth Centuries." *Speculum* 30 (1955): 321–66.

Otis, Leah L. "Municipal Wet Nurses in Fifteenth-Century Montpellier." In *Women and Work in Preindustrial Europe,* edited by Barbara Hanawalt, 83–93. Bloomington: Indiana University Press, 1986.

Patterson, Orlando. *Slavery and Social Death: A Comparative Study.* Cambridge: Harvard University Press, 1982.

Peabody, Sue. *"There are no slaves in France": The Political Culture of Race and Slavery in the Ancien Regime.* New York: Oxford University Press, 2002.

Pelteret, David A. E. *Slavery in Early Mediaeval England: From the Reign of Alfred until the Twelfth Century.* Rochester, N.Y.: Boydell Press, 1995.

Pérez Garcia, Pablo. *La comparsa de los malhechores: Valencia 1479–1518.* Valencia: Diputació de València, 1990.

Perry, Mary Elizabeth. *The Handless Maiden: Moriscos and the Politics of Religion in Early Modern Spain.* Princeton: Princeton University Press, 2005.

Phillips, Carla Rahn, and William D. Phillips. *Spain's Golden Fleece: Wool Production and the Wool Trade from the Middle Ages to the Nineteenth Century.* Baltimore: Johns Hopkins University Press, 1997.

Phillips, William D., Jr. *Slavery from Roman Times to the Early Transatlantic Trade.* Minneapolis: University of Minnesota Press, 1985.

Piles Ros, Leopoldo. *Apuntes para la historia económico-social de Valencia durante el siglo XV.* Valencia: Ayuntamiento de Valencia, 1969.

——. *Estudio documental sobre el bayle general de Valencia, su autoridad y jurisdicción.* Valencia: Instituto Valenciano de Estudios Históricos, Institución Alfonso el Magnànimo,

Diputación Provincial de Valencia, Consejo Superior de Investigaciones Científicas, 1970.

———. *Estudios sobre el gremio de zapateros.* Valencia: Ayuntamiento de Valencia, 1959.

Pitt-Rivers, Julian A. *The Fate of Shechem.* Cambridge: Cambridge University Press, 1977.

———. "Honour and Social Status." In *Honour and Shame: The Values of Mediterranean Society,* edited by J. G. Peristiany, 19–78. London: Weidenfeld and Nicholson, 1965.

Plazolles Guillén, Fabiana. "Trayectorias sociales de los libertos musulmanes y negroafricanos en la Barcelona tardomedieval." In *De l'esclavitud a la llibertat: Esclaus i lliberts a l'Edat Mitjana (Actes del Colloqui Internacional celebrats a Barcelona del 27 al 29 de maig de 1999),* edited by Maria Teresa Ferrer i Mallol and Josefina Mutgé i Vives, 615–642. Barcelona: Consell Superior d'Investigacions Científiques, Institució Milà i Fontanals, 2000.

Pryor, John H. *Geography, Technology, and War: Studies in the Maritime History of the Mediterranean, 649–1571.* Cambridge: Cambridge University Press, 1988.

Ramos y Loscertales, José Maria. *El cautiverio en la Corona de Aragón durante los siglos XIII, XIV, y XV.* Zaragoza: Publicaciones del Estudio de Filología de Aragón, 1915.

Ray, Jonathan. "Beyond Tolerance and Persecution: Reassessing Our Approach to Medieval Convivencia." *Jewish Social Studies* 11, no. 2 (2005): 1–18.

Reyerson, Kathryn. *The Art of the Deal: Intermediaries of Trade in Medieval Montpellier.* Boston: Brill, 2002.

Roca Traver, F. A. *La jurisdicción civil del Justicia de Valencia (1238–1321).* Valencia: Ayuntamiento de Valencia, 1992.

Rodriguez, Jarbel. *Captives and Their Saviors in the Medieval Crown of Aragon.* Washington D.C.: Catholic University Press, 2007.

Romano, Dennis. *Housecraft and Statecraft: Domestic Service in Renaissance Venice, 1400–1600.* Baltimore: Johns Hopkins University Press, 1996.

Rossiaud, Jacques. *Medieval Prostitution.* Translated by Lydia G. Cochrane. New York: Blackwell, 1988.

Rubio Vela, Augustín. "Sobre la población de Valencia en el cuatrocientos (Nota demográfica)." *Boletín de la Sociedad Castellonense de Cultura* 56 (1980): 158–70.

Ruiz, Teofilo F. *Spain's Centuries of Crisis, 1300–1474.* Oxford: Blackwell, 2007.

Russell-Wood, A. J. R. "Iberian Expansion and the Issue of Black Slavery: Changing Portuguese Attitudes, 1440–1770." *American Historical Review* 83 (1978): 16–42.

Salicrú i Lluch, Roser. "Dels capitols de 1413 als de 1422: Un primer intent de fer viable la guarda d'esclaus de la Generalitat de Catalunya." In *Tercer Congres d'Historia Moderna de Catalunya: Les institucions Catalanes (segles XV–XVII),* 355–66. Barcelona: Universitat de Barcelona, 1993.

———. "Propietaris d'esclaus a l'ambit rural de la vergueria de Barcelona segons el Llibre de Guarda de 1425: El Cas del Maresme." In *X Sessio d'Estudis Mataronins,* 115–25. Barcelona: Museu Arxiu de Santa María, Patronat Municipal de Cultura, 1994.

——. *Esclaus i propietaris d'esclaus a la Catalunya del segle XV: L'assegurança contra fugues.* Barcelona: Consell Superior de Investigacions Científicas, 1998.

Sánchez Martínez, M. "Comercio Nazarí y piratería Catalano-Aragonesa (1344–1345)." In *Relaciones de la peninsula ibérica con el Magreb (siglos XIII–XVI),* edited by M. García Arenal and M. J. Viguera. Madrid: Consejo Superior de Investigaciones Científicas, 1988.

Sans, J. Miret y. "La esclavitud en Cataluña en los últimos tiempos de la edad media." *Revue Hispanique* 41 (1917): 1–109.

Saunders, A. C. de C. M. *A Social History of Black Slaves and Freedmen in Portugal, 1444–1555.* Cambridge: Cambridge University Press, 1982.

——. "The Depiction of Trade as War as a Reflection of Portuguese Ideology and Diplomatic Strategy in West Africa, 1441–1556." *Canadian Journal of History* 17 (1982): 219–34.

Scott, James C. *Domination and the Arts of Resistance: Hidden Transcripts.* New Haven: Yale University Press, 1990.

Scott, Rebecca J., and Michael Zeuske. "Le droit d'avoir des droits: Les revendications des ex-esclaves à Cuba (1872–1909)." *Annales. Histoire, Sciences sociales* 59, no. 3 (2004): 521–45.

Setton, Kenneth M. *Catalan Domination of Athens, 1311–1388.* Cambridge, Mass.: Medieval Academy of America, 1948.

Schafer, Judith K. "'Guaranteed against the Vices and Maladies Prescribed by Law': Consumer Protection, the Law of Slave Sales, and the Supreme Court in Antebellum Louisiana." *American Journal of Legal History* 31, no. 4 (October 1987): 306–21.

Sheehan, Michael. "Theory and Practice: Marriage of the Unfree and the Poor in Medieval Society." *Mediaeval Studies* 50 (1988): 457–87.

Simon, Larry. "The Church and Slavery in Ramon Llull's Majorca." In *Iberia and the Mediterranean World of the Middle Ages: Studies in Honor of Robert I. Burns, S.J.,* edited by L. Simon, 345–63. Leiden: E. J. Brill, 1995.

Snowden, Frank. *Before Color Prejudice: The Ancient View of Blacks.* Cambridge: Harvard University Press, 1983

Sobrequés i Vidal, Santiago, and Jaume Sobrequés i Callicó. *La guerra civil catalana del segle XV: Estudis sobre la crisi social i econòmica de la baixa Edat Mitjana.* 2 vols. Barcelona: Edicions 62, 1987.

Solomon, Michael. *The Literature of Misogyny in Medieval Spain: The Archipreste de Talavera and the Spill.* Cambridge: Cambridge University Press, 1997.

Stella, Alessandro. *Histoires d'esclaves dans la Péninsule Ibérique.* Paris: Éditions de l'École des Hautes Études en Sciences Sociales, 2000.

Stewart, Frank Henderson. *Honor.* Chicago: University of Chicago Press, 1994.

Stuard, Susan Moshe. "Ancillary Evidence on the Decline of Medieval Slavery." *Past & Present* 149 (1995): 3–32.

——. "To Town to Serve: Urban Domestic Slavery in Medieval Ragusa." In *Women and Work in Preindustrial Europe*, edited by Barbara Hanawalt, 39–55. Bloomington: Indiana University Press, 1986.

Sweet, James H. "The Iberian Roots of American Racist Thought." Special issue, "Constructing Race: Differentiating Peoples in the Early Modern World," *William and Mary Quarterly* 54 (January 1997): 143–66.

Taylor, Julie. *Muslims in Medieval Italy: The Colony at Lucera*. Lanham, Md.: Lexington Books, 2003.

Teixeira da Mota, A. "Entrée d'esclaves noirs à Valence (1445–1482): Le remplacement de la voie saharienne par la voie atlantique." *Revue française d'histoire d'Outre Mer* 66 (1979): 195–210.

Thompson, Lloyd. *Romans and Blacks*. Norman: University of Oklahoma Press, 1989

Thornton, John. *Africa and Africans in the Making of the Atlantic World, 1400–1800*. Cambridge: Cambridge University Press, 1992.

Torres Fontes, Juan. "Los alfaqueques castellanos en la frontera de Granada." In *Homenaje a Don Agustín Millares Carlo*, edited by J. Simón Díaz. Las Palmas de Gran Canaria: Caja Insular de Ahorros de Gran Canaria, 1975.

——. "La hermandad de moros y cristianos para el rescate de cautivos." In *Actas del I Simposio Internacional de Mudejarismo*, 499–508. Madrid-Teruel: Consejo Superior de Investigaciones Científicas, 1981.

Tramoyeres Blasco, L. *Instituciones gremiales, su origen y organización en Valencia*. Valencia: Imprenta Domenech, 1889.

Vaquer Bennàssar, O. *L'esclavitud a Mallorca, 1448–1500*. Palma de Mallorca: Institut d'Estudis Baleàrics, 1997.

Vauchez, André. "Note sur l'esclavage et le changement de religion en Terre Sainte au XIIIe siècle." In *Figures de l'esclave au moyen age et dans le monde moderne*, edited by Henri Bresc, 91–96. Paris: Editions L'Harmattan, 1996.

Verhulst, Adriaan. "The Decline of Slavery and the European Expansion of the Early Middle Ages." *Past & Present* 133 (1991): 195–203.

Verlinden, Charles. "Aspects quantitatifs de l'esclavage méditerranéen au Bas Moyen Âge." *Anuario de Estudios Medievales* 10 (1980).

——. "L'origine de sclavus-esclave." *Bulletin du Cange: Archivum latinitatis medii aevii* 17 (1942): 97–128.

——. *L'esclavage dans l'Europe médiévale*. 2 vols. Bruges: De Tempel, 1955–77.

——. "Medieval Slavers." In *Economy, Society, and Government in Medieval Italy: Essays in Memory of Robert L. Reynolds*, edited by R. S. Lopez, V. Slessarev, and David Herlihy, 1–14. Kent, Ohio: Kent State University Press, 1969.

——. "Orthodoxie et Esclavage au bas Moyen Age." *Mélanges Eugène Tisserand* 5 (1964): 428–42.

Vincent, Bernard. "L'esclavage en milieu rural espagnol au XVIIe siècle: L'exemple de la région d'Alméria." In *Figures de l'esclave au Moyen-Age et dans le monde moderne*, edited by Henri Bresc, 165–76. Paris: Editions L'Hartmattan, 1996

Vinyoles i Vidal, Teresa. "Integració de les llibertes a la societat Barcelonina baixmedieval." In *De l'esclavitud a la llibertat: Esclaus i lliberts a l'edat mitjana*, edited by Maria Teresa Ferrer i Mallol and Josefina Mutgé i Vives, 593–614. Barcelona: Consell Superior d'Investigacions Científiques, Institució Milà i Fontanals, 2000.

White, Deborah Gray. *Arn't I a Woman? Female Slaves in the Plantation South*. New York: W. W. Norton, 1985.

Willett, Cynthia. "The Master-Slave Dialectic: Hegel vs. Douglass." In *Subjugation and Bondage: Critical Essays on Slavery*, edited by Tommy Lee Lott. Lanham, Md.: Rowman and Littlefield, 1998.

Winer, Rebecca. *Women, Wealth, and Community in Perpignan, c. 1250–1300: Christians, Jews, and Enslaved Muslims in a Medieval Mediterranean Town*. Aldershot: Ashgate, 2006.

Wolf, Kenneth Baxter. "The 'Moors' of West Africa and the Beginnings of the Portuguese Slave Trade." *Journal of Medieval and Renaissance Studies* 24, no. 3 (1994): 449–69.

Index

Abdalla (aka "Abdalla *Alfaqui*," freed *llor* and alleged *ladre de catius* [slave stealer]), 233–35

adultery, as grounds for enslavement, 13, 16

afermament (contract of service or apprenticeship), 84, 87, 92, 95

agency, slave, 5–6, 71–79, 92, 164–65, 268; *see also* claims-making; resistance

agents of the ear (*corredors d'orella*); *see* brokers

agricultural production, role of slaves in, 80, 82–84, 95–99

alfondech (fonduk), 244, 251

Alfonso V (the Magnanimous), King of the Crown of Aragon, 118, 162

Ali; *see* Mena, Pedro de

Amalrich, Johana (freedwoman), 115–16, 246–48

Andria ("defective" black African slave), 60, 64–65, 67, 237, 272

Angelo de Capoa (squire and purported lover of Rosa), 179, 185, 276; *see also* Castello, Arnau; Diego; Rosa

Anna (Russian slave woman, mother of Barbera), 173–74, 215–16, 259

Anthoni (Tartar slave and farmer), 98–99

Anthoni (Tartar freedman, formerly of Barcelona), 239–40, 242–44, 249n36

apostasy, of baptized Muslims, 62n33, 138–39, 183–84

auctions, slave, 12–13, 48–54

Azmet (fugitive slave, owned by Johan Insa, carpenter), 233–35

bailiff general, 20–28, 41–45, 48–49, 52, 54, 70–71, 212, 224–25, 243–44, 271

bakers, as slaveholders, 108–11, 168–69, 232–33

baptism: of Eastern Orthodox slaves, 34–35, 39; impact on slave's juridical status, 128–38, 212–13; of Muslim slaves, 62n33, 129, 135–39, 183–84, 211–12; of "pagan" Canary Islander and black African slaves, 133–34; rate of, 135, 270; of slave children, 130–32, 174–77

Baptist, Edward, 78, 192

Barcelona: as center of debate concerning ethics of Christians enslaving Christians, 33–36; employment of slave laborers in, 102, 117; as slave market, 18, 52, 60, 68, 73–74; status of freed black Africans and "moros" in, 241–42

Barchi, Césaro de, 19

Barreda, Alfonso de la (baker and owner of Maria, a Russian slave woman), 130, 132, 169n51, 177, 181–82, 190–91, *see also* Maria; Yolant (aka Ursola)

begging, as grounds for penal enslavement (*acaptar sin licencia*), 13–15, 105

Benhamet, Caçim (Muslim captive from Tunis), 9, 22–23

Bernat ("llor" [dark-skinned] fugitive owned by Francesch Gomiz, a carpenter), 102–3, 106–7

Black Africans, representations of, 40–45, 64–65, 151–52, 162–68, 228–29, 236–38, 240, 250–51, 272–77 *see also* boçal; race

boçal (bozal) (barbaric, uncivilized), 42–45, 59–60, 217, 271–72

bort/borda (child born in one's household, often illegitimate), 122–25, 130–32

Bossa, Martí and Luisa (married couple, former slaves of Ysabel Puig), 145–46, 253, 269

Bougie, 22, 24–27